D0772614

CAPTAIN
JOHN R. HUGHES

LONE STAR RANGER

John R. Hughes in his prime, the earliest known photograph. *Courtesy Robert G. McCubbin Collection.*

CAPTAIN JOHN R. HUGHES

LONE STAR RANGER

by

CHUCK PARSONS

Number 7 in the Frances B. Vick Series

University of North Texas Press
Denton, Texas

©2011 Chuck Parson
Foreword ©2011 University of North Texas Press
All rights reserved.
Printed in the United States of America.
10 9 8 7 6 5 4 3 2 1
Permissions:
University of North Texas Press
1155 Union Circle #311336
Denton, TX 76203-5017

The paper used in this book meets the minimum requirements of the American
National Standard for Permanence of Paper for Printed Library Materials,
z39.48.1984. Binding materials have been chosen for durability.

Library of Congress Cataloging-in-Publication Data

Parsons, Chuck.
  Captain John R. Hughes, Lone Star Ranger / by Chuck Parsons.—1st ed.
    p. cm.—(Number 7 in the Frances B. Vick series)
  Includes bibliographical references and index.
  ISBN 978-1-57441-304-5 (cloth : alk. paper)
  1. Hughes, John R. (John Reynolds), 1855–1947. 2. Texas Rangers—Biography.
3. Texas—History—1846–1950. 4. Frontier and pioneer life—Texas. I. Title.
II. Series: Frances B. Vick series ; no. 7.
  F391.H88P2 2011
  976.4'05092--dc22
  [B]
                                        2010042776

            Captain John R. Hughes: Lone Star Ranger is Number 7
                    in the Frances B. Vick Series

Dedicated to the Memory of

Robert "Bobby" Nieman

July 11, 1947–October 17, 2009

His love of preserving Texas Ranger history, from the horseback days through the modern era, was unsurpassed.

Contents

Foreword

The author of this fine biography, Chuck Parsons, is a friend of more than thirty years' standing. I first came to know him back in the '70s through our mutual interest in the fascinating characters populating the history of the Wild West. He came by this interest naturally, having been raised in Minnesota near Northfield, where in 1876 the James-Younger gang met disaster in an attempted bank robbery, and Madelia, where a pursuing posse shot up and captured the Younger brothers. After graduation from the University of Minnesota, Chuck taught classes and held administration positions in high schools in Minnesota and Wisconsin. His passion for Old West history led to a sixteen-year post as "Answer Man" for *True West* magazine, fielding readers' questions. After serving many years on the board of the National Association for Outlaw and Lawman History (NOLA) and editing the *Quarterly* and *Newsletter* publications of that organization, he assisted in the merging of NOLA and the Western Outlaw-Lawman History Association (WOLA) to form The Wild West History Association (WWHA) in 2008, and became editor of the *Saddlebag*, the newsletter of the new organization.

During these years he wrote and published numerous articles for popular Western magazines and historical journals. In 1977 he came out with a pamphlet entitled *Shadows Along the Pecos: The Saga of Clay Allison, "Gentleman Gun Fighter,"* which quickly found a home on my bookshelf. Since then a dozen or more books and pamphlets authored by Chuck Parsons have joined *Shadows* there, including a book-length biography, *Clay Allison: Portrait of a Shootist* (1983), and two volumes dealing with the adventures and misadventures of another notorious gun-wielder: *The Capture of John Wesley Hardin* (1978), and *Bowen and Hardin* (co-authored with Marjorie Parsons in 1991). Over the years other famous and infamous figures of the frontier have become the subjects of Parsons's pen: *Phil Coe: Texas Gambler* (1984); *James Madison Brown, Texas Sheriff, Texas Turfman* (1993), and *James Brown Miller and Death in Oklahoma* (2009). A study of one of the violent family clashes for which the Lone Star State is noted, *The Sutton-Taylor Feud: The Deadliest Blood Feud in Texas*, also appeared in 2009.

Work on a book entitled *"Pidge": A Texas Ranger from Virginia*, published in 1985, led him to an ongoing in-depth study of that storied law enforcement organization, the Texas Rangers, and eventually the publication of a series of books recounting the lives and careers of some of the renowned Ranger officers. With co-author Gary P. Fitterer he published in 1993 *Captain C. B. McKinney: The Law in South Texas*. This was followed in 2001 by *Captain L. H. McNelly, Texas Ranger*, co-authored with Marianne E. Hall-Little. *Texas Ranger N. O. Reynolds, the Intrepid*, with Donaly E. Brice as co-author, appeared in 2005. And now in 2010 appears *Texas Ranger John R. Hughes: Lone Star Ranger*, a biography of the man who, together with Captains John H. Rogers, James A. Brooks and William J. McDonald has long been acknowledged as one of the "Four Great Texas Ranger Captains."

Since he was such an important figure in Texas Ranger history, the story of the life of John R. Hughes has been told many times before, notably in *Border Boss*, a flawed biography by Jack Martin published almost seventy years ago, and in the many books devoted to the lengthy history of that organization. But here for the first time is the complete story of the man who, because of his length of service and extraordinary achievements, could well be called THE greatest Texas Ranger captain.

Augmenting the riveting account is a remarkable collection of photographs, a gallery that alone would warrant purchase of this book by anyone with at least a modicum of interest in the history of law enforcement on the advancing western American frontier, the Texas Rangers, the most famous organization devoted to that goal, or the life of the man who best personified the legendary Texas Ranger captain.

Robert K. DeArment
Sylvania, Ohio

Acknowledgments

In spite of our desire to visit all the places where John Reynolds Hughes lived and worked, following in his footsteps from his birthplace in Illinois throughout Kansas and Texas has been impossible due to the constraints of time more than any other reason. A fascinating historical figure can capture the writer's attention until it consumes his entire life; one must set deadlines for research, deadlines for writing, and a deadline to provide the publisher with a satisfactory manuscript. Since traveling over all the miles that John R. Hughes covered was impossible, many others went the extra miles for me, and I thank them profusely here. They are all residents of Texas unless otherwise noted.

Bob Alexander, Maypearl; Richard Banks, Lockhart; Richard Barritt, Lubbock; Correen Basor, Mound City, Kansas; Melleta Bell and Terri Garza, Director and Associate Director of the Archives of the Big Bend, Sul Ross University, Alpine; Tom Bicknell, Crystal Lake, Illinois; Donaly E. Brice, Lockhart; Norman Brown, Justiceburg; Donna Buchell, Carlsbad Public Library, Carlsbad, New Mexico; Cliff Caldwell, Mountain Home; Suzanne Campbell, Head of the West Texas Collection, Angelo State University; Esther Chung, Austin History Center, Austin; Mrs. W. D. Cooper, Austin-Travis Collection, Austin; Teresa Coble, Reference Assistant, Kansas State Historical Society, Topeka; Mike Cox, Austin; Jim Dillard, Georgetown; Donna Donnell, Fort Worth; Doug Dukes, Liberty Hill; Candice DuCoin, Round Rock; Ola May Earnest, President and Curator of the Linn County Historical Museum and Genealogy Library, Mound City, Kansas; Peggy Engledow, Director of the Caldwell County Genealogical & Historical Society, Luling; Will Erwin, Senior Historian Texas State Cemetery, Austin; David George, San Antonio; Ben Hammons, Fort Worth; Joel Hankinson, Lakeville, Minnesota; Kurt House, San Antonio; Diana Houston and her staff of the Texas State Library and Archives; John R. Hughes, Kyle;

Dr. Louis B. Hughes, Baytown; Jan Jones, Fort Worth; Jim Kearney, Columbus; Gary and Margaret Kraisinger, Halstead, Kansas; Ellis Lindsey, Waco; Dennis McCown, Austin; Robert G. McCubbin, Santa Fe, New Mexico; Michael McDermott, Fort Worth; Leon Metz, El Paso; Rick Miller, Harker Heights; Linda C. Pinneo, Deputy Register of Deeds, Linn County, Kansas; Linda Puckett, Director Garza County Historical Museum, Post; Louis R. Sadler, Las Cruces, New Mexico; Richard Selcer, Fort Worth; Betty Shankle, Senior Librarian, Genealogy and History Archives, Fort Worth Public Library, Fort Worth; Claudia Rivers, Director of the Special Collections, C. L. Sonnichsen Department, University of Texas-El Paso and her very helpful staff: Anne Allis, Yvette Delgado, Graciela Galvez; Richard and Ida Saunders, El Paso; Kristy S. Schmitz, Register of Deeds, Linn County, Kansas; Christina Smith, Research Librarian, Texas Ranger Hall of Fame & Museum, Waco; Christina Stopka, Director, Texas Ranger Hall of Fame & Museum Research Center, Waco; Karen and John D. Tanner Jr., Fallbrook, California; Scott Turner, Executive Director, Davis Mountain Educational Center, Fort Davis; Deen Underwood, El Paso; Jackie Sue White, Fort Worth; Keith Wilden, El Paso; Donald M. and Louise Yena, San Antonio.

There are no doubt others whose names I have overlooked: if so, my profound apologies. Several of the above contributed more than they could have realized in their efforts to dig deeper into their archives for what I thought "should be" there; many times the documents were, sometimes not. And as always, I acknowledge the help and encouragement and occasional prodding of my wife Pat who has ridden most of the miles with me. To all a grateful thanks.

Introduction

The light of the moon shone as brothers Will and Alvin Odle worked their herd of stolen horses towards the eastern side of Bullhead Mountain. They were eager to meet the rancher who would buy good horseflesh, no questions asked. The Odles had to be cautious, naturally, as experience had taught them never to relax their guard completely. At any moment, someone might challenge them, demanding to know why they were driving horses so close to midnight on Christmas Eve. Should not all good ranchers be home in bed on such a special night?

But shortly after midnight, someone did yell out "Halt! Halt!" The Odle brothers took no time to determine who challenged their right to be driving horses so late at night. They both jerked their six-shooters, knowing now they had to fight whoever it might be, no matter whom and no matter how many. Was it the county sheriff? An ambitious deputy sheriff? An angry mob of ranchers? Texas Rangers?

What the Odles never realized was the challenge came from a posse, a mixed group of lawmen who had discovered where they were going to be at that late hour of the night. Besides a deputy sheriff and other ranchers deputized just for this specific piece of work, the posse also contained Texas Rangers, young Rangers who were brave and reckless. After the demand to halt, to surrender, no sooner than the words rang in their ears, it became a matter of life and death. Lawmen and horsethieves shooting at each other, in the dark, made it a matter of kill or be killed.

It was early Christmas morning, 1889, and one of the men whom the Odle brothers chose to fight with deadly weapons was Texas Ranger John R. Hughes.

This was not the first gunfight John Hughes experienced, nor would it be his last. Over a decade before, he had handled the big rifles which brought down buffalo, up in Kansas. When hide hunters had nearly wiped out the buffalo herds, he turned to cattle driving, and made more than one trip up the trail to the wild and woolly Kansas end of trail towns, towns where the memory of such lawmen as Wild Bill Hickok, Wyatt Earp, and Bat Masterson was fresh in the minds of the locals. Before becoming a Texan, he had traded with reservation Indians, Comanche and Kiowa, and had lived with members of the Osage tribe. Hunting buffalo, raising cattle, and trading with the Indians was not to be John R. Hughes's role in life. The call from Texas reached his ears, and the idea of raising horses and becoming a successful horse trader appealed to him, and not only him but his brother Emery as well.

The Hughes brothers started a ranch in Central Texas, a few miles northwest of Austin, the capital city. Although cattle had replaced the buffalo and Austin was far from a "wild frontier" community, raising horses was not a child's game. Wolves roamed the unfenced ranches, and Hughes lost more than one young colt to a wolf pack. But whereas wolves could pluck one or two young horses from their Running H Ranch to satisfy their hunger, more dangerous packs existed which could wipe out a rancher's herds in a single raid. Horsethieves were the scourge of the western frontier as well as more civilized areas of Texas.

In 1883 such a pack of horsethieves did raid the Running H ranch, taking sixteen head from his herd as well as a good number of his neighbors' horses. It proved to be a highly successful raid for the thieves, but a devastating loss to the ranchers. John R. Hughes was not a man to go to the local sheriff for help; after all, his authority ended at the county line. Hughes decided he would become the law: he would follow the trail of the thieves and either return with the stolen horses or not return at all. The arrangements made with neighbors and brother to take care of the ranch, Hughes took up what trail remained. The hunt turned into an odyssey, trailing the thieves from Central Texas into the Panhandle, across northern Texas into New Mexico, where in the southern corner of the territory he caught up with them. A gunfight ensued; after the smoke cleared, Hughes had possession of his own horses as well as those of his neighbors. Fifteen days shy of a year and he was back home, ready to continue ranching.

But the life of a peaceful rancher was far into the future. A young Texas Ranger, Ira Aten, asked for his help in tracking down a murderer; Hughes now became a deputy, and the two of them together found the fugitive. Aten was so impressed with Hughes he asked him to join. The decision was not difficult: why not get paid for hunting outlaws? Hughes intended to work as a Ranger for a few months, and then return to ranching. But it was then that John R. Hughes found his true calling in life. He was good at hunting down fugitives, tracking them, capturing them, almost always without resorting to gunplay. But when it was necessary to shoot, there was no ambivalence: usually it was a matter of kill or be killed.

He did have one nagging concern, that perhaps an outlaw's bullet had his name on it. When his sergeant was killed in action in 1890, Hughes was promoted to take his place; when his captain was killed fighting bandits in Mexico in 1893, he was promoted to take his place. Six years after joining the Rangers in 1887, he was by the middle of 1893 captain of Company D, Frontier Battalion. He would hold that rank until his forced retirement in 1915. During those years, he never lost a prisoner, never lost a fight, never was wounded in action; and in so doing earned the respect of his fellow Rangers as well as all the honest men and women of Texas, the Lone Star State. In addition, he earned the respect of fugitives from justice. As a captain he at times had as few as five men under his command, covering an area larger then the states of New England combined. He worked in every county along the Rio Grande, from the farthest western county of El Paso to the most southern, Cameron, and in the Panhandle and the Piney Woods of East Texas. The area included what is today's Big Bend, an area of rough terrain, and at the time of John R. Hughes, an area often frequented by tough men, all hoping to avoid meeting John R. Hughes.

Hughes certainly had sufficient reason to wonder about the bullet fired from a fugitive's gun with his name on it, ending his life. On the Texas side of the Rio Grande, much of the territory was a no-man's land, similar to the "Indian Territory" where Hughes had lived in the 1870s. It was there he had his first altercation with another man, a fight in which his right arm was badly injured. After that fight, he had to learn to do everything with his left hand.

During his long career, he came to know the land, the plains, the Llano Estacado, the tall pines of East Texas and the mountains of the Trans-Pecos. During those years, he gave few interviews and remained, as far as the media of the day was concerned, a lone ranger, as he focused on his Ranger responsibilities. After retirement in 1915, after more than a quarter century enforcing the law, he became reachable, and writers, amateur and professional, sought him out, not only for newspaper copy but also for magazine articles, for book chapters and ultimately for a full-length biography. He willingly gave of his time and related experiences. At times, what the reporter wrote disagreed with the official record, based on reports written within days of the event. Certainly that was due more to the writer's "literary creativity" than Hughes's incorrectly recalling events.

Hughes's willingness to open up to reporters began immediately after his 1915 forced retirement. In January of that year he gave a lengthy interview to a reporter of the *San Antonio Daily Express*. This was certainly the first interview given, as it begins: "Captain John R. Hughes retired from the State Ranger service yesterday." The *Express* readers learned that for twenty-eight years he had been "chasing outlaws of high and low degree in the wild region bordering on the Rio Grande." This full-page interview, with illustrations, boasted that Hughes "had more battles with outlaws than any man in this country. . . ." Further, he knew "every curve of the international boundary stream all the way from its mouth to El Paso" and "is familiar with the haunts in the innermost recesses of the hills and mountains, where hard pressed bandits were wont to seek refuge [and further] he can follow the dimmest trail through the thick-growing chaparral of South Texas. . . ."[1]

These statements are certainly true to a degree but they also are prime examples of journalistic exaggeration. The same reporter stated that when Captain Hughes began a chase there would be only one of two possible endings: "Either the fugitives were captured or killed." Hughes was indeed an excellent man-hunter, as his informal training among the Osage Indians as well as other tribes in the frontier area of Kansas or the wilds of what is now Oklahoma proved of great value to him in his Texas Ranger years. What the reporter failed to point out was the fact that sometimes Hughes, like every other Ranger, sometimes returned to camp with a weary horse, after days of trailing, to report that he had accomplished nothing. Occasionally at least, the fugitive did get away.

Later during that first year of retirement, Hughes shared events of his life with a reporter from the rival of the *Express*, the *San Antonio Light*. A *Light* reporter interviewed Hughes in May of 1915, and stressed that the "oldest" Texas Ranger now "modestly recounts his early exploits." It was not a journalistic *coup* for the *Light*, but if the reader had missed the *Express* article of six months earlier, he may have thought so. Here Hughes reviewed numerous events of his career, which he had earlier shared with the *Express* reporter. But now the tone became more boastful, pointing out, almost apologetically, he had been in several engagements where "desperate criminals were killed." However, Hughes assured the reporter, "I have never lost a battle that I was in personally, and never let a prisoner escape." How was this possible? "The longer I held a prisoner the closer I watch[ed] him." In this interview, Hughes touched on the subject of his bachelor life: "Being single I think I am specially fitted for an officer. An officer who hunts desperate criminals has no business having a wife and family."

Hughes concluded the interview by stating that he had a scrapbook that was "very interesting to all old-timers, and a great many of my friends want me to write a book of my life as a ranger. . . ." However, Hughes did not expect to do so for two reasons: he did not crave notoriety, and he did not need the money. He had accumulated enough of the world's goods "to be able to keep the wolf from the door." He added he was "not rich, however."[2]

Hughes may have shared some thoughts of his past with these San Antonio reporters, but much of what he did share was of the same events. He spoke much more of his pre-Ranger adventures than of his Ranger experiences. He preferred to let the record speak for itself, the monthly returns, muster rolls, and letters to and from the adjutant general. Hughes was the antithesis of the self-aggrandizing raconteur such as Wyatt Earp or James Butler "Wild Bill" Hickok. He was reticent about his accomplishments, and reporters apparently accepted that during his lifetime. The *Express* reporter stated with no doubt a degree of frustration: "The mere suggestion of publishing in a newspaper an account of some of his daring deeds brings a blush to his bronzed face. He not only opposes the idea but he cannot be induced to talk about any of the stirring events of his career."[3]

However, some reporters were able to induce the gray-bearded man to talk briefly about his exciting life. Pearl Virginia Crossley, wife of a Philadelphia-trained doctor, was forty-something in 1925 when she interviewed Hughes. In 1920 she and her husband and family of two children lived in Ysleta Village near El Paso; thus Hughes knew them and it was this knowledge perhaps which allowed her access to the then-former Ranger turned successful farmer. Mrs. Crossley was totally impressed with Hughes's physical appearance and described him as "[t]all and straight-shouldered, with the swinging stride of the college athlete; bright eyes of the kind that never cease to twinkle and sparkle under the slightest animation." Further, she gushed, Hughes had hair "slightly sprinkled with gray, chopped graying beard; a mouth to match the breadth of his varied life and character" and not the least she noted the seventy-year-old man had the "spirit of a thoroughbred" when "he reluctantly allowed the conversation to touch on scattered chapters of his thrillful past."[4]

John Hughes did indeed open up to Virginia Crossley, even though she quoted him as saying, no doubt with a touch of ironic humor, that his life was "too full of exciting events to talk about," suggesting that he may have feared if he revealed all the story of his life to the lady it would be too unbelievable to those who had lived a more sedentary life.

Hughes shared what he knew about the hunt for fugitive Geronimo Parra, the man who had killed Ranger Sgt. Charles Fusselman, with journalist L. A. Wilke. *Real Detective* magazine published the article, by-lined as if Hughes wrote it, in 1936. Wilke also took a number of photographs of Hughes.[5]

Fortunately, much of the paper trail of John Reynolds Hughes has survived. The primary source material from those early years as a Texas Ranger, from his beginning as a private in late 1887, to his earning the rank of captain, is nearly complete. Of his early years, we know but little, because not only did Hughes choose to ignore his youthful adventures, but also he himself doubted there would be anything of interest to later generations. He may have known every dim trail of the "thick-growing chaparral of South Texas" but the beginnings of that long trail stretched back to the tamer land of Lincoln, miles and miles from the "haunts in the innermost recesses of the hills and mountains" of South Texas.

There has not been a serious attempt to provide a complete biography of this noted Texas Ranger, although several books contain a chapter on his career. Those authors did not provide a scholarly approach to their subject, but each one provided a meager base for further research. Dane Coolidge, a writer-photographer of the 1920s and 1930s, provided a chapter on Hughes and several other lawmen in his popular *Fighting Men of the West*, published in 1932. J. Evetts Haley reviewed this book and suggested that Coolidge's "decision to write these biographical sketches, for the most part composed of material that he gathered from the subjects themselves, makes available the historical basis of his novels, and will interest many readers of history not attracted by his fiction." Coolidge did spend some time visiting with Hughes and taking notes, but the long quotations attributed to Hughes must have been heavily edited by Coolidge.[6]

Claude L. Douglas gathered material on various Rangers from the beginnings of the organization through Frank Hamer of the early twentieth century and published his fast-reading chapters in *The Gentlemen in the White Hats: Dramatic Episodes in the History of the Texas Rangers*. The book was first published in 1934 by the South-West Press of Dallas, and was reissued in 1992 by State House Press of Austin with a brief foreword by Roger N. Conger, former President of the Texas State Historical Association.[7] Douglas's book did not reveal in-depth research; it did however prove to be a popular history. Perhaps the most significant contribution Douglas made was to provide Jack Martin with the title for his biography of Hughes, *Border Boss*. Douglas titled his chapter "Captain John R. Hughes . . . Border Boss." Certainly, Douglas's two-word phrase, "Border Boss," not seen in print prior to Douglas's work, was the inspiration for Jack Martin.

Prolific writer of western novels Eugene Cunningham produced a work that proved to be very popular and has undergone several editions: *Triggernometry: A Gallery of Gunfighters*. First published in 1941, this book contains a chapter on Hughes entitled "Bayard of the Chaparral." Cunningham envisioned Captain Hughes as a knight-errant from the days of chivalry, using a six-shooter instead of a lance.[8]

William Warren Sterling, captain of Company D in the 1920s and later adjutant general of the state, devoted a brief chapter to Hughes in his memoirs, *Trails and Trials of a Texas Ranger*, first published in 1959.[9] Virgil E. Baugh wrote a booklet devoted to two Ranger captains entitled *A Pair of Texas Rangers: Bill McDonald and John Hughes* published in 1970. Baugh's bibliography cites only four secondary works as his source material, with no indication of researching in primary source materials.[10] Since Martin's biography appeared in 1942, most writings that contain any mention of Hughes, be they chapters in books or any of the numerous magazine articles, have depended greatly on *Border Boss*. Coolidge's work influenced writers to a lesser degree than Martin's.

To many, these early writings about Rangers and other Western characters are disappointing indeed. There is much created conversation; there is virtually no indication of sources, few if any endnotes, most lacking even a worthwhile "selected bibliography." Jack Martin especially was guilty of creating incidents that he intended to give the narrative additional color, but which had little or no basis in fact. One example will suffice. Martin described how Hughes—prior to his Ranger career—trailed a band of horsethieves from Central Texas deep into New Mexico territory. These thieves were, according to Martin, part of the notorious Butch Cassidy gang, a loosely knit group of outlaws at the turn of the century, but more recently made a household word in the twentieth century thanks to Hollywood. However, in 1883, when the horse stealing raid actually occurred, there was not yet a "Butch Cassidy Gang," nor were people even aware that such an individual existed, outside of his immediate home territory of Utah, far away from Texas. In 1883 the man who became Butch Cassidy was still known by his birth name, Robert Leroy Parker.[11]

Harold Preece carried this fiction further in his biography of Ranger Ira Aten, *Lone Star Man*, published in 1960. Preece also accepted the fictional Butch Cassidy claim of Martin, and described how Hughes had accomplished his task of recovering stolen horses from members of the Cassidy gang. In *Lone Star Man*, it was Aten who advised Hughes to join the Rangers, stating, "You won't have that ranch long, John. Butch Cassidy will send one of his gunmen down from Wyoming to bushwhack you. . . . And he'll keep sending them till one gets the drop. So if you're going to be shot at anyhow, you might as well join the Texas Rangers and get paid thirty dollars a month for it."[12] Not satisfied with merely creating conversation between Aten and Hughes, Preece also identified what was particularly unique about the subject of his biography: "Thousands of Texans came to know John Hughes. But Ira Aten was probably the only one who ever plumbed the depths of that resolute, semi-solitary man."[13] At one time Preece considered writing Hughes's biography, but settled on Aten instead. He had contact with Hughes and could have prepared a satisfactory biography of him as well as that of Ira Aten, but chose instead to fictionalize his writing.

Martin's biography of Hughes, as well as the Preece biography of Aten, is comparable to the Stuart N. Lake "biography" of Wyatt Earp, *Frontier Marshal*, in that in addition to the factual material, there is a significant amount of fiction, in spite of the fact that each author, Martin and Lake, as well as Preece, had access to their subject while he was still alive and could have produced a reliable biography. Perhaps the best compliment for any of these works—Preece, Coolidge or Martin, as well as Cunningham—is that they do provide a basis for further research, but must be used with extreme caution.

An additional work must be mentioned here, that being a lengthy article by George Washington Ogden that appeared in the then very popular publication *Everybody's Magazine*, published in September 1911. Ogden was a prolific writer of Western fiction, but as *Everybody's* was a publication devoted to investigative journalism, his article was an honest effort to provide accurate biographical material on the Rangers including Hughes, while he was still active.[14] How much time Ogden did spend interviewing Hughes, or attempting to interview him, is unknown, but the work does suggest Ogden made a serious effort to give an accurate portrait of a tough Texas lawman on the international boundary line of the Rio Grande: John Reynolds Hughes.

For the Anglo historian, amateur or professional, frequently the names of Mexicans have posed a problem in spelling. Occasionally a Ranger captain has spelled the name of a Mexican two different ways in the same report. Captain Hughes may not have been totally bilingual, but after living for years on the border, he became fluent in Spanish. Nevertheless, his spelling of Mexican names was more phonetic than we would have preferred. This author has attempted to correct his spelling where it appeared he was in error, although there may remain some names spelled incorrectly in the following.

This author has also attempted to present a serious biography of the fourth of the "Great Captains." Paul N. Spellman has authored the biographies of John H. Rogers and James A. Brooks, followed by Harold J. Weiss Jr. providing us more recently a biography of William J. McDonald. These are outstanding works of research and writing. I hope that readers will consider this biography of John R. Hughes a worthy companion volume. Hughes had such a long life, and covered so much ground, it was impossible to visit every place he lived and worked, although that was the intent some years back. Another minor regret is that many communities did not preserve their newspapers, thus no doubt numerous incidents of a relatively minor nature, dealing with Hughes's career, have been lost forever.

⁓ 1 ⁓

A Terror to all the Bad Men

". . . THIEVES STOLE ABOUT SEVENTY-FIVE HEAD OF HORSES
FROM MY RANGE. AMONG THEM WERE SIXTEEN HEAD OF
MINE. I FOLLOWED THEM TO NEW MEXICO, GOT ALL MY
HORSES BACK, AND A LOT OF MY NEIGHBORS' HORSES. THE
BAND OF MEN WAS ALL BROKEN UP."

—*John R. Hughes, interview in the* San Antonio Light,
May 30, 1915

I f Texas Ranger John R. Hughes had been a boastful man, he could
have prided himself on his ancestral background. His grandfather,
Ezekiel Hughes, a native of Montgomeryshire, Wales, came to
America to avoid religious persecution. Ezekiel settled in the Miami
River area in Hamilton County, Ohio, on land that was known at the
time as the Northwest Territory. Looking westward Ezekiel Hughes
could see Indiana; southward Kentucky. He purchased the first land
sold by the government from this territory, paying $2.50 per acre for it.
According to his most complete obituary, Ezekiel Hughes was "a thrifty,
hard working man, a staunch Presbyterian and at his death left each one
of his ten children a good farm." A "good farm" for *each* of ten children
certainly was a sizeable amount of acreage. Among his neighbors was
the U.S. president-to-be, William Henry Harrison, "their farms being
in close proximity."[1] Just when Ezekiel Hughes made the acquaintance
of Mary Ann Ewing of Cumberland County, Pennsylvania, is unknown,
but the pair married on July 10, 1805, in Hamilton County, Ohio. They
gave ten children to the world, all born in Hamilton County: the first in

1806 and the last, two decades later in 1826. They named their fourth child and second son Thomas, born in July of 1812.[2]

Thomas Hughes, the father of future Ranger Hughes, was an adventurous man himself, as in 1839 he crossed the Atlantic to visit his father's home and explore Wales, England, and Scotland. He returned to America but then three years later he crossed the ocean again and this time kept a journal of his travels and his impressions. Some member of the family later bound the notes for the sake of permanence; they proved to contain "many interesting sketches and descriptions of the people and countries that came under his observation." Unfortunately, the journals did not survive, perhaps going up in smoke when the Hughes family home-hotel burned in October 1909. A voracious reader, Thomas Hughes was familiar with the works of such British authors as Shakespeare, Byron, Burns, and Pope. He was educated at Miami University, at Oxford in neighboring Butler County, Ohio. Besides farming, Thomas Hughes taught school for at least one term, providing his pupils with a good education in his home.[3]

On June 1, 1846, Thomas Hughes married Jane "Jennie" Augusta Bond.[4] Less is known of her, other than that she was a native of Venice, Ohio, and was born December 29, 1827, the fourth of six children of Enoch and Jane Sargent Bond. Both the Hughes and Bond families had earlier "left the comforts of good homes, and sought the forests of Ohio, to escape religious persecution."[5] Jane Bond, as a little girl, had received an above average education at the Young Ladies Seminary located at Oxford. Thomas Hughes had been "her neighbor and friend from early childhood," according to her obituary. The Rev. Thomas Thomas, formerly a resident of London, England, had baptized them both. Both Thomas and Jane became full members in the Presbyterian Church.[6] Mr. and Mrs. Hughes became the parents of seven children: Louise/Louisa, generally known as Lou; Bond; Emery Sargent; John Reynolds born February 11, 1855, the man who would become the famous Texas Ranger; William Parker, who also served as a Texas Ranger although a decade earlier than his more famous brother; and twins Thomas F. Hughes Jr. and Nellie. Thomas Hughes Sr. was listed as a farmer on the various censuses on which his name is found, and as the operator of a hotel.

The Hughes couple lived for a few years in Butler County, Ohio, but then ventured into western Illinois in 1855. Deed records reveal Thomas purchased "a parcel of land in the town of Genesee Henry County" for $125.00, purchased from Miner M. DaSano.[7] Another move followed, as in 1856 Thomas Hughes was in Marion County, Illinois, nearly two hundred miles south. Now he is on record as selling to James M. Nye "a certain tract of land situated in Henry County" in the northwest corner of the town of Cambridge, Henry County.[8] Again, we have no indication as to why Thomas Hughes made these particular moves. Perhaps the frequent moves instilled in John R. Hughes a restlessness that he was able to take advantage of a few years later.

Thomas Hughes moved his family ever westward. Although he may have had wanderlust in his veins, a stronger reason for moving was that he had unwittingly settled in an area with strong pro-slavery sentiment. The atmosphere surrounding him was "not congenial and failed to harmonize" with the Hughes family's "ardent anti-slavery ideas" so they moved to Rockport, Illinois, and then farther west.[9]

Main Street, Mound City, Kansas, circa 1893–1894. The Hughes family resided here from 1867 until well into the 20th century. Note the Isaac N. Ray store front sign on the left. Ray was Indiana-born and founded a successful business in Mound City. Photograph by Clarence H. Heckman. *Courtesy the Kansas State Historical Society.*

By the middle of the 1860s Thomas Hughes had established himself and family in Mound City, the seat of Linn County, Kansas.[10] It was a small community in the southeast corner of the state, located some sixty miles due south of Kansas City. In 1865, Thomas Hughes purchased and remodeled a large dwelling operated as a hotel, which he named the Mound City House. Built by Isaac Ellis and his son Benjamin H. in 1859, it was the first hotel in the county. The Ellises later moved to violent Lincoln County in New Mexico Territory. Four different owners had operated the hotel unsuccessfully before Thomas bought it. He continued to farm and to operate the hotel until his death in 1890.

The Hughes Family plot in Woodland Cemetery, Mound City, Kansas. This stone is inscribed: "In my father's house are many mansions/ Thos. Hughes/ Died 1890 Aged 78 Yrs." and for his wife, "Jennie A. Hughes/ Died 1903/ Aged 76 Yrs." On same stone: "Nellie Coleman/ Died 1943/ Aged 83 Yrs." and "Enoch Bond/ Died 1876/ Aged 88 Yrs." *Photo by Pat Parsons.*

Mrs. Hughes acted as hostess until the infirmities of age dictated she turn over the operational duties to her daughter. The name of the popular establishment was changed to the Commercial House by daughter Lou Coleman.[11] An advertisement, carried regularly in the *Border Sentinel*, the Mound City newspaper, informed the traveler that it was "newly refitted" and was "one of the most comfortable and best houses in Southern Kansas." In the early days $5.00 per week provided the traveler with board and lodging. In addition there was an "excellent stable and stock yard attached, which makes it convenient for Drovers and the Travelling [*sic*] Public."[12] Tragically, a fire cost the Hughes family many of their possessions in October 1909: their home and the hotel business. Citizens were able to save some three-quarters of the building's contents. The only loss of life was the death of Bond Hughes's dog Bowser, who normally slept under Bond's bed. Bond was away in Kansas City at the time of the fire, and Bowser refused to leave due to the absence of his master.[13]

While young John Hughes worked in the "excellent stable and stock yard" attached to the hotel, he certainly became aware of Linn County's rich history of Civil War engagements, most notably the Marais des Cygnes "massacre" that had taken place in 1858, only a dozen years before and less than twenty miles from their home in Mound City. On October 25, 1864, the last important Civil War battle in the area had been fought nearby at Mine Creek: 2,500 Union cavalrymen defeated 6,500 Confederate cavalrymen.[14] The knowledge of the fighting that had taken place not long before and relatively close only added to the excitement of the Hughes children's lives, and perhaps especially for John. The wanderlust and urge for adventure compelled him to seek his fortunes elsewhere.

John R. stayed at his family's new home in Kansas for at least one year "before the fascination of Indian Territory made him run away," as Hughes admitted years later in an interview with an El Paso newspaper reporter.[15] His leave-taking was coyly expressed, stating that "if he neglected to obtain the consent of his parents, it was only because he deemed himself capable of making his own decisions."[16] The Federal census shows that Hughes was still considered "at home" at least as late as 1870, when he was fifteen years of age. He was still residing with his parents and siblings: Emery S., William, Thomas Jr., sometimes called Forester, and Nellie. At the time of the census, Emery was working as a printer, a profession he followed most of his life. Census enumerator William R. Biddle listed the other siblings as simply being "at home."[17] Sometime after 1870 John did leave Mound City as the Kansas state census of 1875 shows only Thomas and Jane with children William, Thomas Jr., and Nellie still at home. Enoch and Jane Bond, Mrs. Hughes's parents, now lived with them in the Mound City House.[18]

John R. Hughes was a courageous and responsible individual; leaving home and living resourcefully for a young man aged somewhere between fifteen and twenty years old proved that. Whatever work he did initially to earn room and board is unknown, but he knew horses and could work hard, and no doubt was proficient with firearms, at least in hunting animals, which could not return fire. His skill in handling weapons would later prove invaluable in tracking human prey that could and often did return fire. His skill with weapons was only one of the sterling characteristics of John Reynolds Hughes.

John Reynolds Hughes sought new horizons and adventure at this young age. He avoided living in the white man's world at this early point in his life, spending several years among the tribes in what government mapmakers identified as "Indian Territory." Just west of Linn County, Kansas, lived various tribes, primarily the Osage, and Hughes may have initially lived with them before going farther south into the Indian Territory in what is now Oklahoma.[19] By living with the Osage, Hughes gained "invaluable knowledge on tracking down horse thieves, outlaws and other enemies of society."[20] He later found work on the reservation at Fort Sill, built in 1869 in the Wichita Mountains. It was from this fort that army troops with their frontier scouts applied such pressure on warring Kiowa and Comanche bands that they surrendered. Once proud lords of the plains, they had no choice but to move to the U.S. government's reservation after their defeat at Palo Duro Canyon in the Texas Panhandle in September 1874. Among the experienced scouts Hughes became acquainted with during the 1870s was Simpson E. "Jack" Stilwell; it was from Stilwell that he learned of Custer's defeat in June 1876.[21]

While working out of Fort Sill as a reservation trader Hughes became acquainted with noted Comanche Chief Quanah Parker, once the feared leader of the Comanche tribe in the war against the buffalo hunters. Quanah, the warrior son of a white woman and Comanche chief, realized the futility of continued struggle against the white man and with one hundred warriors and some three hundred women and children brought his people into Fort Sill to live.[22] That Hughes and at least some of the Comanche were on friendly terms is revealed from Hughes's own keepsakes: one photograph is of Quanah and two of his wives, Topai and Chonie; another is of Kicking Bird, also known as Humming Bird.[23]

We know some details of this early portion of Hughes's life, thanks to an interview with Pearl Virginia Crossley in El Paso in 1925. From this accounting, it becomes clear that his living among the Osage, Comanche, and Kiowa may have been no more isolated or primitive than being on the reservation at Fort Sill. He explained that when he became a Ranger living in a tent, this was "not his introduction to the wilds" because "he had spent six exciting years of his youth among the Indians of Oklahoma." He explained:

> The traders went out from the agency loaded with a limited variety of provisions, such as red calico, red blankets, colored glass, beads, green coffee, flour and sugar, which they traded for buffalo robes. Leaving one of the men to carry on the business with the Indian chief, the remainder of the wagon train returned to the agency with the buffalo robes they had on hand. For six years I was the man left behind.

In 1872 Hughes was for the first and only time injured in a scrape with another man. We know few details of this incident, but in an interview with Ernie Pyle, before Pyle himself became an American icon, Hughes told of how he nearly lost his life. "He was shot, however, by an Indian when he was 17, and he suffers from the wound to this day," Pyle wrote. "His right arm was shattered and is weak and smaller than his left. He had to learn to do everything with his left hand, even shoot."[24] There is no doubt the right arm was badly damaged, but did the Indian do it intentionally, as Pyle recorded, or was it an accident as Mrs. O. L. Shipman described in her article on Hughes, published in 1923? She wrote, telling of his experience with the traders, that the accident happened "while he was in the territory that made his right arm stiff and caused him to shoot with his left hand, but he developed a direct fire that made him a terror to all the bad men along the entire stretch of the Rio Grande."[25] Although the cause of the injured right arm may be open to historical question, the fact remains that he became a "southpaw" for the remainder of his life. There was no question that many thought he was a natural-born left-hander.

That some believed he was born a southpaw was apparently part of family lore, as Hughes's nephew, Emery H. Hughes, son of brother Emery Sargent Hughes, shared the notion with author William Cx Hancock. Hancock may have added additional "color" in identifying the man with whom Hughes engaged in the fight.

> He had caught on as a cowhand in Oklahoma Indian Territory with an outfit supplying cattle to the reservation Indians. A feared breed rustler named Big Nig Goombi tried to run off the stock Hughes was herding. The tenderfoot puncher killed the dangerous thief, but was himself maimed by wounds in the right arm which permanently slowed his draw from that side. He quickly taught himself to fire from the left side with such speed and accuracy that few subsequent acquaintances suspected that he had not been born left-handed.[26]

Hughes learned the business of driving cattle as well as breaking horses and hunting buffalo during these Indian Territory years. He went on at least one significant buffalo hunt, as he recollected to interviewer Crossley: "In 1871 when I returned to civilization from my first buffalo hunt I heard of the Chicago fire," which charred that city on October 8.[27] He also worked with cattlemen who contracted with the army to deliver beef to the reservation. Hughes, years later, wrote to Roy Aldrich[28] a brief summary of these years:

In the Spring of 1877, I was working at Fort Sill, Indian Territory, issuing cattle to the Comanches and Kiowas, to keep them from going out on buffalo-hunts. The contractors, Powers and Buckley, lost their contract that Spring, so we had to move what cattle we had left on hand to Kansas, to sell them.

The firm of Powers, Buckley & Co. trailed the herd north from Texas early. It was the first herd of the season to reach famed cattle town Dodge City, arriving in May. A correspondent identified only by his *nom de plume* of "Nemesis" wrote from Dodge City to the editors of the *Ellis County Star* of Hays City, the rival cattle town's newspaper, that the first herd of Texas cattle "had made their appearance on the sunny slopes of the Arkansas [River]." Although with no mention of the hands accompanying the herd, such as Hughes, Nemesis did write that the first herd had been brought up by the "genial and well known Mike Dalton" and in their conference regarding the drive,

The Midwest of John R. Hughes.

Dalton informed Nemesis that the cattle were in excellent condition and everything "moved lovely on the trail." It was fortunate for them, as some drovers lost many head through storms, raiding parties, or stampedes. Dalton, so Nemesis wrote, was in charge of the Powers & Co. cattle and would cross the Arkansas River on the fourteenth, bound for Ellis.[29] Hughes did not state the reason Dalton chose not to sell in Dodge and drove his herd on to Ellis in Hays County, some eighty miles north. The *Star* announced the good news (for merchants and businessmen): "The first drove of 'long horns' reached Ellis on Tuesday [May 22], Powers & Buckley are the owners; thousands more are on the trail destined for Ellis."[30] Powers & Buckley's herd made up only a small portion of the estimated 200,000 head of cattle driven north from Texas during 1877.[31] Hughes's recollection continued:

> We drove them to Ellis, Kansas, and herded them there until November, 1877, then sold them. The boss of the trail herd was Mike Dalton. One of the cowboys was Charley Nebo, one was Jim French, one was John Middleton, and one an ex-soldier named Steel.[32]

Hughes recalled that the cattle were from deep South Texas, "all in the Running W brand; all old longhorns from the King Santa Gertruda [*sic*, Gertrudis] ranch. Most of them were old outlaw brush steers and fit only to feed Indians."[33]

It was about November 1877, that Hughes had the opportunity to leave the excitement of the Kansas cow towns and engage in an economic conflict in far-off New Mexico. His narrative continues:

> About the time the cattle were sold and delivered, a man from New Mexico was there. He hired Jim French and John Middleton as fighting men, to go to New Mexico and fight in the Lincoln County War. These two are mentioned in connection with Billy the Kid's exploits. John Middleton was with Billy and their employer, Tunstall the Englishman, when Tunstall was murdered on the road to Lincoln, February 18, 1878. Middleton was also with the Kid when Sheriff Brady was ambushed in Lincoln. He was indicted for

murder but left the country before the term of court in the Spring of 1879, forfeiting bond. He was in the Kid's party in the battle at McSween's house.

Nevertheless, young Hughes remained in the cattle business. In one of the fascinating ironies of history, when French and Middleton arrived in Lincoln they certainly became acquainted with Isaac and Benjamin Ellis, former residents of Mound City and the original builders of the Hughes family hotel. They were considered non-combatants in the Lincoln County War, whereas French and Middleton were fighting men for the Tunstall-McSween faction.[34]

Driving cattle in southern Kansas enabled John to see the town of Ellis and no doubt Hays City, both in Ellis County, Kansas, as well as at least one trail drive going to Dodge City. In 1878 cowboy Hughes went up the trail again, now with Cross P cattle working for the well-known Ohio-born rancher, Major Andrew Drumm, who was part-owner of the herd.[35]

Meanwhile, John's older brother Emery S. who later joined him in ranching in Texas, found his calling in the printing business, which employment he engaged in the early 1870s. Perhaps John at one point considered following his older brother in the printing trade. An undated Mound City newspaper, in reporting the resignation of Ranger Captain Hughes, included this tantalizing statement about his activities of decades before:

> After coming here [Mound City] John R. remained about a year when he and another brother, Emory [*sic*] Hughes, a printer, bought a printing press and outfit and moved it to Oxford, Sumner county [Kansas], and started a newspaper. This was the first printing press ever located south of the Arkansas River. The printing business being too tame an occupation for him, he about a year afterward engaged as a cowboy for the then well known Drum[m] & Snider [*sic*, Snyder] Cattle Co.[36] in the Indian Territory, in whose employment he remained about eighteen months and then started ranching for himself near Austin, Texas[.]

Oxford, Kansas, was a small gathering of buildings nearly 150 miles from Mound City. When Emery S. Hughes arrived, Mound City was not much more than a nascent community, a "city" made up of hastily built structures standing amid buffalo-hide tepees on the west bank of the Arkansas River. It had no newspaper in the area and Emery S. Hughes recognized an opportunity. Emery began the *Oxford Times* newspaper, a weekly that announced its birthing with a date of Thursday, June 22, 1871. He and William H. Mugford opened issue number one with a poetic "Salutatory":

> With this issue commences the existence of THE TIMES, though its birthplace still retains the frames of the Indian wigwam, the embers of whose camp fires are as yet scarcely cold. In our county, west of us, the buffalo slowly gives way before the invincible march of progress and civilization and the fleet-footed antelope yet lingers around us, both to leave the banks of our noble river, the home of its race for centuries past.

Senior Editor Mugford, only recently from Linn County as was his partner Hughes, enthusiastically stated the aims of the publication:

> It shall be our constant aim, however, with all the ability we may possess, to spare no effort to make THE TIMES worthy of the community and interests which it is intended to represent, and, we trust, a faithful exponent of all that pertains to the welfare of our county at large.

Emery Hughes was three years older than John R. He seemingly intended to make Oxford, Kansas, his home, as he boasted of the qualities of the land: "With the richest lands of the State around us, and a county that is receiving the major part of western immigration, we issue the first and only paper in Sumner county—the only paper west of the Arkansas River—the first number of which we regard as the commencement of the work of our future life." He concluded the salutatory by stating he and Mugford would rely upon the "intelligence and support of the inhabitants" and that they would identify themselves with both, "with the firm conviction of success for each."[37]

Emery Sargent Hughes, older brother of John R., as he appeared in later years. John R. and Emery S. Hughes operated the Running H horse ranch when they first arrived in Texas. *Courtesy Mike Cox.*

John may have seriously considered the printing business with his brother, but the thought was of short duration. Only once did editors Mugford and Hughes mention John in the columns of the *Times*, and then only briefly. In the fourth issue in the personal columns one learns that Clarence Chandler, E. R. Curtiss, and "Johnny" Hughes—"our 'little' brother"—had arrived the previous Saturday, July 8, from Linn County.[38] No indication is given as to what the trio was doing in Sumner County, but considering the numerous times buffalo hunting was mentioned in the columns of the *Times* one suspects they were hide hunters. The names of Chandler and Curtiss appear only this once in the life of John R. Hughes. C. H. Chandler within the next few years returned to Mound City, where by 1880 he was in the printing business, living in the house adjacent to the Thomas Hughes hotel, now with wife Almeda and a three-year-old daughter.[39] E. R. Curtiss remains but a name.

It is apparent that Mugford and Hughes intended to settle in Oxford for some time. On July 26 senior editor Mugford went back to Linn County to gather up his family and then together find a permanent home in Sumner County.[40] But all was not idyllic for either editor, in spite of the praises they had given the town and county three months earlier in their columns. On September 21, 1871, the readers found on page two in bold letters a "valedictory" signed by Em. S. Hughes: "My connection with the TIMES ceases with this issue. Ill health, and the desire to engage in other business, are the causes which have led me to sever my connection with the paper and its associations, for whose prosperity and welfare I have consistently labored, and in which I shall ever feel a deep interest."[41] Senior editor Mugford's plans did not bode well either. His "valedictory," appearing three weeks later, was downright abrupt: "My connection with this journal has ceased."[42] That was how be announced his leave taking. Hughes felt there was no need for further explanation and the real reasons for both discontinuing their association remain unclear. Thus, the newspaper, which had outwardly held so much promise back in June, was now going into the hands of others. Both Mugford and Hughes saw their futures in Texas.

Emery Sargent made the printing profession his career, as did younger brother William Parker Hughes. William Hughes, born October 14, 1857—two years younger than John—also followed the printer's trade, but prior to finding success in that career he served as a Texas Ranger for a short time. Sometime after an unidentified census enumerator counted the Mound City residents in 1875, William P. Hughes moved to Texas, where on September 1, 1877, he enrolled in Company E, Frontier Battalion. His commander, a Pennsylvania-born adventurer and former Union soldier Nelson O. Reynolds, but known to his men by the nickname of "Major" or "Mage" Reynolds, had had three years' experience in leadership behind him, besides a successful soldier's career combating Confederate guerrillas. After several years of travel in the Midwest and Central America and a brief stint as a jail guard in Hays County, Reynolds then enlisted in C. R. Perry's Company D, Frontier Battalion. Lieutenant Reynolds was in his mid-thirties when he took command of Company E.

William P. Hughes entered as a private but served for only three months. As to why his term of service was so short, he later wrote that "a reduction of the force was called for and I being a young man and inexperienced received my honorable discharge at Camp Bear Creek, November 30, 1877. I regretted it, as I liked the service and all the boys. . . ." Following his discharge he worked for various newspapers and learned the printer's trade. After working with newspapers in such cities as Denver, Colorado, and Laramie, Wyoming, he journeyed to Northport, Washington, where he began that town's first newspaper, the *Northport News*, the premier issue appearing on July 4, 1892. Northport became his home for life. In time he became the first postmaster, and then received further honors when the citizens elected him mayor. The city leaders continued their trust by appointing him police judge. After leaving Texas in 1877, William P. Hughes did not see brother John again until December 1936, a separation of six decades.[43]

By 1878, Emery was ready for a break from the printing business and in the fall, John R. and Emery S. Hughes started a ranch to raise horses, located on the border of Williamson and Travis counties, in central Texas. This "Long Hollow Ranch" would be John's work for the next nine years.[44] For strong young men it may have been possible to stock a ranch in the 1870s simply by capturing wild mustangs, but at least some of the horses acquired for the Long Hollow Ranch were purchased. In the fall of 1878 Emery S. Hughes, now a resident of Austin, placed an advertisement in the *Daily Democratic Statesman* reading: "WANTED—To buy a stock of horses of 50 to 100 head. Address, stating price and place of delivery, E. S. HUGHES. Austin, Texas."[45] The Hughes brothers were now in partnership. Fortunately, the brothers preserved their dealings in raising horses in a ledger, which they had printed for keeping their records, stamped "Hughes

Brothers' Horse Record."[46] In their ledger they *named* each horse acquired—be it by purchase or trade or natural increase—as well as the sire and dam, when acquired, valuation, how disposed of —be it trade or sale and if so valuation—and remarks.

The advertisement brought results as the record shows the brothers purchased five horses on September 20, 1878. They named these five Maggie, Dolly, Bill, Snoozer, and Bettie. On November 4, they acquired another horse that they named Kitten. These acquisitions seem unusual, as instead of purchasing them they obtained them as the result of a trade. They had acquired this first group of five in exchange for a "House & Lot." Their total value was determined to be $135.00. Kitten's value was $20.00. Of particular interest is the fact that of these six initial acquisitions, one was later sold for $22.50; one traded for "19 cords wood"; two were "Stolen"; and there were no remarks for the other two. This was in the days before barbed wire was common, when there was still open range, thus providing horsethieves easy access to any horses not corralled.

Emery Hughes was earning a regular paycheck as a printer, while at the same time building the ranch and considering the racing circuit. A brief note in the *Statesman* in the following year provided this information: "Mr. Hughes, of this office, now owns Tom McKinney, a famous racer, and invaluable to farmers and stockmen in this county."[47] Tom McKinney is the first horse named in the Hughes brothers' ledger: a stallion with bay face and nose and hind feet, fifteen hands high. It was purchased on January 7, 1879, for $160.00 cash, a large investment considering a cowboy received $1.00 per day.[48]

John R. with brother Emery S. now were established proprietors of the Long Hollow Ranch, their brand the Running H, certainly inspired by Richard King's Running W brand. An ownership title preserved by Hughes bears on it a crude drawing of several horses standing peacefully by a fence with a building in the background, also showing the brand which was placed on the left shoulder of horses and the left side of cattle. Although the ranch itself was located in Travis County, their post office was Liberty Hill in adjacent Williamson County. The title provides the location of the ranch as well. For the traveler who wanted to visit it was thirty-three miles northeast from Austin, Travis County; eight miles northwest from Bagdad in the same county and six miles southwest from Liberty Hill. [49] They recorded their brand at the Williamson County courthouse in Georgetown.[50]

It was not an easy task to suceed in the business of raising horses. They purchased Frankie, a sorrel sired by Steel Dust, on January 28, 1879, along with six other steeds. Those seven were valued at $100.00. Frankie did not live long on the Hughes ranch as she was "Killed by Tom McKinney" in April. Later, in May 1879, two horses were lost: Minnie was lost in breaking and Susie died from fistula. Later Kitty Wells, sired by Tom McKinney on Sallie, lived but a day as the foal fell victim to natural predators, one of several who were lost to wolves.[51]

Although working in the *Statesman* office and devoting energy to the ranch as well, Emery S. Hughes found time to court a young lady from Travis County, Miss Selma Bastian. The pair met perhaps due to the occupation of her father, Frederick Bastian, as he was a bookbinder by trade.[52] The Bastian family were natives of Prussia. Exactly when Emery S. and Selma Bastian met is uncertain, but she was still in her teens. They were well acquainted by March 1880, as on the sixteenth of that month a colt was born on the Long Hollow Ranch, sired by Tom McKinney on Sallie and was named Fred Bastian, in recognition of Selma's father.[53] Emery and Selma were joined together in matrimony on October 9, 1882, at the home of the bride's father, with Elder J. J. Williamson officiating. Mr. and Mrs. E. S. Hughes left the same evening on the train for Waco to honeymoon. One wedding announcement reported what perhaps everyone knew, that Hughes was "a most worthy young gentleman in all relations of life" and the bride was "equally estimable"; no doubt Austin sorrowed in their departure.[54]

The years living among the Indians proved invaluable as Hughes was put to the test in tracking human prey not long after the brothers formed their partnership. They were developing a respectable herd of horses, but sometime in August 1883, horsethieves raided the

Williamson and Travis counties area. The raiders, variously identified as the Cravens gang or the Johnson brothers gang, visited the area of the Long Hollow Ranch. The thieves stole horses bearing the Running H brand as well as many belonging to Hughes's neighbors, in all making a sizeable herd of stolen stock. Hughes was confident enough, or foolish enough, to believe that he could recover the stolen property by himself. He left alone, not knowing if he would recover the stock or even if he would return alive. His object was to recover the sixteen of his own and as many others of his neighbors as he possibly could. From Hughes's record book we know the names of the sixteen horses stolen. They were Flossie, Bee Creek, Moscow, Dinah, Bessie, Matilda, Fraulien [*sic*], Diamond, Quarter Horse, Sam, Kurg, Lee, Nancy, Magnolia, Elias, and Satilla. Moscow was John R. Hughes's favorite horse; he had sired four of the horses the thieves had stolen: Diamond, Quarter Horse, Sam, and Satilla.[55]

Most ranchers would have preferred companionship on such a venture, but Hughes began his odyssey alone, certainly his preference. With his property stolen, Hughes knew he was facing near financial ruin if he failed to recover his herd. Hughes made a simple agreement with his neighbors: he would track down the thieves and bring back the stolen property, if they would watch his place during his absence.

From the tracks remaining Hughes determined there were at least three men driving the stolen horses, but possibly a half dozen. The trail led westward, and Hughes resolutely followed it, ignoring the dangers of being alone on what was still frontier. He trailed them across the interior of Texas, into the vast Texas Panhandle, across the Llano Estacado, then into New Mexico Territory. The chase turned into weeks and then into months. Along the way, one of the thieves dropped out, leaving only two. At a point now lost to history, Hughes caught up with the thieves. It was a situation of two against one, two desperadoes against a relatively untested man. When Hughes challenged the pair to surrender, they resisted. Their resistance was costly as he killed one but he allowed the other to escape with his life, no doubt on a very fast horse. Hughes's first biographer, G. W. Ogden, writing in 1911, summed up the result of the engagement with a twist of ironic humor: "After confrontation one lay dead and the other fleeing, riding for his life. . . . and the whole herd of horses was in the hands of the young rancher who would not sit quietly by and be robbed like a gentleman."[56] Hughes was absent from his ranch for nearly a year; he estimated he had traveled a total of three thousand miles. He recited the details of his long trek to G. W. Ogden; matter of factly and with no bravado.

> Before I enlisted in the ranger force, I was a ranchman on the line of Travis and Williamson counties. A band of thieves stole about seventy-five head of horses from my range. Among them were sixteen head of mine. I followed them to New Mexico, got all my horses back and a lot of my neighbors' horses. The band of men was all broken up. Two of them were convicted for stealing my horses, and sent to the New Mexico penitentiary.[57]

About four years after the interview with G. W. Ogden, Hughes told a *San Antonio Express* reporter the story of his pursuit of the horsethieves, only with slight changes. Now it was in 1885 when a band of outlaws raided the area where he was living and stole seventy horses, sixteen of which were his. It was "the very daring of the nefarious enterprise" that angered Hughes, "and he proposed to his neighbors that if they would look after his ranch while he was gone he would 'go and get the thieves.'" The trek after the stolen horses was, according to the *Express* reporter, "the most remarkable criminal chase that was probably ever made. . . . One man against a desperate gang of six cut-throats." Was the increase in the number of horsethieves a creation of Hughes or the reporter? The outlaws had several days' start but Hughes finally found their trail. "For days, weeks and months he silently and relentlessly followed the thieves. At night he would throw his saddle upon the ground, hobble his horse and go into camp. Close around him howled wolves and coyotes. These and the myriads of twinkling stars that looked down upon him from the broad canopy of heaven were his only company in the solitudes, with the exception of his patient, endurance-bearing horse."

The *Express* reporter's story follows Hughes from Central Texas, northward through the Texas Panhandle, then south again into New Mexico Territory. Somewhere in New Mexico, according to this version, Hughes came upon their camp. "The memory of the long, silent ride, the hardships he had encountered and the promise that he had made to his neighbors that he 'would get the thieves' put bravery into his heart and he made the attack upon the outlaws with such vehemence and boldness that they were able to offer but little resistance." One significant detail stands out in this version: the action must have been brief, as when the gunfire ended there were four dead thieves. He delivered the two surviving thieves to the New Mexico authorities. They were tried, convicted, and sentenced to prison.[58] Obviously this reporter chose to take considerable license in his version of the confrontation of Hughes and the thieves. One man challenging six horsethieves, killing four of them: could it really have happened that way? One writer, acquainted with Emery H. Hughes, may have learned of the meeting between his uncle and the thieves. William Cx Hancock related the version he had learned from the nephew as follows:

> At last he overhauled the robbers. Characteristically disregarding the odds, the furious young rancher attacked without hesitation. When the echoing thunder of gunfire died away in the New Mexico canyon, four rustlers lay dead and two wounded survivors were begging for a chance to surrender. He turned the pair over to the nearest sheriff.[59]

Yet a third version was born when Hughes stated to an unidentified reporter in May 1915 that before enlisting in the Rangers, he ranched on the line of Travis and Williamson counties when a "band of thieves stole about seventy-five head of horses from my range. Among them were sixteen head of mine. I followed them to New Mexico, got all my horses back and a lot of my neighbors' horses. The band of men was all broken up. Two of them were convicted for stealing my horses, and sent to the New Mexico penitentiary."[60] In this interview Hughes made not even an allusion to killing any of the thieves when recovering the stolen horses.

The saga of Hughes and the horsethieves varied with the telling, but how much was Hughes's own accounting of the experience and how much was created by the reporter or historian is anyone's guess today. The number of thieves varies, as does the year; and the distance involved also varies: was it 1,000 or 3,000 miles? The answer to these questions only John R. Hughes knew, other than what the record book shows: that thieves stole sixteen head from his herd in August of 1883. The salient fact from the various accounts strongly indicates that Hughes was a man determined to right the wrong inflicted upon him; his bravery and resoluteness were unquestioned; his ability to persevere in a time of danger and uncertainty was predominant. He determined his course of action and remained true to it, and in so doing not only recovered his own property but that of his neighbors.

During the years of the Works Project Administration (1935–1943), Vera P. Elliott interviewed Hughes in El Paso. During her brief interview with him he did touch on his early experience of recovering his stolen horses. Elliott recorded that Hughes "talked of a time, when, merely to ride the trails and live was a daily struggle. . . . As a young man he caught wild horses on his ranch, a start toward independence. When horsethieves drove off most of them, he followed the thieves month after month, overtook them and recovered his property. This led to his enlistment with the Texas Rangers. . . ." Perhaps Hughes was too modest to bring up the bloody recovery of his property with Miss Elliott, ignoring the gunfight that may have left one or more men dead.[61] Unfortunately most of it is recorded in Elliott's paraphrasing, rather than Hughes's own words.

The Elliott interview provides the identity of the thieves as the Craven brothers. They have also been identified as the Johnson brothers. No contemporary accounting or notice of the raid in the Williamson-Travis counties area records has yet surfaced. Of interest, and it may only be coincidental, is that in 1870 there was a household in Williamson County with Johnsons and Cravens living together. James Johnson is shown as head of household, with five others: a twenty-eight-year-old female, Nanee; Henry and Jesse Johnson, aged fifteen and twelve years respectively, and two others named Craven, Jennie and James, aged nineteen and seventeen years respectively. James Johnson was a native of Alabama while all the others were born in Arkansas. The males of this configuration, a few years later, could have become the Craven-Johnson brothers gang.[62]

However, in spite of the various accounts of the recovery of his stolen horses, whether he acted alone in taking them back from the thieves, or if he had the assistance of an unidentified New Mexico officer, a rare letter signed only "Farmer" and published in an 1885 periodical may be closest to the truth after all. What prompted the letter to the editor of the *Texas Farm and Ranch* publication, an agricultural journal first published by Franklin Pierce Holland in Austin in 1883, was an early issue that pictured on the cover what appeared to the reader to be a "cow thief."[63] At least that is what "Farmer" ostensibly accepted the illustration to represent, as it pictured the man carrying six-shooters. Farmer wrote with irony, stating that if

> our all wise Governor [John Ireland] had not declared that no occasion existed in West Texas for carrying pistols the vagrant Indians and the Mexicans, who murdered poor Merrill and his wife, last week, might have been hurt. . . . And again if honest men were permitted to carry pistols, such good men as the Craven brothers, who stole sixty horses from the poor people in Travis county at one "swoop," might not be permitted to carry on the professions they have devoted their lives to . . . These gentlemen then were followed 3000 miles by a brave citizen of Travis county (being a law-abiding man, of course unarmed), and caught and jailed in [New] Mexico.

Farmer wrote the letter from Georgetown, county seat of Williamson County, and dated it January 3, 1885. The Merrill couple referred to was Thomas Merrill and his wife, both murdered near Van Horn, Texas, by Mexicans on Christmas Eve, 1884. "Farmer" was obviously an educated man, capable of writing such a letter using irony to make his point that there were still plenty of areas of Texas in which Texans should have the right to carry their gun.

Could "Farmer" have been John R. Hughes himself? Alternatively, more likely brother Emery, recognized for his mastery of words while editing the newspaper back in Oxford, Kansas. John no doubt shared his adventure with Emery, but Farmer omitted certain details about the New Mexico experience, which only later John revealed, almost by chance. In 1907, an Austin reporter provided a review of Hughes's life up to that time, headlining his contribution "Ranger Leader Whose Career is Thrilling One" with sub-headline "Captain Hughes, of Retiring and Religious Nature, Hero of Many Daring Battles."[64] The report states that before spending most of his career on the Rio Grande border he "worked on ranches as a cowboy in New Mexico and Western Texas before he joined the Ranger force." Furthermore, Hughes "was personally acquainted with many of the noted characters of the frontier" and "has been compelled, in the exercise of his duty as an officer, to arrest many of his old-time friends and associates." The specific incident referred to was the arrest of William D. Barbee in 1892. Hughes and Barbee had "worked on the Las Animas ranch in Sierra County, New Mexico, together in 1884 and were close friends. Barbee turned out bad. . . ." Hughes spent nearly a year away from the Williamson County ranch, 350 days by his own accounting, tracking the thieves who had stolen his horses and those of his neighbors. In reality, it did not take a year to track them to Sierra County, New Mexico, but Hughes may have finally determined where the stolen horses were held and over a period of time befriended the owners-thieves before revealing the horses were his. William D. Barbee may have been one of the thieves he had trailed, and the close friendship Hughes exhibited with him may have been only a sham. The details of what happened in New Mexico may forever be unclear.[65]

Hughes, once in Texas, had intended to be a rancher. No doubt while trailing the recovered herd back to Williamson County he envisioned simply the continuation of what he and brother Emery had started: to raise horses profitably. When he returned to his ranch, he unbuckled his gun belt "and went about attending to my stock and wanted to be at peace with the world."[66] But events would force him to again change his plans.

~ 2 ~

"Hold up, Wesley!"

"YOU WILL OF COURSE BE ON THE LOOKOUT FOR ANY FUGI-
TIVES FROM JUSTICE WHO MAY BE ON OR NEAR YOUR ROUTE."
— *Captain L. P. Sieker to Private Hughes, December 24, 1887*

By 1884 the future looked bright indeed for John W. Braeutigam, a popular and respected businessman residing near Fredericksburg, Texas. He had, years before, chosen to leave his native Saxony and had brought his wife Christine to the "new world," where he became a successful businessman. After more than three decades he could look with pride on his family—a wife and eight children—besides his successful business. It was on the former United States army post known as Fort Martin Scott, long abandoned by the government for lack of any military need, where he established a beer garden. Described by some as an amusement center, *Braeutigams Garten* to the native German-speaking population or simply Braeutigam's Garden was used for local "gala celebrations," including the Fourth of July. Local residents established the first Gillespie County Fair in 1881 and chose Braeutigam's "garden" for the fairgrounds. The businessman was popular and respected in the community.[1]

He certainly had been aware of the dangers of living in this western territory, but the threat of outlaw raiding parties causing havoc was rare in an established community such as Fredericksburg. County sheriffs as well as Texas Rangers had established by the 1870s a high degree of law

24

and order. The dangers to a businessman such as Braeutigam in 1884 were few: minor thieves or ruffians, or natural disasters such as a fire. He may have heard about the trek of John R. Hughes, but the Long Hollow Ranch was some seventy-five miles east, although Hughes may have passed through Gillespie County.

However, in spite of the good work of local law officers, tragedy struck the Braeutigam family on the night of September 3, 1884, shortly after Hughes had returned from his hunt for the horsethieves. Four armed men entered J. W. Braeutigam's place of business intending to steal whatever they wanted. He proved to be a brave fighter, but at the age of fifty-four years his resistance against the armed quartet was not enough to drive them away. One of them shot him to death. Ten-year-old son Henry Braeutigam, who was the first to come upon the scene, no doubt heard the shots that killed his father.[2]

The murder shocked the community. Gov. John Ireland, who had many friends in the primarily German community, resolved to find the murderers and give them their just punishment. How the authorities determined who made up the guilty party is unknown but an indictment was filed on November 17, 1884, that named three men: Wesley Collier, Ed Janes, and Jackson Beam.[3] The name of the fourth man, James Fannin, was later added to the list, although this might be a pseudonym. One week later Gillespie County Sheriff John Walton had the trio in his custody, captured at New Braunfels, Comal County, some forty miles northeast of San Antonio.[4] The jail in Fredericksburg, according to Ranger Sergeant Ira Aten who knew the place well, was "an old rock and wood affair," which could contain ruffians and drunks. Aten further recalled that "knowing the feelings of the people there were very bitter against the men," authorities transferred the prisoners to the Bexar County jail in San Antonio for their own safety. The Bexar County jail may have been considered among the best in the state but within four months' time the prisoners managed to escape.[5] In the meantime another one of the fugitives was arrested and locked up in the Fredericksburg jail. "This building," as Sergeant Aten wrote, with tongue in cheek perhaps, "almost immediately and mysteriously burned down upon the prisoner."[6] There was no mystery, as clearly it was an example of "popular justice"—Wild West style.

Two of the three remaining fugitives were re-captured, although the details of how this was done have been lost. The law caught up with Wesley Collier and Jackson Beam and placed them in the Mason County jail, forty miles north, for safekeeping until a new facility could be constructed in Fredericksburg. But the jail in Mason was not escape-proof either, as on September 12, 1885, Collier and Beam escaped yet again. When they were still not re-captured in the spring of 1886, Ranger Adjutant General King[7] decided it was time for the Rangers to become involved. He called Ira Aten to Austin and gave him certain instructions and sent him into the governor's office. According to Aten, Governor Ireland "lost no time and came right to the point." He was given orders to bring the murderers in, "dead or alive."[8]

A young John R. Hughes, from a photograph by David P. Barr of San Antonio. *Courtesy Western History Collections, University of Oklahoma Library.*

After several failed efforts to capture the escaped prisoners Aten determined he needed help. A mutual friend must have introduced the young Ranger to rancher John R. Hughes, whom Aten didn't know, but who was willing to listen. Aten recalled:

I had never seen Hughes before and don't think he had ever seen me. He had the usual cowman's frankness and hospitality, and, although I was so dejected that I felt I had lost my last friend, his presence seemed to react upon me. I liked his looks and it seemed that I could see a spark of sympathy in his eyes, so I just opened up and told him my whole story. After I had finished, Hughes said in his quiet, mild, sympathetic manner, "I will go with you and help you."[9]

Hughes's reaction cheered up the dejected Aten who now knew he had found a new and worthy friend. The fact that Hughes, older than Aten by eight years, *listened* to him no doubt contributed to the respect the young man held from the onset.[10] First, Aten deputized Hughes in order for him to work officially; then the pair outlined their plan together. Neither Hughes nor Aten recorded the details of their hunt, but Ranger Aten and deputy Hughes were quickly on the trail of Wesley Collier. After some weeks of hard tracking, they found him at the home of rancher Nicholas Dayton,[11] near Liberty Hill in Williamson County, not far from the Long Hollow Ranch of Hughes. It was going to be a case of kill or be killed once Ranger Aten[12] uttered the words of "Hold up, Wesley" to accused murderer Collier. It was Sunday morning and they wanted to take him then by surprise, hoping to avoid bloodshed— Collier's or their own. All day Sunday they lay in wait, watching the Dayton house. Their intentions were to take the house during supper time but that proved impossible due to the sharp ears of the numerous dogs, which put up "a terrible rumpus every time they approached the house." Instead, the pair decided to wait until the next morning. After the Dayton family and their "guest" had retired for the evening, Hughes and Aten hid in the corn-crib for the night. One of them alternated with the other for the night's watch, as they knew that at sunrise members of the family would begin to stir.

In the early morning Hughes managed to sneak—somehow without disturbing the dogs this time—to the west door of the house where Collier was believed to be sleeping, while Aten entered the front, also not alerting the guard dogs. By chance Collier, just awakening from the night's sleep, noticed Hughes, as some sound or movement attracted his attention to the back door. Perhaps as Hughes had turned the knob to try the door, only to discover it was locked, did the slight sound alert Collier. With the fugitive thus distracted, Aten entered and uttered the words of "Hold up, Wesley," having the drop with his pistol in his hand. Ignoring the fact that Aten had him covered, instead of reaching upwards Collier reached under his pillow for a pistol. Aten had no choice but to react with gunfire. He fired once. There was no need for a second shot.[13]

Wesley Collier had been staying at the Dayton ranch for about a week, the family apparently having no indication he was a wanted fugitive. He gave his name as Martin, saying he was a relative of Judge Martin of nearby Blanco County. Collier, certainly realizing there were men hunting him, had found a suitable place to lie low. He had had a "skirmish" with Aten back in April; there were no fatalities in that exchange of gunfire, but Collier had received a wound in the right hand.[14]

Within hours after Aten's bullet ended the life of C. W. Collier, alias Martin, Dr. Henry H. Thorpe of Williamson County arrived to examine the body.[15] Whether Hughes or Aten had gone for the medical examiner is unknown, but Dr. Thorpe arrived, accompanied by a newspaper reporter who described the scene:

> Upon entering the room we found everything just as Mr. Aten had left it three hours before. The murdered man lay across the bed as he had fallen, one hand convulsively clutching at the ghastly wound in his breast. He was partially dressed, being in the act of putting on his clothes when he was shot. He had on his pants, one sock, and was in the act of drawing on his boot when his attention was attracted to Aten. His face was not as distorted as we thought it would be, considering the violence of his death. The leaden missile entered his breast

about three inches to the left side of the right nipple, coursed down-ward, struck a rib and glanced off, probably into the intestines, though the range of the ball may not have carried it that low.

After Aten's first bullet found its mark, he immediately cocked his pistol for another shot, but now Collier was able to speak for the first—and last—time. "Don't shoot, I am dead," he uttered, and fell back upon the bed.

After the fatal shot Hughes and Aten examined the dead man. In his pockets they found an assortment of items: several cartridges and strings, a comb, a knife, a match box and whet rock, a purse with $5 in gold and $1 in silver, a piece of soap, a handkerchief and a piece of paper with the initials "M.L.D." which meant nothing to Aten nor Hughes, although the initials matched those of Mary L. Dayton, the mother, as well as the daughter. In addition to these miscellaneous trifles they found Collier had three pistols: a .45 caliber Smith & Wesson, a .45 Colt's, and a smaller .38 Invincible, the latter an unreliable hideout pistol. All these were "loaded all around and in prime condition." What really attracted their attention was the unusual manner in which the dead outlaw had carried his weapons. Typically a man wore his handguns in holsters on either side, or if a two-gun man, on both hips. Collier however, wore his pistols *under* his vest, one on each side, with another in an inside pocket. They were arranged in an "ingenious manner, being connected together by a strap which passed over his shoulders, terminating at each end in a scabbard. . . ." He had worn his principal weapons in concealed shoul-der holsters, not in scabbards on his hips.

In the barn Hughes and Aten examined Collier's saddlebags. Here they found more cartridges and a pair of wire snippers, which he "prob-ably had with him to cut his way out should he become hemmed up in a wire lane by his adversaries." The unidentified reporter concluded that Collier's "complete outfit showed him to have been a man who was strictly up to his business in every particular."[16]

Ira Aten succinctly reported his first kill as a Ranger to his supe-rior: "on the 25th of May met and killed Collier who resisted arrest."[17]

Hughes, being at this time a deputized citizen who had only assisted Aten in tracking down the fugitive, left no account of his active participation. Apparently he only observed what Aten had accomplished, but no doubt catching up with Collier was due to Hughes's tracking ability, which led the pair to the fatal doorstep of the Dayton home.

What Aten omitted from his laconic account was that prior to their approach to the house, they had made a prisoner of a young son of Nicholas Dayton to prevent him from warning Collier that the law was about. George Porter Dayton slept in the same room with Wesley Collier. He was seven years old at the time, and it was his early rising that also awakened the Dayton "house guest." George normally arose early and part of his chores included tending the horses first thing prior to breakfast. Naturally his mother arose as well to start breakfast for her family.[18] With the young boy coming out, and knowing there was a chance of gunplay, Aten and Hughes locked him in a corn-crib. They then approached the house, one hundred yards away. As Aten entered the house and went through the kitchen, Mrs. Dayton certainly expressed surprise if not shock and Aten must have told her to keep quiet. Mr. Dayton never forgave the law for having killed a man in his home; that he was a thief and murderer fleeing the law made no difference in his mind. The sanctity of his home had been violated by the law.

The official records fail to provide additional details on this killing of outlaw Wesley Collier, or what happened to the other defendants. The court documents identify only Collier, Janes, and Beam but the fourth man was later identified as James Fannin, possibly an alias. Robert Penniger edited the *Fredericksburger Wochenblatt* then and later compiled a "Festival Edition" for the Golden Anniversary of the Founding of Fredericksburg, which provided a "brief account of the German Colonies in Texas Established by the Mainzer Nobleman's Society and Chronicles of the City of Fredericksburg." One of the articles discussed the Braeutigam killing, in which he told of the quartet robbing the man. According to Penniger, one of the four was shot to death by a Ranger; one was burned to death "when the jail was destroyed by fire"; one was shot to death near Mason; and the fourth man, "presumably the one who committed the murder, a fellow named Fannin, escaped."[19]

If Aten and Hughes had not been consciously aware of their developing friendship before, the act of their being in a life-threatening situation certainly contributed to that friendship. "From this introduction grew a friendship that has steadily ripened as the years passed," Aten recalled. "Not only that, but this incident was the beginning of a life of service to Texas given by Captain Hughes."[20] His successful experience as a deputy working with Ira Aten convinced John R. Hughes to join the Frontier Battalion the next year.

On August 10, 1887, John Reynolds Hughes stood before Williamson County Clerk J. W. Hodges and his deputy John N. Ellyson to swear the following oath:

> I do solemnly swear (or affirm) that I will faithfully and impartially discharge and perform all the duties incumbent upon me as a member of the Frontier battalion until August 31, 1887, unless sooner discharged, according to the best of my skill and ability, and agreeably to the Constitution and law of the United States and of this State. So help me God.

He signed his name "John R. Hughes" boldly and clearly. Then Hodges and Ellyson signed their names. Hughes, successful man-hunter as proven by the recovery of the stolen horses in 1883–84 and then as a deputy working with Ranger Aten, was now a Texas Ranger.[21] He intended to serve for a short while, "expecting to stay only six or eight months" as he later recalled.[22] Aten was with Hughes when he took the oath, and on the day following he mailed the oath to Adjutant General King, confident the new recruit would be accepted into the Frontier Battalion. Aten added that they would leave for Lampasas County that very day, August 11.[23] Neither Ranger could have envisioned that Hughes would eventually rise to the rank of captain and serve the state for nearly three tumultuous decades until his retirement in 1915.

Three weeks after enlisting in the Ranger service, Hughes received his first "Certificate of Indebtedness" or pay voucher, for the twenty-one days of service. He had earned a dollar a day and now had $21.00 to show for it. The voucher was signed by his commanding officer, Capt. Frank Jones. Thirty-two-year-old Hughes must have stood a little taller than his normal five feet eleven inches, presenting an imposing and impressive presence with his dark complexion and brown hair and eyes.[24]

Captain Jones of Company D, Frontier Battalion, was one of the six sons of William E. and Kezziah Rector Jones. His brothers who also served as Rangers were Emmett, Gerry, Pinckney "Pink," and the twin brothers William Kenner and James Russell. Frank L. Jones began his career in 1875 under Capt. Ira Long of Company A of the Frontier Battalion. He next served under Capt. Pat Dolan in Company F and then under Capt. Daniel W. Roberts in Company D and then under Capt. Lamartine P. Sieker. By 1884 he was a lieutenant in Company D and

Courtesy Linda Wolff.

Captain Frank Jones of Company D, Frontier Battalion, killed in action on Pirate Island.
Courtesy The Centennial Collection, Archives of the Big Bend, Bryan Wildenthal Memorial Library, Sul Ross State University, Alpine, Texas.

then was promoted to captain on May 1, 1886. His first wife, Grace O'Grady, died young, and he later married Mrs. Helen Baylor Gillett, the daughter of Texas Ranger Capt. George W. Baylor. By the time Captain Jones and Hughes met to work together, the captain had behind him an impressive career as a Ranger.[25]

Sgt. Ira Aten had been a Ranger since June 1, 1883, thus giving him four years' experience as a lawman, which enabled him to judge John R. Hughes as a good candidate for the service. The exact date of Hughes's decision to set aside raising horses to become a Ranger for good is unknown, but it was probably during that year of 1887.

In addition to the search for Collier, Aten had on his mind train robbers John Barber and Bill Whitley.[26] Hughes was on his Running

H Ranch during that time, but even in Williamson County, only miles from the state's capital and not far from where the Dayton family lived, danger was ever present. On August 6, 1887, just days prior to Hughes's oath taking, Williamson County Deputy Sheriff William J. Stanley was shot to death, lured from his home at night by three men telling him his fence had been cut. The trio of assassins riddled his body with eight shots, killing him instantly. It was generally understood that he was killed because he had been "very active in hunting up criminals," or so reported the popular *Galveston Daily News*.[27] Hughes was certainly aware of the killing of Deputy Stanley; it was the general belief that members of the train-robbing Whitley-Cornett gang murdered him.

One of Ranger Hughes's first acts was to join up with friend Aten to continue the pursuit of these train robbers. Captain Jones convinced Adjutant General King to enlist Hughes "to assist Sergt. Aten in the capture of John Barber & Bill Whitely wanted for train robbery."[28] The most recent assault on a Texas train was at McNeil, twelve miles north of Austin. On the evening of May 18 a gang, the number estimated to be between twelve and fifteen, forced the train to stop by placing a log across the rails. They bound station agent S. R. Ely and then showered the train cars with a fusillade of bullets, forcing passengers to drop to the floor for safety. Estimates of the amount of money taken ranged from the relatively small amount of $4,000 to a huge estimate of $55,000. Passenger Harry Wanda was wounded, but was able to provide authorities and the press with details. A brakeman was also wounded.[29]

A month later, on June 18, ten or twelve robbers assaulted a Southern Pacific train near Schulenburg, in Fayette County. This time the estimate of loot taken from the express car and the passengers ranged from $8,000 to $15,000. As train robbery was big news, the press covered any robbery or attempt at robbery with considerable detail. The *New York Times* called the Schulenburg robbery "the most daring train robbery that ever occurred in Texas," a statement perhaps true at that date. El Paso County Sheriff James H. White happened to be on the train and was able to identify the man considered the leader, "Captain Dick," whose real name was Braxton "Brack" Cornett, a fugitive from

Goliad County.[30] The frequent train robberies now placed every lawman, amateur or professional, searching for clues to their identity and whereabouts.[31]

On September 10, Private Hughes and Sergeant Aten were in Cisco, Eastland County, some 150 miles west of Fort Worth and on the trail of the train robbers; but now they had to separate as Aten was called to testify in court in adjacent Brown County.[32] Hughes was now literally a "lone star ranger"[33] for the first time, and was ordered to report to Company D headquarters in Edwards County, some two hundred miles due south. On September 16, 1887, Hughes reported to Captain Jones, ready for orders.[34]

What specific duties were initially assigned to the new recruit—other than working with Sergeant Aten—are unknown. Certainly Private Hughes quickly made a point to get acquainted with the other Rangers of Company D, and the actions that had taken place in recent months before his arrival. He certainly learned of the Ranger efforts to capture the Odle brothers, John, Will and Alvin, the former wanted for murder and all three wanted for horse theft in Burnet County. Lawmen did arrest John, Will, and Alvin Odle in April and jailed them in Burnet, the county seat, but they escaped from jail and became fugitives again.

The day before Hughes's enlistment, Ranger Baz L. Outlaw, popularly known as "Bass," with three other Rangers returned from an unsuccessful nine-day scout after train robbers. No doubt Hughes looked forward to as much action as possible. Hughes was well aware of the ever present danger facing a Texas lawman in the 1880s—and for decades to come. Only a year before, Privates Outlaw and J. M. Mize experienced a near deadly encounter with fugitive James Davenport. No one was killed but Outlaw received two wounds: one over an eye and one in the hip; Davenport's shots also left a wound in Mize's shoulder.[35] Davenport escaped to fight another day.

Hughes's first orders were to scout after fugitives, not identified in the monthly returns. He and two other Rangers were away from camp on detached service, and did not return until October 16. Apparently they were unsuccessful in capturing any fugitives as the monthly return

Camp of Company D. From left, Baz L. Outlaw, Charles Fusselman, James R. Robinson on horse, Ira Aten, Walter W. Jones, J. W. Durbin on horse, Calvin Aten, Frank L. Schmid on horse, John R. Hughes, Jim King, and Ernest Rogers. *Courtesy Robert G. McCubbin Collection.*

fails to mention any arrests. Two weeks later Company D broke camp after orders were received from Adjutant General Wilbur Hill King to move to Starr County, down on the Rio Grande. The company moved through the communities of Uvalde, Carrizo Springs, Laredo, and Carrizo on the way to Starr County.[36] By the twentieth of November Captain Jones and Company D had established their camp near Rio Grande City, the county seat. The one commissioned captain, sergeant, teamster, and ten privates had covered over three hundred miles during those twenty-two days.[37]

On Christmas Eve 1887, Hughes was at Uvalde, west of San Antonio. He received orders to take certain state property to Barksdale in Edwards County and turn it over to Sgt. James A. Brooks, later to be Captain Brooks. Following this transfer he was to return to his company "by nearest and best route taking wood water and grain into consideration." What supplies he might need were to be obtained from the firm of F. A. Piper & Company. Capt. L. P. Sieker added the following to his orders, not realizing perhaps that Hughes would naturally be alert for wanted men: "You will of course be on the lookout for any fugitives from Justice who may be on or near your route." By the end of December Hughes was in Laredo, and requested permission to take the train to Realitos where Company D was to be stationed. Hughes's request was denied, as Sieker could see no reason to ride the more expensive means of transportation. Unless there was "something urgent," Sieker advised, he was to ride his horse.[38]

On December 10 Captain Jones broke camp in Starr County, leaving a detachment there, and moved to Realitos, Duval County. He found suitable water and grass for his command in a pasture belonging to a Mr. Savage, the site now becoming "Camp Savage" for the Rangers.[39] It was here that one of the most famous group photographs of Texas Rangers was made, although unfortunately Hughes was part of the detachment left behind and out on scout when the photographer visited. Hughes was away from camp from December 18, 1887, to January 10, 1888, dealing with state property and hunting fugitives.

During the decades prior to the 1880s one of the fears of western settlers was a raid by Comanches, Kiowas, or Lipan Apaches, but the threat of a child or an adult being killed or captured by them for slavery purposes was now diminished due to the success of the Rangers. But now Hughes had to deal with the kidnapping of a Mexican by Mexicans. Hughes was one of the five men with Captain Jones hunting the men charged with the kidnapping of Juan García Barrera, a fifty-two year old prominent Mason and stockman of Starr County. Barrera had left his ranch on August 31, 1887, near San Pedro in Starr County, intending to travel to Mier, Mexico. At a place called La Retamosa, three miles from his ranch, Barrera met four men who he first believed were Rangers. Too late did Barrera realize his mistake, as they were bandits who captured him, took what arms he had, his food, and $200 in his valise and then informed him his life would be spared if he paid them $3,000. Barrera, no doubt speaking truthfully, responded that he could not possibly raise that amount of money, but could within a week's time raise half the amount. He was then forced to give instructions that $1,500 should be turned over to the bandits, the instructions to be delivered to his son. Nearly three weeks later the money was delivered and the bandits, after much quarreling among themselves, released Barrera. He had been "taken blindfolded through the thicket, his clothes torn to fragments, wet with rains and drying on his person, subject to the constant insults of the bandits who threatened his life."[40]

How the men suspected of the kidnapping were captured is not recorded in the monthly returns, but on December 6, Captain Jones with five men and Starr County veteran Ranger and now Sheriff William W. Shely,[41] scouting down the Rio Grande covering Starr and Hidalgo counties, arrested two of the suspected kidnappers: Viviano Díaz and Cicilio Barra. The two were turned over to Sheriff Shely. The Rangers then left Rio Grande City to make additional arrests, but in their absence during the night of December 7 "about 7 o'clock, the sheriff was waylaid by a band of from fifteen to twenty armed Mexicans who took the two prisoners away from him and hung them both."[42] Shortly afterwards one Frank Gardiner discovered the pair, "dangling at the end of a rope upon the same tree." A coroner's inquest declared officially what everyone already knew: they were both dead. The coroner determined they "had been hung but a few hours."[43]

Lynching the kidnappers of Barrera did prove that some Mexicans disapproved of the maltreatment of lawabiding citizens. The thieves and kidnappers who quarreled whether to allow Barrera to live or to die were not lynched summarily by Anglo ranchers but were "hung by Mexican vigilantes. . . ."[44] In case there were other members of the kidnapping band still in the area, Private Hughes, serving as his body guard, took Barrera to Roma in southwestern Starr County on the Rio Grande. Barrera had no further terrifying experiences; he reached Mier, his original destination, and by January 10, 1888, Hughes was back in camp.[45]

Five days later Hughes wrote to Captain Sieker that he had been ill, explaining that he "had an attact [sic] of bilious fevor [sic] and a very bad cold do not know the cause of my sickness unless it was laying out in the cold weather." Besides this report he enclosed the expense account for himself and his two men.[46] Although Hughes failed to capture any fugitives on his most recent scouts, he had proved his leadership abilities.

In the early months of 1888 Hughes experienced one of the more perplexing problems of that decade: fence cutting. Fence cutting had become a real problem as early as August of 1883, the same month thieves had stolen horses from the Running H Ranch. Talk was already common that there existed a "wide-spread organization to destroy the wire fences around large wire pastures." A Shackelford County resident complained that this organization "throughout the stock raising district" had just cut 2 ½ miles of his fence, cutting it at every post. There were other reports, in which smaller stock raisers were suspected of eradicating fences "to have free pasturage over the whole country." It was generally understood that the small number of Rangers were "utterly unequal to the task of protecting the large pastures unless their number was increased to thousands," which would be an impossible task. The *Fort Worth Gazette* predicted this "growing practice of fence cutting" would trouble the stock growing country "for some time."[47]

The adjutant general and governor received complaints regarding fence cutting almost daily. Certainly the problem was exaggerated by some, such as a lengthy report from Montague County that compared the fence cutting organization to the Ku Klux Klan: fence cutters operated in darkness; the meetings were under the cover of darkness; its membership was "deeply veiled." The fence cutting "league" had as its goal the extermination of the wire fence, and "it's [*sic*] power is amazingly illustrated in the terrible blows which have already been dealt."

The situation was approaching a dangerous point. A man in Jack County was reportedly lynched for "interfering" with a party cutting the wires. Fence cutters were so strong and well organized that all that was needed was "but a signal from the leaders of the secret organization to inaugurate a terrible, deadly unflinching contest, a border warfare, in which the black flag would be raised, brother arrayed against brother, friend against friend, neighbor against neighbor."[48] This writer feared the Civil War would be fought again, only over the question of fences rather than the question of slavery.

A question frequently asked: Why would not the Rangers prevent the destruction of fences? The *Statesman* of Austin provided the answer with word from the governor: "It would be about as easy for five policemen of Austin to protect every citizen" as for the Rangers "to watch every man's fence in the country."[49] Too many miles of fence, too few Rangers was the simple answer.

The conflict over fencing proved one of the more perplexing problems of the 1880s for Governor Ireland. The invention of barbed wire had changed the range drastically as ranchers could control their land holdings. Some placed fences around precious water holes, which resulted in antagonism from smaller ranchers whose cattle required access to those water holes. Many ranchers believed in the concept of the open range and free grass, but wire fences curtailed that practice. In addition, fencing did allow the big ranches to require fewer cowboys to patrol the range. These

Ranger camp on the Leona River three miles below Uvalde. From left: Charles Fusselman; Ira Aten (in background); Walter W. Jones, seated; Jim King, cutting meat off deer hide; unidentified boy in background; Ernest Rogers, making bread; Cal Aten, squatting down at skillet; Frank L. Schmid, directly behind Aten; J. Walter Durbin, between the two trees; James Robinson, to right of tree with wash tub; and John R. Hughes seated at far right. *Photo from the M. T. Gonzaullas Collection, courtesy the Texas Ranger Hall of Fame and Museum, Waco, Texas.*

were only a few of the reasons that brought a new problem into Texas, as cutting a fence amounted to the destruction of private property. The legislature, under leadership of Governor Ireland, had, by early 1884, created laws that should have reduced fence cutting drastically. The law read, in part, that anyone who "wantonly, or with intent to injure the owner, and willfully cut, injure or destroy any fence, or part of a fence, . . . shall be deemed guilty of an offense." Punishment ranged from a prison term of one year to not more than five years. In addition the law required that a gate be placed in every three miles of fencing; it had to be at least eight feet wide and remain unlocked. Violation of this misdemeanor amounted to a fine of $100 to $200 for each offense. The laws against fence cutting became effective on February 6, 1884.[50]

Sergeant Aten had had experience with fence cutters before Hughes joined the Rangers. Adjutant General King had entrusted Aten to work up fence cutting cases in Lampasas County in the summer of 1886, then later in nearby Brown County and then in Navarro County, then working with Ranger Jim King.[51] In Navarro County Aten devised a system involving booby-trapping the wires with dynamite, killing or at least injuring the wire cutter. Aten was proud of his "invention" but when he informed the governor of this device he was ordered to "take up the bombs," which of course he did. His method of dismantling amounted to detonating them, "and they were heard for miles around." Aten allowed the rumor to spread "that there were bombs planted on all the fences." Aten was never again ordered to deal with fence cutters, which pleased him "mightily."[52]

But even knowing the dynamite bombs might be a possibility, fence cutters continued to operate. On May 12, Private Hughes received orders to proceed "without delay" to Navarro County. There he was to report to District Judge Samuel R. Frost, his work now to detect fence cutters in that county.[53] Frost, a Montgomery County, Texas, native, received an above average education and was licensed to practice law as early as 1870. In 1876 he settled in Navarro County at Corsicana where he continued to reside. In 1886 he became district judge of the Thirteenth Judicial District.[54] He was at the beginning of his impressive career when he met Ranger Hughes.

The most historic Ranger badge, a coin silver watch with original chain and key carried by Capt. Frank Jones when he was killed. It was a gift from Company D men: "To Captain Frank Jones from the men of Co. D Rangers, Realitos, March 12, 1888." Inside watch case is inscribed: "Capt. John R. Hughes to Eddie Aten, 1936." *Courtesy Mr. and Mrs. Donald M. Yena Collection, San Antonio.*

Hughes left camp on May 14, 1888.[55] His efforts at combating fence cutters produced no positive results, but not because of any inability on his part. On the eighteenth of June he was back in camp, having "Failed to accomplish anything, out 34 days. Marched 1000 miles." The fault lay not with Hughes, but a careless cattleman. The official ledger relates: "In Navarro County Hughes was unsuccessful in locating fence cutters by the indiscretion of one of the stock men, who gave the case away."[56] Back in camp, Hughes no doubt was pleased to have the fence cutting assignment behind him, as Aten had been. Even though he had made no arrests he was back with his Ranger companions.

What began as a seemingly inconsequential arrest turned out to be a near riot with the potential for numerous casualties. The Rio Grande City Riot of September 1888, resulting in press coverage not only in Texas newspapers but in papers as distant as the *New York*

Times, had its origins in May when Starr County Sheriff William W. Shely arrested Abram Resendez, a Mexican-American resident of Rio Grande City, for robbery.[57] Following the peaceful arrest Resendez was killed, allegedly while attempting to escape, shot by Victor Sebree, then a U.S. Inspector of Customs but once a Texas Ranger of the Frontier Battalion.[58]

Not surprisingly great anger was expressed by the Mexican-American community of Starr County, in particular against the Anglo sheriff as it had been on his watch that two other Mexicans had recently been lynched. The outrage of the anti-Shely group did not merely simmer: Augustine and Silurio de la Pena organized opposition to Shely in hopes of having him removed from office. To aid them in their efforts, they employed Catarino Garza, a well-known orator, journalist, and revolutionary who through his newspapers criticized not only the action of Sebree but also the regime of Mexican President Porfirio Díaz.[59] Sebree brought libel charges against Garza for his journalistic efforts. Private Hughes and one other Ranger were sent to arrest Garza. Hughes arrested the noted firebrand peacefully on August 19 and then delivered him to camp, keeping him there for his own safety.[60] He later told of the arrest in modest terms: "I arrested Catarina Garza in August, 1888, for criminal libel, complaint being made by Victor Sebra [*sic*]." [61] On the next day, August 20, Pvt. James R. Robinson[62] and three other Rangers delivered Garza safely to Rio Grande City.[63] Garza gave bail and then was released.

But on Friday, September 21, Garza, with a companion named Lopez, met Customs Inspector Sebree on the street of Rio Grande City. Both men intended to kill the other, but no shot proved fatal. "The feud" reported one newspaper, "between these two resulted in threats, and upon their meeting on the streets of Rio Grande City both opened fire and Garza and another Mexican were shot."[64] Former Texas Ranger as he was, Sebree wisely chose to flee from the angry mob of Mexicans that quickly formed.[65] After shooting Garza, Sebree "mounted his horse and made a break for Ringgold barracks pursued by a gang of mounted Mexicans firing on him."[66] Ringgold barracks, otherwise known as Fort

Ringgold, was less than a mile east of Rio Grande City, so it was a rela-tively short gallop to safety.

An angry mob numbering nearly two hundred "armed men" entered the garrison and demanded Colonel David R. Clendenin "to give him up to them, which request was promptly refused and they were ordered out of the reservation." That night the mob took over the streets of Rio Grande City, "the whole town was . . . delivered over to mob vio-lence." The mob "besieged" the telegraph office, but a call for help was sent prior to the wires being cut.[67]

At first it was believed that Garza's wound would prove fatal, but two days after being shot he was resting well and, according to the Fort Ringgold surgeon, his condition was judged to be fair.[68] As Garza's condition improved, the telegraph wires hummed to bring assistance to prevent further mob violence. And help did come, in the form of Cam-eron County Sheriff Santiago Brito with eighty men, the deputy sheriff of Hidalgo County with forty-five men, and the sheriff of San Patri-cio County with thirty men. These posses had arrived in Rio Grande City by the twenty-fourth.[69] In addition to the sheriffs' men Colonel Clendenin had 135 soldiers under his command. Rangers from Captain Jones' Company D and also from Capt. John F. Rogers' Company F were there, presenting a total force of over three hundred men to control the streets, "a force largely in excess of any that could be mustered by rioters."[70] It would not be the first time that John R. Hughes and Cap-tain Rogers would be on duty together to prevent violence.[71]

On September 26 Colonel Clendenin sent a dispatch which calmed the nerves of the new governor, Lawrence Sullivan Ross. He wrote:

I have protected Sebree and others from the mob. No property has been destroyed or depredation committed in Rio Grande City. Affairs are not so bad as represented. If any real danger had existed I would have used the troops to prevent bloodshed. Posses from adjoining counties arrived last night and to-day. All quiet.[72]

On September 29 Sheriff Brito and his posse left Rio Grande City for Brownsville to deliver Sebree there for his safety. Garza continued to improve. It was, in the opinion of his doctors, "his critical day," but if he should die then it was expected that the riots would resume.[73]

Garza did not die, and things remained peaceful. During the next few weeks Rangers investigated the "shooting scrape which had caused so much trouble" and arrested two dozen men on charges of conspiracy to murder and for assault to murder. They appeared in court and were released on bail in amounts ranging from $500 to $5,000 to appear before the next term of district court. Again this was a combined effort by Rangers from companies D and F together. In this matter no individual Ranger's name appeared, merely that men from both companies made the arrests.[74]

Captain Frank Jones and men of Company D at Camp Leona, Uvalde County. Standing from left: Unknown, Dr. Martin, a civilian; Frank L. Schmid, on crutches due to wound received in August 1889 at Richmond; John O'Grady; Baz L. Outlaw; Captain Jones; Walter W. Jones; Solon Costley; Tom Baker, a civilian; "Old Hous," the camp cook, seated. At least one other image was made of this group, only with the men posed differently. In that rarely seen image they are from left, Dr. Martin, standing; Frank L. Schmid seated, with crutch; Walter W. Jones; "Old Hous" seated with the unidentified civilian standing behind him; Captain Jones, Baz L. Outlaw, Solon Costley, John O'Grady and then civilian Tom Baker. *Image shown here is from the M. T. Gonzaullas Collection, courtesy the Texas Ranger Hall of Fame and Museum, Waco, Texas.*

With a non-violent ending to the rioting in Rio Grande City, Hughes now turned his attention to detective work. A stagecoach was robbed between Rio Grande City and Pena in late October; Privates Hughes and Marcellus Daniels of Company F were sent there to investigate. They left on October 27 but were unsuccessful in finding any leads and returned to camp on November 4. Someone must have provided an additional clue as Hughes returned to Pena on the thirteenth and investigated further. He now began following the stagecoach robber's trail, tracking him to San Antonio. There Hughes determined the man he had followed those many miles was the wrong man. By December 11 he was back in camp.[75]

If John Reynolds Hughes relaxed in camp, pondering the first sixteen months of his life as a Ranger, he could have considered some accomplishments, but also some failures. He had accomplished nothing in Navarro County dealing with fence cutters, and he had failed to bring in the stagecoach robber, after the many miles of trailing. But he had made peaceful arrests, and he had not had to kill a man in the line of duty. That would change in 1889.

～ 3 ～

Challenging the Odles

"Presidio . . . is a centre point for all evil doers."

—*Corp. Charles H. Fusselman to Capt. L.P. Sieker,*
July 20, 1889

anging during the early months of 1889 was relatively quiet, as no
significant action took place on the part of Hughes according to
the monthly returns until April. While scouting in the Edwards
County area he made several arrests, probably considered inconsequential, although of course one never knew when an arrest could turn
deadly. On February 16 he and Pvt. Charles B. Barton[1] arrested Dave
Sweeten, charged with theft of cattle. On the next day Sergeant Aten
was out on scout with five others, unidentified, and arrested Sweeten's
brother John. On the eighteenth Hughes with Captain Jones arrested
John Chapman, charged with theft of cattle. These three men were all
delivered to Edwards County Sheriff Ira Wheat.[2]

Between March 7 and March 12 Hughes and two others scouted
in the area around Kickapoo Springs on the West Fork of the Nueces
River. They gathered in William and Joseph Thurman, charged with
assault to murder in Uvalde County, and one C. E. Tucker who was
charged with hog stealing. Hughes turned this trio of alleged malefac-
tors over to an Edwards County constable.[3]

In mid-February 1889, a notorious murder case created an opportunity for Hughes and Aten to hone their detective skills. Several

47

members of the Williamson family of San Saba County were murdered, their bodies found floating in the Rio Grande seven miles above Eagle Pass in Maverick County. Their skulls had been crushed and the bodies weighted down with stones tied around their waists. No one in Maverick County could identify the victims. When authorities requested assistance from Captain Jones he immediately assigned Hughes and Aten to "ferret out the murderer of these four people." The pair soon remembered that two men had "created a disturbance" in the small community of Barksdale in southeastern Edwards County only a short time before. They also recalled having seen the pair riding with three women and a young man; this recollection now aroused their suspicions. Without intentionally doing so, they were working more as detectives than Rangers, as they had made a mental note of the wagon the party had been driving and that it bore the name of a San Saba dealer. Their investigation led them to San Saba where they learned that a Mrs. Williamson, her son, and two daughters had sold their farm to Richard H. "Dick" Duncan. The Rangers now determined the identity of the four victims: the sixty-year-old widow, Mary Ann Williamson; her twenty-two-year-old son Ben; her fifteen-year-old daughter "Bula"; and her thirty-year-old daughter Levonia, now a widow after the death of her husband Mr. Homes.[4]

The detective work by Hughes and Aten over the months, searching for clues and locating evidence, led them to believe that Duncan and his brother George T., better known as "Tap," were the men responsible for the multiple murders. Sergeant Aten wired San Saba County Sheriff Samuel B. Howard[5] to arrest the Duncans. The Rangers also believed a third man was involved in the murders, H. W. Landers.

Aten left camp on the twenty-second of March to go to San Saba after the Duncans and Landers. Both Dick and Tap Duncan had been arrested but Landers could not be located. A habeas corpus trial was held in Burnet on April 11; both Aten and Sheriff William N. Cooke[6] of Maverick County, where the murders had taken place, were kept busy rounding up witnesses for the trial. George T. "Tap" Duncan[7] was ultimately released for lack of evidence but his brother Richard was found guilty. The third man, Landers, alias "Picnic" Jones, was indicted as an accessory. He remained at large with a $200 reward offered for his arrest and conviction. Ultimately the authorities suspected Landers had been murdered by Duncan as well, although his body was never found.[8]

With the charges in place and witnesses secured, the two Rangers then went on about their regular scouting duties. At his trial, presided over by Judge Winchester Kelso, the jury found Duncan guilty of murder. Judge Kelso sentenced him to death by hanging, setting his date

J. T. Gillespie (April 28, 1856–January 14, 1890). From the original photograph made by the H. B. Hillyer "New Gallery" in Austin, Texas. *Courtesy the C. B. Casey Collection, Archives of the Big Bend, Bryan Wildenthal Memorial Library, Sul Ross State University, Alpine, Texas.*

of execution as September 4, 1891, but due to various delays, Duncan avoided the walk to the gallows until September 18, at Eagle Pass, Maverick County. Without the dedicated detective work of Hughes and Aten, the case may have remained unsolved.[9]

Hughes was now frequently in charge of small detachments going out on lengthy scouts. He was in charge of a scout that took them away from camp between April 8 and April 20. Spencer Morris during this time had escaped from the Brewster County jail. J. T. Gillespie, former Captain of Company E, Frontier Battalion but now serving as the first sheriff of the county, notified the Rangers of this man's escape. Hughes searched the area around Sabinal, Uvalde County, with a squad of three men. He and Pvt. James R. Robinson managed to trail Morris to Kerr County where they arrested him on April 25. He was delivered back safely to Sheriff Gillespie, who was no doubt relieved he had his prisoner in custody again.[10]

Because of his successful work as a beginning Ranger, an opportunity arose to earn more money but with added danger. Captain Jones's brother-in-law, John G. O'Grady, needed dependable guards at his mining operation in Mexico. O'Grady[11] operated the Fronteriza Mines in Sierra del Carmen in the state of Coahuila, Mexico, and needed tough men to guard the mines. Captain Jones recommended Hughes and Pvts. Baz L. Outlaw and Joseph Walter Durbin and the three were eager for a change. In addition, the pay was significantly higher, although the work may have been considered more dangerous.

Pvt. Baz L. Outlaw resigned on May 16 to work for O'Grady; then on the seventeenth Hughes and Durbin resigned.[12] From mid-May until December 1 these three privates were temporarily out of the service working in the state of Coahuila, across the Rio Grande in northeast Mexico. J. Walter Durbin later recorded his memoirs and had this to say about Outlaw: "This man was with me two years in [a] Ranger company and went to Mexico with me and I must say of all the bad men I have knew [sic] he was one of the worst and most dangerous. He never knew what fear was."[13] Although Baz L. Outlaw was recognized by all who knew him as an excellent man to have in a fight, he was

Baz Lamar "Bass" Outlaw. *Courtesy Robert G. McCubbin Collection.*

troublesome to everyone when drinking, even to his friends. The trio
of former rangers traveled by rail to Barroteran, then left the train for
horseback over some of the roughest country they had ever experienced.
The trip took fourteen days.

The duties of Hughes, Durbin, and Outlaw were simple: protect the
shipments of silver bullion and assure their safe arrival to the railroad at
Barroteran. Each shipment was valued in excess of $60,000. The trio no
doubt expected gunplay; however, there was none as potential ore thieves
recognized it was not wise to challenge this trio. In August, perhaps
due to the lack of action, Private Outlaw left Hughes and Durbin to
return to Company D in Richmond, Fort Bend County. He re-enlisted
on September 1. Then it was Durbin's turn to return to Company D,
leaving Hughes alone. When the mines closed in the winter of 1889,

Hughes also returned to Company D where he re-enlisted on December 1.[14] Captain Jones welcomed these men back into the service. Ironically, while the three ex-Rangers were protecting sliver ore without trouble, two groups in far-off Fort Bend County, over three hundred miles from Company D's usual territory, were feuding. History calls the conflict the Jaybird-Woodpecker Feud, somewhat humorous names for two groups each vowing vengeance on the other. Although their nomenclature might bring a smile to the unwary, their animosity resulted in bloodshed on the streets of county seat Richmond. Even with the presence of a detachment of Company D Rangers, the feudists continued their defiance of each other with guns.

During his absence from the company, Hughes learned that Governor Ross had ordered Rangers to Richmond to settle the feud, and that Captain Jones had sent friend Ira Aten with seven men to prevent further

Rangers of Company D at Camp Leona near Uvalde. Ira Aten, standing. Others from left: Jim King; Frank L. Schmid with crutch; Ernest Rogers; Cal Aten, brother of Ira; Walter W. Jones; Charles Fusselman; J. Walter Durbin; James R. Robinson; John R. Hughes; and Baz L. Outlaw. *From the M. T. Gonzaullas Collection, courtesy the Texas Ranger Hall of Fame and Museum, Waco, Texas.*

violence. On August 16, 1889, the two feuding factions turned the court-house square into a battleground that left four citizens dead and numerous others wounded. One of the wounded was Pvt. Frank L. Schmid of Company D. He had received a severe wound in the right thigh during the gunfight. Schmid suffered for almost four years, dying from the wound on June 17, 1893.[15] He was the first of Hughes's Ranger companions to die, not in action, but as a result of wounds received in action.

Trouble still brewed in Burnet County. County authorities wanted certain members of the Odle family, in particular John D., Alvin C., and Walter P. called "Will." They bore a hard reputation with both robbery and murder on their records. The family experienced tragedy within itself as well as causing trouble for neighbors. John D. had married Miss Annie M. McCarty on July 20, 1882,[16] but the relationship became strained between Odle and his father-in-law Bryant V. McCarty to a point resulting in violence. On November 25, 1885, John Odle shot McCarty.[17] The several witnesses testified that the shooting was unprovoked, and that McCarty was "shot in the back while unarmed and unprotected." He died three days later on November 28. John now became a fugitive. William M. Spitler, district clerk of Burnet County, prepared a petition signed by sixty-six Burnet County citizens praying the governor would offer a reward. Odle was described as "a man of bad reputation and considered to be a horse-thief."[18]

Governor Ireland offered a reward of $200, and by May 1886, Burnet County Sheriff John W. Wolf believed Odle was in Monclova, Mexico, nearly one hundred miles from Laredo.[19] Apparently Sheriff Wolf was content to leave him there, if indeed he was hiding out in Old Mexico; nothing came of this. Then on April 26, 1887, Sheriff Wolf wrote to the new governor, L. S. Ross, informing him that the two younger Odle brothers, Alvin and Will, were now in jail in Burnet. Hughes's friend Ira Aten had arrested them and recovered the ten or twelve stolen horses in their possession. Sheriff Wolf expressed the belief that the brothers would have gotten away with them into New Mexico Territory if the water and grass had been better. "The Odles," Wolf wrote, "know every hog trail in this county and stay in the Cedar brakes when here so that

The historic Burnet County jail, built in 1884, as it appeared in 2009. The Odles escaped
from this building. *Photo by Pat Parsons.*

it is impossible to get them." Further advising the governor, he recommended Ira Aten be given the assignment of hunting up John Odle.
Wolf certainly knew about Ira Aten and John Hughes's gunfight that
had resulted in the death of Wesley Collier, and reminded the governor:
"May the Lord prosper him, [Aten, as he] has rendered inestimable service in this county in killing Collier, running off Jim Fannin, capturing
and convicting Beam and last arresting two of the Odles and Henry
Cavin. . . ." To reinforce his request, Wolf enclosed another petition
signed by numerous Burnet County citizens.[20] That was in late April.
On May 18 Sheriff Wolf had reason to believe John Odle was jailed in
Fort Smith, Arkansas, but offered no explanation as to how he learned
this important information.[21]

However, the Burnet County jail was not secure enough to hold
the Odle brothers. Just when they made their escape is uncertain, but
by mid-October 1887, Rangers were scouting for the fugitives. They

now added the name "Ep. McCarty" to their wanted list for helping the Odles to break out of the Burnet jail. This was probably William E. McCarty.[22] The brothers were now escaped fugitives, ready to fight back against any lawman trying to apprehend them. But after two years on the run, the end of the trail was near for Will and Alvin Odle.

Lawmen learned that the Odles had arranged for stolen horses to be delivered to a rancher near the little community of Vance, in the far western corner of what is today Real County, but in 1889 part of Edwards County. Sheriff Ira L. Wheat sent Deputy Will Terry to organize a posse to attempt their capture. Terry informed the Rangers and Privates Hughes, Outlaw, and Calvin Grant Aten,[23] younger brother of Sgt. Ira Aten, now joined the posse. He also deputized Paul Jones, Dan Crier, Jim Rhodes of Barksdale, and Henry Wells of Vance, making a good-sized posse of men who had no patience with livestock thieves. About a mile above Vance, near the eastern slope of Bullhead Mountain, the posse lay in wait for the anticipated arrival of the Odle brothers. It was a little after midnight, the beginnings of Christmas Day 1889. The demand to surrender, yelled out by Hughes, Outlaw, or Aten, or all three, brought only gunshots from the Odles. Challenged, totally without warning, in the darkness the pair had little chance to escape or survive the Rangers' shooting. Captain Jones commented on the event in his report to Assistant Adjutant General L. P. Sieker several days later, revealing his overall satisfaction in what his men had accomplished:

> I guess you have seen in the papers where some of my men celebrated Christmas day by killing the two Odles in Edwards County. It is a great strain off that country and the good people are rejoicing. John Hughes, Outlaw and young Aten and some citizens did the work.[24]

The report to Adjutant General King provided no real details but presented what happened in a more official tone: "Private Hughes and two men with Deputy Sheriff and posse in attempting the arrest of Will and Alvin Odle wanted for murder was fired on by them. The shots were returned resulting in the death almost instantly of both. Out 2 days. Marched 25 miles."[25] None of the posse was injured according to the official report. None of the lawmen claimed his bullets were the fatal ones, taking no pride in having brought about the death of a man, but no doubt also experiencing relief the gun battle had resulted in death to the outlaws alone, and that there would be two fewer thieves to deal with. It was Hughes's first gunfight as a Ranger that resulted in the death of an outlaw. He had no desire to claim the kill as his own.

Walter J. Lockhart, Edwards County rancher, resided in the immediate area of the gun battle and claimed to have gathered details of the fight from one of the posse members. According to Lockhart's account, an unidentified Edwards County rancher—described only as "a prominent cow-man of the Nueces Canyon"—was charged with cattle theft and was facing conviction. He volunteered to betray the Odle brothers in exchange for dismissal of the charges against him, thus avoiding a prison term. Rancher Lockhart knew where the Odles were going to be and notified Sheriff Wheat, who then gathered the posse and Rangers to lay the trap. Lockhart claimed that it was Ranger Outlaw in command of the posse, and whose demands to "Halt! Halt!" were ignored. The Ranger bullets killed one of the brothers instantly, but severely wounded the other. "But after falling," Lockhart recorded, "he tried repeatedly to raise his pistol to fire again, but he was too weak. Outlaw snatched it from his hand. The fight was over. Outlaw had one ear burned. Several others had felt the hiss of lead, but there were no casualties." The wounded man lived about fifteen minutes before expiring from his multiple wounds.[26]

As Calvin G. Aten was not in charge of the party, there was no need for him to make any type of a report. But years later, in 1936, brother Ira, then a California resident, visited his brothers in Texas and a flood of memories were brought back as they discussed their younger days. Later Cal wrote a lengthy letter to Ira in which he reviewed some of the incidents they had discussed. Cal called the gunfight the "Battle of Bull Head Mountain." He recalled how the Odles "were assassinated. That is all it was just plain assassination." Nevertheless, Aten did not consider it murder, as he continued: "How ever there would have been someone else assassinated if we hadn't got in the first shots." . . . *if we hadn't got in the first shots* . . . Did Aten mean to say that the call to surrender came after the first shots were fired? Regardless of which came first, the reality of the situation was a matter of kill or be killed for the lawmen, as the Odles would not surrender.[27]

The Rangers buried the Odle brothers near where they fell, the only ceremony consisting of placing their bodies into hastily dug graves on the east side of Bullhead Mountain near a large rock. Sometime later Zac Eppler carved their names on the rock and placed a fence around it. It is known by some as the "Historic Odle Brothers Cemetery" but contains only the final remains of the duo who resisted Ranger law.[28]

With the new year of 1890 Hughes was to experience more dangerous work on the border along the Rio Grande. He was fortunate in that he seemingly bore a charmed life. Presidio County was notorious for criminal activity. Private Charles H. Fusselman of Company D, stationed there in July 1889, stressed the isolation, writing that the community of Presidio was "75 miles from Rail Road or Telegraph [and] it is a centre point for all evil doers."[29] He later reported to Sieker that since August 17, 1889, there had been seven murders in and near Presidio County, "& the murderers take refuge in Mexico."[30] Fusselman's concerns about murderers seemed to foreshadow events to come: rustlers killed ex-Ranger James W. King, once a Company D man like Fusselman and Hughes and Aten.

Fusselman had enlisted as a private on May 25, 1888, and on May 18, 1889, Captain Jones promoted him to the rank of corporal following Durbin's resignation, and on Durbin's recommendation. Captain Jones had reservations, feeling Fusselman was "a good man but is somewhat lacking in experience, he having been in the service only a year."[31] Fusselman did not disappoint Captain Jones during the next few months, however, as on August 21, 1889, he promoted him to the rank of 1st Sergeant of Company D.[32]

The dangerous scouting and at times tedious pursuit of fugitives began to tell and as Christmas 1889 neared, Fusselman felt homesick. On November 26 he asked for a fifteen-day furlough, pointing out to Adjutant General King that he had "Ranged since May 1888 & have never had a furlough[.] I was private until June 1st then Corpl until

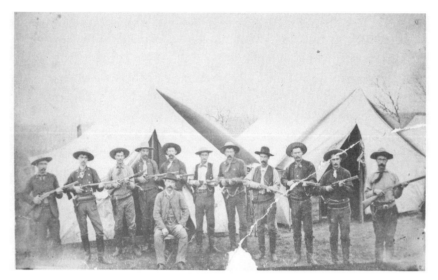

A view of Company D camp in South Texas. Capt. Frank Jones is seated. Standing from left Ira Aten, Frank L. Schmid, Charles Fusselman, James R. Robinson, John Woodard Saunders, John Reynolds Hughes, Joseph Walter Durbin, Baz Lamar Outlaw, James Walter Durbin, Ernest Rogers, Gerry Jones. *Author's Collection.*

Aug 20 & now am Sergt & you will confer a great favor on me if you will grant me about 15 days furlough[.]" He wanted to leave on or about December 12, intending to return two days after Christmas. He wanted to spend Christmas at home near Lagarto, in Live Oak County. Apparently Adjutant General King granted the request as the monthly returns make no mention of him during the period he requested.[33]

Fusselman had impressed other lawmen as well, as U.S. Marshal Paul Fricke appointed him as his deputy on June 19, 1889, but apparently no one informed Captain Jones or Adjutant General King until after the fact. A Ranger holding another office was technically against policy, but Jones chose to let it pass, as "the two positions dovetail."[34]

The apparently innocent dovetailing, however, would bring about a tragedy in Ranger history. By also being a deputy, Ranger Fusselman placed himself in harm's way when rustlers raided the ranch of John Barnes. This act brought Fusselman into action as a deputy rather than a Ranger. Fusselman was in El Paso attending district court on April 17,

1890. During a break he went to the office of El Paso County Sheriff James H. White.[35] The casual visit was interrupted when rancher John Barnes burst in and informed everyone that bandits had stolen his horses during the night, as well as killing a calf and carrying off the meat. He had followed the trail of the thieves until one of them confronted him; the "vicious looking Mexican" was "well equipped" and Barnes, being unarmed, chose to retreat and appealed for help from the sheriff's office.[36] Sheriff White was out but his deputy Frank B. Simmons was there. As Simmons could not leave the office vacant during court, Ranger Fusselman volunteered to pursue the thieves. Former Ranger George Herold was also present and joined him along with several others, forming a small posse, perhaps a half-dozen men. Herold was an experienced fighting man, having survived the Civil War, fights with Indians, and fights with outlaws during his years as a Texas Ranger. He also had served as city marshal of Laredo. In contrast to Fusselman's youth and inexperience, Herold was a veteran of many engagements and nearly sixty years old.[37]

The lawmen apparently did not realize just how many thieves there were. They came upon one Mexican who they believed had lagged behind and captured him as well as his horse. They recognized him as Ysidoro Pasos, a "well-known horse thief." With this bandit arrested, they perhaps let down their guard and continued—not suspecting what lay ahead. It was then the outlaws sprang the trap and fired a volley into the posse. In the confusion Pasos managed to escape.[38]

"Boys, we are in for it, and let's stay with it!" Fusselman, in the lead, called out. No sooner had he yelled out those words than Fusselman fell, his body "riddled" with bullets, two going through his head and one through his body.[39] Seeing the loss of their leader the posse hastily retreated and returned to El Paso for reinforcements, leaving the brave Fusselman dead on the ground. Sheriff White organized "a posse of six of the most fearless men in the county" to retrieve Fusselman's remains. A wagonload of provisions followed.[40] By the time the posse recovered the body, the bandits were well into Mexico. Ironically, the bandits were part of a gang who a few days before had appeared in court charged with horse theft and had been acquitted.[41]

Hughes later recalled the incident and related it to friend and *El Paso Herald-Post* editor L. A. Wilke, who recorded his thoughts:

Until the last light of day had gone, the posse followed their trail, but the job was hopeless. The start of the outlaws had been too great. Long after night had fallen, the tired and dusty men straggled back to El Paso. In their wake was a buckboard and in the buckboard was the body of my sergeant, Charles Fusselman . . . one of the finest men ever to take the trail that law and order might pave the way for civilization, for progress. And he was dead.[42]

Final resting place of Charles Fusselman, killed by bandits in 1890. His remains were delivered to the Lagarto Cemetery in Live Oak County, Texas, and rest under a four-foot-tall obelisk. Lagarto today is nearly a ghost town. *Photo by author.*

Sheriff White brought the body of Charles Fusselman back to El Paso and turned it over to the undertaker. Adjutant General King ordered Private Hughes to El Paso to attend the burial as well as to pursue the murderers. He and a posse of citizens scouted and searched several ranches, perhaps hoping the murderers had remained on the northern side of the Rio Grande. They were out six days and covered almost four hundred miles, but found no trace of the gang who had killed Ranger Fusselman.[43]

Pvt. Calvin G. Aten was in Marfa when he learned of Fusselman's death. His communication to Capt. L. P. Sieker included the following expression of regret: "A good boy and energetic ranger has been laid away through the Deviltry of a lot of cowardly thieves and murderers in which this country abounds. Much regret is expressed here among the people and I hardly know what we can do without him."[44] Young Aten certainly had no hesitancy in expressing his feelings. He may have felt confident that Ranger Hughes would find the murderers of Fusselman and avenge his death.

How authorities determined the identity of the bandit who actually fired the shots that killed Fusselman is unknown, but they believed the guilty man was Geronimo Parra, a noted desperado. Hughes intended to avenge his friend's death and would eventually have Parra in custody, but it would be a long time coming. Marshal Fricke immediately offered a $100 reward, since Fusselman had also been his deputy. Gov. L. S. Ross offered a reward of $250 for the arrest and conviction of the "unknown murderers" of Fusselman. The reward announcement was deliberately vague, as any member of Parra's gang could then be captured and charged with murder, even if only Parra fired the fatal shot. This reward would stand for six months "and conviction thereafter."[45] Hughes was certainly aware of this, but he wanted revenge, not a reward.

With the death of Fusselman on April 17, Adjutant General King had to determine who would take his place. On the following day, John Reynolds Hughes became 1st Corporal of Company D, Frontier Battalion of the Texas Rangers.[46]

~ 4 ~

Another Ranger Killed

"[CARRASCO] GOT DOWN AND DELIBERATELY SET ABOUT
GETTING HIS RIFLE OUT OF HIS SCABBARD. ONE OF US
KILLED HIM."

—*Alonzo Van Oden, June 1892*

For the Rangers of Company D, or any other company of the Frontier Battalion, boredom sat in on occasion; at times matters of seemingly little consequence had to be dealt with. One such incident had originated with Fusselman, and now that he was dead the matter fell into Hughes's hands: what to do with a "locoed" mule? Back in late February, Sergeant Fusselman had informed Quartermaster Sieker that one of the mules, property of the State of Texas, was "locoed" and "unserviceable & likely to remain so" and inquired as to what was best to do with it. Sieker responded with instructions that if the mule had any real value to have it sold; if the mule could not be sold then it should be shot.[1] Apparently Fusselman had not attended to the matter in a timely manner, as on April 11, 1890, Sieker wrote again to Fusselman advising that if the mule was "impossible to cure" it should be sold or shot. Expenses were always a prime concern to the quartermaster, and the sick mule was costing the state fifty cents per day just to keep it in a stable. He was told to get a certified statement from a disinterested witness once it was sold or shot.[2]

No doubt the fact that Hughes spent some time dealing with the death of Fusselman made the matter of the locoed mule a lesser concern.

62

Sieker now wrote to Corporal Hughes advising him to deal with the mule as Fusselman had been ordered to do, and presumably Hughes did so, although there is no follow-up in the correspondence as to the fate of the "locoed" mule.

On May 7 Corporal Hughes, now trusted to be in charge of a detachment, moved from Marfa to Presidio. Later that same month Captain Jones also moved the main camp from La Salle County to Presidio. The work of the Rangers in the counties of La Salle and Brewster had been so effective that their efforts would now be better spent elsewhere.

During the summer months Hughes rode many miles scouting after wanted men. On May 14 he and four other Rangers scouted on the Bustamento and Barnhart ranches. They located and arrested two men charged with smuggling: Antonio Bustamento and Comela, or Camillo, Kellas. Hughes turned the pair over to a deputy sheriff of Presidio County. That action was in May, but in June the monthly return indicated "Corp. Hughes did not scout any this month" with no explanation or reason given. Perhaps Hughes was ill during June.[3]

July was different as Hughes was active again. On the nineteenth he arrested Juan Garcia and Jose Martinez for horse theft. They both were turned over to a justice of the peace in Presidio. Then with one other unidentified Ranger he scouted up to Marathon after smuggled horses. Apparently this scout proved fruitless as the return does not indicate any horses were recovered nor were any arrests made.[4]

Concerns of a forgotten locoed mule and unsuccessful scouts may have caused ordinary men to relax, but a gunfight in which another Ranger lost his life brought the reality of the dangers of being a Ranger to the forefront. A riot erupted near Shafter in Presidio County on August 4, and during the turbulence John F. Gravis, a Ranger private with little experience, was killed. He had been a stockman prior to his enlistment into Company D on February 24, 1890, through Adjutant General King, at Encinal, La Salle County. He was twenty-two years old. His final pay voucher was made out for $64, but he owed Pvt. Solon L. Costley $35; thus his final payment was a mere $29. The contemporary press made little mention of his death, nor are there details in the Ranger records, perhaps because he had served such a brief time. A report from Alpine dated August 4 headlined his passing: "A Fight With Desperadoes/ A Desperate Battle Between the Rangers And Outlaws—One Ranger Killed." The dead Ranger was incorrectly identified as *Graves*; in the same engagement Deputy U.S. Marshal Ike Lee[5] was wounded. When the shooting ceased, about seventy-five Mexicans "were corralled." At press time there were no particulars available, either of the battle nor of the killing.[6]

Captain Jones took six men to Shafter to investigate the riot and determine who was guilty of killing Gravis. They left camp on August 4 and returned on the seventh, having arrested seven Mexicans, who were placed in jail. Privates Charles Barton, Walter W. Jones,[7] William Kipling,[8] and John C. Mayfield,[9] with the assistance of several citizens, arrested a dozen more and turned them over to the deputy sheriff. They

Ruins at Shafter, Presidio County, after the wild mining days. Today Shafter is a ghost town. Note the Chinati Mountains in the background. *Courtesy the Elton Miles Collection, Archives of the Big Bend, Bryan Wildenthal Memorial Library, Sul Ross State University, Alpine, Texas.*

were charged with riot, murder, and assault to murder.[10] Private William Kipling delivered the body of Gravis to Marfa and had it shipped to Laredo at the request of the family.[11]

During that same month of August, Corporal Hughes began a lengthy scout throughout Brewster and Pecos counties. The records provide no details, other than stating that Hughes "assisted" Deputy Marshal Cook "in search of stolen and smuggled horses." In contrast to the sad fate of Private Gravis, who fell in the line of duty with limited experience as a Texas Ranger, Thalis T. Cook had already served with distinction in the Ranger service. He began his long career as a lawman when he enlisted in Company F of the Frontier Battalion on June 4, 1876, at the young age of sixteen. Capt. Neal Coldwell then commanded Company F. After serving only three months Cook resigned, but then in September 1876, he again joined Company F, but his Irish-born uncle, Capt. Patrick Dolan,[12] now was commander. Cook served under Captain Dolan two and one-half years, resigning in early 1879. He then joined Company D on April 25, 1889, and served until November 30. Continuing his career in law enforcement Cook moved to Marathon where he worked as a deputy under Sheriff James B. Gillett.[13]

Neither Hughes nor Cook found anyone to arrest during all their scouting: no smugglers, no horse or cattle thieves, no fugitives from justice. On September 10 Hughes was back in camp, having been out seventeen days. The monthly return merely indicates that he had covered a total of 350 miles, but he had "accomplished nothing."[14] October proved to be no more exciting than September. Corporal Hughes with a deputy marshal now went to Green Valley in the western portion of Brewster County in search of one John Chambers, charged with bribery and smuggling. Four days later they had to give it up, with another 120 miles logged in but nothing to show for their efforts.[15]

The month of November proved to be somewhat more rewarding. Beginning on November 3, he and one other Ranger were at Patterson's Ranch for two days, keeping the peace during the election. All was peaceful, and the office of greatest concern, if not the most important, was that of sheriff. William Russell, elected for the first time in

November of 1888, was re-elected and served until November 8, 1892. He was followed in office by Denton G. Knight who would work often with the men of Company D.[16] While Hughes was at Patterson's Ranch, Ranger Carl Kirchner[17] and one other were at Marathon with the same orders. Everything remained quiet due to their presence. Captain Jones and one other were at Alpine, and then on November 5 Hughes and one other Ranger joined them in Alpine to "keep peace at U.S. Criminal Court." On November 10 Hughes and three others were still in Alpine to preserve order while new officers qualified. Then on November 28, still in Brewster County, he caught up with the elusive John Chambers and arrested him. When turned over to authorities, Chambers managed to make bond and was then released.[18]

During this time Pvt. Walter W. Jones and Brewster County Sheriff James B. Gillett trailed and arrested E. L. Vandergriff, who was charged with train robbery. Gillett was a highly respected lawman, having served back in the 1870s under Frontier Battalion Company E's commander, Nelson O. Reynolds, and later as city marshal of El Paso. He became well acquainted with Hughes during his years in El Paso, and may have recalled his brother William P. Hughes, as both served at the same time under Lieutenant Reynolds. He also worked as a guard on the Santa Fe railroad, and then began a new career in ranching. Gillett provided historians with a self-serving autobiography that placed his name among the great Texas Rangers.[19]

Five days before Christmas 1890, as he was traveling 150 miles to Shafter for an unspecified duty, Corporal Hughes could reflect on the previous year and perhaps consider that after beginning as a private in mid-1887, he was now a corporal. That promotion had resulted from his own solid and dedicated work in spite of some failures, but also from a Ranger losing his life in the line of duty. Hughes had been promoted after Segeant Fusselman's death on April 17. That his advancement was caused by the death of another must certainly have been a subject of sober reflection.

Then on January 31, 1891, Hughes's friend Deputy Thalis T. Cook and Ranger Jim Putman, two men who would work frequently with

Hughes, met up with Finus "Fine" Gilliland, wanted for the murder of the one-armed Confederate veteran Henry Harrison Powe. The heavily armed trio engaged in "a desperate fight," which proved to be deadly to Gilliland, felled by Putman. A shot from Gilliland hit Cook in the leg, giving him a dangerous wound, and Putman's horse was fatally shot by Gilliland.[20] Hughes certainly became aware of this notable fight, and no doubt would have preferred to have been a participant.

Whereas Cook and Putman experienced excitement and danger in the Gilliland gun battle, Corporal Hughes had much more prosaic duties to perform: escorting the tax collector from Shafter to Marfa. On January 27 in Marfa he did arrest J. B. Humphries, who had been charged with assault to kill.[21] Apparently this arrest was without incident, as were so many arrests made by Ranger Hughes. On February 1 he escorted two attached witnesses to El Paso. While there he arrested Will Ward and Mateo Durán for theft of property valued at over $20. He then traveled to Midland "in a murder case," although no details were provided. Later, on February 16 he and one other man investigated a reported murder but determined the report was false as no murder had occurred.[22] The March monthly return fails to mention Hughes or any of his activities. Captain Jones did enlist one man who would become a friend of Hughes, as well as a man who would provide history with a fascinating journal of his experiences along the border: Alonzo "Lon" Van Oden.

Oden enlisted on March 1, 1891, and soon he and Hughes became fast friends. One of the most famous Ranger photographs from this period shows Hughes, Oden, Jim Putman, and Robert Speaks in a studio image, their weapons prominently displayed. A second image shows the quartet with their horses, on a scout. An itinerant photographer may have taken the photographs at Shafter. Oden wrote and collected poetry and also kept a diary, later edited by Ann Jensen and published by the Kaleidograph Press of Dallas in the Texas centennial year of 1936. She apparently gathered a few lines about some of the Rangers mentioned in the book, and quotes Hughes as saying: "Alonzo Oden was a member of my Ranger Company for several years. He was a good Ranger and a good citizen."[23]

Among the most famous photographs of Texas Rangers is this showing Alonzo Van Oden and John R. Hughes seated; Robert Speaks and Jim Putman standing. *University of Texas at El Paso Library, Special Collections Department.*

The eighth entry in Oden's "scrapbook" places him at Shafter, noting, "John Hughes is here, our corporal. Folks trust John. Bob Speaks is also with us. Bob is older, and has done just about everything that can be done—reckon that's because he was born in Missouri."[24] When Oden wrote these lines he may have been thinking back on when that now famous photograph was made.

Unfortunately the monthly returns are never as complete or detailed as one would like. The April 1891 return reports that on April 12, Hughes and one man arrested José Milleto and Calisto Flores; they were both drunk and disturbing the peace.[25] On the next day Hughes was with Alonzo Oden and arrested John Faver and Garnacindo Subia and delivered them to a deputy sheriff in Presidio County. Perhaps Oden was with Hughes when he arrested Milleto and Flores as well. Perhaps it was in Shafter or Presidio where the arrests were made. From April 18 through April 22 Hughes and two others scouted through the Pool and Burton ranches in Brewster County to investigate reports of rustlers changing cattle brands. Their investigation brought no evidence against any one.[26]

Throughout the next few months Hughes continued to scout throughout the area: on May 12 he and one other scouted to Burton's "Ranche Ruadoza" [*sic*, Ruidosa] and Hot Springs and then another forty miles down the Rio Grande to Presidio. They made only one arrest, a man identified as Quirinio Ramírez, wanted for criminal libel. After delivering him to a deputy sheriff Hughes continued down to Polvo to investigate rumors of an unidentified disturbance. All was quiet when they arrived; and perhaps it was merely their appearance at Polvo that prevented any riotous action.[27]

The monthly returns for the remainder of 1891 reveal little significant action on the part of Hughes. He covered many miles scouting, and made some arrests. On July 25 Hughes arrested P. Mano, F. Orcon, and F. Mano for theft of cattle, but the return fails to mention the result of the arrests or to whom they were delivered for prosecution.[28] He and two others did go to Presidio in an attempt to capture Estanislado Arios but he eluded the lawmen. That was on the seventh; on the fifteenth he and two others scouted to the "Grand Cañon" through the community of Polvo in search of Ursulo Galindo, charged with horse theft. The Ranger trio did not locate Galindo.[29] On August 26 Corporal Hughes arrested P. Ormendina for aggravated assault; then from September 14 to 18 he and one other scouted for stolen horses. The horses were not found but they did arrest J. Butler for assault to kill, and A. Ochoa for theft of a horse.[30] The only arrest recorded in the October return is on the nineteenth, of Bill Dunman, charged with receiving stolen horses.[31]

Elsewhere during the month of October Captain Jones with a scout of seven men trailed a gang who had robbed the Galveston Harrisburg & San Antonio train near Sanderson. The gang, composed of John Flynt,

James Lansford, John Wellington, and Tom Fields, had stopped the train on September 2; after dynamiting one of the cars the gang helped themselves to the money entrusted to Wells Fargo & Company.[32] The Rangers left camp on October 8 and went to Beaver Lake to strike the trail of the train robbers; the tracks led to the "upper edge of Crockett County," where they "overtook them."[33] Jim Lansford, Jack Wellington, and Tom Fields were all arrested, but gang leader John Flynt chose to take his own life rather than surrender to Captain Jones. The three survivors were delivered to the jail in El Paso.[34] Corporal Hughes was with a detachment down at Shafter, or else he would have been in charge of the scout after the train robbers.

As the man in charge of the Shafter detachment Hughes had ample opportunity to make arrests and pursue wanted fugitives. This he did during November and December: on November 9 Hughes and one other man went on scout to Polvo and Presidio in search of Prejedes García wanted for theft; they were out four days but could not locate García. During the next week Hughes and two men were on scout to Ruidosa, a small community located some fifty miles south of Marfa, and did arrest José Corrasco for assault to murder. He was placed in the Shafter jail. They had been out five days this time, traveling 150 miles. Apparently on the same day he arrested Jim Pool for carrying a pistol. Pool was able to give bond. Then on November 25 Hughes arrested Anicito Nunez for theft of a horse. He too was placed in the Shafter jail.[35]

On December 13 Hughes arrested Sabin Gallego for aggravated assault somewhere in Presidio County and then delivered him to the Shafter jail. Three days later Hughes and three others scouted after smugglers and arrested Francisco Hernandez. They recovered two horses, one mule, a saddle, and gun, which were delivered to the proper authorities; Hernandez was placed in the Shafter jail. This scout lasted seven days, covering 210 miles. Then on Christmas Day Hughes arrested Jesús Flores for horse theft. He also was placed in the jail at Shafter.[36]

Shafter, due to its proximity to the Rio Grande—less than twenty miles—became more and more attractive for smugglers in spite of the presence of the Rangers. The wild country attracted thieves and desperadoes of all sorts because of its rough terrain and closeness to the border. Fugitives could easily roam over Presidio County as well as evading lawmen from adjacent counties. On January 23, 1892, Captain Jones with a squad of three men—Carl Kirchner, M. R. Daniels, and one other—scouted to the Glass Mountains in Buchel County (now part of Brewster County)[37] in search of fugitives. The quartet of Rangers caught up with three men: a man identified only as Eduardo, José Blanco, and Pedro Eureto. They were charged with conspiracy and murder but instead of surrendering they chose to fight the Rangers. Pedro Eureto was killed for his efforts. The surviving pair were delivered to Alpine. Kirchner and Daniels[38] remained behind to locate a flock of stolen sheep but were unsuccessful.[39]

While Captain Jones was dealing with those fugitives, Corporal Hughes had, on January 7, arrested F. E. Miller for theft and embezzlement in Presidio County. He was jailed. Then on the twelfth Hughes located Matilde Carrasco, wanted for theft of ore from the Shafter mines. He was with two other men, also wanted for the same theft: José Velata/Villeto and Quinlino/Guintino Chaves/Chavez. How many men Hughes had with him is unknown, as he was certainly not a "Lone Ranger" on this occasion. Hughes called out to them to surrender, but instead of a peaceful arrest the men chose to resist and the result was a bloody gunfight. It was a very dangerous situation with three smugglers battling three Rangers, although in the report of operations there were no dramatics, nothing to suggest the adrenaline pumping up during a gunfight. The three men who challenged Ranger firepower were shot to death. Hughes, after checking with his companions to see if they had suffered wounds, examined the trio of dead men. He offered no detailed explanation of what was said or who shot whom, but merely provided a brief statement of the action to the adjutant general's Austin office: "Corpl Hughes and detachment attempting to arrest thieves of ore from the Shafter mines killed Matildo Carrasco, José Velata & Guintino Chavez whilst resisting arrest."[40]

In *Border Boss*, Jack Martin identified ex-Ranger Ernest "Diamond Dick" St. Leon as being involved in the fight as well, although he is not named in Hughes's report. Martin also adds a romantic—but unrealistic—touch with Hughes burying the three dead thieves: "Corporal Hughes located relatives of the dead men the next day, but they would not claim the bodies. So he buried them, side by side, on a mountain top near the robbers' trail, and in such a position that on a moon bright night, the three white crosses marking the graves would reflect a grim warning to anyone venturing up the trail." [41]

During the next few months Hughes made a significant number of arrests, although occasionally he could not locate the man he wanted. The February monthly return shows Hughes scouting with a three-man squad and spending three days and covering ninety miles in "Pinto Canon after Mexican horse thieves." They were not found. But on February 9 he arrested Tiburcio Lujan who was wanted for assault in Presidio County; he was placed in jail. In Shafter, on the sixteenth, he arrested two Mexicans for "Shooting in town," probably two men celebrating something of little consequence and placing emphasis on it with their six-guns. Two days later he arrested Elejio Magillanos for swindling. He too was placed in the jail in Shafter. [42] The March return shows that on the fourth Hughes arrested Marcus Justo for theft of a pistol and placed him in jail in Shafter. Then on the fourteenth a more informative entry is found: "Pvt. Speaks [43] and 2 men went to Barnharts ranche and arrested Geraldo Rodriguez charged with bringing stolen horses into the State. Met Corpl[.] Hughes at Polvo and returned to Shafter via Presidio. Delivered the prisoner to Sheriff Samuel R. Miller." This was a five-day scout, with mileage recorded as 150 miles. Were the other two men with Speaks Ranger Oden and Putman? A week later, on the twentieth, Hughes rounded up four men in Presidio for being drunk and disorderly: Arundio Ruicez, Andreas Vagaro, Elejio Magillanos, and Ronaldo Castella. All were placed in jail. [44]

In June 1892, Hughes, with Privates Putman and Oden, scouted down into the Mexican settlement known as San Antonio Colony, intending to locate and capture fugitive Desidario Durán, charged with theft. Oden, recalling the life and death situation, unintentionally provided history with a step by step construction of a wild west gunfight by one who was a participant. He began his narrative:

Just last week, [on June 20] John Hughes, Jim Putman, and I went down to the San Antonio colony, a Mexican settlement on the Rio Grande, to get Desidario Duran, who had raided the section house at Chispa. On our way back with Duran, we dropped in Jim Windham's store for some supplies. We saw three Mexican men trying to get a fourth man, who was drunk, to get on his horse. They were down at the end of the bosque. A farmer said that one of the men was Florencio Carrasco.

At this point the simple arrest of Durán entered a more dangerous phase with the presence of another fugitive.

We've had orders to arrest Carrasco, as he had a bad record—everything from horse stealing to murder. Well, Hughes and I got on our horses and started toward them. They quickly mounted and started firing on us, running as they fired, all except Carrasco. He was mounted, but got down and deliberately set about getting his rifle out of his scabbard. One of us killed him. My horse was shot and killed by the fleeing bandits.[45]

It was another situation of kill or be killed. Apparently Carrasco was shot to death before he was able to fire his Winchester at the Rangers. No Ranger was wounded in this engagement, but now they had a live prisoner, Durán, and a dead desperado, Carrasco, to deal with, in an area where the prisoners both had friends.

When the Rangers got back to Jim Windham's store there was "considerable excitement" and groups of Mexicans could be seen "congregating and talking in excited groups." Oden admitted they feared trouble from the mob, but within a few hours things returned to relative normalcy. They may have made some arrangements for the burial of Carrasco, but then it was necessary to return to Marfa with prisoner Durán. Hughes realized that if they took the Marfa road there would be plenty of opportunities for an ambush, so after getting out of sight of the settlement they turned off onto the road to Valentine. It took them longer, but they made the trip without incident and Durán was delivered safely to the Marfa jail.[46] The official record merely indicates the men were disturbing the peace and carrying pistols, then resisted arrest and fought back while on the run. Florencio Carrasco was killed, and Oden's horse wounded. No doubt it was so badly wounded it had to be shot to put it out of its misery.[47]

That was in June 1892. Later, on August 18, Hughes and three others returned to the San Antonio Colony after Bacinto (or probably Vicento) Durán, who had been charged with robbing a section house. They failed to find him, even after five days of intently searching for him. On August 23, Pvts. Putman and Oden scouted after William D. Barbee, a former acquaintance of Hughes, charged with murder in Crockett County. They were more fortunate this time and arrested him on the Presidio Road and delivered him to jail.[48] Hughes had known Barbee years before, and he had somehow gone bad. A newspaper reported his capture:

> William D. Barbee, alias "Pecos Bill," was arrested Aug. 23rd, 1892, near Presidio for the murder of a man in Ozona, Crockett county, on Aug. 16th, 1892. Barbee passed through Shafter on the 22nd, and the account of the killing came in the San Antonio Semi-Weekly Express the same evening. State Rangers Oden and Putman followed him on the 23rd and caught him on the road about four miles from Presidio. Corp'l. John R. Hughes worked with Barbee on the Las Animas Ranch, in Sierra county, N.M., in 1884, when Bill Barbee was foreman and was a very popular and honest man. He was born in Texas, is 38 years old, has been a cow boy all his life, but is well educated. His description is in the San Antonio Semi-Weekly Express of the 19th inst. He is held at Shafter, awaiting word from the authorities of Crockett Co.[49]

Barbee obviously had intended to lose himself in Mexico but didn't quite make it across the river due to the diligence of the Rangers. While waiting for the Crockett County authorities, he "sat staring into space ever since we locked him up" according to Private Oden's diary. Oden recalled that while "Pecos Bill" Barbee was in jail he ate very little and would "talk even less; but I feel rather good about Bill as I watch him. Bill may be staring into space; but the space is full of meaning for Bill, and Bill, at last, is seeing himself. I can not explain how I know this, but I do know it; and when a man sees himself, he has found himself—and he is no longer afraid." Oden also reinforced the belief that Hughes, years before, had spent considerable time in New Mexico infiltrating the horse thieves who had stolen his herd, stating: "Bill used to work with John Hughes on the Las Animas Ranch in Sierra County, New Mexico, about eight years ago. At that time he was well liked, and considered even tempered, honest, and fine." Oden and Putman had arrested Barbee for the murder of Albert Von Kleeser at Ozona, Crockett County, and he also was charged with the murder of a man named Staggs.[50]

Then in September, Captain Jones had to make a difficult decision regarding his sergeant, Baz L. Outlaw. His service record merely indicates he was honorably discharged on September 18, 1892.[51] Although Captain Jones did not record the reason for dismissing his sergeant, it was because the man continued to abuse alcohol. On the following day Corporal Hughes was promoted to the rank of 1st Sergeant, replacing the discharged Outlaw. On that same day Captain Jones promoted Carl Kirchner to take Hughes's place as 1st Corporal.[52]

~ 5 ~

Battling the Olguins

"I Expect trouble here[.] can you send sergeant Hughes and outfit up tonight[?]"

— *Corporal Carl Kirchner to Adj. Gen. W. H. Mabry,*
June 30, 1893

During late 1892 and the early months of 1893, Hughes daily scouted after fugitives and frequently arrested wanted men. Charges against these men included simple theft of miscellaneous goods; obtaining money under false pretensions; theft of a horse; aggravated assault; assault and battery; and theft of a saddle or theft of a horse and saddle. He probably considered much of the work routine. His scouts were of course not always successful. On January 17, 1893, Hughes and one other man scouted to Fort Davis "and other points" in search of one Marcos Justilla, charged with theft of a mare and a gun. After eight days scouting they had to give up without having found him. They had covered over 200 miles in their unsuccessful hunt.[1]

Ironically, on that same day, Captain Jones penned a letter to Adjutant General Mabry praising his sergeant. Captain Jones noted that he was "very much of the opinion" that his company could do excellent service in El Paso, and that "it will be a new field and we will be more interested and can work with renewed energy." He praised Hughes, but recommended he be left at Alpine. "Sergt. Hughes should, in my opinion, be left at his present station. He is a fine officer and is in full accord with the best people in the Country and is very familiar with the entire

76

section for several Counties along the Rio Grande." Further, "Hughes Knows the people and Country and can do better service than any one I can think of unless he was in the country for many months."[2]

Later that same month ex-Ranger Baz L. Outlaw entered the office of County Judge W. Van Sickle[3] and discussed his situation. He had been dismissed from the service and now wanted to be reinstated, either as a full Ranger or at least as a Special Ranger. He was aware of the conversation the judge had held with Captain Jones about adding him to the rolls again. Apparently certain individuals had complained

A young Wigfall Van Sickle, circa 1895. *Courtesy the C. B. Casey Collection, Archives of the Big Bend, Bryan Wildenthal Memorial Library, Sul Ross State University, Alpine, Texas.*

about Outlaw's character, but he would admit to only one fault: "where I was wrong only in one thing, and that was drinking too much Some times but not when I was on duty, for it never caused me to neglect any Business." He explained that any officer who "Ranges over Texas Several years" and used any vigilance, or activity, "makes many enemies among the criminal class of people." And it was this class of people who were always eager to make some negative report against an officer, "& especially if it be a Ranger." Outlaw had gone before the county judge that very morning, January 26, and taken an oath which was left on file at Van Sickle's office "not to drink liquor of any kind for the next five years & I intend to Stick to it for I realize that it has already injured me financially and otherwise." His wish was granted, and Baz L. Outlaw became a Special Ranger assigned to Company D.[4] Unfortunately Baz L. Outlaw was unable to keep his pledge.

In February Hughes and two others scouted via Cleveland's Ranch to San Antonio Colony in search of stolen horses, but found none. They learned later the horses had already crossed the river into the state of Chihuahua, Mexico. Later that same month Hughes and an unidentified Mounted Inspector of Customs spent five days searching for smuggled goods but only recovered one horse, some wine, and some mescal.[5]

Meanwhile, former Ranger and ex-member of the Texas House of Representatives George Wythe Baylor was writing Adjutant General Mabry requesting that he send a squad of Rangers to Ysleta. Just the day before two men had been killed driving off stolen cattle within twelve miles of El Paso, and "theft of horses and cattle is nearly an every day matter [and that fact] would seem to emphasize very strongly the pressing need of some thing more than the [local] officers of the law to give protection to the citizens. . . ." Baylor reminded the adjutant general that the men who had killed Ranger Fusselman had not been caught, as local officers could not follow them. But Rangers "with their pack mule & 20 days rations would have Kept on the trail with out regard to State or national boundaries & captured or Killed the murderers." Baylor further reminded the adjutant general that when he was in charge of a squad of Rangers, many outlaws were driven out of the state and "did not dare to come back."[6]

In March the decision of where to send Sergeant Hughes was still pending. Captain Jones was inclined to send him to Ysleta in order to provide protection along the river, stating in a letter to Adjutant General Mabry that "the men who are with Hughes are all 30 years or more in age, and are tried and true, and that class of men are more needed in a small detachment than under my immediate control."[7] The problem of too few Rangers and too vast a territory was vexing for Captain Jones. His men had broken up a gang planning to attack the Southern Pacific Railroad; further concerns were that Langtry, "one of the toughest places on the S.P." line, continued to be a hotbed of trouble.[8] Only two men were there to control the roughs and deal with cattle thieves. Mabry considered sending a squad of four men to El Paso County, but Captain Jones believed that "4 men will simply be murdered and will do no good." The gang that was causing so much trouble numbered at least fifty, and the gang was well organized.[9]

Another group of hard cases, although considerably fewer in number, were of great concern to Reeves County Sheriff George A. "Bud" Frazer,[10] son of Reeves County Judge George M. Frazer. Sheriff Frazer had served as a Ranger prior to becoming sheriff, first serving under Capt. Sam McMurry May 3–31, 1882, in Mitchell County, then under Capt. George W. Baylor from October 24, 1883, to February 19, 1884. He received an honorable discharge at Ysleta. In spite of his record as a Texas Ranger, Sheriff Frazer did not have great faith in his own abilities and now expressed his concerns to Gov. James Stephen Hogg, stressing that he had only three Rangers, courtesy of Captain Jones, but would like them to be retained for the "next four or six months." Sheriff Frazer believed their presence was necessary "Owing to the condition of affairs here—the number of hard cases—and amt of crime . . ."[11]

The hard cases causing Sheriff Frazer such trouble included the notorious James Brown Miller, his brother-in-law Emanuel "Mannie" Clements, and Martin Quilla Hardin as well as various others of their clique. Miller had arrived in Pecos in 1891 and became deputy under Sheriff Frazer. Miller and his friends quickly became thorns in Sheriff Frazer's side. Miller had married Mannie Clements's sister, whose father, Emanuel Clements Sr., had lost his life in a saloon brawl. Clements was a cousin of John Wesley Hardin who would be pardoned out of Huntsville State Prison in 1894. The exact relationship of Martin Q. Hardin to John Wesley Hardin is unknown, but the group of Miller, Clements, and Hardin were a formidable outfit of hard cases. In 1892 Miller ran against Frazer for the office of sheriff, but lost; nevertheless he attained the position of constable, allowing him to wear a badge and legally go armed. Miller then began to plot against Frazer. In May 1893, he intended to cause a disturbance at the train depot when Frazer returned from a business trip, and during the created "disturbance" and confusion a shot would "accidentally" hit Frazer. A witness friendly to Frazer learned of the plot and informed the sheriff. Charges of conspiracy to murder were brought against Miller, Clements, and Hardin, specifically that on or about May 22, 1893, the trio plotted "with malice aforethought to then and there kill and murder G. A. Frazer."[12] The three were held briefly in jail, then released on bond to later stand trial. With the trio now on the loose naturally Frazer became even more concerned for his safety; he would live under constant fear of assassination. The Frazer-Miller feud would smolder until late 1896. John R. Hughes found that the hard cases of Reeves County gave many lawmen "concern," due to the "condition of affairs."

Learning that Captain Hughes was to be sent to Ysleta, attorney and State Senator John M. Dean heard Shafter citizens express their concerns about his removal. Dean wrote that "Shafter is the most important place on the west side of the Pecos river for a detachment of rangers. . . . John R. Hughes is a splendid officer and he has had an excellent detachment with him at Shafter and I hope that if he is ordered elsewhere that you will replace him at Shafter with an equally efficient officer and detachment."[13] Dean did not know of anyone who could truly replace Hughes, but he apparently had enough faith in the Ranger service in general that any commander would satisfy him.

Captain Jones investigated personally the area with the intention of determining the best place for a permanent Ranger camp, considering water, grass availability, and terrain. He determined that Ysleta would be best, and that a squad of Rangers "will be more effective stationed at this place than any where else in the Valley." At Ysleta the command would be centrally located and could operate in both directions along the river.[14]

Meanwhile, after suffering from his leg wound for almost four years, Frank L. Schmid of Company D died. Hughes learned of Schmid's untimely death only after arriving in Ysleta, El Paso County, having been ordered there by the adjutant general. He and eight men had spent ten days on the road, traveling 250 miles. Ysleta, San Elizario, and El Paso would become home for Hughes for many years, well into the twentieth century. In addition to the common hard cases he knew he would have to deal with, Hughes as well as every other Ranger knew of the Olguins, also known as the "Bosque Gang," the most notorious of the desperadoes in the contiguous corner of Texas, New Mexico, and Mexico. Parts of the area they inhabited were swamps or wetlands, hence the name the "Bosque Gang." The region covered was a swamp-like area between Fort Fillmore, New Mexico, running down to the San Elizario region south of El Paso. Their primary headquarters were on an island in the Rio Grande, frequently termed "Pirate Island." An El Paso newspaper commented on the Olguin Gang's territory, decrying "the nature and extent of the Island and Fort Fillmore bosques or swamps, and their capability of affording a safe hiding place for the horse and cattle thieves, smugglers and murderers who have so long infested the border. Between these two great jungles the distance is about thirty-three miles, and by avoiding the roads and keeping in the mesquite thicket along the foot of the mesa a man or a party of men might travel the whole distance without at any point being seen by a person fifty yards from the line of march."[15]

Some years before, the Rio Grande had changed its channel, which caused this unusual land formation. Due to the unstable nature of the river, an imaginary line was established to mark the border between the two countries. In June 1893 the invisible line divided the island. In this instance, one could cross the river and still be in Texas; but crossing the imaginary line placed one in Mexico. The island was several miles long and had a population of about three hundred, mostly populating a small community known as *Tres Jacales*. It was on this land that Captain Jones intended to challenge the Olguins on the thirtieth day of June, 1893.

The Olguins were composed of an extensive family. At this point in time the head of the family, Clato, was over ninety years old and perhaps going blind. His son Jesús María was in his mid-forties. Severio and Antonio, sons of Jesús María, were both young and now considered leaders among the thieves and murderers who infested the "neutral ground" along the Rio Grande.

Only recently Jesús María, his sons Severio, Sebastian, and an unidentified Mexican, had all defied R. E. "Ed" Bryant, a deputy sheriff of El Paso County.[16] Captain Jones's father-in-law, George Wythe Baylor, later described them as "a hard set, the grandfather, Clato, his sons, Jesús María, Antonio (ex-convict) and Pedro Olguin. The sons of Jesús are Severio, Sebastian, Pecilliano, and two younger ones. All live on the Island on Texas soil, except the ex-convict, Antonio, who was sent to the penitentiary and escaped." By reputation, the Olguins composed a "gang of thieves, murderers and smugglers that have for years infested an island that has been a sort of neutral ground." On or about June 25 several of the Olguins "got on a drunk" in the village of Guadalupe in Mexico and killed one man and wounded three others, one of whom was expected to die.

The members of this gang and others created a reign of terror among many inhabitants of the greater El Paso area. Petitions had gone to the governor for Ranger protection. Finally, in June 1893, Adjutant General King responded favorably to their pleas; he sent Captain Jones to provide "protection from these border thieves and murderers." One of the first things Jones did on arrival was to set up tents in Ysleta "for the avowed purpose of ridding the island below and the bosque above of the desperate characters that have for years infested them."[17]

On Thursday, June 29, Captain Jones with a squad of five men— Corporal Carl Kirchner, privates Edward D. Aten, T. F. Tucker, John W.

Saunders, and El Paso County Deputy Sheriff R. E. "Ed" Bryant—left camp with warrants for certain members of the Olguin family. Jones believed that since the Olguins had recently been in more trouble they would now seek refuge temporarily on the Rio Grande island. The evening of June 29, the Rangers camped opposite La Quadrilla, five miles below San Elizario, on the east bank. The next morning they were in their saddles by 4:00 a.m. and rode straight across the island for the Olguin ranch, some five miles distant. Rounding up the ranch, they found old Clato Olguin, Jesús María's wife, two other women, and a boy. The old man was very surly, and the fugitives were aware of the scout, as their friends in Ysleta or San Elizario had apparently alerted them to what was coming. The fugitives had crossed over to the Mexican side to the house of Antonio Olguin.

According to Kirchner's official report, they then started "in the main road, which crosses backward and forward from our side to Mexico several times, the river being very crooked and being overgrown with chapparal [*sic*], it is difficult to determine which one is in Texas or Mexico."[18] The Rangers searched several houses—whether these houses were in the little village of Tres Jacales or elsewhere is not clear in any of the reports—with no results and were on their way back when they saw two mounted Mexicans approaching them. The pair turned their horses and ran, causing the Rangers to suspect they were the men they wanted. Within half a mile, Corporal Kirchner and Private Saunders overtook them and demanded their surrender. The two Rangers were well ahead of their companions as they had faster horses. Then from inside the building the Mexicans fired two shots at Kirchner and four shots at the others. One shot hit the magazine of Kirchner's Winchester, not ruining it but damaging it in such a way that he had to reload after each shot. The other Rangers, having now caught up with Kirchner and Saunders, dismounted to engage the men hidden in the adobe house. Immediately Captain Jones received a bullet in the thighbone, breaking the bone, but he continued to fight, shooting at his assailants. [19]

George W. Baylor, Captain Jones's father-in-law, provided additional details about the last fight of his son-in-law, although slightly in disagreement with what Kirchner reported. As Baylor wrote, it was Captain Jones and Private Tucker in the lead who met the two Mexicans who then "wheeled and ran back." After some three or four hundred yards Kirchner, Aten, and Saunders passed Jones and Tucker "and ran on the Mexicans." Jesús María Olguin fell from his horse and ran, finding sanctuary in the adobe house of Antonio Olguin. The other rider threw up his hands. The little settlement had but four adobe houses, three of them on the right side of the road about fifty yards apart, and one house on the left. As Kirchner passed one of the buildings, someone fired at him from inside, the bullet hitting his weapon, disabling it in part so he could only fire one shot and then reload. Bullets flew close to Saunders as well as Aten, and they both returned fire. Now it was a situation of the Rangers being in the open and their assailants behind adobe walls, both inside the houses and from behind the walls connecting them. The house had a porthole allowing the shootists the advantage. Baylor continued:

> The Mexicans would open the door & fire and two Mexicans on the right & left of the house would rise from behind an adobe wall & fire also. The door would then close. Kirchner, Saunders & Aten whirled and came back, dismounted & Bryan[t] came up back of & within 15 or 20 feet of Capt Jones & Tucker, and every time the door was opened, and a volley be fired Capt Jones and the men would return it.

In the second volley, a bullet hit Captain Jones's thigh, breaking his leg causing him to fall. He managed to straighten his wounded leg in front of him and fired two or three more shots. In great pain, Captain Jones continued to fire, leaning forward, and firing at the Mexican who fired at him. Then he was hit again, the ball knocking him flat. Tucker saw him fall and asked, "Captain, are you hurt?" Captain Jones replied, "Yes, shot all to pieces." In spite of his leg wound the captain continued to fire his pistol, emptying it but even in the confusion managing to hit two of his targets. Now a Mexican from behind an adobe wall rose up and fired again at the captain, this time a fatal shot. He managed to utter "Boys, I am killed" and collapsed.[20]

Tucker, close to his captain when he was hit, stayed with him, intending to take the body back to Texas. He later explained that when the fight
started Jones probably did not realize he had crossed the imaginary line and
was in Mexico. Now Deputy Bryant told him, "We had better get across
the line, we are in Mexico." They were within a mile or so from the plaza
of *Tres Jacales* (Three Shacks), and knew that there would soon be a force
of Mexicans coming to investigate. Young Lujan, a youth who had accompanied the scout in an effort to try to recover a stolen horse, informed the
Rangers a courier had gone to nearby Guadalupe for soldiers.

The Rangers had to leave Jones's body where it fell. Tucker was now
in command of the squad. The concern became whether reinforcements
for the Olguins would arrive to finish them all off. When the firing
stopped, the Rangers rode up the road to *Tres Jacales*. Bryant asked a
Mexican to take care of the captain's body, which he promised to do, but
said they could not deliver the body to the Rangers on the United States
side as it was against their laws.

The Rangers had lost their captain, but two of the Olguins were
injured: a bullet had gone through the right hand of Jesús María Olguin
and two bullets had grazed his head. His son Severio "had his arm broken near the body."[21]

There was nothing more for the Rangers to do other than return
to Texas. At San Elizario Corporal Kirchner sent a telegram to General Mabry:

> Have just had fight with Mexican outlaws near line of Mexico[.] Capt
> Jones killed[.] we were overpowered and have just come in for rein-
> forcements[.] only had six men[.]

A second telegram to Mabry expressed his concern:

> I Expect trouble here[.] can you send sergeant Hughes and outfit up
> tonight[?] the railway co[mpany] will furnish transportation free[.]

Kirchner must have also quickly informed George W. Baylor of the
death of his son-in-law as Baylor then telegraphed Mabry:

Corporal Kirchner reports Capt Frank Jones Killed by Mexicans on the Island near Tresjacales [*sic*] —can you send Sergt Hughes and squad here at once[?][22]

Kirchner, besides informing his superiors of the tragedy, now resolved to recover Jones's body. El Paso County sheriff Frank B. Simmons quickly called for volunteers to go across and recover not only the body but Jones's personal effects as well. Superintendent Martin of the Southern Pacific provided Simmons with a special train: a coach for the men and a stock car for their horses. Within two hours additional men volunteered, many who were friends of the Rangers and were heading to the scene "to avenge the death of their friend and to capture the body of the fallen man from the keeping of the pirates and cutthroats that took it." Members joining Sheriff Simmons's command included officer

El Paso County Sheriff Peyton J. Edwards (1910–1916). *From the Hughes Personal Photo Album, courtesy the Texas Ranger Hall of Fame and Museum, Waco, Texas.*

Albert C. Ross, Deputy Sheriff J. C. Jones, Frank McMurry, Peyton F. Edwards Jr., Will Davis, Thomas A. Bendy, Paul Logan, George A. Scarborough, J. D. Ponder, and Fred Stevenson—the latter two reporters "of the afternoon papers"—and Thomas O'Keeffe of the *El Paso Times*. Ranger R. B. Chastain[23] later joined them. Attorney T. T. Teel also was with the group.[24]

The news of the death of the Ranger captain spread rapidly. From Alpine, Special Ranger Baz L. Outlaw telegraphed Mabry: "Capt Jones was killed near Ysleta by thieves today[.] will go up on first train [and] do all I can to capture murderers." Hughes was also at Alpine and telegraphed Mabry the same day, "I will go to San Elizario by first train." Now Kirchner telegraphed further news to Mabry, that the fight had taken place in Mexico, and that he had recovered the body of Captain Jones and secured the arrest of the men who had killed him. Baylor also informed Mabry of the news of recovering Jones's body. "The Mexican authorities have Shown every courtesy in their power in given [*sic*, giving] us the body of our dead Ranger & promise to return the Gun, pistol, watch, money & horse left at the scene of the fight."[25]

Sheriff Simmons did not realize that Kirchner had recovered the body, and anticipated trouble in attempting to do so. He met with the *jefe político* of Juarez—Lieutenant Colonel Rafael García Martínez— and together they headed for the scene of the tragedy, intending to recover the remains. Colonel Martínez had an escort of soldiers and by chance, this group met three of the Olguins who were intending to sneak around Juarez to hide out in the upper bosques. Sheriff Simmons recognized who they were and Colonel Martínez ordered his escort to arrest them. Mexican officials delivered the prisoners to the military prison at Juarez. They were Jesús María Olguin, his son Severio, and another son, Antonio.

Hughes arrived at San Elizario at 9:30 the morning of July 1 and found Corporal Kirchner had left word for him to go on to Ysleta, as there had been arrangements for the recovery of Jones's body. At 2:00 p.m., Kirchner arrived at Ysleta with the body. The Masons of the El Paso Lodge No. 130, A.F. and A.M. laid Captain Jones to rest at 6:00

p.m. that evening with full Masonic honors. His brother, Judge William Kenner Jones[26] of Del Rio, as well as John R. Hughes, attended. Mrs. Jones, prostrate, was unable to attend. Special Ranger Baz L. Outlaw arrived too late from Alpine to assist in recovering the body but perhaps attended the funeral with the seven men he had brought with him. He doubted the widow Jones would recover from the shock of her husband's death.[27] Perhaps the other Rangers of Company D attended as well, their thoughts on the tragic death of their captain, but also wondering who would replace him.

"I found that Corpl. Kirchner had done good work in getting the body and securing the arrest of three of the criminals on the Mexican side of the river," Hughes wrote to Adjutant General Mabry. As yet, Jones's personal effects, his arms, watch, and money, as well as the horse and saddle of Private Tucker, were still in the hands of the Mexican officials. They were to be delivered to Juarez, and Hughes, Kirchner, and Tucker would "try to get them back." Hughes continued sharing his observations with his superior, noting that El Paso County was "in

The Frank Jones badge is made of brass and copper and has gold letters "F.B." (Frontier Battalion) mounted to badge face. The watch and badge were returned to Sergeant Hughes with the body of Captain Jones by Mexican authorities. *Courtesy Mr. and Mrs. Donald M. Yena Collection, San Antonio.*

a very bad condition [and] the depridations [*sic*] of the 'Bosque gang' as they are called have not been interfered with for so long that they think they can do as they please and can not be arrested."[28] That of course would be work to do for whoever replaced Captain Jones, as well as completing the June monthly return for Company D.

In the official records of Ranger scouts and activities, summaries of the death of a Ranger were recorded. The clerk who summarized scouts in the adjutant general's official operations ledger wrote in *red ink,* that on June 29

> Capt Jones & 5 men Scout to Pirate Island with writs to arrest Jesus & Severino [*sic*] Olguin[.] Camped for the night 7 miles below Tres Jacales Mexico. No arrest. On returning Scouted up old river. Saw two Mexicans wheel & run. Capt. Jones & party gave chase[.] Capt Jones & party followed them to Tres Jacales not knowing that he was in Mexico. The fugitives took refuge in a house & fired upon the pursuers, and Capt Jones was killed.

In the margin is written, again in red ink, "Capt. Jones Killed," and in the same margin, but in pencil, "1 Horse wounded of a Ranger."[29] Adjutant General Mabry now had the difficult task of selecting the man who would replace Frank Jones as captain of Company D.

To add even more excitement in the lives of the law-abiding of the area, and perhaps more particularly to Sergeant Hughes, was the announcement in the *El Paso Times* that U.S. Deputy Marshal Ben Williams of Las Cruces, New Mexico, was in El Paso the night of July 5. He was described as "the officer who recently shot and captured Geronimo Parra, one of the Bosque gang who killed young Fusselman . . ."[30]

~ 6 ~

Scouting on Pirate Island

"I WAS FOUR YEARS SHERIFF OF REEVES COUNTY AND WHILE I
WAS SUCH SHERIFF THIS TROUBLE CAME UP AND IT HAS BEEN
GETTING WORSE ALL THE TIME AND WHILE I WAS SHERIFF I
DONE MY WHOLE DUTY AND NOW IT IS A YOUNG WAR."

— *George A. Frazer to Gov. C. A. Culberson, February 24, 1895*

Adjutant General Mabry as well as Governor Hogg now faced
the decision of who would be the best man to replace the dead
captain. State Senator John M. Dean telegraphed the governor recommending Hughes, "next in line of promotion please appoint
him Captain."[1] El Paso's mayor, W. H. Austin, even though out of town
on a visit to McMinnville, Tennessee, quickly learned of the sad news.
He telegraphed the governor that he "earnestly" endorsed Hughes.[2]
Acting Mayor James P. Badger agreed, stating simply that Hughes "is
the man we want." Trevanion Theodore Teel, attorney, Mexican War
hero and veteran of the Confederacy's failed New Mexico Territory
campaign, not only fully endorsed Hughes but telegraphed that he was
"the best appointment that could be made" as he was "sober capable
honest brave."[3] Robert Cross, an El Paso policeman, also telegraphed
the governor, stating: "I know him to be tried and true[.] I have been
an officer on the frontier long enough to know."[4] Atkins Jefferson "Jeff"
McLemore, member of the House of Representatives from the Corpus Christi district, nearly 700 miles east from Ysleta, telegraphed that
the appointment of Hughes "will be gratifying to the people of this
section."[5] Attorney Peyton F. Edwards Sr. telegraphed the governor "our

90

people want Hughes."[6] W. W. Turney "heartily" recommended Hughes for the position.[7] Sheriff Frank B. Simmons telegraphed both the governor and Adjutant General Mabry indicating he personally preferred Hughes but in addition Hughes was "the choice of the people of this County to Succeed Capt Jones."[8] J. D. Escajeda, District Clerk of El Paso, requested Hughes be appointed, stating he knew him "to be tried and true."[9]

Besides telegrams, letters and petitions flooded the offices of Mabry and Hogg, but not all agreed that Hughes was the best man to replace Captain Jones. H. H. Kilpatrick, county judge of Presidio County since the 1892 election, forwarded a petition to Adjutant General Mabry signed by Denton G. Knight and over thirty others requesting Baz L. Outlaw take Jones's place. Their petition stated, "Mr. Outlaw is thoroughly acquainted with the Western part of the state & is widely known as a brave & efficient officer."[10] In addition, Brewster County Judge Wigfall Van Sickle forwarded a petition signed by over eighty citizens recommending him as the man to select. They had "faith & confidence in B. L. Outlaw & believing him to be a man of undaunted courage and fine generalship, and from his long Service in the frontier Battalion of this state, & valuable services rendered to his country & his fit qualifications gained from his experiences of many years upon the frontier . . ." believed him worthy.[11]

Some people also believed that George W. Baylor would be a good choice for the captaincy. Baylor certainly had considerable military experience, having served on the staff of General Albert S. Johnston during the late war, rising to the rank of colonel of the 2nd Texas Cavalry and had excelled in leadership qualities. He did not feel inclined to run however, and made it clear to Adjutant General Mabry. "In this connection," Baylor wrote, "I wish to say that Sergt Jno. R. Hughes had the entire confidence of Capt. Jones and my daughter heard him Say in case he resigned he would use all his influence in the Sergts behalf & I believe in regular line of promotion he should have the position, & trust you will give it to him." Baylor concluded his letter by stating that he would try and recover the horse and equipment of Private Tucker, as well as the gun, watch, and other items of Frank Jones, and thanked the general for his expression of sympathy.[12]

Special Ranger Baz L. Outlaw also wrote the adjutant general, but not to recommend Hughes. He was not shy about his wishes and indicated that it was at "the Solicitation of many friends, and stockmen in the Surrounding Counties . . . I will respectfully request that I be appointed to Succeed Captain Frank Jones." But in addition, still concerned that others might doubt his willingness to avoid alcohol, he promised "to do all in my power, to imitate the Example Set by my old and honored Co. Commander—in temperate habits, and will faithfully discharge all duties incumbent upon me, as an officer."[13] He had the very best of intentions.

William Noyes, superintendent of the Presidio Mining Company of Shafter, learned that Hughes was a candidate for the captaincy. "If this is so," he wrote on July 5, "I desire to state in Mr. Hughes behalf that he is a thoroughly reliable and very energetic man—that while stationed here he and his men preserved excellent order, and that everyone I know was highly pleased with his efficiency as an officer."[14] From Leander, northwest of Austin, J. H. Faubion wrote that since learning that "the place of Capt Jones of the Rangers is to be filled soon" he recommended his friend John Hughes. Faubion declared that he knew of "no man who would So well fill the vacancy, and I hope you will feel about the matter as I do."[15]

However, perhaps most influential of all was the petition Carl Kirchner and the men of Company D forwarded to Mabry. Kirchner wrote that Hughes was the choice of the company "to fill the vacancy caused by the death of our beloved Captain." He reminded Mabry that Hughes was an "honest brave & efficient officer with sober & industrious habits." Furthermore, he had "given the utmost satisfaction & has been on the Rio Grande border long enough to speak Spanish sufficient to be of great help along the border." Hughes, according to Kirchner, had worked in every county as a Ranger from El Paso to Brownsville, the entire length of the border along the Rio Grande. Corporal Kirchner and privates J. V. Latham, E. D. Aten, J.

W. Fulgham, Robert Speaks, T. F. Tucker, Ike Herrin,[16] J. W. Saunders, and R. E. Bryant all signed the petition.[17]

Samuel R. Miller, longtime resident of the Trans-Pecos area and resident of Marfa in 1893, wrote Mabry stressing his acquaintance with Hughes. He wrote that he had a "great deal to do with the Rangers while I was Sheriff" and more especially Hughes. He "was brought to my notice" and Miller appointed him a deputy. Miller remarked that Hughes was in every way capable and well acquainted with the country and knew "more or less about the ways of the Outlaws in this country" than any one else. Hughes was a sober, brave man, and was "allways [*sic*] on duty and trying to keep peace and order." Miller claimed to have worked with Hughes, going after outlaws, for two years, and knew him to be "Suitable to fill any place."[18]

And what of 1st Sergeant John R. Hughes, the man himself? He wrote and placed his name in consideration, "to fill the vacancy caused by the sad death of our Brave and Beloved Captain Frank Jones." He asked the adjutant general to consider the telegrams and letters from his friends, "which you will see are all men of high standing in the country where they live and where I have worked as a ranger."[19]

In spite of the high regard for Frank Jones, reality brought the feelings of some to consider expenses. Sheriff Simmons complained of "quite an expence [*sic*]" in getting the body back from Mexico and believed the State of Texas should reimburse him. He stressed to Governor Hogg that his office "pays but little" and it would be "quite a hardship on me" if he were not reimbursed, at least partially. Besides asking for money to cover his expenses Simmons also asked for a full company of Rangers "if only for a few months." He concluded, "I am going to try and catch all these Mexicans that had been doing the Stealing and Robbing [*sic*] in this county for years."[20] One wonders why he had not already attempted to do just that.

Sheriff Simmons also penned a letter to Adjutant General Mabry on the same day, in which he also asked for a full company of Rangers. Simmons believed that within a few months, with a sufficient number of Rangers, and with the promised cooperation of Mexican authorities, he could "raid all the Bosques." The mayor of Juarez, Mexico, Rafael Martinez, requested fifty mounted men so that at any time the Rangers could go down the Bosque on the Texas side, he would send his men down on the other side "to prevent any one we may encounter from crossing." Simmons again stressed that Hughes was a good man and he would like to see him appointed captain of Company D. With Hughes in charge of a full company, Simmons was confident that no mob could storm the jail and lynch the men involved in the murder of Captain Jones. First, someone had to capture those still at large and deliver them to the El Paso County jail. He intended to bring the Olguins to justice and gather the necessary papers "preparatory to applying to the Mexican authorities for the extradition of the Olguins" from their cells in the military prison in Juarez. [21]

All those individuals who wanted John R. Hughes to replace Frank Jones as captain of Company D received their wish. On July 8 Hughes wrote his superior, W. H. Mabry, that he had received the appointment: "I will try to do my duty impartialy [sic] and try to be a credit to the Frontier Battalion."[22]

Ira Aten, Hughes's friend and Ranger companion from the 1880s, now wrote to Mabry concerning Hughes. He had been in New Mexico after a fugitive and had just learned of "the sad death of my old Captain." Jones's death was "a sad shoke [sic] to me for he was almost the same as a brother as we have often been where I [sic, our] lives depended upon one [a]nother & always came out victorious. One by one the old boys go how sad, how dreadful." Aten obviously had not forgotten the gunfight he and Hughes had experienced tracking down Wesley Collier, and now recommended Hughes to replace Jones. At the time Aten was serving as sheriff of Castro County, Texas, hundreds of miles northeast of El Paso County.[23]

On July 16, Hughes, with Deputy U.S. Marshal George A. Scarborough, and eight other men, scouted to Pirate Island in search of Espiridon Gabaldon, believed to be one of the Bosque Island gang. Only four days before he had quarreled with another Mexican and ended the quarrel by killing him.[24] Gabaldon was the prime target of their search, but there were others wanted for cattle theft. Certainly while watching for Gabaldon they also remained alert for any members of the Olguin gang who may have still been in the area. Hughes recorded no arrests in his report of this scout.

What the captains omitted in their official reports is their use of lynch law, occasionally used by the Rangers, men sworn to uphold Texas law. A San Antonio newspaper report indicated that two weeks after Jones's death a Mexican identified only as "Jaso" was found hanging from a tree on the lower end of Pirate Island. His corpse had been hanging for a day or two and according to the Mexicans there, "the man was a Mexican citizen and that Texans hanged him." The implication was clear that the bandits responsible for the death of Captain Jones were marked for death, Jaso being one of them.[25] Years later Captain Hughes, long since retired, admitted to a reporter that *nineteen* members of the gang responsible for the death of Captain Jones were found "where they committed suicide by hanging with Rangers' ropes around their necks."[26] Grassroots historian C. L. Sonnichsen knew Hughes in El Paso, having arrived there in 1931, and learned from him that the death of Captain Jones "was a great grief to him" and "he saw to it personally that the eighteen men involved were run down and brought to justice in one way or another."[27] Eighteen or nineteen . . . were *brought to justice in one way or another*. Occasionally lawmen became their own judge, jury, and executioner in the Wild West.

On July 23 and 24 Hughes with seven men led another scout up the east side of the Franklin Mountains, to the upper bosque, as far as Anthony, New Mexico Territory. They were hunting Geronimo Parra and Desidario Pasos. Parra was the bandit the Rangers believed had killed Sergeant Fusselman. While at Anthony, Hughes met with Ben Williams, a deputy sheriff from Las Cruces, New Mexico. Williams told Hughes that Parra was now in jail at Las Cruces, charged with horse theft and assault to murder. Williams felt certain that Parra would be convicted for the crimes he was charged with—in New Mexico. Hughes, however, wanted him tried for murder in Texas, as he was confident Parra would be found guilty and receive the death penalty. At this point, though, Hughes could do nothing to get Parra into Texas for trial, but he would not forget him.[28]

On the twenty-eighth Hughes with nine men and lawman George A. Scarborough scouted down the Rio Grande near Fort Hancock in search of thieves. They arrested three men, but Hughes did not indicate their names or the specific charges against them. They arrested two men for smuggling on the following day and turned them over to Deputy Scarborough in El Paso. There Hughes also arrested Gregorio Yberra for theft of a steer. He was delivered to the El Paso jail.[29]

By August 1 Captain Hughes was "on scout to Pecos City on official business."[30] Here Captain Hughes and James Brown Miller, reputed professional man-killer for hire, met for the first time. In spite of Miller's outward respectability, in reality he was a con artist at best and a hired murderer at worst. Hughes no doubt suspected Miller would continue to be troublesome in spite of his efforts to prove respectability.

As described in Chapter 5, Sheriff George A. "Bud" Frazer and Miller were involved in a longtime personal feud. To add to the conflict between the two parties, Miller was now city marshal of Pecos City, so the two lawmen feuded with each other with the real potential for bloodshed. Hughes could not let himself get involved in such personal difficulties, however, and for now he allowed local officials to deal with the troubles.[31] He did, however, leave a three-man detachment there to assist in keeping the peace. Reeves County Judge Clarence N. Buckler was well aware of the situation and wanted Rangers stationed in Pecos City, the county seat. He expressed his concern in a letter to Governor Hogg, describing the "Sense of consciousness of the powerlessness of the peace officers to cope," with those lawless elements that opposed them. He believed that keeping two or three Rangers in the county "would Serve a good moral effect."[32] Others agreed with the request, including Judge George M. Frazer,[33] his son George A. the sheriff, District Clerk J. B. Gibson (brother of Con Gibson, recently killed in New Mexico Territory by a Miller associate), and attorneys Octavious A. Larrazola and Robert Holman. The presence of Hughes's Rangers ought to have calmed down their nervousness somewhat. On July 13 Private T. F.

Tucker and two others arrested James B. Miller, A. D. Ervine, Martin Q. Hardin, and Mannen Clements Jr. They placed them in the Pecos jail, charged with conspiracy to murder the sheriff. They would make bond and be released.[34]

Special Ranger Baz L. Outlaw, seemingly more aware of the troubles of other people than his own, was acutely aware of the potential for violence in Reeves County. As a "special" he was obliged to provide a report monthly to his superior, but on this occasion he was delayed in getting his report in on time due to "the heavy rains." He was aware of and reported what everybody must have already realized, that

> There seems to be a feud existing between the Sheriff of that county &
> the city marshal of Pecos City, & some cittizens [*sic*] which is liable to
> terminate in trouble at any time, in fact I don't think it will be Settled
> So long as the present Sheriff holds office—if I have been correctly
> informed by some of the citizens.[35]

The Reeves County problems would continue and would involve John R. Hughes, and they would remain a concern for other lawmen as well. The grand jury in Pecos did indict James B. Miller and Martin Q. Hardin for conspiracy to murder Sheriff Bud Frazer. The date for the trial was set for October and it would be held in El Paso.[36]

During the remainder of the summer and fall of 1893 Hughes was kept busy with his small company of Rangers covering a huge area of Texas, filled with criminals and fugitives of all types. His business frequently placed him in Fort Hancock, or Pecos City, or Shafter. On August 14 he led a nine-man scout to Fort Hancock in search of Juan Rodriguez and others. Three days later he arrested a man identified by Hughes as Lauro Albillar for sodomy; he delivered him to the county jail in El Paso.[37]

But not all was serious law work for Captain Hughes, as on Thursday, August 24 he, along with Colonel George W. Baylor, his wife and daughter Mamie, Miss Mary Ten Eyck, and Elliott C. Hull, left El Paso "for an outing" at Hueco Tanks. They intended to be gone a week.[38] It must have been an enjoyable change for man-hunter Hughes, but no further notice of this "outing" was reported in the newspapers or monthly returns.

As captain, Hughes was concerned not only with arresting fugitives, but also with enlistments, as many men served only a few months and had to be replaced, as well as dealing with the problems of his men. On August 24, Private J. W. Fulgham killed a man at Pecos City, one Charles Carroll, and Hughes had to investigate.[39] An early report indicated only that an "unknown man was killed to-day by Ranger Fulgham. . . . He was ordered under arrest and offered resistance and was thereupon shot by the officer." The only identification found was a small book in his pocket bearing the name of Charles Carroll, address Suggs, Indian Territory, dated May 3, 1893. Whether the man was indeed Carroll or someone else remains a mystery. The body was turned over to the county for burial.[40]

At the same time Hughes had to make a decision about another man wishing to enlist: Ernest St. Leon. The application went to the adjutant general, who apparently had some doubts about St. Leon's character, and it was referred to Hughes. Hughes responded that he had known St. Leon for about three years and considered him a man of "more than ordinary intelligence and industry." Hughes continued his praise: "I feel that he could do more good in this country as a ranger than any man that I know of." Hughes was aware of St. Leon's previous experience when he had been discharged, but that was on a report of E. S. Fisk who himself was dishonorably discharged. There had always been a doubt in Hughes's mind that St. Leon was guilty of what he was accused of: petty theft. Hughes now admitted that he "ought to be careful and enlist only men of good character [and] I also realize that I have got to have a few men who are industrious and understand the class of criminals that we have to deal with" and therefore wanted St. Leon. St. Leon had already made an unspecified promise to Hughes, and Hughes said that if St. Leon would "stick to his promise he has made me he will make a good ranger." Of course, if St. Leon did not keep his promise then Hughes would discharge him. In the same communication Hughes had good news: Private Fulgham had been tried in El Paso for the August killing of Charles Carroll. The jury took only twelve minutes to determine the verdict of acquittal.[41]

Fortunately all arrests did not end in gunplay. Some were made and received no attention in the press at all, such as the arrest of Catarino Nieto in El Paso. No details have been preserved, other than the fact that on September 8 Captain Hughes, with Robert E. "Ed" Bryant, arrested Nieto, who was charged with murder.[42] This was only one of many such arrests, as now Hughes's reputation was often enough to cause offenders to submit without resorting to violence. Bryant was with the Rangers and Captain Jones on Pirate Island. He was then a deputy sheriff, but now a Ranger, having enlisted on June 26 at Ysleta. Prior to serving under Hughes he had been a private in Company A commanded by George W. Baylor.

Hughes had not forgotten the loss of Charles H. Fusselman, killed by bandits back in April of 1890. Now in November 1893, he made a scout along the river above El Paso to see what he might learn about the men responsible for Fusselman's death. He learned that Geronimo Parra was still in jail in Las Cruces, New Mexico; Desidario Acosta was working on a ranch on the Rio Grande in Sierra County, New Mexico; and a third man, unidentified, was in Willcox, Arizona. All had been indicted in El Paso County but Hughes doubted they could be convicted on the evidence then at hand. Hughes would have worked longer on the Fusselman case but news reached him that he was needed back in El Paso, due to rumors of another Mexican revolution.[43]

A week later Hughes wrote again to Adjutant General Mabry. Horses had been stolen by "Revolutionists" near San Elizario and Hughes sent men in pursuit of them. His report indicated they had been taken into Mexico, then driven around Juarez and were headed for Deming, New Mexico, but his Rangers did not follow them out of the state. For some good news Hughes reported that the horse Corporal Tucker had lost in the fight on Pirate Island had been recovered, but as yet neither the pistol of Captain Jones nor the handcuffs of Tucker had been returned. He was able to include a list of all the items that had been recovered, and the value of those items. At the time Jose [*sic*, Jesus] Maria and Severio Olguin were still in jail in Juarez.[44]

With the legislature ever decreasing the funding needed by the Frontier Battalion, each captain had to discharge men. After another scout to Pirate Island on December 19, and various other scouts including one to Pecos City on "official business," Hughes made out the December monthly return: Company D now was reduced to one captain, one sergeant, one corporal, one teamster, and but thirteen enlisted men—privates. It was a drastic change from the first Company D monthly return made out in the summer of 1874, three decades earlier, by Capt. Cicero R. Perry in Blanco County. Perry had listed *seventy-five* names on his first muster roll. The drastic reduction in the number of men mustered into the Frontier Battalion was due in part to the success of the Rangers themselves. After the 1870s the primary concern was no longer the threat of Indian raiding parties, but outlawry: enforcing law and order on the Texas frontier.

Besides the regular scouting duties Hughes now had to deal with what might be best termed "administrative paperwork." Private A. V. Oden was injured somehow and Captain Hughes turned in the bill for medical attention received in February. Quartermaster G. H. Wheatley rejected the bill, and explained that "at the time he was wounded he was not in the discharge of his duties as a Ranger [and] therefore cannot allow the bill." No further details of this injury have been learned, nor is there mention of it in Van Oden's diary.[45]

An unusual call to duty came with the advent of a portion of the so-called "Coxey's Army," which had the potential for violence. Jacob Coxey, in Ohio, had organized a protest march, intending to march on Washington, D.C. The purpose was to protest widespread unemployment caused by the Panic of 1893 and to lobby the government to create jobs by building roads. Although Coxey himself never made it to Texas, a group of protestors from California traveled through the southwest, including the Lone Star State. The numbers, nicknamed "Coxey's Army," grew along the route, men on foot as well as any other means of transportation they could obtain. The protest march involved the Texas Rangers when on the night of March 22, General Lewis C. Frey, leading the "first California regiment of the industrial army," arrived in El Paso on the Southern

Pacific. The regiment filled one flat car and ten boxcars. Captain Hughes with seven Rangers, as well as County Sheriff Frank B. Simmons, was there to assist in patrolling the huge number of men. The presence of the lawmen proved to be unnecessary as the leaders of the "army" had trained them to be well behaved and to conduct themselves as peaceful protestors. In El Paso a thousand people met them as they disembarked from the train cars. As the crowd cheered, "the notes of a bugle rang out and the regiment immediately formed into twelve companies, each in command of a captain, whose orders were obeyed without any hesitancy." The companies marched towards city hall, each one with a color bearer carrying "a good-sized American flag . . . preceded by two drums beating a quickstep." The city fathers had already prepared "an immense amount of eatables" for them. General Frey, according to an El Paso reporter, then

> stepped to the center of the square and called his officers where they held a consultation. Several more bugle calls followed and a small square of ground was marked out for each company, the blankets were plied [*sic*, piled] in the center, large fires were built with wood provided by the city and then the men began washing themselves and eating.

The muster rolls for this crowd of men showed 807, "over four-fifths of whom are young men of good appearance and American parentage. . . . They are well-behaved, quiet, and orderly, and no man is allowed to leave the place set apart for his company, nor do they attempt to."[46] Presumably the companies behaved so well that there was nothing for Captain Hughes and his men to do, other than to observe. A week later "Frey's Regiment" reached Sierra Blanca, some ninety miles east of El Paso. The marchers were now estimated to number only five hundred, and news had reached the governor's office that the Rangers were now working for the railroad. Governor Hogg telegraphed Hughes that he was not to be in the service of the Southern Pacific guarding their trains, nor to interfere with either side unless there was violence. Hughes responded that "I am not serving the railway company. Sunday morning a railway switch was displaced, a train side-tracked and a seal broken. To protect property I ordered them off the train. . . ."[47]

Railroad officials legitimately were concerned that the hundreds of men in Coxey's Army, traveling on the trains, would do severe damage to railroad property, opening cars and pillaging whatever was found inside. But the Rangers made no arrests and the hundreds moved on towards San Antonio. In 1894 Sierra Blanca was a small community in eastern El Paso County, but is today the county seat of Hudspeth County.

In April tragedy struck, affecting many of the men in Company D, as it involved former Ranger Baz L. Outlaw, Ranger Private Joe McKidrict, and Constable John Selman Sr., one-time fugitive from Texas justice but now a working lawman in El Paso. Born in 1871, McKidrict had enlisted in Company D at Shafter on July 15, 1893. Marauding Indians had killed his father while he was a child. His mother later married prominent attorney Albert O. Cooley, giving rise to the mistaken belief that his real name was Joe Cooley. In the early 1890s, McKidrict traveled to Presidio County where he found work as a mine guard, but later, as he had originally intended, he became a Ranger with Captain Hughes his commander.

Baz L. Outlaw had not kept his vow to avoid alcohol and his state of intoxication now resulted in the deaths of two men and severe wounding of a third—and all lawmen. Baz L. Outlaw's good friend Ranger Oden described what happened to this tragic figure after he arrived in El Paso. Outlaw "came up from Alpine and headed for Tillie's place," a brothel located at 307 South Utah Street, considered the city's "most elegant," operated by Tillie Howard.[48] After a few drinks, according to Oden, one of the girls "took him in hand" and a half hour later he was "half under, but not in an ugly mood." He then left the brothel and headed up Utah Street, stopping in various places to have another drink. He met Walter James "Frank" Collinson, an acquaintance who had over a decade before hunted buffalo in the area of Fort Griffin where John Selman worked as a deputy sheriff. English-born Frank Collinson was well acquainted with the drunken former Ranger, who now complained to him how Deputy Richard C. Ware "had been treating him," apparently over fees earned for serving court papers. As they ambled along, the pair met a mutual acquaintance, Ernest Bridges, and they together tried to take the drunken man back to his room to sleep it off. He resisted, and insisted on going back to Tillie Howard's to see a certain girl. There, in Tillie's parlor, they met John Selman Sr., and all began conversing.

For some reason known only to himself, Baz L. Outlaw then exited the parlor and "wandered out into the back hall leading outside." Moments later the men heard a shot. Selman, whose past was filled with violence and gunfire, joked: "Bass has dropped his gun." Selman started toward the back when Tillie came running, blowing her police whistle to alert any law officer within hearing distance there was trouble. She must have been distraught as there were sufficient lawmen present to handle a drunken customer.

Joe McKidrict arrived on the scene in the back of the brothel first, observed the drunken man with a smoking revolver in his hand and innocently asked, "Bass, why did you shoot?" Angered over the perceived insult, Outlaw answered, "You want some, too?" and shot McKidrict in the head and again in the back as he collapsed. By then Constable Selman was within a few feet of the struggle with his weapon in hand. Senselessly, Baz L. Outlaw turned on John H. Selman and fired. The shot was so close the discharged powder burnt Selman's face, but fortunately, it missed. The near blinded Selman returned fire, and shot his assailant through the body, just above the heart. The dying man retreated but continued shooting, now hitting Selman twice in the right leg. Although he was temporarily blinded and unsteady on his feet, Selman, with one hand over his eyes, did only what he knew best to do in that kind of situation: cock the pistol and squeeze the trigger. Selman could not know if his bullets hit Outlaw or not, but Outlaw was mortally wounded, so badly that he was no longer a threat. Amazingly the dying man again started to walk up Utah Street—managing to walk nearly a full block—where Pvt. Francis M. "Frank" McMahan of Company D demanded his surrender. Selman's bullets had taken all the fight out of him and he gave McMahan his pistol, begging him to protect him from a mob. McMahan and an unidentified Mexican helped him inside the Barnum Show Saloon where they found a prostitute's bed in a back room and made him as comfortable as they could.[49] He kept crying over and over, "Oh God, help" and then repeatedly asked, "Where are my friends?" He died mourning for those absent friends. His good friend Alonzo Van Oden summed up the reason for the tragedy:

> Bass Outlaw is dead. Bass, my friend is gone. Before he died he shot and killed Joe McKidrict. Maybe all of us knew something like this would come to Bass—Bass, who was so brave and kind; who could laugh louder, ride longer, and cuss harder than the rest of us; and who could be more sympathetic, more tender, more patient than all of us when necessary. Bass had one weakness, that—at last—proved to be stronger than all his virtues. Bass couldn't leave liquor alone, and when Bass was drunk, Bass was a maniac; none of us could handle him; none of us could reason with him, we just stayed with him until he sobered up.

Alonzo Van Oden summed up both the dead men with this statement, "Joe McKidrict was a fine ranger. Bass Outlaw was my friend."[50] Oden did not date his journal entries, but the gunfight took place on April 5, 1894. Pvt. Frank McMahan had arrested the drunken ex-Ranger for the killing of McKidrict, but death came before any paperwork was completed. Captain Hughes's official report agreed with Oden's, that Joe McKidrict "a member of Co[mpany] D was killed tonight while attempting to arrest B. L. Outlaw[.] Outlaw is dead also." He explained that Outlaw held commissions as deputy sheriff of the Western District of Texas and as a Special Ranger attached to Company D. Hughes made the necessary arrangements for him to be buried in El Paso and for McKidrict to be buried in Austin where his family resided.[51]

On April 12, just over a week after the McKidrict-Outlaw tragedy, Reeves County Sheriff Frazer chose to take the law into his own hands and end the feud with James Brown Miller. He found Miller on a Pecos street and shot him; Frazer's aim was good but Miller was only wounded. Unknown to Frazer his intended victim wore a breast plate, which saved his life. This act did not sit well with the county citizens and Frazer was ultimately defeated in his race for another term as sheriff. Daniel Murphy became county sheriff on November 6, 1894.

Even with Frazer out of office, the Miller-Frazer feud still caused work for Company D. Reeves County Sheriff Murphy, Bud Frazer's successor, anticipated trouble when case against Frazer came to trial and on February 21, 1895, wrote to Mabry that "there has already been two shooting scrapes over this afair [*sic*] and as both parties have many friends and as I am unable to keep down troble [*sic*] I would ask that you send me some rangers to remain here during Dist. Court." Sheriff Murphy specifically wanted men who were not acquainted with either Miller or Frazer and who would be "wholey [*sic*] disinterested."[52]

Sheriff Frazer had twice attempted to kill J. B. Miller and failed, once back on April 12, wounding him, and then again on December 26, 1894. He was indicted with assault to kill, but Judge Buckler transferred the trial to El Paso County. The jury was unable to reach a verdict and was discharged. A second trial was scheduled to take place in Colorado City in Mitchell County. During this tumultuous time between trials Frazer was demonstrably in fear for his life, fearful of an ambush by Miller or his henchmen. Part of the time he hid out in Eddy, New Mexico. In late February he wrote Texas Gov. Charles A. Culberson a long plea for Ranger protection, a basic cry for help.

> I hereby make application for a detachment of State Rangers to be sent to Pecos Texas for the reason that I have to be there at the opening of the next term of District Court which convines [*sic*] on the 4 day of March 1895 and I deem my self in secure and unsafe as J. B. Miller will be there and he is a dangerous man, . . . [H]e has John W. Hardin a man only out of the pen a short time here and Clemins [*sic*, Mannen Clements Jr.] his brother in law and a great many others with him. I do not want any trouble but I do not feel like going down there when I know if we meet there will be trouble. I left Pecos to keep from having any trouble and all I ask is that I be protected and for this reason I ask for the rangers.

Frazer felt an explanation was needed and continued:

I was four years sheriff of Reeves County and while I was such sheriff this trouble Came up and it has been getting worse all the time and while I was sheriff I done my whole duty and now it is a young war and I want peace and law and order and in order that the law may have its course I do ask that you grant my [h]umble request.[53]

This petition had the desired effect. Adjutant General Mabry ordered Hughes to take a detachment to Pecos City. Hughes immediately responded that he would take three men who had no acquaintance with anyone there and he would go with them. They arrived the evening of March 3, 1895, and Captain Hughes, determined to prevent any trouble during court, placed Frazer under arrest, which was a technicality as he had come to court willingly. Perhaps it was as much for his own protection as anything. Before the court session began he placed two men at the foot of the stairs leading up to the court room and had them disarm everyone who intended to go up the stairs, with the exception of the sheriff and one deputy. However, the case was delayed until the next day. Hughes anticipated the case would be changed to El Paso County as it "will be impossible to get a Jury in this county as it is such a noted case." He explained that "citizens here are badly scared and are expecting trouble." Scared citizens or not, Hughes had given "all parties to understand from the start that the first man that displays a pistol will be put in Jail at once." Hughes was correct in believing the case would be transferred: it was changed to El Paso, trial date set for April. The citizens, he informed Adjutant General Mabry, were pleased that the Rangers had kept the two parties separated, and were "anxious that we be present at El Paso court when the trial comes up at that place."[54] While in Pecos Hughes did arrest Brannick Riggs, brother of Barney Riggs, considered one of the Frazer faction, for public drunkenness. Captain Hughes noted the scout for the Frazer trial had lasted five days, and covered 430 miles—by rail.[55]

Later that month Hughes received a totally different assignment as General Mabry now ordered him to report to Temple in Bell County, south of Dallas, and protect railroad property due to the railroad strike.

In 1893 the pioneer American Labor Union (A.L.U.) leader Eugene Debs helped to form the American Railway Union (A.R.U.). In the following year in Chicago the A.R.U. ordered a boycott by workers, essentially resulting in the first significant labor strike in American history. President Grover Cleveland ordered federal troops to keep the U.S. mails moving, and strikers were careful not to interfere with the delivery of the mail. Not knowing when or where violence might break out between strikers and non-union men, Governor Hogg ordered Rangers to key cities along the railroads, placing them along the lines from Galveston through Fort Worth and on up to the Red River. There were some minor disturbances, but with the presence of federal troops and various court injunctions, the strike was broken.[56]

One of the frequently published group photographs of nineteenth-century Texas Rangers shows Captain Hughes along with seventeen others, including Captain J. A. Brooks of Company F, posed in front of

Texas Rangers who protected the U.S. Mail during the Temple Railroad Strike, July 1894. Standing from left: Capt. J. A. Brooks, Co. F; Capt. J. R. Hughes, Co. D; Pvt. John F. Nix, Co. E; Pvt. E. D. Aten, Co. D; Pvt. Ed F. Connell, Co. B; Corp. Tom M. Ross, Co. E; Pvt. R. L. Queen, Co. B; Pvt. A. A. Neely, Co. B; Pvt. G. J. Cook, Co. F; Pvt. Dan Coleman, Co. E.; Seated from left: Pvt. Jack Harwell, Co. B; Pvt. William Schmidt, Co. D; Pvt. C. B. Fullerton, Co. B; Pvt. George N. Horton, Co. F; Pvt. Ed Palmer, Co. D; Pvt. Joe Natus, Co. F; Pvt. James V. Latham, Co. D; Pvt. Ed E. Coleman, Co. F. *University of Texas at El Paso Library, Special Collections Department.*

railroad boxcars. The Rangers are heavily armed, gun belts and Winchesters prominently displayed, obviously indicating strength. Along with Hughes from Company D were Corporal E. D. Aten and Privates William Schmidt, Ed Palmer, and James V. Latham. In addition to the five men from Company D and Captain Brooks there were four men from Brooks's Company F; three from Company E; five from Company B—a total of eighteen.[57] Their responsibility was to guard trains and other railroad property. The only arrest recorded by Hughes was that of Jack Gifford, taken in by the captain and one unidentified Ranger. Gifford, charged with assault and battery, was turned over to City Marshal William Taylor of Temple.[58] The men of Company D returned to camp on July 27, apparently having experienced no trouble with the striking workers.[59]

Over the next few months Hughes spent considerable time working with deputy U.S. marshals. On September 4 Hughes and a deputy went to San Elizario and arrested Jose Perez, who had been charged with violating the United States Pension Law. On the sixth Hughes and three others scouted to Anthony, New Mexico, after Secario Hernandez. Apparently they did not locate Hernandez, but while returning they arrested two smugglers and recovered one horse, a saddle, and some dry goods. It was another peaceful arrest. On the eleventh Hughes was again in New Mexico, now in Las Cruces, scouting after Santos Morales and stolen horses. He accomplished his mission.[60] No doubt Hughes continued to work on getting Geronimo Parra released to his custody so he could be tried in Texas.

If the Rangers had believed the Reeves County troubles were over with the quieting of the Miller-Frazer Feud they were wrong. While Captain Hughes and five of his men scouted on Pirate Island again, Carl Kirchner and Joe Sitter remained at Pecos City. On September 26 Kirchner arrested W. P. Matthews and Oscar W. Williams for failure to pay an occupation tax. On the same day Sitter arrested Sheriff A. J. Royal of neighboring Pecos County for assault and battery.[61]

Sheriff Andrew Jackson Royal was born in Lee County, Alabama, in 1855. By the 1880s he had settled in Kimble County, Texas, owning the

Star Saloon in Junction with D. T. Carson who later became a member of Company D. Curiously Baz L. Outlaw also lived in Kimble County in the 1880s before joining Company D. In 1889 Royal had moved to Fort Stockton and entered into politics. He developed a reputation for being an abusive and violent man but in spite of those weaknesses in his character he was elected county tax assessor on November 10, 1890. On May 30, 1892, he killed Apollinar Mendoza. In spite of his explosive personality he was elected on November 8, 1892, to the office of county sheriff. At the same time Oscar W. Williams was elected county judge and W. P. Matthews county and district clerk. Then on November 23, 1892, Judge Williams dismissed all the cases against Sheriff Royal.

But Sheriff Royal, having gained many enemies during his term, decided he needed help due to the threats and angry citizens. On August 7, 1894, he telegraphed Adjutant General Mabry to send Rangers. Two days later Sergeant Kirchner with four men arrived at Fort Stockton. On the twelfth, Judge Williams asked that Rangers be stationed there until after the elections, due to "outrages, abuses, and threats on the part of our Sheriff against some of our best citizens." It was a drastic situation with county officials feuding with each other.

Sergeant Kirchner met with the sheriff and convinced him to "be quiet now until the court meet[s] in September" and determined there was no need for Rangers to remain. Exactly what Kirchner told Royal is speculative, and Kirchner returned to Ysleta. But Judge Williams still was not satisfied, if he was even aware of Kirchner and Royal's conference, as on the twentieth he wrote asking for Ranger protection for the next three months, which would keep them there until well after the elections. On the next day Sheriff Royal wrote to Mabry stating he had been shot at several times, but now requested specifically Sergeant D. L. Musgrave of Company F. He also sent the governor a petition requesting "a sufficient force of Rangers to be stationed at this place, to prevent bloodshed and keep the peace." Besides Royal's own signature, other names of note included hard case Barney K. Riggs[62] and his brother Tom as well as several attorneys and county commissioners. On August 26 Sergeant Kirchner with four men left Ysleta to return to Pecos

County.[63] Captain Hughes obviously had great faith in his sergeant to deal with the troubles in Fort Stockton.

The close proximity to Mexico naturally caused many problems for Texas Rangers, problems not only caused by Americans but by Mexican bandits as well, as well as "Revolutionists" who were against the regime of President Porfirio Díaz. One of the first insurrectionists was Victor Leaton Ochoa, a native of Ojinaga, Chihuahua, Mexico. Born in 1850, Victor moved with his family to Presidio County three years later. As an adult Ochoa entered the political arena but was unsuccessful. In 1889 he became a naturalized U.S. citizen and entered into a career in journalism. In 1892 he began publishing two Spanish-language newspapers in New Mexico and became president of the Spanish-American Press Association. A year later he joined the rebellion against President Díaz and in November of that year was arrested by Deputy U.S. Marshal George Scarborough, charged with violation of the neutrality laws. Arrested on November 30, he was released on the next day due to lack of evidence. In January 1894, he was in Mexico with a guerrilla band. Attacked by Federal soldiers, he and several others barely escaped with their lives, returning to the safety of Texas soil. In October Ochoa was indicted by an El Paso Grand Jury for violating the neutrality laws, by planning the overthrow of a friendly government on U.S. soil. Ochoa was arrested in Fort Stockton by Company D Ranger J. W. Fulgham, Sheriff A. J. Royal, and two other Rangers.

U.S. Marshal Richard C. Ware sent Deputy Scarborough to Fort Stockton to verify the man was indeed Ochoa. The controversial Royal at the time was more concerned about being re-elected to the office of Pecos County sheriff and promised Ochoa he would be released if he—Royal—had the support of the Mexican vote. Consequently, Ochoa was allowed to escape. He didn't get far, as Rangers caught up with him in the village of Toyah, Rangers Fulgham and Schmidt making the arrest on October 22. Other arrests followed: Sergeant Kirchner arrested Barney Riggs on the first of November; on the next day Private Schmidt arrested A. J. Royal, both charged with assisting prisoners to escape.[64]

Of special interest, years later a different report appeared in a most unusual source, giving Captain Hughes the credit for Ochoa's arrest. The *Times-Democrat* of Muskogee, Oklahoma, carried a brief article about the Texas Rangers, headlining the article "Fearless Texas Rangers, Waiting to Jump Across Rio Grande; Never Wound, Always Kill." In spite of such absurd hyperbole, the article stated that the "prowess" of the Rangers proved that one Texas Ranger was "equal to a whole company of state militia." To prove the writer's point there followed a description of the capture of Ochoa.

> Their captain, John R. Hughes, is considered capable of putting down any Mexican trouble that may arise. He has already stifled one Mexican rebellion, single handed! It was in 1894. The leader of the rebellion, Victor Ochoa, a bandit and all-round bad man of the bloodiest variety, ventured onto American soil at Fort Stockton. Captain Hughes of the rangers met him on the street. Ochoa pulled his gun, Hughes looked him square in the eye, laid his hand on his shoulder, and arrested him, without a move of violence![65]

Texas could probably boast of being the home of more notorious outlaws than any other state, but north of the Red River in the "Indian Territory," where Hughes had formerly worked as a cowboy, there were hundreds of law breakers as well. In the early 1890s members of the Bill Cook gang were among the most wanted. Gang leader William Tuttle Cook, born in 1873, was the son of a Tennessee-born Union Army veteran and a quarter-blood Cherokee.[66] After growing up to become a cowboy with not much education beyond learning how to drink whiskey, drive cattle, and play cards, he was a tough young man. He joined up with another young tough named Jim Turner and the pair continued in their careers of minor acts of criminality. Cook's ability to avoid capture did not last long and he spent a short term in jail for selling whiskey illegally. He did not change his ways after serving time and by the mid-1890s he was worth a reward of $500 to the man who could capture him. In December 1894, he battled with Texas Rangers, including Sgt. W. J. L. Sullivan of Captain McDonald's Company B, Frontier Battalion.[67]

Sullivan intended to capture Bill Cook for the reward and began an intensive man hunt, putting aside any notions to capture Jim Turner for the more lucrative Cook. Others with the same intention included Chaves County, New Mexico, Sheriff and Deputy U.S. Marshal C. C. "Charley" Perry and Sheriff Thomas D. Love of Borden County, Texas.[68] Sullivan followed the Cook trail to Pecos, then on to Eddy, New Mexico, and to Roswell. There, at Roswell, Sullivan became convinced that Cook was bound for Mexico. He hurried to El Paso and arrived there on January 11, 1895, where he met up with Captain Hughes. Sullivan and Hughes together searched El Paso but found no trace of him.[69] Then Sullivan learned that Perry and Love already had captured Cook. Sullivan recalled this disappointing episode in his autobiography:

> The next morning I left for El Paso. Captain J. H. [sic] Hughes was camped at Ysleta, twenty miles from El Paso, and I wired him to meet me at the train and go to El Paso with me, which he did. We made a thorough search, both in El Paso and across the river in Old Mexico, but did not find Cook. That night I heard that Cook had been captured at White Oaks by Sheriff Perry; . . . I boarded the east-bound train and went back to Pecos, where I met the train Cook was on. I found him with Perry, Tom Love and one McMurray [sic] of Colorado City.[70]

Apparently this was Hughes's only official work with Sergeant Sullivan, other than their acquaintance preventing the prizefight later in 1896. Sullivan believed lawmen Perry and Love had unfairly beaten him out of the reward as he had spent many weeks trailing Bill Cook. Although there was a question as to whether there were any valid rewards for Cook, Sullivan claimed he deserved at least one-fourth of the reward, and stated he received word from Wells Fargo & Company that they recognized his claim in full, but "I have never received any part of this reward."[71] If Sullivan later shared his complaints with Captain Hughes he made no mention of so doing in his autobiography.

Now in January 1895, a difficult matter was brought to the attention of the captain of Company D. Henry W. Reynolds, deputy collector of customs at Eagle Pass, expressed his concern in a letter written to Judge Van Sickle about a little village springing up across the Rio Grande, some hundred miles south of Alpine. The sub-post was known as Las Boquillas and had been open since November 1, 1894, for import duties on lead ore and live stock. Quite a little community was springing up on the Mexican side of the river which, Reynolds estimated, contained six or seven hundred inhabitants and of which "several hundred are the worst desperadoes and renegades on the western border." Reynolds feared that unless the mines began working again these people would resort to depredating on the stockmen of southern Brewster, Buchel, and Foley counties. Reynolds believed it was "highly necessary to have a detachment of State Rangers down in this vicinity where they can be near the border."[72] Van Sickle forwarded Reynolds's letter to influential attorney W. W. Turney in Austin, adding that he endorsed everything said by Reynolds about that area around Las Boquillas. He delighted in adding that Fort Stockton then was quiet as a grave, and that a detachment of Rangers would do good work at Las Boquillas.[73]

In deploying his handful of Rangers across the huge Trans-Pecos, Hughes occasionally had to defend his men against unwarranted attacks: not by outlaws but by citizens who employed their personal and negative agendas. Such an example is the effort of one J. L. McAleer who wrote a bitter letter about the Rangers and sent it to the adjutant general's office. General Mabry sent Hughes an extract and expected his response. McAleer had stated in the February 1 letter that the part of El Paso County that included El Paso and Ysleta was "the most demoralized Section of the state." Further, McAleer assured, "Gamblers, drunkards, thieves & notorious libertines have long been, and still are, at the head of affairs, and the Saloon interest is omnipotent." McAleer said he had been asked to sign a petition asking for an appropriation for the Rangers but he refused. He explained why by adding: "there are few, very few, who have the moral courage to refuse to Sign any of these petitions got up by, or advocated by the Saloon interest." This was not enough as McAleer fumed: "I refused, because I am Satisfied that the Same men or better ones than compose the company of Rangers now stationed here, could be had at $20 per month, and rations for men and horses, whereas they receive each $40 per month & rations." And the wages earned by the Rangers were not the full extent of his complaint, as "a lot of the ranger company can most always be found loafing at the drinking & gambling Saloon which like every store in Ysleta, except those run by Jews, is Kept open on Sunday as well as on week days." But the most outrageous claim followed: a "respectable old citizen" was arrested and fined before "a crazy, prejudicial Justice of the Peace" but as he could not pay the fine he was sent to the Ranger camp, and "was put under *ball & chain*, although the Rangers had nothing else to do but guard their prisoner." This unfortunate man was "Kept in this barbarous manner away from his family until some of his friends came & bailed him out."[74] Hughes, upon receiving this extract by McAleer through the adjutant general, indicated he would respond to it within a few days. His initial reaction was simply to state that McAleer "did not confine his statements to the truth."[75]

In the meantime he had to deal with detaching men to Chispa, a newly birthed railroad stop on the Southern Pacific line, as Sheriff D. G. Knight of Presidio County had requested four men at or near Chispa where there were some twenty-eight miles of railroad track being laid "in a wild mountinous [sic] district and a long distance from any settlement."[76] Sheriff R. B. Neighbors was concerned about moving the Rangers from Pecos County, but felt that if either Ed Palmer or William Schmidt were kept there due to the "inquiet feeling in this county" that would satisfy him. Palmer and Schmidt were both aware of the county's conditions and had the confidence of the people.[77]

Chispa was then nothing more than a siding on the railroad some miles northwest of Valentine. A side track ran south to the coal mines. A rough and tumble place for John R. Hughes's Rangers then, but today it is nothing; not even remnants exist to justify it as a ghost town. Hughes agreed that Chispa "would be a good place" for four or five men as on the other side of the river was a settlement called San Antonio Colony, which was composed of "hard characters, a great many of which are fugitives from Texas, & make frequent raids into

Texas selling mescal and Stealing property from Texas when they return to Mexico."[78]

Before Hughes could prepare the response to the McAleer letter he received another from Adjutant General Mabry inquiring about the trial of Pvt. J. W. Fulgham. He had neglected to inform the adjutant general of it, but did remind Mabry that he had written to the quartermaster about the expenses incurred for attorney fees. Now he explained to Mabry that both Fulgham and G. P. Leakey, who at the time of the incident was a deputy sheriff of Reeves County, had been involved in a difficulty with Charles Carroll who was killed. This had occurred back on August 24, 1893. Now Hughes merely explained to the adjutant that the pair had been indicted by a Reeves County Grand Jury; their trial was moved to El Paso on a change of venue. The judge dismissed charges against Leakey and the jury needed only twelve minutes to acquit Fulgham.[79]

On February 18, 1895, Hughes replied to General Mabry's request on the matter dealing with J. L. McAleer. His response is a long typed letter; certainly Hughes himself did not sit down and type it out as it bears no strikeovers, which are typical of many typed letters of his from this period. Hughes discounted immediately the statement that the "gamblers, drunkards, thieves & notorious libertines" were the responsibility of the Rangers; on the contrary, that was a matter of other state and county officers. Further, during the previous summer many of the gambling establishments had been closed. Hughes pointed out the ignorance of McAleer as to the pay Rangers received for their duties. The idea of his Rangers frequenting, or loafing about saloons, was a "misrepresentation arising either from mistake or malice." Conduct that McAleer described would not be tolerated by Captain Hughes, "and the men know it." Further, there was only one saloon in Ysleta. The men occasionally did go into a saloon but it occurred sometimes "that the men from the very nature of their duties and in seeking and tracing criminals are compelled to visit saloons but I countenance their presence there only upon business, and I have not what is known as a 'drinking man' in my command." And further, Hughes stated, there was no such thing as a ball and chain in his possession. The hand-cuffs and leg-irons were items furnished by the state. Prisoners in his camp, Hughes explained, were guarded during the day and chained at night.[80] Hughes must have breathed a sigh of relief when this was finished, as it had taken valuable time away from other duties.

On February 20 County Clerk W. H. Harris found it his duty to also respond to the McAleer charges. The charges against Hughes were "uterly [sic] false" he wrote. Of the men in Captain Hughes's command, and the question of their being "drinking men" Harris stated, "I know of no set of men more free of such acts than they are." Harris concluded his missive by stating that he "should pay no attention to charges by such men" as McAleer.[81]

But rumors surfaced again that Hughes's men had been abusive to various citizens. Hughes had to accept this type of complaint as a matter of course, and responded on March 11 defending his men, stating in part "they are as good *moraly* [sic] if not a little above the average citizen of El Paso County."[82]

When Hughes had enlisted in Company D back in Williamson County in 1887 he may have thought that his responsibilities would focus on such typical Ranger activities as pursuing horse thieves and murderers. He could not have envisioned dealing with religious fanaticism in which people lost their lives, or so the reports indicated. On March 21 Hughes wrote to Mabry expressing his concern about the rumors of a woman claiming to be a saint who had developed a significant following. At this point Hughes anticipated the possibility of violence. On the twenty-eighth he telegraphed Mabry: "Trouble on the border at Presidio. Sheriff Knight asks my assistance. Shall I go?" Naturally Mabry ordered his captain to assist Sheriff Knight and to report back to him what the trouble was. On the following day Hughes wrote, "Parties wanted in Texas and Mexico [and] resist arrest with arms."[83] On the thirtieth, Presidio County Judge H. H. Kilpatrick expressed his concern about the woman and "a fanatical war in progress."[84]

The details of this curious incident are meager but a group of individuals, described as a "band of fanatics," were led by Incarnacion

Lorez, called "The Hunchback," and a woman who claimed to be a holy woman, going under the name of Santa Teresa.[85] Born Teresita Urrea in 1873 in the Mexican state of Sinaloa, she was the illegitimate daughter of Don Tomas Urrea and Cayetana Chavez. In 1880 Urrea moved his family to Cabora, Sonora, to escape President Díaz. Not long after the move Teresita went into a "cataleptic state" in which she remained for several months. Upon recovering she found she had the power to heal the sick and crippled, providing not only physical health but also becoming an inspiration to the poor. Word of her healing powers spread rapidly; she quickly became a "symbol of hope for the downtrodden." Her message of hope inspired the poor to rebel, or at least that is what Díaz's dictatorial government believed. She and her father were ordered out of the country in 1892. By the time they were located in El Paso the illegitimate daughter was called the Mexican Joan of Arc because of the various uprisings she had supposedly inspired.[86]

To Hughes's way of thinking "Santa Teresa" and "The Hunchback" operated a fraud in which they sold "medicines," which guaranteed their followers "a sure hold on the next world" as well as the ability "to resist the bullets of their enemies," in other words, the local authorities—or the troops of President Díaz. Reportedly the pair together had sold more than $2,000 worth of their products, the money coming "from the poorest people in Texas and Mexico." Hughes, on arriving at the scene of the conflict with Sheriff D. G. Knight, two deputies and four of his men, "found every thing in a very troubled and unsettled condition." He explained that a woman had been traveling with a stone image, pretending to cure the sick by faith. The governor of the Mexican state of Chihuahua ordered her arrested but the "Gendarmies" failed to catch her. They did arrest one of her followers and took custody of the stone image. Both the man and the image were jailed in Ojinaga, across the Rio Grande from Presidio. Now the followers of Santa Teresa banded together and demanded the release of the prisoner as well as the return of the stone image. The Ojinaga *alcalde*, or mayor, refused, which resulted in threats of force from the fanatics. Now the mayor summoned a posse of thirty-one men to arrest the entire threatening party. Their demand to surrender was answered by the fugitives' firing into the posse, killing one and wounded several. Four of the "fugitive party" were killed and several wounded. Not wishing to continue this uneven battle the fugitives began their flight across the river. Captain Hughes ordered them back across.[87] The *Galveston Daily News* reported that the chief of the Mexican posse, Cisco V. Amarillas, and four of his men had been killed but the woman who created the troubles had eluded the authorities as well as her faithful followers—with the money collected—and had disappeared somewhere, perhaps in Texas. In all, ten men had lost their lives. This is how the press reported the conflict, although Hughes did not identify the Hunchback, Incarnacion Lorez, by name.[88]

Hughes was back in Ysleta on April 5 and reported that he had made no arrests as the fugitive followers had all returned back across the Rio Grande and surrendered to Mexican officials. "But," he added, "the trouble is not settled on the Mexican side and may not be for some time and they may come to the Texas side again. It was rumored that the leader of the fanatics was organizing a band in the mountains in Mexico on April 3d." Hughes apologized to Mabry for not finishing his report as "there is a severe sand storm blowing" but would finish it the next day.[89] Santa Teresa would appear again in the troubled area, this time with George A. Scarborough—who would barely escape with his life.

Of the numerous fugitives from justice, Captain Hughes undoubtedly wanted to take Geronimo Parra most of all, but with Parra in a jail in New Mexico he could do little. But there were other concerns keeping him busy. On April 14 Hughes arrested Eugene Sullivan, who had been charged with assault and battery; three days later he arrested Leonard Lee, charged with threatening to murder. There are no details available on these two arrests. On the first of May, Hughes was called back to Pecos, but apparently left no report of his actions there. May and June passed relatively quietly, with few arrests, only recovering of stolen horses. Ranger Oden on May 10 arrested Nicholas Olguin, brother of Jesús María Olguin, charged with assault to murder. It is not clear if Nicholas Olguin was involved in the Pirate Island affair, but presumably to the men of Company D any man with the name of Olguin was suspect. Then on June 11, Hughes took a five-man scout to Pirate Island where they arrested Apolonio Piquant and Victorio Maldonado and recovered three stolen horses.

In April, Jefferson Davis Milton, then the El Paso chief of police, applied to be a Special Ranger. Hughes knew him and recommended him as a "good officer" who would "not be a drawback to the Frontier battalion but on the other hand may be of great advantage to us." In Milton's letter to Hughes requesting the appointment he reminded him that for experience he had served under Ranger Captains Ira Long, Bryan Marsh, and Charles L. Nevill.[90] His application was accepted and Jeff Milton now became a Special Ranger attached to Hughes's Company D. Milton would play a significant role in El Paso history in the months ahead.

Former Company D Ranger Homer L. Nix was working for the firm of Murphy & Co., a large firm of merchants doing business at Chispa and on the line of a new railroad being built from Chispa to the San Carlos coal mines. Nix, who had served in Company D only from October 14, 1890, to March 14, 1891, receiving an honorable discharge, complained of the amount of lawlessness in that section and wanted Rangers. Hughes of course would like to have obliged, but he had none to spare, as there was "plenty of work in El Paso County."[91]

State Senator John M. Dean could not have realized the amount of work for Captain Hughes as now he allowed his wife to invite Adjutant General Mabry to accompany them on an excursion to the Sacramento Mountains and into New Mexico and invited Captain Hughes to accompany them. H. B. Wood and wife, A. P. Coly and wife, a Mr. Logan, a Mr. Burges, and Senator and Mrs. Dean—in all a group of ten excursionists—would make up the party. The request was written on June 13 but there was no immediate response. Hughes did later write to the adjutant general that he doubted very much if the excursion would happen, but if it did, "I expect to make a business trip of it, as there are a great many fugitives passing from here to the country where we expect to go."[92] In other words, if he were to accompany the group it would not be just a pleasure jaunt, but combined with manhunting.

Two weeks later, on June 24, Hughes was in El Paso endeavoring to capture Martin Mrose and Victor Queen, both wanted men suspected of rustling. He failed to find either man, apparently unaware they were just across the river in Juarez avoiding Texas officials including new Ranger J. D. Milton and Deputy George A. Scarborough. Hughes wanted Martin Mrose because he was "indicted by the El Paso grand jury for bringing stolen property into the state of Texas." Scarborough had convinced Mrose he had arranged a meeting between him and his estranged wife to take place on the Texas side of the river. Mrose correctly suspected his wife and John Wesley Hardin were having an affair. In reality, however, Scarborough's story was a ruse to capture Mrose. In the middle of the railroad bridge over the Rio Grande on the night of June 29, Scarborough and Mrose met. With Scarborough were J. D. Milton and Frank M. McMahan. When officers ordered, "Up with your hands!" Mrose covered Scarborough with his pistol, and then the firing began. Mrose received eight bullets in his body, dying instantly. El Paso Deputy J. C. Jones made complaint against the officers who each gave a bond of $500 to appear before the next grand jury. Hughes finished his report, stating there was "some feeling among the citizens here against Scarborough for betraying Mrose but no one seems to doubt that Mrose resisted arrest, and that the killing was purely a case of self defence [*sic*]." [93] Milton gave few details in his monthly report listing his activities as a Special Ranger: "Attempt to arrest one Martin Mrose on 29th warrant was for Fugitive [*sic*] from Justice from Eddy N.M. charge Theft of cattle and Horses[.] Mrose resisted and was killed." [94]

Hughes's request for a two-week furlough to go to Williamson County, presumably to visit friends from his pre-Ranger days, did not receive a positive response. He continued his work. On July 5 he, with three men, went to Fabens to investigate an attempt to wreck a train on the G.H. & S.A. Railroad. Someone had placed two steel rails on the tracks. Hughes spent two days investigating and did arrest Herminio Ruiz, charging him with the attempt. He had located two witnesses. Additional rumors were spreading and had to be investigated as now he was called to scout around Comstock, Del Rio, and Spofford to investigate the actions of some parties who were suspected of plotting to rob a train on the G.H. & S.A., but this time there were no arrests.[95] But what happened on the night of August 16–17 was reality, not a rumor, and a man died. Two masked bandits held up the store of Keesey & Company, at Valentine, Presidio County. Owner Whitaker Keesey was not present but John J. Edgar, the G.H. & S.A. manager, and railroad brakeman L. Lardo were, as was a young boy. Also present by chance was Everett Ewing Townsend, a Mounted Inspector of Customs, who was spending the night in the Keesey store, Valentine not having a hotel at the time. As both storerooms were occupied— one by Mr. Edgar and the other by the store clerk Mr. Holly Hester— Townsend made his bed on the floor of Hester's room. As he had had

Edward Ewing Townsend as a young Ranger who later gained fame as the "Father of the Big Bend." Photo by Frank J. Feldman of El Paso. *Courtesy Archives of the Big Bend, Bryan Wildenthal Memorial Library, Sul Ross State University, Alpine, Texas.*

virtually no rest the previous three days and nights he retired early, about nine o'clock. From a sound sleep he was awakened by a masked man thrusting a Winchester in his face. He first thought someone was playing a joke on him, but quickly realized it was no joke. The masked man had Townsend's two six-shooters and a third weapon belted around his waist, and held Townsend's brand-new .38-55 Winchester carbine, now pointing at him. The robbers had all the advantage but unknown to them the young boy had observed what was transpiring and ran to alert what authorities Valentine had. Within moments "Captain" Richard Ellsberry and seven others arrived to challenge the robbers. Inspector Townsend wrote in his journal:

> About the time the robbers had got all the money and some jewelry, the rescuing party knocked on the front door. [The robbers] marched us to it and ordered Mr. Edgar to open it—seemed as if they were going to put us up front and fight their way out but changed their minds and ordered us to the back door on double time [and] of course we obeyed[.] Mr. Edgar opened the East "Corral" gate according to instructions and we scattered. The robbers went out of the gate and were met by the citizens and about fifty shots were fired[.][96]

In the melee—two masked men shooting at the hastily assembled posse, which returned fire—someone shot Ellsberry who died instantly. An elderly man who had worked for the Southern Pacific Railroad for a number of years and was now the town's watchman, he represented the law in Valentine. He had met the two robbers as they exited the back door of the store, ordering them to halt. Instead they fired back, killing the old man. The robbers then fled the scene.

Presidio County Sheriff D. G. Knight, Captain Hughes, George Scarborough, and Pvt. Joe Sitter were quickly on the trail. A heavy rain worked to the advantage of the robbers whose tracks were soon washed away. Apparently the pair had been recognized in spite of their masks, however, as in early September, Hughes and Joe Sitter were scouting in Sonora, Sutton County, hunting two brothers named Holland, wanted for the robbery and murder. On September 9 Hughes reported he was hunting evidence in Valentine; six days later he was in Marfa before the grand jury. On that day, September 15, the grand jury indicted Samuel L. and Thomas A. Holland.[97] They were two of the five children of David A. and Susanna Holland, the boys aged thirty-three and twenty-two respectively.[98] Townsend learned the outcome of the hunt for Ellsberry's killers: "Later a man named Ramsey [Samuel Lorenzo, "Ramzey"] and Tom Holland were arrested near Sonora and were charged with the robbery. Tom, however, proved an alibi . . . Ramsey was tried and convicted at El Paso and was given a sentence of fifteen years. But he won a reversal and the case was sent to Eagle Pass, where it was finally dismissed."[99]

With such tragic events as the store robbery and murder of an elderly watchman, Hughes must have felt depressed at times, and knowing his force amounted to a mere handful, but effective men. Quartermaster W. H. Owen inquired of Hughes as to the nature of his work, to which he replied that he had enough work there to keep twenty Rangers busy. "I have calls every week that I cant attend to."[100]

~ 7 ~

Spectators on the Rio Grande

"I WILL KEEP A CONSTANT WATCH ON THE MOVEMENTS OF
THE SPORTING CLASS AND THE ONLY WAY THEY CAN HAVE
THE FIGHT IN TEXAS IS TO HAVE IT OVER WITH BEFORE I
REACH THE PLACE FOR IF I CAN LEARN WHERE IT IS GOING
TO BE IN TIME TO GET THERE I WILL PREVENT IT."

—*John R. Hughes, November 8, 1895*

In the nineteenth century, bare-knuckle fighting was among the most popular "sports" in the country, although in most states it was illegal. To those who favored the contests, boxing was the prime example of American manliness; to those who opposed boxing, it was no different from Emperor Nero throwing early Christians to the lions, a simple act of barbarity. The bare-knuckle contests ended with the implementation of the Marquis of Queensberry rules, requiring fighters to wear gloves and giving them to the count of ten to recover if knocked down. Sporting man Dan Stuart, a Vermont-born gambler and entrepreneur, arrived in Texas in 1872 at the young age of twenty-six intending to find success on his own terms within the sporting world. One historian described him as a "portly, genial, prosperous-looking man with a fashionable full mustache and dark hair parted straight down the middle." He had integrity as well as a vision: he planned to erect a "monument to sport" in the form of a 52,500-seat coliseum in Dallas. This structure would feature, at its grand opening, a contest between two recognized champions of the ring: James J. Corbett and Robert P. Fitzsimmons, the latter recently declared the heavyweight champion of the world by the prestigious New Orleans Olympic Club.[1]

However, Texas Governor Charles Allen Culberson was not a fan of prizefighting, and in addition was "an old political foe" of Dan Stuart. In 1890 and again in 1892 he had been the choice of the people for the position of Texas Attorney General. In 1894, he defeated the Populist candidate for the governor's office on the conservative platform. To defeat Dan Stuart's vision, Governor Culberson called a special session of the legislature with the sole intent to make prizefighting a felony in Texas. "Gentleman Jim" Corbett called this a "grandstand play for the voters" but Culberson convinced the Senate and the House to agree to his wishes, and Culberson won his battle.[2] The essence of the law, to take effect immediately, was that any "pugilistic encounter" between a man and a man or between a man and a beast was a felony with a punishment of not less than two years or more than five years.[3] Only five members of the House and one in the Senate voted against it, the single Senate vote cast by John M. Dean of El Paso. Three hours elapsed from presentation of the bill to its passage, a record. Governor Culberson signed it into law on October 3, 1895. In spite of the new law, Texas, and the nation, began to witness preparations for the intended fight. If Dan Stuart somehow managed to hold his contest on Texas soil, he as well as promoters and boxers would be charged with a felony.[4]

Stuart, with his dream on the ropes and in debt due to the huge expense of his Dallas Coliseum, did not surrender his dream. Governor Culberson was just as determined to prevent the fight even starting; he was less concerned about the potential legal battles that might follow if it did take place. He ordered his adjutant general to send the Rangers to track Dan Stuart, the fighters, and their assistants, consuming time and energy that could be better devoted to preventing crimes against people and property. This "fistic carnival"—the attempts to prevent it and the actual event itself, which ultimately did take place but not on Texas soil—attracted the attention of not only the state but also the nation. Stuart considered numerous places for his event, and played a near hide and seek game with authorities, sending the fighters from city to city. In late 1895, John R. Hughes was on the trail of Corbett, while other Rangers of Company D followed Stuart.

On November 11, Hughes was in Dallas, but all he could learn was what was reported in the newspapers.[5] Private William Schmidt was also there but he had learned that Stuart was also in Dallas and observed that "he seems to be very thissatisfied [*sic*, dissatisfied] about somithing" [*sic*] and had learned nothing about the fight.[6] Hughes returned to Ysleta and wrote a summary of his actions of the previous days. He had left Dallas on October 30 and arrived at Texarkana on the thirty-first, then left to go to Hot Springs, Arkansas. He arrived there on November 2 and learned that Corbett was going on to Little Rock. Hughes managed to get on the same train as Corbett, leaving on the evening of the third, and watched Corbett until he left. Then Hughes went to a gambling house where Fitzsimmons was stopping and by chance met the brother of James M. Bell, the consumptive member of Company D. After Hughes learned from Bell that Stuart had returned to Dallas he concluded that Corbett would not be returning to El Paso and decided to "give up the chase." On November 4 Hughes left Little Rock and returned to Texarkana, then on to Dallas and Fort Worth. Hughes and Schmidt were back in Ysleta on the seventh where Hughes now learned from the newspapers the latest on the proposed fight, that the El Pasoans had not given up on holding the fight in their town. Hughes wrote,

> [W]hile I dont think there is any danger of having the fight there, I will keep a constant watch on the movements of the sporting class and the only way they can have the fight in Texas is to have it over with before I reach the place for if I can learn where it is going to be in time to get there I will *prevent it*. I was informed by good authority that if the fight comes off near El Paso it will be in Juarez and the sports intend to bribe the officials of Juarez and have the fight over with before the President [Porfirio Diaz] can stop it.[7]

On November 11 Hughes wrote again to Mabry, informing him that he was keeping an eye on the "sporting men of El Paso very closely and I think if there is attempt to bring the fight off, I will be there in time to prevent it."[8] Before year's end Hughes learned that Corbett had withdrawn from the contest. Promoter Stuart now planned the fight to be between Fitzsimmons and Peter Maher, somewhere in Texas. He had spent considerable time keeping track of the fighters and promoters. He had learned that a surveyor had been to a disputed strip between Texas and New Mexico, but had not learned yet who had employed him. Hughes intended to go back to Las Cruces, New Mexico, and "learn more about the matter."[9]

The monthly returns of early 1896 do not reflect the excitement that was seemingly everywhere; the sporting news had never before reached such prominence, filling front-page columns in nearly all area newspapers. Of course, such an event, which the leading officials of Texas, New Mexico, and Mexico were determined to prevent, drew headlines. On February 10, 1896, the *San Antonio Express* reporter, operating in El Paso, notified his paper that "Capt. Hughes' company of rangers from Ysleta is now here and with the companies of Capts. Brooks and McDonald has gone into camp near the Texas & Pacific depot." He anticipated the other company, not named but that of J. H. Rogers, would arrive the next day.[10] Hughes's monthly return merely reported that the entire company moved to El Paso "in preventing prize fight from taking place in Texas. Returned to Ysleta Feb. 23rd, out thirteen days."[11]

El Paso now became the site for a great variety of lawmen, their presence not in the interest of upholding the laws, but in order that they could witness the historic pugilistic contest, wherever it might occur. U.S. Marshal Edward L. Hall came from Santa Fe, New Mexico. Besides his obligation to prevent the fight from taking place on New Mexico soil, he also had the recent disappearance of Colonel A. J. Fountain on his mind. Authorities suspected Fountain and his young son had been murdered, since they had not been seen since January 30. In addition to that concern, Hall was aware of a certain forty-acre tract of land along the river "alleged to be of uncertain national ownership."[12] Could that have been the chosen site of the prizefight?

Some who believed the fight would take place intended to preserve it on film for posterity, or at least for a financial return. Enoch J. Rector, pioneer moviemaker, arrived in El Paso with thousands of dollars' worth of equipment, intending to profit from motion picture ticket sales for those unable to see the fight in person. His intention was to not only profit financially from the film, but also to promote boxing.[13] Naturally, he too became a person for the Rangers to follow. Adjutant General Mabry believed he had spotted the railroad cars in which the "kinetoscope, platform and other carnival paraphernalia are loaded," and was keeping track of them.[14] Early on the morning of Friday, February 14, Rangers discovered two cars loaded with what they believed were "carnival paraphernalia, attached to a Southern Pacific train just pulling out for the west." Hughes ordered the train delayed until he obtained permission for four of his men to accompany it to the state line. With permission granted the Rangers rode away on the rails.[15]

The *El Paso Herald* provided considerable space to the efforts of the Rangers to prevent the fight. In the popular column, "On the Qui Vive," the *Herald* reviewed what the governments of Mexico, New Mexico Territory, and Texas were doing, but at times found important news was slow. "Adjutant General Mabry," readers were informed, "had nothing for publication as yet, but did not appear at all harassed [but] has been a very busy man." While he and the Rangers appeared to be "taking things easy," they were kept busy and thought they had spotted the location of the fight, but where it was to be was not revealed. There was one bit of embarrassment for the Rangers, and that occurred at El Paso's Pierson Hotel. Captains Hughes and Brooks were having breakfast when Hughes accidentally tipped over a glass of milk, its contents landing on Brooks. The press found this "upsetting" of "a glass of milk between Captains Hughes and Brooks, and the ruination of the latter warrior's togs" amusing and worthy of reporting. The ensuing "racket" gave General Mabry some "amusement."[16] Mabry may have been amused by observing Captain Hughes spilling milk on Captain Brooks, but he was not amused when two sporting men engaged in "a lively shooting affray" on a San Antonio street the next night, the fourteenth, and even less amused with the report that he was "rousing much hostility among the citizens, . . . by having his men dog everybody connected with the carnival."[17] All Mabry could do, however, was to continue his efforts to prevent the fight, and in so doing enforce the law of Texas.

Texas Rangers in El Paso to prevent the Fitzsimmons-Maher prizefight, 1896. Front row from left: Adj. Gen. W. H. Mabry, Captains J. R. Hughes, J. A. Brooks, W. J. McDonald, J. H. Rogers. Second row from left on bottom step: George N. Horton, J. H. Evetts, Sgt. Julian G. Throckmorton, Robert Chew, John Hess, C. T. "Creed" Taylor; third row: William J. "Billy" McCauley, standing on plinth with rifle, R. L. "Lee" Queen, G. W. Bell, Ed Flint, James Fulgham, Ed Donley, Sgt. W. J. L. Sullivan, Jack Harwell, Robert McClure, Edward F. Connell; back row: George Tucker, Dr. Lozier [?], R. E. "Ed" Bryant, Edgar T. Neal, Doc Neely, Curren L. Rogers, Thalis T. Cook, Charles F. Heirs, John Moore, William M. Burwell, Andy Ferguson. *From the M. T Gonzaullus Collection, courtesy the Texas Ranger Hall of Fame and Museum, Waco, Texas.*

At noon on Thursday, February 20, El Paso photographer J. C. Burge arranged General Mabry, his four captains and twenty-seven Rangers in front of the county courthouse where he made at least two exposures.[18] The most-often-reproduced image shows Captain McDonald with rifle muzzle resting on the sidewalk; in the other he is holding it at nearly a "present arms" position like Brooks and Rogers. Neither General Mabry nor Captain Hughes show their Winchesters. Nor did any of the captains exhibit their pistol belts and Colt revolvers, typical of so many Ranger photographs. Commented the *Herald*, "It was such an unusual occasion that called them together, that they thought they would celebrate in this way. The officers stood in front, and the men were armed with their Winchesters and cartridge belts. It was a determined looking crowd, ready for most any kind of business."[19] Burge's photograph has become one of the celebrated images of nineteenth-century Texas Rangers. Presumably it depicts all the Rangers who were in El Paso but there were others elsewhere throughout the state.

Not all of the Rangers in El Paso were allowed to take the February 21 train to Langtry where the fight ultimately did take place—four hundred miles down the Rio Grande. As the *Herald* initially reported, Mabry took with him the men under Captains Brooks and Rogers and left the remainder in El Paso. The *Herald* reported that they were "under Sergeant Sullivan," and were left in El Paso as "there was more or less uncertainty as to the character of some of the toughs left in this city."[20]

Apparently, however, the newspaper was misinformed, as in the next day's issue readers learned that a train carrying both fighters, their trainers, and their managers, a "number of sports wishing to witness the battle, General Mabry, Captains Hughes, McDonald, Brooks, Rogers with twenty rangers and a number of through passengers" left the depot at 11:20 that evening.[21] The city of El Paso was actually left with very little protection. Bunco artists and pickpockets presented another concern during this time when everyone's thoughts were on the prizefight. As the *Herald* expressed it, since the train from the west was late in getting to the Southern Pacific depot, "the people stood around and chewed the cud of reflection, and the pickpockets began to circulate." Sergeant W. J. L. Sullivan of McDonald's Company B and Robert M. Loeser, a Special Ranger of Company D, reported that some twenty people had had their pockets picked. Private Loeser, in his monthly report, noted he had arrested five individuals, three for theft, identified merely as "bunco," and two others, including one man for assault to murder and a John Doe.[22]

Bat Masterson, a gambler-lawman who had gained a reputation as a gunfighter in the Kansas cattle towns of the 1870s, now a professional sport, had $900 taken from him, or so the press reported. El Paso Chief of Police Ed Fink contradicted this statement, saying that he was on the platform all evening and no pockets had been picked. However, certain unidentified Rangers stated that people did come to them with information "that leaves in their minds no doubt whatever, but that the pockets were picked as charged." Sergeant Sullivan said that some thieves had cut pockets with a sharp instrument allowing the thieves to easily remove the contents.[23]

Sullivan wrote his memoirs that were published in 1909 and devoted several pages to the El Paso prizefight event. He recalled that the Rangers stayed in El Paso eighteen days to see that the fight did not take place. They also "had to put down the tough element of the town, as thieves, robbers, pickpockets, and other classes of criminals were giving a great deal of trouble." Sullivan also wanted to see the fight, but General Mabry "requested" him "to remain in El Paso with eleven rangers and help guard the three banks, which I did."[24]

After many days of fruitless watching, the Rangers finally received a relevant lead when a Galveston and Harrisburg freight train, pulled by Engine No. 807, left the El Paso station on February 21, two hours late. Stephenson, the *El Paso Herald* sports editor, sent the following dispatch from Alpine at 11:45 a.m.: "Two engines and ten coaches going east. All pugs aboard, and cars crowded. Two hours late. Weather threatening." Stephenson followed with a second dispatch at 1:00 p.m. from Sanderson, stating that the fight would take place "near Langtry at 4 o'clock. Everything O.K."[25]

In spite of all the efforts of Texas Rangers from four companies as well as other lawmen to prevent the fight, it did take place, hundreds of miles from El Paso, with perhaps hundreds witnessing it, including most of the Rangers as well as Adjutant General Mabry. It did not take place on the soil of Texas, Mexico, or New Mexico or Arizona, but on a sandbar in the middle of the Rio Grande, only a short distance from Langtry in Val Verde County. Just how Stuart and Judge Bean managed the arrangement remains mysterious, but there, Justice of the Peace Roy Bean, self-proclaimed "Law West of the Pecos," provided liquid refreshments for all the thirsty sports and other spectators after the long train ride. Moreover, there would be thirsty throats as well after the fight, no matter how long it might last or who emerged victorious.

James G. Reagan,[26] a Val Verde County deputy sheriff, was at Langtry but did not know how to respond when the crowds converged on the tiny community. Apparently, he could not locate Sheriff W. H. Jones and telegraphed Governor Culberson for advice: "Prize fight takes place across river[.] whose Jurisdiction are we under yourself or Judge Roy Bean[?] await your instructions."[27] Culberson's response, or that of his assistant, has not survived, but with the fight in the middle of the Rio Grande, the Austin executive had no authority.

Once the passengers were off the train, and presumably had quenched their thirst, courtesy of Judge Bean, he directed them towards the river, a third of a mile distant. "The path," reported the El Paso reporter, "led down a steep rocky cliff into the river canyon, about two hundred feet below. After the bottom was gained the crowd followed the river bed down for three hundred yards and the tent loomed up to the view of the 'sports.'" But there was yet an improvised pontoon bridge across the river to the sandbar that the sports had to traverse. This done, they could finally view the tent and arena, "located on a sand flat with steep, rocky cliffs towering two hundred feet high on either side, . . ." Although not close to the combatants, the best view of the fight from the outside was from the cliffs on the Texas side of the river. On that "precipice" the Rangers "planted themselves" so they could see the action, their Winchesters across their laps. There were some two hundred spectators looking down into the middle of the ring.[28] Apparently, Adjutant General Mabry, Hughes, and the other three captains were among the two hundred. Sergeant Sullivan, following orders, remained in El Paso as the *Herald* reported, and maybe a few others as Sullivan recorded, including the consumptive Ranger James Maddox Bell of Company D.

There were some two hundred inside the canvas arena and about the same number outside on the cliffs. After the fighters selected the gloves, referee George Siler called Maher and Fitzsimmons to the center of the ring for final instructions regarding clinching and breaking away, stating that "each man must step back one step after a clinch. Both contestants said they understood the instructions."[29]

Fitzsimmons struck early, "at arms length, hit left, right and left on Maher's temples; Maher struck out and Fitz got away." Then they clinched but as they were breaking away, "Maher drove out and hit Fritz on the right cheek." Several cried out that was a foul, and Referee Siler warned Maher that if he did that again he would decide the fight against him. Fitzsimmons said to Siler, "Let it go, I'll lick him any way." Then "hard fighting" began and the "licks were passed so fast that it was hard to tell when they landed." After feints, clinches, and missed punches, Fitzsimmons "shot out a half arm hook that caught Maher on the left jaw. Maher's head dropped, his frame trembled, and he fell to the platform, and his eyes turned white. In this position he lay until Referee Siler counted nine and out."[30] After the count Martin Julian, Fitzsimmons's manager, stepped up to ring side and declared, "Bob Fitzsimmons is now champion heavy weight of the world. He has fought his way up from the bottom. He will be ready at all times to meet any one who is worthy of his notice." The hundreds yelled for Fitz and then headed back to Langtry; they had indeed worked up a thirst and Roy Bean was waiting for them all.

The *Herald* headlined its Saturday, February 22, issue with "Fitz the Champion" and opened its lengthy report,

> The battle that has been attracting the attention of the civilized world for over a year has been fought, despite the action of congress, legislatures, supreme court decisions and the assertions of the president and several governors of Mexico. A battle that attracted the world and caused people to travel thousands of miles to see, was fought in just one minute and twenty-five seconds.

The brevity of the fight was a terrible disappointment for all. Everyone who had bet on Maher lost money. History also lost as Enoch J. Rector's filming of the great event proved worthless; the day was so overcast there were no satisfactory images on the film. Nevertheless, Fitzsimmons and his backers, and Roy Bean, were certainly among the happy sports. They were the winners. Noteworthy among the vast amount of documentation regarding this prizefight, involving Rangers traveling into other states shadowing the promoters and fighters, was Mabry's concern for Frontier Battalion expenses. The Legislature was continually stingy with the appropriation that funded the Rangers, and

Mabry frequently reminded his captains to curtail expenses. Of course, Hughes responded he would keep them "as low as possible in the future." If anyone in the governor's office—Culberson had wired Mabry that he would rely upon him "to prevent fight on any territory claimed by Texas regardless of consequences"—added up the expenses occurred in trying to prevent the fight, the figure has not been discovered. Looking backwards it would seem that nearly the entire Frontier Battalion had been sent to El Paso to stop a prizefight, which would harm no one and would not destroy property, and which most Rangers watched and enjoyed. But Dan Stuart was an old enemy of Charles Culberson, and perhaps that explained the governor's determination to stop the prizefight, "regardless of consequences," rather than the stated reason to uphold the laws of the great State of Texas.[31]

Famed lawman, newspaper reporter, and sportsman William Barclay "Bat" Masterson later wrote negatively of his experience in El Paso. His biographer, Robert K. DeArment, wrote that Masterson suspected the Rangers had spread the rumor that he had lost nine hundred dollars "to the light-fingered gentry in El Paso." As noted above, however, Police Chief Ed Fink denied the rumor. Further, DeArment asserts, the "entire episode left Masterson with contempt for the Texas Rangers." Years later, when Masterson wrote a sports column appearing regularly in the *New York Morning Telegraph*, he called the Rangers "a four-flushing band of swashbucklers" and described Adjutant General Mabry as a man full of "affected dignity and self-importance." Masterson not only disparaged the Rangers but also dismissed the Mexican *rurales* as "a body of armed horsemen [who] were nearly all outlaws at one time or another."[32]

Although much of the state focused its attention on the activities of Dan Stuart and the fighting pair, cattle thieves continued to work. During the early excitement of the prizefight, in December, Rangers were called to Green Valley in Brewster County. Judge W. W. Turney, in a state of near panic, had written to Adjutant General Mabry, advising him that thieves were stealing hundreds of cattle, that they had no fear of the law, and begged him to do "something for us."[33] General Mabry ordered Hughes to respond to the request; he answered with his typical reply to orders that he would attend to it at once. On December 20, 1895, Hughes advised his superior that he had sent Sergeant E. D. Aten and one man to Turney's ranch and that Private John C. Yeates would report for duty to Aten.[34] The three men were now protecting the ranching interests of Judge W. W. Turney. Aten and Hughes would discover that Private Yeates was not the kind of man the Frontier Battalion wanted or needed.

During all the genuine news and reported rumors and the presence of four companies of State Rangers, as well as U.S. Marshal Hall from New Mexico, and famed lawman Pat Garrett of Uvalde, crime did continue in El Paso. John Selman Jr., son of the constable who had shot to death Baz L. Outlaw and in August of 1895 John Wesley Hardin and an unknown number of others, was patrolling El Paso Street at 4:30 a.m. on February 17, when he was jumped by five or six men while passing

Company D, Frontier Battalion. From left standing: Deputy U.S. Marshal Frank M. McMahan, William Schmidt, James V. Latham, Joseph R. Sitter, Ed Palmer, Thalis T. Cook; Seated: unidentified prisoner, George Tucker, J. W. Saunders, Carl Kirchner, Captain Hughes. *Courtesy Robert G. McCubbin Collection.*

a stairway close to the Gem Saloon. Selman recognized one of them as a man he had arrested some time before for drunkenness. The man slashed at Selman while his companions tried to hold him down, evidently intending to cut his throat. Selman fought back violently, struggling for his life; his resistance was more than the thugs had bargained for and they fled, leaving Selman bleeding from slashes on his left wrist. His overcoat, thick enough to deflect the blade but now ruined, had saved his life.[35]

Captain Hughes and the other Rangers could easily forget about all the work needed to prevent the fight on Texas soil: after all, most of them had enjoyed watching it. The Rangers continually had to deal with such ordinary things as theft, but now, new to Hughes, was the necessity of enforcing a recently passed quarantine law. The phenomenon, which potentially could ruin the Texas cattle industry, had its origins decades before, but only recently had become a major concern to Texas cattle ranchers. Following the Civil War, many ranchers drove their cattle to northern markets, as far north as Illinois. But in 1868, many cattle of the northern herds were stricken with a disease that was nearly always fatal. Finally, veterinarians realized that what was fatal to nearly all northern cattle did not affect the longhorns driven from South Texas. Stock raisers called the disease "Texas fever." Northern states, although not knowing why the disease did not affect Texas cattle, established quarantine lines to protect their herds. The state of Kansas in 1885 outlawed driving Texas cattle *anywhere* in the state. During the decade of the 1880s, pioneer bacteriologists Robert Koch of Germany and Louis Pasteur of France continued to seek methods of control, including vaccinations. It was not until 1893 that Theobald Smith and Fred Kilborne were able to isolate the pathogen of Texas fever. The disease, they demonstrated, was caused by a "microscopic protozoan that inhibits and destroys red blood cells." The culprit of Texas fever was the tick, which, after sucking blood from an infected animal, would drop off into the grass and lay eggs from which young ticks would hatch. Long after the infected tick dropped off the longhorn, other cattle became infected. Longhorns were immune, but remained carriers that infected other cattle.[36]

But cattle in Texas were not always exempt from the dread disease. Cattlemen exerted enough pressure on the administration that by February 1896, Governor Culberson had signed and sealed at Austin the proclamation adopting regulations regarding a quarantine line that would work against Texas fever, also known as southern or splenetic fever, in cattle within the state. The quarantine affected many counties, and included nearly a third of the state's land, from the Rio Grande to the Red River. The new law produced more work for Rangers as it stated that between February 15 and November 15, 1896, no cattle were "to be transported by rail, driven or moved in any manner whatever from said area [of quarantine] south or east of said line . . . situated north or west of said line." Cattle were not to cross from the Republic of Mexico into the state. On February 15, sheriffs along the county lines set forth were enjoined to enforce the law, and Culberson did "especially enjoin the Frontier Battalion, to vigorously enforce these regulations and use every effort to apprehend violators of them."[37]

In addition to enforcing the urgent quarantine, Rangers had to address the continuing common rustling of stock. On March 11, a band of Mexicans crossed the Rio Grande in Presidio County and stole 2,500 head of sheep from stockman Steven W. Pipkin.[38] Pipkin telegraphed the governor for help, who turned it over to the adjutant general, who ordered Hughes to act at once. Pipkin had asked, "how can I get them?" On reverse of the telegram was written, "Telegraph Jno. R. Hughes." It was a simple answer to a desperate request, with no explanation offered as to why the county sheriff could not initially respond. The same day Hughes sent Ranger Charles Davis to investigate the thefts. The response was a telegram of classic simplicity: "Will do all in our power." On March 18, Hughes responded to the urgent plea; he had recovered the stolen property although he offered no details as to how his men had recovered the 2,500 sheep so quickly.

Coincidentally the annual report of the Rangers' work was released at Austin and the *Galveston Daily News* combined the two reports into one lengthy and praiseworthy article. The sheep were returned to Pipkin, but Hughes "did not state how he had recovered them, and, as the captain had orders from the adjutant general not to cross the river into Mexico, it is presumed that some of the Mexican *rurales* lent a help- ing hand in getting back the stolen sheep." That act alone, according to the Austin reporter, was "a big mark to the credit of the rangers of this state."[39] The details were not recorded, and the initial reports were contradictory: one report stating that Pipkin's *own herders* stole 2,000 sheep and crossed them over into Mexico, and "Pursuit impossible."[40] That was the word from Van Horn, but on the same day telegraph wires hummed with the news that a gang of Mexicans from across the river had stolen 2,500 sheep. Apparently, the collector of customs assisted Hughes in recovering the stolen sheep—2,000 or 2,500—and, no doubt, Hughes encouraged the Mexican *rurales* to deal with the thieves.

Hughes did not waste time basking in his glory but now turned his attention to the enforcement of the quarantine law, sending Sergeant Aten with a detachment from Alpine to Pecos. However, he had to accept the resignation of Private James V. Latham, who now intended to go to New Mexico to live. He again enlisted Thalis T. Cook who had been working for the railroad but now wanted a change. Further changes saw Private Fulgham turning in his request for a discharge.

From the middle of March to April 4, Hughes was in the Pecos area "watching cattle." He reported everything was quiet at Pecos, and "No cattle have attempted to cross the line since my men have been stationed at Pecos."[41] Over the next few months Hughes reported from such distant places as Pecos, Midland, Sweetwater, and Colorado City, all locations where he worked in matters relevant to the quarantine law.

In spite of the presence of the Rangers and the rationale behind the quarantine, some ranchers ignored it. On May 9, Hughes reported to Adjutant General Mabry from Sweetwater, using letterhead of the City Hotel, informing him that he had arrived there the day before at the request of W. B. Tullis of the Sanitary Board to assist in enforcing the law. Two men had already been arrested and were awaiting trial. In addition to Hughes and Tullis, a Mr. Bush, Capt. W. J. McDonald of Company B, Sergeant E. D. Aten, and Special Ranger R. M. Clayton were present.[42] Ranger Clayton had stopped a herd numbering 450 head belonging to Jink Clark that had crossed the line from Nolan County into Fisher County. Clark attempted to get an injunction to restrain officers from interfering with his cattle, but District Judge William Kennedy refused to grant it. The cattle would have to remain on the south side of the line, and Hughes believed the trouble would be over "for a while." He expected to return to Ysleta that evening and Aten would go on to Pecos.[43] Special Ranger Clayton was doing impressive work and that did not go unnoticed. Tullis wrote Adjutant General Mabry that Clayton was "one of the best men in the line."[44]

In addition to recovering stolen livestock and enforcing the quarantine law Hughes certainly expended some energy with concerns for friends and the dangers they continually experienced. An incident involving friend George Scarborough nearly cost the lawman his life. Revolutionists always created work for men on the border and revolutions and rumors of revolutions were frequent. Two editors of a Spanish language newspaper, *El Independente*, printed in El Paso, were charged with fomenting a Mexican revolution on U.S. soil.[45] The notorious Santa Teresa, who had caused work for Hughes back in April of 1895, apparently owned their paper. Scarborough located the editors—Lauro Aguirre and Flores Chapa—in the early morning hours of March 11, 1896. What should have been a peaceful arrest turned deadly when Aguirre pulled his pistol and shot Scarborough, the bullet entering "just to the right of the center of the chin and followed the jawbone for about three inches before it made its exit." In extreme pain, Scarborough resisted the impulse to shoot back and made the arrest, in spite of his bleeding face. Scarborough took the editors before the commissioners court where their cases were dropped, but they were immediately re-arrested on warrants from Arizona charging them with the same offense. Scarborough chose not to charge them with assault to murder, which he certainly was justified in doing.[46]

In addition to law enforcement problems Hughes had to deal with resignations and men applying for commissions as Rangers, demanding additional paperwork that concerned officers. In early April, George A. Scarborough resigned his commission as Deputy U.S. Marshal, and now applied for a commission as a Special Ranger. In the aftermath of the Martin Mrose killing, newspapers portrayed Scarborough as a bad character indeed, but Hughes contradicted this. However, Hughes set aside friendship in favor of making sure nothing harmed the reputation of the service, or reflected badly upon his superiors. He explained to Mabry that Scarborough had resigned because of his trouble in El Paso, and the newspapers were "so bitter against him" that "it might be a draw back to the Ranger service to have him become a member." Hughes continued in his assurance to Mabry that Scarborough was a good friend not only to the Frontier Battalion but also to him personally, and would like to see him prosper; but "I thought my duty as a member of the Frontier Battalion to try and post you as to his character. . . . I am only afraid the News Papers would use it against Governor Culberson or yourself."[47] On the reverse of this communication Secretary Henry Orsay wrote that Hughes's letter "puts the Adjt Genl on his Guard about appointing him." Scarborough did not receive an endorsement to become a Special Ranger.

At the end of April, Jefferson Davis Milton, former acquaintance and friend of Scarborough, wrote the adjutant general to explain why he had not made a monthly report as he should have and why he had resigned. He stated he was out of the state, now working for Wells Fargo & Co., guarding the trains on the Southern Pacific railroad. He still wanted to keep his commission as a Special Ranger however. But apparently because Milton was now working for Wells Fargo & Co. he had to surrender that commission. The fact that he was still under indictment for the Mrose killing, as were Scarborough and Frank McMahan, with a trial set for June 15, may have entered into Mabry's decision as well.

Back in Ysleta, Private James M. Bell came in. Hughes was concerned for his health issues, and on the twenty-ninth Hughes wrote to Quartermaster W. H. Owen that Bell "came in O.K. and is looking pretty well but have not seen much of him as I have been so busy and away from camp lately."[48] Bell had taken the oath on September 2 at Alpine before Judge W. Van Sickle. At Ysleta, Hughes wrote on the reverse: "I sent blank oath of office to Presidio to Sitter, Bell & Yeates but they were on scout to Alpine & got sworn in there on the enclosed blanks. If it does not answer let me know and I will have them sworn in again. Yeates did not come to town. Stopped at Turney's Ranch and had not been sworn in yet but will be soon."

In June, rumors again surfaced that there were twenty-five or thirty armed Mexicans near the Guadalupe Mountains opposite Fort Hancock, and they were followers of Santa Teresa, now identified as Teresa Urrea, which may have been her real name. She was then in El Paso, or at least that was what was believed, and some feared a revolution or "a fanatacal [*sic*] war of some kind." Hughes indicated that if he found out anything definite he would report it to Adjutant General Mabry.[49] With the frequent rumors of a revolution in Mexico, Hughes now left three men in Presidio County "to protect life & property of the citizens of Texas."[50]

Not only did Rangers occasionally have to resort to violence in defending their very lives, but also frequently Rangers had to appear in court to defend their actions in making an arrest. George A. Scarborough, J. D. Milton, and F. M. McMahan had to face the charge of murdering

Ranger James Maddox Bell served nearly two years under Captain Hughes before the "white death" of consumption claimed his life. *Courtesy Western History Collection, University of Oklahoma Library.*

Martin Mrose. Milton hired W. W. Turney to defend him and the case was called for June 1896. Turney was confident that he could present all the facts in the case and the jury "will speedily acquit him."[51]

But certainly, the most significant event during this period of Hughes's long career occurred in late September. The incident that ended with shots fired and blood flowing began when former Brewster County Sheriff James B. Gillett[52] learned that five men had robbed a ranch of horses and guns and suspected they intended to rob a train. Gillett informed Railroad District Superintendent W. R. Martin what he had learned, who in turn passed the information on to Captain Hughes. Gillett indicated he would gather a posse of citizens and attempt to follow the thieves. Hughes gathered what men he had—Privates Thalis T. Cook and Robert E. "Ed" Bryant—and at 10:30 p.m. on September 24 the Rangers boarded Engine No. 19, placing their horses and a pack mule "in the blind end of the mail car." Deputy Sheriff Jim Pool of Presidio County joined the Rangers at Marfa. About daybreak on the twenty-fifth the Rangers and deputy arrived at Alpine where Hughes unloaded the horses and men but remained on the train and went on as far as Marathon "for the purpose of guarding the train in case of an attack." There was no attack and at Marathon he met Engine No. 20 and then returned to Alpine.[53]

There Hughes and his posse saddled up and started for the Glass Mountains, a range extending from northern Brewster County to southern Pecos County. In the western portion of the range some peaks reached an elevation of over 5,700 feet.[54] It proved to be difficult terrain, hard on both men and horses. The heavy rain that cooled the land also added to the difficulties of tracking the gang. W. C. Combs now joined Captain Hughes and his man hunters. Combs had a valid reason to be involved in this chase: he had lost a good horse to the thieves. Hughes later wrote:

> On reaching the Glass mountains we found where they had been camped and had driven horses back & forth over a scope of about 5 miles. We were bothered some by the tracks of some of the posse who had been there before us. Mr. Jim Stroud, who had also lost a

fine horse, joined us here and he proved to be a great help to us as he was a good trailer.[55]

On the morning of the twenty-seventh the lawmen again started out on the trail. It rained all day and the job became increasingly difficult, what with the trail already four days old and washed out by heavy rains. But Hughes, perhaps with the help of Jim Stroud, managed to find the outlaws' trail due to the years of early training while living among the Osage. They followed it all that day and the next morning, the trail leading into the pasture of the McCutchen Brothers, near the foot of the Davis Mountains. There they found an empty sack that the outlaws had discarded; Hughes surmised they were getting low on provisions from this bit of physical evidence. He believed that the robbers' method was to hide in the mountains and when they saw people leaving the ranch houses they would go down and rob them to replenish their supplies. Hughes also realized that they likely could be seen, and if seen as a group with a pack mule the thieves would conclude they were Rangers. Hughes's narrative continues:

> Mr. McCutchen had kindly offered to send his cow boys to hunt the trail for us. I sent Jim Pool with one of the cow boys (Mr Tip Franklin) to look at one mountain pass while Mr. McCutchen [,] Jim Stroud and Cook went up into the [other] pasture. When they had gone about 7 miles they found the trail and followed it into a little side canon in the mountains, when two men raised up and presented their guns at them and order[ed] them to turn back if they did not want to be killed.

Cook realized this challenge came from the men they were hunting, and he played along with them, asking them if they were not joking. They claimed there were seven of them with guns; they cursed Cook and told him that if he and his group came closer they would kill them all. Cook obviously did not believe there were seven men against him and tried to get his cowboy companions to charge the outlaws with him but they refused, stating they were not armed well enough for a gun battle. But before they left Cook borrowed a shotgun from one cowboy, so he was now armed with a Winchester and a shotgun as well as his sidearm. He intended to keep the thieves from escaping; they fired several shots at him, and it became a wait and watch game which lasted about three quarters of an hour. Finally, Cook decided to go back and join Hughes and the others.

Now all together the posse headed back to where the outlaws remained hidden. This gave them time to plan their next move. "3 of us were to charge them at full speed until we gained a good position to fight from, the others were to scatter out and come in from the other side. When we were within about 300 yards . . . there was a shot fired at us." Cook looked at Hughes and said, "Where was that shot" and Hughes pointed with his gun, saying "from that mountain top." They then spurred their horses "and started to take the mountain away from them. We could not see anyone on the mountain but the bullets kept coming by us. We ran on our horses almost to the top of the mountain when the fight was so hot that we left our horses." Here Mr. Combs received a wound, a bullet going through his left ear.

The Ranger fire was heavy and one of the thieves dropped, shot to death, but no one knew whose bullet had killed him. Then the other one, wounded, called out "I have got enough." Cook ordered, "Hands up then and come out." But the wounded man foolishly raised his weapon and fired again. This act resulted in a volley from the posse and the man dropped. Meanwhile one man was seen running in the valley. Ordered to surrender, he kept on running until he found a horse and got away. Now that the battle was over, the Rangers investigated the outlaw camp. They found five horses, one the property of Mr. Combs, one the property of Jim Stroud, and two others belonged to neighboring ranchers. All the guns and pistols were also determined to be stolen property. Jim Pool and Tip Franklin, who had earlier left to return to their ranch, heard the roar of the guns and now rushed forward hoping to get into the action, but they were too late. Never had Hughes seen two men as disappointed as they were, having missed all the action.

While the Rangers were still at the ranch, a young boy had approached and volunteered to go with them but he had no horse.

Hughes had offered him one, so he was now mounted, but with only a pistol for a weapon. Hughes thought he was not strong enough to handle a Winchester but

> When we made the charge on the mountain he was right with us, and using his pistol. When the heat of the fight was over I looked and saw the boy by my side with a gun & I said where did you get that gun, [and] he said he got it from that man[,] pointing to a dead man. I asked him if he had plenty of cartridges, he said no but there [was] a belt full on the man. I told him to get them.[56]

The young man's name was Arthur McMaster; he had been sick and was staying at the McCutchen ranch but could not resist the impulse to join the man hunters.

Hughes borrowed a buckboard from the ranch and took the two bodies into Fort Davis where they were given a decent burial. They were

Within recent years an impressive granite marker has been placed in the Pioneer Rest Cemetery on the outskirts of Fort Davis to mark the final resting place of the Frier brothers. Ranger George Bingham of Company D was killed by outlaws in Presidio County in 1880 and is also buried there, although his grave remains unmarked. *Photo courtesy Pat Parsons and Scott Turner.*

brothers, Jube and Arthur Frier.[57] Hughes concluded his lengthy eight-page report to Mabry with an interesting final thought: "We reached home on Oct. 2nd and found more work awaiting us."[58] In Hughes's monthly report he summarized the deadly incident with fewer words:

> We struck their trail in Glass Mountains and trailed them about 80 miles and found them in the star pasture in the Davis Mountains. They would not surrender but fired on us. When we charged on them and returned the fire killing two of them, the third man escaped. The names of the killed are Jube Frier and Arthur Frier. We had four citizens with us at the time of the fight. We came to Marfa and took the train to Ysleta.

They had been out eight days and had traveled a total of 625 miles.[59] What Hughes did not state in his report was that among the property recovered were seven stolen horses, some of them very valuable. One was a race horse, valued at $500. "A lot of other stolen property, such as rifles, pistols, razors and blankets, was found. All of the property has been identified by the owners."[60] Curiously Hughes made no comment regarding the youthfulness of one of those killed. Arthur Frier was born August 9, 1879, thus he was all of seventeen years, one month, and twenty-eight days of age when he challenged experienced Rangers in a gunfight. A reward notice, printed on a postcard directed to Sheriff D. G. Knight at Marfa, indicated the pair was wanted for horse theft. A $10 reward was offered for each horse recovered; $50 was offered for each of the three thieves.[61]

From Sanderson, Ranger Ernest St. Leon also sent Mabry a report, and provided the identification of the two dead men as well as that of the one who had escaped: Burke Humphreys. St. Leon described him as "a general hard character and the man who murdered J. Bundren at Lavernia [*sic*, La Vernia] Texas 3 years ago escaping, but I understand the Boys are still after him." He informed Mabry that Humphreys was heading north as he had friends in Abilene [Texas] and several in Oklahoma. He was facing robbery and assault to kill charges.[62]

Hughes did catch up with the fleeing Humphreys. In mid-October, the fugitive was held in the El Paso jail, waiting for Sheriff Gerome

W. Shield of Tom Green County to come after him.[63] Hughes assisted Shield in getting the prisoner safely to the jail at San Angelo to await his trial, leaving El Paso on October 17. Humphreys stood trial on December 23 with Captain Hughes and Private Cook present as attached witnesses.[64] In spite of defense attorney F. E. Allen's attempt to have him declared insane and numerous delays and continuances, he stood trial and was found guilty, his denial of ever stealing a horse and ever having been in the fight with the Rangers to no avail. The judge sentenced Humphreys to six years in the penitentiary for theft of a horse.[65]

While Hughes was in court as an attached witness, he had to depend on his men to deal initially with a train robbery. He had left Ysleta on the evening of December 20 to go to San Angelo on the Texas & Pacific Railroad but on the train a telegram from District Superintendent W. R. Martin was delivered to him, stating that the westbound passenger train had been held up near Comstock. Pvt. Thalis T. Cook managed to get to the scene of the holdup, as well as the few Rangers left at Ysleta, Hughes having wired Superintendent Martin to take them to the scene

Rare photograph of Company D in camp outside Ysleta, Texas circa 1894. George Tucker standing by horse. Seated from left: Thalis T. Cook, Deputy U.S. Marshal Frank McMahan, Capt. John R. Hughes, William Schmidt, James V. Latham, Carl Kirchner, J.W. "Wood" Saunders, Joe Sitter, Ed Palmer. *Photo courtesy Jake Sitter and Bob Alexander.*

of the robbery and do what they could in determining the robbers' identity and where they were headed. Hughes was confident he knew the identity of the holdup men, and surmised they would go into Mexico for a few days and then return to Texas. It was not a significant amount the robbers obtained, Hughes stating it was two packages with a value of only $70.00.[66]

Following the Humphreys trial Hughes quickly returned to Ysleta and immediately went to Comstock where he discovered that his men had already arrested the train robbers, and believed they had good evidence against them. Four men were in custody: Rollie Shackleford, Alan Purviance, Frank Gobble, and Bud Newman. T. T. Cook had brought the prisoners in and placed them in the El Paso jail. Privates J. W. Saunders and Samuel Newberry were still at Comstock with the horses.[67] Cook with several deputies delivered the quartet to Del Rio, Val Verde County, where Judge J. G. Griner oversaw their arraignment on the morning of December 30, all charged with stopping the U.S. mail.[68] On the same day they had a hearing before U.S. Commissioner Augustine Montaigue Gildea.[69] Purviance and Gobble were allowed bail in the sum of $2,000 each; the other two, Newman and Shackleford, were placed under bond of $1,500 each.[70] Gildea may not have met Captain Hughes at this point, but the two would later meet. Gildea had buried his outlaw past; if Hughes was even aware of it he made no mention of it. Hughes warned the adjutant general that his report would be "a few days late as I am expecting the men home this evening or tomorrow and want their work in my report."[71] With all the necessary traveling, and doing good work, the timing of the paperwork was not a high priority.

Captain Hughes, years later, related some of his adventures to publisher J. Marvin Hunter. In 1944, the ninety-year-old Hughes visited the editor of *Frontier Times* magazine. Hunter, nearly three decades younger than Hughes, wrote that the visit was "a short time ago" and that Hughes was "well preserved and quite as active and alert as a man in his sixties. He has the most outstanding record of any of the Texas Rangers of the old days, and did more than any other one man to rid the Texas border of outlaws and desperate characters." Among other events in his life he related to Hunter was a description of the Glass Mountains fight. "Captain Hughes," looking back on his career, "regards this [fight] as the toughest and perhaps the most dangerous fight in which he has ever engaged during his long service as a State Ranger," wrote Hunter.[72] With two men dead, one wounded, and one being pursued by Rangers, it certainly had been a dangerous fight.

On arriving home from the Glass Mountains engagement, Hughes found he indeed had work to do: there was still the enforcement of the quarantine law to deal with; Special Ranger R. M. Clayton had, in November, reported having stopped 1,300 head of cattle from crossing the line in November. In addition, there was a great deal of area to protect and very few men to cover it. At year's end, Hughes counted his men and miles traveled: he had under his command one sergeant— E. D. Aten—and five privates, leaving Company D with an aggregate of only seven men. During that month, the command had traveled a total distance of 3,132 miles.

~ 8 ~

The Hardest Man to Catch

"I CONSIDER THE LEADER OF THE LOZIER TRAIN ROBBERS
THE HARDEST MAN TO CATCH THAT WE HAVE HAD IN TEXAS
FOR MANY YEARS."

—*John R. Hughes, May 27, 1897*

Hughes entered his tenth year as a Ranger in 1897, rising from private to captain in ten dangerous but exciting years. His work had dealt with such various activities as following the tracks of sheep thieves, enforcing a quarantine line, trailing fence cutters, and challenging desperadoes to surrender, only to be met with gunfire. Although occasionally under fire, as yet he had not been wounded.

Hughes as well as any of his men faced the possibility of sudden death in gunfights or from some deadly disease: in addition to the shooting deaths of Joe McKidrict, Charles Fusselman, and Frank Jones, Hughes had experienced Company D Ranger George P. Leakey's death from tuberculosis on the train between Pecos and El Paso in April 1896.[1] In early 1897 Hughes feared Ranger James Maddox Bell would not long survive, and discharged him so he could be nursed by relatives. Bell, discharged on January 31, 1897, died from tuberculosis on July 29 of the same year at the young age of thirty-two. Relatives had cared for him, and provided a large memorial marker above his final resting place in the Stockdale City Cemetery in Wilson County.[2]

Bell's terminal illness was only one of many concerns of the captain. A combination of medical bills and a diminished force became a major consideration in early 1897. When Bell was ill in Pecos a Ranger companion was with him, but now that companion was needed elsewhere. Because Deputy U.S. Marshal A. B. Cline asked for "help very badly," the Pecos detachment was now sent to Presidio and Brewster counties.[3] Bell was not the only Ranger ill, as 1st Sergeant E. D. Aten was lying in misery on a simple mattress suffering from typhoid, with fever, abdominal pains, and possibly intestinal bleeding. Hughes, always a frugal man, saw the medical bills and believed they were simply too high. He informed Quartermaster Owen that he had corresponded with several of the doctors and felt confident the bills would be reduced. Hotel keeper Philip S. Elkins[4] had reason to be concerned as he feared his bills would not be paid: "I received today all the Bills during Atens sickness at Pecos, they were returned by the Quarter Master stating that they were entirely too high." Hughes explained further that Owen "thinks your board bill too high when Aten lived on Beef Juice and Whiskey 3 or 4 weeks." He expressed the subtle suggestion that if Elkins could cut the bill some it would be "advisable," and because the appropriation for the Rangers was running low "if we hang fire too long the money may be entirely gone and you will have to wait until the new appropriation is made which may be 4 or 5 months."[5] Hughes could be subtle at times.

The matter did not get simplified in spite of Hughes's efforts. On January 19, Judson Heard, the man who had been hired by Dr. Ira J. Bush to act as nurse to Aten, wrote Hughes.[6] His letter in response to Hughes's request to lower the bills was on the letterhead of the troublesome J. B. Miller, Proprietor of the Commercial Hotel of Pecos, and said that even if he did "loose [*sic*, lose] the whole amt of my bill" he would not "scale it one cent"; further, if he could not get paid he would turn it over to Attorney at Law T. J. Hefner[7] for collection. The daily rate for a room at the Commercial Hotel was $2.00 per day, which included board. The fact that the Judson Heard correspondence was on James B. Miller's letterhead was not lost on Hughes. He informed Quartermaster Owen that at $2.00 per day for nursing for thirty-seven days that amounted to $74.00, which was twice the amount Hughes had authorized the sheriff to pay. Hughes had supposed the amount was

$1.00 per day until he received the bill. Now Hughes was willing to let the matter go to court. "I don't think he can possible [*sic*] collect more than one dollar per day if he sues for it. You will notice that he writes on letter head of J. B. Miller who is a bitter enemy of Rangers and the sheriff at Pecos and in fact all officers. I think Miller has influenced him to do this."[8] Perhaps he had. In early February Judson Heard had not yet received payment from Captain Hughes; he now complained that he had "nursed" Sergeant Aten during his sickness for forty days, was employed by attending physician Dr. Ira J. Bush, and had been told by him that payment would come through Captain Hughes. Sergeant Aten, apparently recovered, told Heard that whatever the state did not pay on the bill he would make up. Judson Heard felt that the state should pay the whole amount.[9] Finally, Philip S. Elkins decided it best for him to "take a reduction of $15.00" in his bill for board and room for Sergeant Aten during his sickness, "and avoid any trouble with the State Although I think my first bill was not too large." He did finally receive payment for the reduced bill. Perhaps some of that money had to be used to replace the mattress, which Heard determined was utterly worthless after Aten's bout with typhoid.[10]

Reduced funding for the Frontier Battalion now became a reality. On February 8 Quartermaster Owen ordered Hughes "to strike from my pay roll" five men; since he had already dismissed J. W. Bell on the first of the month he now dismissed four more: Sergeant E. D. Aten,[11] and Privates S. H. Newberry, J. N. McMurry, and Sam Noling. He chose to retain T. T. Cook and J. W. Saunders, "as they are the oldest men on the list except the Sergt."[12]

Additional concerns faced the captain, concerns which would not have been his in the early years as a private. The case of John C. Yeates is a prime example: a young man wanting to be a Texas Ranger, but not having the skills or character to become one. Hughes at least gave the young man the opportunity to prove he could become a worthwhile member of Company D. Yeates had been appointed a Special Ranger in June of 1895 and was discharged October 31 of the same year. In February 1897 he now wanted to regain his commission as a Special Ranger and to be attached to Capt. J. A. Brooks's Company F. In his communication to Adjutant General Mabry he pointed out that he had made twenty-five arrests, that he had had ten years' experience as a law officer, and that he wanted to have a Ranger's legal right to carry a weapon. "I know a great many of the Lawless Characters who infest this Border," he wrote, and explained that he had been "instrumental in sending a great many of them to the Penitentiary and that my Life is in Constant danger. [In addition] my own Stock interests have suffered from the depredations of Horse and Cattle thieves, and that I can render good service to Capt. Brooks . . . and materially assist the Ranger force in Making a good showing in their Annual Report."[13]

Hughes had had experience with Yeates and was willing to endorse the man. He reminded Mabry that he had initially taken Yeates into Company D on the word of the sheriff of Kinney County who recommended him. On arrival at camp Hughes and Yeates had a long talk, and Hughes learned that his applicant had lived for nine or ten years with a Mexican woman, without the benefit of marriage. Hughes explained to Mabry that living with a Mexican woman "is not considered so very bad in this western country any way, unless they make it public." Apparently, according to Yeates, this co-habitation resulted in his being ostracized from society, and because of that "he wanted to get away from the county and turn over a new leaf." Hughes must have had some reservations about Yeates, but was willing to include him on his roster. But Hughes was disappointed in his man quickly, as on his first scout, the captain learned his new man knew nothing about scouting, nor did he know how to ride; further, "he was in the way when it came to trailing."

Yeates failed to redeem himself when another opportunity arose: sent out to find evidence in the Ellsberry murder case, he was gone eight days but accomplished nothing. Further, in November, Hughes had "started him in the same work again" but again Yeates was gone a month and accomplished nothing, even after Hughes had clearly told him what he wanted done and how he wanted it done. "I then concluded that it was no use to ever send him out of town again but still had hopes of making him useful around the Justice court until he could find some other work as I always dislike to discharge a man unless he does something disgracefull [sic]."

Then, Hughes recalled, in May he was in Colorado City to keep peace during the G. A. Frazer trial, with Sergeant Aten and Private Yeates along. The sheriff of Mitchell County asked Hughes to send him one of his Rangers to remain with the jury all night. Yeates was assigned this task, which should have been of no great consequence. But during the first trial of Frazer, amazingly, Yeates obtained a copy of the 18th Court of Appeals volume in which he learned that Miller—now a chief witness for the prosecution—had been convicted of murder and had been sentenced to life in the penitentiary. This information Yeates *shared with the jury*, which obviously influenced their decision.

Hughes kept Yeates at Ysleta until July 1, 1896, not having any work he could trust him with. Hughes at least found some responsibility for him: Yeates was placed in charge of the camp while the rest of the company was away on other duties. But while he was supposedly watching camp he "took up" with a Mexican woman and Hughes "was told by several citizens that he stayed away from camp at night most of the time." When confronted with this, Yeates denied it. But Hughes had proof of the man's dishonesty: he had trailed him from the woman's house to the camp not once but on three different mornings. Hughes could have justifiably issued him a dishonorable discharge, but strangely declined to do so. He sent him to join Private Sitter's detachment on the W. W. Turney ranch. The detachment made several trips to Presidio then and while at Presidio Yeates went to live with some Mexicans. W. W. Turney now advised Hughes to get rid of the man, as he was unreliable "and would never make a good ranger." In fact Turney felt strongly enough that he didn't want Yeates to ever be on his ranch property again. Hughes still didn't want to simply dishonorably discharge the man, but Turney advised him that he owed him no favors.

Hughes also learned that at this point Yeates had applied to Richard C. Ware for a commission as Deputy United States Marshal. Ware informed Hughes of what he knew, that Yeates "was a man of bad character" and that he knew Yeates was an ex-convict. "I saw," Hughes wrote on October 31, 1896, "that I had made a great mistake in enlisting Yeates and wanted to drop him with as little fuss as possible as I dont [*sic*] want it to get before the legislature that I had an exconvict in my company." He concluded, "I dont consider Yeates a good officer and I dont want him any longer. . . . I dont consider Yeates an honorable man, and don't want him to have an honorable discharge with my name signed to it."[14] Curiously, Yeates did receive an *honorable discharge* on that same day, signed by Captain Hughes.[15]

Hughes certainly was not ashamed to admit that he had made a mistake, but this exchange of letters between the adjutant general and his captain also reveals that Hughes honestly had tried to make Yeates a good Ranger and had given him numerous opportunities to prove his good intentions. He was also astute enough to know that it was a time to keep such bad news out of the public eye because if the truth be known that

A quiet moment at an Alpine Saloon. Standing left is Dr. Devenport; at right Wigfall Van Sickle. Seated is Doctor "Doc" Wilburn Gourley. Photo made circa 1885. *Courtesy the C. B. Casey Collection, Archives of the Big Bend, Bryan Wildenthal Memorial Library, Sul Ross State University, Alpine, Texas.*

at one time an ex-convict was a member of the State Rangers it could be used against the governor and adversely affect the decision of the Legislature when it came time to determine the appropriation for the service.

On February 17, 1897, Brewster County Sheriff D. W. Gourley requested assistance. He wanted two men to be stationed at Marathon for two or three months. Sheriff Gourley explained that the new road had come in from the mines and the influx of young men was "causing a good many loose white men and Mexicans [;] no end to them to come to Marathon and they are a good deal of trouble just now." Gourley further explained: "the Boys could pick up a few men wanted in other counties if they were their [*sic*]." The response of course was that it would be an impossible request to fulfill due to the shortage of manpower. Possibly, and this must have been simply a caveat to give Sheriff Gourley some degree of satisfaction, with the new Ranger appropriations some men could be sent to Marathon. But did not Captain Hughes wonder why Sheriff Gourley could not handle the Marathon situation with a few good deputies and his own ability? After all, he had had considerable experience: Gourley had served as a Ranger under Captains Neal Coldwell, Dan. W. Roberts, and Charles L. Nevill, from the Indian fighting days of early 1875 until his honorable discharge dated August 31, 1882, having attained the rank of corporal. And now he was serving his third term as sheriff. In March of the previous year he escorted three prisoners from Alpine to Eagle Pass, delivering them due to a change of venue, alone and without incident. The trio was John Chambers, Antonio Hernandez, and Jefferson Davis Hardin, the younger brother of the late John Wesley Hardin. Hardin was charged with attempted bribery; Chambers was facing nine indictments of cattle theft; Hernandez was also charged with theft of cattle.[16]

Captain Hughes could not forget the Miller-Frazer troubles. Frazer had expressed his fear of Miller, but Miller also had to be continually on his guard, having survived two attempts by Frazer to kill him. Both men necessarily lived in a near-constant state of awareness of where the other was. Miller, having recovered from the wounds inflicted on him by Frazer, now decided to show everyone how to kill a man. He had already killed an unknown number of men, preferring the shotgun as a weapon. Frazer now was to be the next victim. Miller had various friends who kept him informed of where Frazer was, one of whom was William M. Earhart.

On September 14, 1896, Frazer was in Toyah, a small community in southwestern Reeves County. He now habitually carried a Winchester wherever he went, with a pistol stuck in the waistband of his trousers. On that day about 9:30 in the morning he entered the Welch & Company Saloon[17] intending to play some cards. William Earhart was one of the men there playing the popular game of Seven-up. When Frazer entered, Earhart "gave up" his chair and then sat on a barrel along the saloon wall. The other players were Andy J. Cole, S. J. Tate, and J. E. Jarrell. J. D. Shelton and Earhart now watched the progress of the game. Pat Flowers was on duty behind the bar.

Earhart, sitting to one side, now observed Frazer as he continued the game. No doubt Frazer was unable to concentrate fully on the game due to the presence of Earhart, a known friend of Miller. By chance, or by design of Earhart, Frazer's chair faced the saloon door. Frazer looked up from his cards when he saw a figure in the door facing him, about twelve feet away. That figure was James B. Miller and he had a shotgun in his hands.

Frazer instantly recognized the danger. He knew it was now a matter of kill or be killed and dropped his right hand to draw his pistol, but he was too late. At that movement by Frazer, Miller fired one barrel of his double-barreled shotgun, the slugs striking Frazer in the face. Pat Flowers turned to see what the shooting was about as the other card players scattered after the first shot. Miller then fired the second barrel, even though he knew Frazer was a dead man. Miller's second blast struck Frazer in the neck.[18]

On the day following the killing, Captain Hughes was in Pecos, there to prevent any possible trouble in the aftermath. Dr. Ira J. Bush, an acquaintance of Hughes, bravely expressed strong words against Miller as to how he had killed Frazer. The arrogant Miller took Dr. Bush "to task about something I had said concerning the killing." Miller was not above killing or threatening to kill a doctor, or anyone else, and may have threatened Bush. No one was there to record the exchange but the discussion was getting heated, and if the matter got beyond words Dr. Bush would be helpless. Then Dr. Bush noticed Captain Hughes standing only a few feet from him and Miller, observing the exchange. Hughes must have taken a step forward, or adjusted his gun-belt, something which drew the attention of Miller. When Miller noticed Hughes so close and aware of the situation he realized he was now in danger, but he knew better than to challenge John R. Hughes. Miller quickly changed his tone and decided his presence was needed elsewhere. It was obvious that Miller was a cowardly killer, choosing to walk away rather than tangle with the Ranger. Hughes watched Miller until he was out of sight entering his hotel. "I was watching that top button of his vest" Hughes said later, suggesting that he expected Miller to reach inside his coat for a concealed pistol, and Hughes would be ready for him if that happened.[19]

Miller surrendered to Sheriff Daniel Murphy. He was charged with the murder of Frazer but the case was transferred on a change of venue to Eastland in Eastland County, some two hundred miles northeast. On March 12, 1897, Hughes traveled to Eastland to assist Reeves County sheriff John Leavell in guarding the prisoner Miller. In two days he traveled 1,000 miles.[20] Miller's first trial ended with a hung jury; on the second trial in January 1899 he was acquitted on a plea of self-defense. The jury believed what Miller had done to Frazer was no worse than what Frazer had tried to do to Miller, thus the verdict.

Sheriff Gourley again called for Ranger assistance in April 1897, now asking for two men to be stationed at Marathon, stressing "We need them very badly."[21] Meanwhile Special Ranger R. M. Clayton was busy enforcing the quarantine law. In the month of April he had prevented 2,700 head of cattle from crossing into Sterling County, placing them in quarantine; then he quarantined another seventy-five head in Fisher County.[22]

In May another assault on the railroad drew Hughes to tracking train robbers. Three men attacked the Galveston, Harrisburg & San Antonio Railway about 2:00 a.m. on May 14 at a watering stop one and one-half miles west of Lozier, Texas. The lonely spot was some fifteen miles west of Judge Roy Bean's "West of the Pecos" community of Langtry. Two of the robbers, believed by Hughes to be Tom Ketchum and Will Carver, climbed aboard the tender and covered engineer George Fries and conductor James Burns with their pistols. Then they stopped the engine at the next cut where confederate David Atkins had cut the telegraph wires and was waiting with horses and explosives. To get to the contents of the safes, the trio placed dynamite on top of the through safe and then placed the small local safe on top of the charge. It took four blasts to open the safe, also blowing the roof and part of the side off the express car. They removed loot that Wells, Fargo & Company ultimately admitted was $42,000. After first heading towards the Rio Grande, the trio then turned and headed north and crossed the Pecos River, knowing they were being trailed but managing to evade lawmen. Back in the home country of Knickerbocker in Tom Green County the suddenly rich cowboys spent their ill-gotten wealth. When it was time for a new robbery the gang headed west to New Mexico to rob again, even though in the New Mexico Territory it was a hanging offense to assault a train.[23]

Captain Hughes learned of the train robbery and by May 18 he and others had trailed them to Ozona, county seat of Crockett County, stopping in the office of County and District Clerk Frank Olney to report his movements to Adjutant General Mabry. They had trailed them eighty miles before finding where the robbers had divided the spoils and killed a "played out" horse by cutting its throat and then had cut out the brand. Hughes suspected who the train robbers were. "One of them has a brother near San Angelo but he will hardly stop there as he is wanted for murder in Tom Green Co."[24] Hughes guessed correctly the leader was Tom Ketchum, the same man who had erroneously been reported killed a short while before near Clifton in Arizona Territory. The brother living near San Angelo was Sam Ketchum, also involved in numerous crimes. Tom Ketchum, known in Western history as "Black Jack" Ketchum, had reportedly killed a man in Tom Green County in 1895.

Hughes was still on the trail of the Lozier train robbers nine days later. By now the other posse members, O. Lattimer and Val Verde

County Sheriff W. H. Jones, brother of the late Capt. Frank Jones, had returned to Del Rio.[25] On the twenty-seventh Hughes arrived at San Angelo where he visited with Assistant Superintendent McKinney of Wells, Fargo & Company. "I don't think there is any chance of catching them soon," Hughes wrote to Mabry. "I have no doubt but what they came to this country as they have lots of friends here. They have a big range and have probably left this county temporarily." Hughes indicated he had sent his men back and would return that night or the next, concluding his letter with words of doubt: "I consider the Leader of the Lozier train robbers the hardest man to catch that we have had in Texas for many years."[26]

During Hughes's long trek attempting to capture the robbers, W. H. Mabry determined he was not being kept adequately informed. He sent letters to Hughes dated only two days apart, informing Hughes he did not have his superior's blessing for such a long pursuit. On returning to Ysleta Hughes found the two letters waiting, and although these letters of May 23 and May 25 no longer exist, Hughes's reply to them reveals what the messages from Mabry were about. "I will be very careful in the future," Hughes wrote, "to notify you by wire when I start on a trip of the character of the Lozier train robbery." Continuing his explanation, Hughes wrote that he had returned home to Ysleta on the first of June, but "would have come by Austin to see you but had no pass on I. & G.N. [International & Great Northern Railroad] so I came by Rosenbery Junction. I expect to go to San Angelo in a very few days in company with Captain R. C. Ware,[27] to work on the Lozier train robbery case, and will stop off a day at Austin as I wish to advise with you on the case."[28]

Much of May and June was spent in tracking the criminals. From June 6 until June 18 he was with U.S. Marshal Richard C. Ware working on the case, traveling to San Antonio, Austin, San Angelo, and Llano, but with no strong clues.[29] Hughes was not the only Ranger captain endeavoring to capture these men. In mid-October Capt. W. J. McDonald of Company B reported to Adjutant General Mabry that it was suspected that Tom Ketchum and his outfit were in San Angelo County.[30] Apparently McDonald could not devote the time necessary as he had bigger concerns with the mob activity working in San Saba

County. Neither McDonald nor John R. Hughes ever did catch up with the "hardest man to catch," but Tom Ketchum did not evade the law for long, nor did he ever repeat the success of the Lozier robbery. In July 1899, brother Sam Ketchum was severely wounded in a gun battle with lawmen. During his incarceration in a Santa Fe hospital, gangrene set in the wounded arm, but against the advice of his doctor he refused to allow his mangled arm to be amputated. Death came in a penitentiary cell on July 24. Later Tom Ketchum attempted to hold up a train single-handed, and he too was severely wounded by an express messenger; having received a shotgun blast in the arm he was in a similar position as his brother Sam had been. Weakened severely from loss of blood and shock the outlaw was easily captured, but he did allow the arm to be amputated. He later stood trial and was found guilty of the charge of "assault upon a railroad train with intent to commit a felony" and was hanged in Clayton, New Mexico, in 1901.[31]

The balance of 1897 was a continuous search, going out after men who committed a great variety of crimes. On July 15 Hughes left on a scout to recover stolen cattle. He recovered twenty-four head but reportedly uncovered no evidence of the identity of the thieves. On July 25 he and T. T. Cook were in Comstock, some thirty miles northwest of Del Rio in southern Val Verde County, guarding the train on the G.H. & S.A. Railway.[32]

Hughes and Cook were together again in August traveling to Spofford Junction at the request of Wells Fargo to guard a heavy shipment of money going from Spofford to El Paso. Spofford Junction, a depot on the G.H. & S.A. Railway line established in 1882, then consisted of numerous saloons, two hotels, a grocery store, and a school. The presence of the two Rangers prevented any attempt to steal the shipment of money.[33]

The year ended with additional typical Ranger work. Hughes and three others arrested seven men charged with cattle and horse theft; he arrested Juan Madrid charged with the serious charge of assault to murder. They were all delivered to the El Paso jail. But much more unusual, and certainly Hughes's first arrest of this nature, was his arrest of Harold R. Lotz for theft of a *bicycle*. It was valued at $100. Considering the fact that the bicycle at that time was not yet priced for the general public's consumption but considered the sport of the elitist, the hundred-dollar bicycle was not the top of the line, or else it was merely a used one. As more and more of the public chose the bicycle as a popular form of transportation, prices were lowered. The arrest of the bicycle thief was on October 12; three days later Hughes arrested Seth Burr for the more common crime of cattle theft.[34]

Hughes had not forgotten the killing of the elderly night watchman at the Valentine store, back in August 1895. No details of how the arrest was made are known but on November 19 he arrested and then delivered to the sheriff of El Paso County Samuel L. and Thomas Holland for burglary.[35] They had been prime suspects in the robbery of the Valentine store and the killing of Ellsberry. The brothers did stand trial, although the charges against them had been built on circumstantial evidence. Tom Holland was able to prove an alibi but it took him a year to do so. Samuel Lorenzo, or "Ranzey," was acquitted of the murder of the night watchman but was found guilty of the robbery and was sentenced to a fifteen-year term in prison. Retried in Maverick County in November 1899, he was found not guilty.[36]

Nor had Hughes forgotten the man who had killed Charles Fusselman. That killing remained uppermost in his mind, and giving justice to Fusselman's memory may have become almost an obsession. The fugitive Parra, apparently surmising that Hughes would never give up his pursuit, had absented himself from Texas and hid out in New Mexico Territory. But there he could not avoid trouble, trouble which eventually led to his downfall. In Lincoln County, Parra, now going under the name of Jose Nunez, was captured following a house burglary and sentenced to a year in the penitentiary. His prison record shows he was twenty-eight years of age, was single and his occupation given as "laborer." He had two bullet scars on the calf of his left leg; these were an entrance wound and an exit wound. Parra managed to escape on October 29, 1891, but was recaptured at Tularosa on November 24. Free again, in 1894 he found himself in difficulty with Dona Ana County Deputy Sheriff Ben Williams who wounded Parra in the fight. The wound was not fatal, and he was now sentenced to a term of seven years in the penitentiary. Parra had led a dangerous life, and was now looking at additional prison time.[37]

Ben Williams notified Captain Hughes that the man he wanted was in the New Mexico penitentiary, and with this knowledge Hughes went to see for himself to verify identification. The man was indeed Geronimo Parra, but was known as prisoner Jose Nunez and it was probably the different name that prevented Williams from immediately realizing he was the man Hughes wanted. Now Hughes began working on obtaining extradition papers to place Parra in his custody to stand trial in Texas. On October 13, 1898, he met with William J. Ten Eyck and District Attorney John M. Dean to complete an application for requisition upon the governor of New Mexico Territory, Miguel A. Otero. Dean completed the application, nominating Hughes to be appointed and commissioned as agent of the state of Texas to return Parra, boldly stating that Hughes had "no private interest" in taking Parra before a Texas court, which of course was not quite true. The application was signed by Ten Eyck as well as Attorney Dean on October 13.

On the fourteenth, Hughes wrote to Adj. Gen. A. P. Wozencraft of his concern. "It is not any use to get the Requisition unless the state will pay my expenses after the man as I cant afford to pay them. I would like very much to get him as Fusselman was a Ranger and a good officer. I think the expense would not be more than $50 and perhaps not that much. Geronimo Parra's time expires about Nov. 9th." He quickly had the agreement in writing that he was authorized to "receive and return" Parra, "to the proper officer inside the jail door." He would be reimbursed for "actual necessary expenses" not to exceed the $50 amount.[38]

Initially the prison superintendent pointed out that Parra had more time to serve and did not wish to overlook that fact. Parra would have been eligible for a "good conduct" allowance, but in confinement he had been "bad and vicious." With this information before him, Governor Otero at first refused to give Parra over to Hughes, but finally "the governor yielded to Captain Hughes's argument and honored the requisition."[39]

Just when Hughes met the noted Sheriff Patrick Floyd Garrett is unclear, but once the Ranger had his prisoner, the lawmen were together on the same passenger train, bound for Las Cruces, then on to El Paso. Ironically, on the same train were two men charged with murder who were without lawmen guarding them. The two were Oliver M. Lee and William Gilliland, charged with the murder of Albert Fountain and his son. They were described as men "who have defied the officers of the law for the past eighteen months, having killed one Deputy Sheriff while so doing."[40] Lee and Gilliland had agreed to surrender to Judge Francis W. Parker at Las Cruces, having resolved never to surrender to Sheriff Pat Garrett, believing if they were in Garrett's custody he would kill them. Thus, on the same train were three men charged with murder: Parra, Lee, and Gilliland, and two of the most celebrated lawmen of the Southwest—John R. Hughes and Pat Garrett. The possibility existed that Garrett would recognize the two men he had hunted but never succeeded in capturing. Or what if they recognized him? Would there be a gunfight on the train?

As each lawman took occasional walks up and down the aisle, it was fortunate that Garrett did not recognize the wanted pair, or if he did he made no sign of recognition. The two were in disguise, and if they did recognize Garrett they wisely kept it quiet. Later it was learned that Lee and Gilliland "were so changed in appearance that Sheriff Garrett . . . did not recognize them, and that many persons who have known them for years did not recognize them." Did the lawmen actually recognize the two wanted men? Or did the long beards of Lee and Gilliland prove to be such an appearance-changing disguise that they were indeed unrecognizable by a lawman who had wanted desperately to take them? Much has been written on that question, but Garrett stated to a newspaper reporter that he did not; Captain Hughes also stated that although he had known Lee for years, "he failed to recognize him."[41] At any rate, Hughes and Parra, the latter chained to a car seat, continued from Las Cruces to El Paso.

At Parra's trial he was found guilty of the murder of Fusselman and sentenced to hang. But he would not be alone on the gallows, as while waiting in the El Paso jail cell, contemplating his fate, another tragedy occurred. On March 19, 1899, Antonio Flores murdered Ramona Vizcaya "in cold blood." Flores had met Senorita Vizcaya, fell in love with her, begged her to become his mistress, and on her refusal begged her to marry him. Still she refused. The hot-blooded spurned lover then stabbed her to death, "saying as he dealt his murderous blows: 'If I cannot have you then no other man shall.'"[42] There was no self-defense plea in this matter; the judge sentenced Flores to die on the same day as Parra. The date set for execution was Friday, January 5, 1900.

Sheriff James H. Boone[43] was in charge of the necessary preparations to carry out the double execution, set for 1:00 in the afternoon. In spite of all the safeguards and preparations, the two condemned men had managed to acquire sharpened wires which they intended to use to escape. It was later believed they had taken the handles from their waste buckets and sharpened them to serve as weapons.

When jail guard Jim Hunter opened the cell door both Parra and Flores leaped out with their improvised daggers in hand. Parra attacked Hunter while Flores sprang toward Deputy Ed Bryant. Deputies Timothy C. Lyons, Eugene Bruce, and Sheriff Boone were instantly there and managed to overcome both prisoners and return them to the cell. Also present were Policeman Christly and W. J. Ten Eyck. Once order was established, Antonio Flores was led to the gallows. Sheriff Boone read the warrant while Ed Bryant translated it into Spanish. At 1:31 Boone released the lever and Flores dropped through to his death. Four minutes later four doctors examined him and declared that he was dead. The body was then pulled up and the rope removed—*to be used on Geronimo Parra.*

Now it was Parra's turn. Knowing how dangerous he was, and knowing he would kill if it meant his escape, and that he possibly had another secreted dagger, Boone showed his leadership and courage, taking chances he did not care to allow a deputy to take. "Gentlemen, we have had an unfortunate happening," he said. "The second prisoner may make an attack on the man who enters his call. I cannot afford to have good citizens or my deputies murdered by this lawless man. I propose to do my duty. If it is necessary to kill this man, I must do it. I shall go in myself and take him out." Boone was more than willing to do his duty, adding, "If it takes a bullet to do the work, that bullet will be fired. I will give him fair warning through an interpreter that resistance means death."[44]

Parra offered no resistance this time. At 1:57 he took his place on the scaffold. When asked if he had any last words, he asked that anyone he had offended forgive him, as he forgave anyone who had offended him. At 2:04 Sheriff Boone told everyone to be quiet, and then in the silence came the sharp clang of the lever releasing the drop. Instead of the rope breaking Parra's neck, it tore the jugular vein, which erupted. The head was nearly severed from the body. Although death was certainly instantaneous, the body was not taken down until twenty minutes later.

Jack Martin devotes several pages to Hughes' obtaining custody of Parra. Instead of Ben Williams informing Hughes that Parra was in a New Mexico prison, he wrote of how Pat Garrett, after retiring from the position of New Mexico sheriff and working on his Uvalde County ranch, was asked to return to Las Cruces to "restore order" as "outlaws had gotten out of hand" there. On his way to New Mexico Garrett stopped to visit "his old friend" Captain Hughes. The pair made a handshake deal, that Garrett would turn over Parra if Hughes would locate a New Mexico outlaw named Pat Agnew. Hughes spent "several weeks of patient detective work" and finally located Agnew and arrested him without resistance. Finally, after Garrett conferred with the governor he was given custody of Parra "and at the border turned him over to Captain Hughes."[45] As yet no record of a Pat Agnew living in New Mexico or Texas during the time period of the late nineteenth century has been located. The original documents in the Texas State Archives make no mention of Garrett being involved or a "trade-off" deal with Hughes. One must conclude that this description of how Hughes obtained custody of Geronimo Parra by Martin is pure fiction.

Although the extensive newspaper coverage of the double hanging failed to mention him by name as being present, as a witness or as one of the officials, John R. Hughes certainly was there. He had resolved to bring the murderer of Sgt. Charles Fusselman to justice; he had gone to New Mexico after obtaining credentials to bring the man back to Texas, and he was stationed at nearby Ysleta. Certainly he was there among the witnesses to see justice carried out.

~ 9 ~

From Ysleta to Alice

"... AS YOU WELL KNOW A RANGER SEEMS TO HAVE A HEAP
MORE INFLUENCE OVER THESE UNRULY CHARACTERS THAN A
COUNTY PEACE OFFICER."

— *Sheriff Denton G. Knight to Capt. J. R. Hughes,*
May 12, 1900

Historically, the days of the horseback Ranger ended during the early years of the twentieth century. The men of Company D continued to pursue lawbreakers on horseback, but now with the use of the railroad the time spent getting from one point to another was greatly reduced. Nevertheless, intrigues along the Rio Grande became an even greater reality than the changes in how to get from one place to another. Revolutions and talk of revolutions as well as the threat of Germany involving Mexico in the events leading to World War I were a constant concern.

The area around Shafter in deep Presidio County continued to pose problems for lawmen, especially Texas Rangers. On May 11, 1900, Harry S. Gleim, manager of the Cibolo Creek Mill and Mining Company of Shafter, wrote Hughes complimenting the work of two of his men who had made an impression on the six-shooting characters there. Rangers John W. Matthews and H. B. Elliot had only arrived the previous week but their presence alone "had a very quieting effect at once on our turbulent population," which resulted in three of the "worst six shooter offenders" being arrested and fined. That "made quite an impression," commented Gleim.[1] The mining manager, aware of not only the good

167

work of Rangers Matthews and Elliot, now learned the unwelcome news that they were going to be ordered elsewhere very soon. "It is regretted by all good citizens here," agonized Gleim, "and we trust it is [only] temporary." Gleim felt confident that somehow Hughes had enough influence with the adjutant general that some Rangers could be sent there to continue the good work initiated by Matthews and Elliot. Several of those good citizens had asked Gleim to write for such a favor, and he reminded Hughes: "I know you have a friendly feeling towards all your old friends down here and will do so if you can." He concluded his missive by pointing out that if there was anything they could do "in the way of punching up the legislature" Hughes should call on his friends at Shafter.[2]

Harry S. Gleim was not the only concerned citizen of Presidio County who would miss the good work of Hughes and his men. Sheriff D. G. Knight wrote on the following day, May 12, to indicate how sorry he was to hear that the strength of Company D had to be reduced. Sheriff Knight did thank Hughes for the way he helped him out "down there" in Shafter, some eighteen miles north of county seat Presidio on the Rio Grande. The boys, meaning Matthews and Elliot, "did good work and I am sorry they could not stay for I had a good deal of work planned for them."[3] Sheriff Knight did not explain what kind of work he had in mind, but it was perhaps nothing more than keeping the peace in general among the miners. The town had a permanent population of only a little over one hundred in 1900, but there were also two saloons and a dance hall, which could provide the necessary ingredients for trouble: young single men, alcohol, and ladies of easy virtue, always a potentially dangerous mixture. The miners were primarily Mexican citizens and black Americans, all living in company houses, all doing their necessary shopping in a company store, and occasionally obtaining medical care from the company doctor.[4] What certainly contributed to the making of the Ranger mystique was Knight's concluding comment:

> I believe the people of Shafter are going to petition you to have one or two men stationed there permanently, and I hope you will be in a

position to comply with their request, for as you well know a ranger seems to have a heap more influence over these unruly characters than a County peace officer.

Sheriff Knight was more than a little concerned about potential problems that he and Deputy Richard P. Porter[5] could not handle. The very next day he again wrote to Hughes, now asking the captain "to do what you can" to have one or two of his "Boys" assigned to Shafter "as they are needed at that place [as much] as any place I know of." Although there were no "murderers or anything of that Kind but the people of Shafter ask for protection as to lawlessness in the way of Shooting up the town and raising cane [*sic*, Cain] in general."[6] One cannot help but ask why Sheriff Knight with his deputies could not have initially dealt with the problem of men shooting up the town with their six-shooters.

As times changed so did the type of work Rangers were expected to perform. The monthly returns of early 1901 show Captain Hughes involved in more administrative work. Perhaps occasionally Hughes considered his required reports closer to needless "administrativia" than necessary reporting, certainly less fruitful than the stereotypical Ranger work of chasing down fugitives from justice. In January he scouted to Fort Hancock to arrest Mauricio Apodaca but found it had been a wasted trip as his bondsman had agreed to deliver him to El Paso. That was on the twentieth; three days later Hughes traveled to Marathon to visit the detachment and consult with Cattle Inspector Thalis T. Cook, former Company D man, regarding a scout on the Pecos River. Hughes met with Cook at Longfellow—then a thriving station on the tracks of the Southern Pacific Railroad, but today a ghost town—sixteen miles west of Sanderson. He was back at headquarters in Ysleta on the twenty-seventh.[7]

The month of March, however, did prove more interesting as Hughes with John J. Brooks[8] and Oscar Carrillo scouted down on "The Island"—where Frank Jones had lost his life—and then on to Fabens on what was termed a "prospect scout" after some lost horses and a stray mule. They started out on March 3 but finding no trace of the animals they returned empty handed two days later.[9]

Then on the thirteenth John R. Hughes received his first wound while on active service, not from a disgruntled citizen or from a fugitive from justice, but by accident. It was not dangerous, but a wound nevertheless, which he had to report to his superior. Painfully and with no doubt considerable embarrassment, Hughes wrote to Adj. Gen. Thomas Scurry:

> I was accidentally shot in the foot this evening but don't think it a very serious wound as no bones were broken. I will not be able for duty for a few days. Expect I will go to Hotel Dieu Hospital tomorrow, at El Paso. I will keep you posted as to my condition.[10]

Hughes placed Lieutenant John Woodard "Wood" Saunders in charge of the company during his recuperation. Hughes had to keep his superior informed during this period of enforced idleness, and reported in the same letter that Privates J. J. Brooks and E. B. Jones[11] had started on a scout near the New Mexico line that afternoon, and would be gone about five days. They knew good horse flesh, and Hughes had sent them there to buy saddle horses for the company's use. Of additional concern was a party who had been robbing boxcars in the vicinity of Fort Hancock and Sierra Blanca, and Lieutenant Saunders with Private Carrillo were to start on a scout to determine who the guilty parties were. They expected to be able to get to a telegraph station nightly to keep Hughes informed.[12]

Private H. E. Delany[13] assisted Hughes in dressing his wounded foot prior to going to see a doctor in El Paso. The sixty-year-old doctor, Marcus O. Wright, told his patient that the dressing "was as well as he could have done"; and Hughes now explained how the accidental shooting happened.

> I had bought me a new pistol 38 cal. Smith & Wesson that has a safety notch in the hammer and I thought it was perfectly safe to carry all six chambers loaded—but last night I went to buckle it on and it slipped out of the scabbard and the hammer hit the floor and shot me through the right foot from the inside. The doctor promised to send me a pair of crutches by train tonight and I think I will be out on

them tomorrow. I expected to go to El Paso today but the doctor said I would do just as well here.[14]

Dr. Wright did provide Hughes with the crutches, but how long he needed them is uncertain. Months later he was in Austin conferring with the adjutant general on conditions in West Texas. Commented an Austin reporter:

Captain Hughes is an old ranger and is regarded as one of the coolest and most capable men in the service. After a record of having arrested many desperadoes and participation in numerous fights and small pitched battles without receiving a wound, he was injured by accident, having dropped a pistol and shot himself through one of his feet. As a result he is now on crutches.[15]

May did prove to be a more interesting month as United States President William McKinley visited El Paso on the fifth. Whether Captain Hughes was there close to the president, acting as a body guard, is unclear but Lt. John J. Brooks and Privates E. B. Jones, Oscar Carrillo, and E. D. Aten of Company D were. Apparently all remained peaceful as the monthly return does not indicate any arrests by the Rangers, nor did the extensive coverage of President McKinley's visit in the newspapers report any troubles. They were back in camp on the sixth, ready to help move camp from Ysleta to Fort Hancock.

The move was started on the eighth and completed the next day. Such a seemingly insignificant thing as moving the camp proved to be copy for the press, as the *Daily Herald* noted: "Captain J. R. Hughes, of the state rangers, has removed with his detachment from Ysleta to Fort Hancock, where he will remain during the summer." The *Herald* explained the move was made because the Fort Hancock camp "was more centrally located."[16] On the fifteenth Hughes went to Van Horn to meet with "some cattle men from down the river" and returned the following day. On the twenty-seventh Pvt. J. W. Saunders went to Alamogordo, New Mexico, to investigate some cattle there supposed to have been stolen in Texas. He did not return until the first of June, with fifty-seven head of smuggled cattle recovered. That trip covered three hundred miles.[17]

In June Hughes had to report to El Paso as a witness in a murder case against Bruno Carmona. After staying in El Paso for three days he left for Valentine on the night of the tenth. He did not return to Fort Hancock until the twenty-second, after what must have been a grueling trip of nearly three hundred miles. The very next day he traveled to Sierra Blanca to see about a captured team of horses. This was probably the team that Lieutenant Brooks, Privates E. B. Jones, Stafford Bland, and H. E. Delany had recovered a few days earlier. The El Paso owner of the recovered team and buggy declared it was worth $350. To Private Delany fell the duty of returning the recovered property to its El Paso owner.

In July 1901, the 27th Legislature made another change for the men who enforced law and order in the State of Texas. Dated July 3, the new act was published "for the information and government of all concerned." The Frontier Battalion ceased to exist with that name; it was now the Ranger Force. The stated purpose of the Ranger Force, not really any different from under the previous name, was "protecting the frontier against marauding or thieving parties, and for the suppression of lawlessness and crime throughout the State." The Force would consist of not more than four companies of mounted men, each company not to exceed more than one captain, one first sergeant, and twenty privates. There would be one quartermaster for the entire force. The captains and quartermaster would be appointed by the governor, "and shall be removed at his pleasure," each to serve two years. Naturally, as before, each man had to furnish his own horse, horse equipment, and clothing. If his horse was killed in action he would be reimbursed for it by the State at fair market value at the time when killed. Each man also would "be clothed with all the powers of peace officers, and shall aid the regular civil authorities in the execution of the laws." Each man in addition was to take an oath to "faithfully perform the duties in accordance with law."[18]

In conformity to the act, which had been approved March 29, 1901, all officers, non-commissioned officers, and privates of the Frontier Battalion, now the Ranger Force, were honorably discharged on July

8. Each company commander then had to forward to the adjutant general's office the pay rolls of his company covering the period up to and including that date. As of July 8 the Force would be organized as follows: four companies known as Companies A, B, C, and D, Ranger Force. Each company would consist of one captain, one first sergeant, and eight privates. It was a drastic reduction from the original proposed number of twenty privates, probably as a cost-saving measure. The captains of the four companies were named as follows: J. A. Brooks, Captain Co. A with headquarters at Alice; W. J. McDonald, Captain Co. B with headquarters at Amarillo; J. H. Rogers, Captain Co. C with headquarters at Laredo; and J. R. Hughes, Captain Co. D with headquarters at Fort Hancock. Each captain also was required to make a monthly report of the company's activities, including "character of scouts made, distance traveled, names of parties arrested, disposition of prisoners and full account of service rendered." Further, no member of the Force could, directly or indirectly, aid or abet the election of any candidate for official position. Perhaps more importantly for the image of the Force, members would "keep within the bounds of discretion and the law under all circumstances."[19] Each captain had great leeway in selecting the men who would serve in his company. If Brooks, Rogers, McDonald, and Hughes had not earned the status of "The Four Great Captains" prior to this change, they now had the opportunity to do so by their accomplishments in the early years of the twentieth century. Perhaps as a reminder of how society had changed since the earliest days of the Frontier Battalion, created in 1874, Lamartine P. Sieker was commissioned captain and quartermaster; he had come a long way from entering into the service to fight Indians back in 1874.

A most unusual case of property theft occupied the time and energy of Hughes and members of the new Ranger Force in July. Hughes left on the eighth to go to El Paso to work on the case of stolen hats, Stetsons or sombreros or what specifically is not indicated, which had been stolen out of a Texas & Pacific Railroad boxcar. Twenty dozen hats had been stolen. The stolen headwear was recovered but the thieves had not been identified or captured. Hughes was back in camp on the tenth but two days later was back in El Paso to continue working on the case. He returned on the fourteenth. Two days later Hughes, with Lieutenant Brooks and Private Delany, began a scout down the Rio Grande to the Cavett Ranch and Hot Springs. No explanation is given in the monthly return for the eleven-day trip, which covered only 160 miles. Nothing more was accomplished on the hat case in August, but Hughes did deliver prisoner Candalario Hernandez to the El Paso jail, leaving camp on the twenty-fifth and returning two days later. Lieutenant Brooks had arrested Hernandez on the twenty-first for theft.[20]

In September Hughes was still working on the stolen hats case but apparently had made no progress. He did, however, arrest three men who were charged with assault to murder: Miguel González, Octaviano Gonzáles, and Domingo García. Hughes left Fort Hancock on the third to go to El Paso; two days later he left Ysleta to go to Midland where he testified as a witness in the Zacario Romero case, although no further details have been learned of this matter. He was back in camp at Fort Hancock on the eleventh of September.

The hat case was taking up an inordinate amount of time and energy, as now on the thirteenth Lieutenant Brooks went down to San Elizario for further investigation. He did not locate the culprits but did arrest two men for disturbing the peace: A. J. Love and J. T. Patterson. He was back in camp on the fifteenth.

Hughes, now on the eighteenth, began a hunt that lasted nearly a week, pursuing a man charged with forgery and theft.[21] The monthly return gives no details but the pursuit and capture resulted in positive attention in the press. Frank Rogers was a young man who apparently chose to become a desperado by first forging the name of J. C. Jones, his employer, and then stealing a horse. Mr. Jones, working with a geological team at Hueco Tanks, some thirty miles east of El Paso, had sent young Rogers to obtain needed supplies. At the mercantile store of Fassett & Kelly's[22] he forged Jones's name in order to obtain a rifle and cartridges, then stole a horse and disappeared. Hughes began the search, heading east and making inquiries at Van Horn, Pecos, and as far north as Odessa. He returned to camp and then began the hunt anew with Lt. J. J. Brooks on the twenty-fourth. Just how the Ranger pair located him is unclear, but on September 24 Hughes with Brooks arrested Frank Rogers; he was delivered to the El Paso jail. Rogers was not yet twenty-one, claimed to be part Indian, his grandmother being a Creek. Now in jail he was interviewed by a reporter from the *El Paso News* who stated, "[t]he young man says he is sorry for his escapade. He had evidently started out to be a desperado. He was hard to trail, as he never stopped at any ranch or house, and killed all the food he needed." The *News* headlined its article with "Rangers Caught Him" in bold followed by the subheadline, "Frank Rogers Captured After a Long Tiresome Chase."[23] It certainly had proved to be long and tiresome, as Hughes noted the chase had covered 938 miles. Time and energy of man and horse was at work, but the Rangers did get their man.

Company D Rangers in 1901. At left is E. B. Jones holding pack horse; at right is Joe B. Townsend. *University of Texas at El Paso Library, Special Collections Department.*

In spite of the good work of Lt. J. J. Brooks, he was discharged on October 14. Five days later a young man who had developed an enviable reputation as a lawman replaced him: William Davis "Dave" Allison.[24] Allison enlisted on October 19 but his name does not show up in Hughes's monthly reports until later that year when Private Allison and Sgt. Enoch Cook[25] went to Langtry scouting after train robber Bill Taylor.[26] There were rumors that Taylor had been seen in the Langtry area but if he was there he avoided being spotted by the Rangers. Cook and Allison scouted for Taylor on December 5 and did not return until December 8, having covered 340 miles on their unsuccessful hunt. Hughes then attempted the same thing, to gather in Bill Taylor, leaving on the eighth, but he fared no better than Cook and Allison. On December 18 Hughes with Privates T. F. McKinney[27] and E. B. Jones scouted down to Fabens and Pirate Island after a horse thief, identified as Felix Magallon. The Rangers had better luck this time than their failed hunts for Taylor, as they arrested Magallon and recovered the stolen horse. Magallon was placed in the El Paso jail on Christmas Eve, 1901.

Perhaps Hughes and the other Rangers rested themselves as well as their horses on Christmas Day as the Monthly Return does not indicate any action. But on December 26 Hughes went to Van Horn, still trying to obtain solid leads on the whereabouts of Bill Taylor. He returned on the same day, having covered 144 miles via rail, but not with the fugitive.[28]

Celebrating the end of one year and the beginning of a new year has traditionally been a time of calm enjoyment and reflection, or disruption, including riotous behavior. Apparently trouble was anticipated at the Midwinter Carnival in El Paso, as on January 14, 1902, Captain Hughes, and Pvts. J. H. Baker and Tom Ross went to El Paso to assist Sheriff Boone. Tom Ross was "detailed to work secretly." On the same day Private Allison left Marathon to "assist in keeping peace at [the] carnival." There were no riots at the carnival, but Pvt. Joseph B. Townsend, brother of E. E. Townsend, having also come to assist, arrested four men: Dan Taylor, Lawrence Banks, Claud Mipauge, charged with disturbing the peace, and A. Miller for theft, all for their misconduct during the Carnival.[29]

Private Townsend could not remain in El Paso as he was on the trail of parties accused of burning bridges on the Texas & Pacific Railroad. He went as far as Abilene, over four hundred miles north, but apparently made no arrests. Townsend returned on February 6 from Abilene, the same day Enoch Cook was discharged.[30]

Private Allison was an experienced lawman, and on February 7, 1902, Captain Hughes promoted him to the position of sergeant. In addition to being a dependable, honest, and hard-working man he had had experience that would be helpful to any Ranger captain. On November 6, 1888, the people of Midland County, midway between El Paso and Fort Worth, had elected him sheriff, only the second sheriff of the county. Born June 21, 1861, Allison thus became the youngest sheriff in the state of Texas. He proved his worth to the good people of Midland County as they re-elected him two years later on November 4, 1890, and then four more times, until he stepped down on November 8, 1898.[31] On December 28, 1899, he applied for a commission as a Special Ranger, explaining why: "That I may be instrumental in Suppression of crime, and bringing to Justice Criminals."[32] When he pledged his oath to the State of Texas and Company D he brought with him ten years as an elected official and experience in law enforcement. He knew people—good men and bad—guns, horses, and how to handle bad men with guns.

An unusual theft occurred on or about May 19, 1902, when allegedly Mrs. Dave Creswell did "fraudulently take the corporeal personal property of one Tom M. Ross" who was a member of Company D. She was accused of stealing one mattress for a single bed, one home-made quilt, two double blankets, one bed sheet, one feather pillow, one small looking-glass, a half load of wood—all of the value of $15. The complaint was sworn out on June 13. John R. Hughes signed the complaint as well as Ranger Ross. Not only that, but on the same day Captain Hughes swore that the same Mrs. Creswell took from him two galvanized water buckets, two stew pots, one bread pan, one tin quart cup, certain empty fruit jars, two tin plates, one china plate, one hammer, five pounds of lard, one can of baking powder, two packages of oatmeal, one package of rice, two or more cans of canned meat, one frying pan—all being of the value of at

least $5.00.[33] Ironically while Hughes and Ross were busy signing com-
plaints against Mrs. Creswell, the *El Paso Herald* was giving them positive attention. Hughes reported "everything very quiet" but he would be
busy as he had "about six cases to present to the grand juries." The *Herald*
reminded its readers that Hughes had been shot in the foot about a year
before, "but he is able to ride on horse back quite well now."[34]

With the ever-increasing use of the railroad, problems also increased,
and much of the work for the Rangers dealt with attempts to damage
railroad property or inflict injury to railroad employees. Such was the
case back in April when two men shot at a conductor, who was apparently not injured. Hughes and Private Townsend arrested the pair at
Hueco Tanks.[35]

Men still occasionally attempted to rob a train, looting a safe in the
express car or taking money from the passengers themselves. On July
29, Captain Hughes traveled to El Paso to learn about a train robbery at
Bermejillo, Durango, Mexico. From his investigation, Hughes believed
the robbers were heading north to Texas to lose themselves across the
Rio Grande. The village of Bermejillo was located over two hundred
miles south of the southern tip of today's Big Bend. Hughes concen-
trated on hunting the train robbers during that month; because of that,
he felt he had neglected other aspects of law enforcement. He explained
in the August monthly return that his men "had spent most of this
month watching the Border for the Bernajillo [*sic*] Train Robbers and
for that reason we have made no arrests."[36] While Captain Hughes was
in Marfa on August 2, apparently investigating a possible clue, Allison
and Townsend were scouting on the Rio Grande seeking the train robbers as well, riding down through Terlingua, Lajitas, on down the river
to Boquillas "and further south."[37] The Ranger pair made no arrests.

September 1902 found Sergeant Allison of Company D, Ranger
Force on his own scouting after wanted men. In late September he
was hunting fugitive George Isaacs in the eastern part of New Mexico,
intending to meet up with Sheriff Cicero Stewart of Eddy County.
Apparently Allison determined that if he was already out of the state
of Texas he might as well continue the hunt. Did he believe he had

authority outside the boundaries of Texas? Sheriff Stewart failed to show up at the agreed upon time and place so Allison continued the hunt "on horseback alone." On the twenty-first he was some fifty miles north of Carlsbad where he arrested a man who fit Isaacs's description. But the man had to be released after what Allison described as "a rigid examination." No further details were provided. Isaacs had become a real problem for the Rangers. A jury in Hardeman County had found him guilty of first degree murder on December 9, 1896. He was delivered to the state prison at Rusk in Cherokee County, on August 11, 1897, but managed to escape with a forged pardon on September 30, 1899. On one occasion Rangers had traveled to Nebraska searching for him, but he continued to evade Texas lawmen. A. Y. Baker[38] of Captain Brooks's Company F had scouted after Isaacs in Roswell, New Mexico, but again, it was an unsuccessful hunt.[39] Later, in April 1906, Rangers Milam Wright and Herff Carnes would also scout to Roswell in search of Isaacs, but no indication of his capture was recorded.[40] His eventual fate as a fugitive from Texas justice is unknown.

Continuing his hunt, Sergeant Allison, back in Texas, arrived in Pecos City on the twenty-fifth where he learned of a lawless situation in Midland and went there. He met County Judge E. R. Bryan who requested assistance in helping prevent a mob from taking prisoner George Arthur out to lynch. Allison, along with Deputy Sheriff L. P. Heard, took the prisoner "to a place of Safety" that night, keeping him alive for an examining trial set for the next day. He was remanded to jail but placed in the Howard County facility until the grand jury called his case, which was set for 1903. Allison and Cattle Inspector William L. Calohan[41] delivered Arthur to Big Spring, the county seat. In addition to delivering the prisoner safely to jail, Allison made two arrests: W. T. Greenhaw on the twenty-sixth for carrying a pistol, and the next day he arrested Dr. W. D. Littler for the same violation. He made complaints against both of these individuals before the county attorney. As a Ranger sergeant he now had to make out his monthly report giving Captain Hughes back at Fort Hancock, details of his activities while on the lengthy scout. He summed up his report stating that he had traveled 1,370 miles in Texas and New

Mexico, and had been absent from camp twelve full days. Averaging over one hundred miles daily, he obviously spent a good portion of the dozen days traveling via the railroad, although he would, if asked, still consider himself a "horse-back Ranger." He signed his communications, "Yours to Command."[42] He had proved to be a valuable asset for Company D, as well as saving the life of a prisoner who otherwise would have ended up the victim of a lynch mob.

Railroad workers struck in October. On the ninth Captain Hughes, Sam McKenzie, W. C. Beach, and Joe B. Townsend started to Laredo to assist Adjutant General Scurry during the strike. A week later they returned to camp at Fort Hancock, except Scurry who then went to Brownsville. On October 29 Hughes, now with Tom Ross and Joe Townsend, joined him in Brownsville to assist Scurry and the authorities in keeping peace during the elections. Celedonio Garza was re-elected Cameron County sheriff on November 4 but the Rangers remained there until November 10. Garza remained in office until January 1, 1911.[43] Possibly the heavy work load and the occasional trouble with the wounded foot resulted in Hughes reporting illness during the last days of November. He entered the El Paso hospital on November 22 and remained four days, until the twenty-fifth. Fortunately he had recovered by late December as he now had orders to move Company D headquarters to Alice. The men arrived there on Christmas Day, after having covered 770 miles.[44]

Alice was then a small community in Nueces County, which would, in March 1911, become the county seat of newly created Jim Wells County. South Texas was not entirely new to Captain Hughes, but it was quite different from the Big Bend and El Paso areas in climate and terrain. The change in location did not mean a change in the types of crimes committed, however. Hughes and his men were required to attend numerous district court sessions, their presence almost guaranteeing a quiet session of the court. On February 12 Captain Hughes started to Floresville in Wilson County to enlist Herff A. Carnes who would prove to be a valuable recruit.[45] Two days later Sergeant Ross with three men met Hughes at San Antonio. The group of Rangers then traveled to Fredericksburg, county seat of Gillespie County, to assist the sheriff in preserving the peace during district court. It was necessary to safeguard a prisoner named Samuel Locklin, so the group delivered him to San Antonio for safe keeping. Sentenced to life imprisonment in Huntsville, the forty-one-year-old prisoner was received there on May 13, 1905. Eight years later, on October 18, 1913, Locklin received a pardon.[46]

Hughes made a very positive impression on the citizens of Gillespie County, especially District Judge Clarence Martin, Sheriff John Klaemer, and District Attorney Dayton Moses. The three officials decided to put their thoughts into writing. On February 26, they wrote out their "To Whom It May Concern" statement, beginning with:

> We take pleasure in saying that . . . Captain John R. Hughes, Sergeant Tom M. Ross and Privates J. F. Harrod, W. C. Beach and Albert R. Mace [were] of great assistance in helping all of the officers

Company D, drastically reduced in size. From left standing: Herff A. Carnes, Sam McKenzie, Arthur C. Beach. Seated Thomas M. Ross, Arthur R. Mace and John R. Hughes. *Courtesy the Texas Ranger Hall of Fame and Museum, Waco, Texas.*

throughout the entire term [of District Court]. They were at all times prompt and attentive to business, polite and courteous to the entire court and at all times willing and anxious to assist all connected with the court in any way whether technically within the line of their duty or not, and it affords us much pleasure to here tender to them our thanks for such service and to lend our endorsement, to the Adjutant General, that in these gentlemen he has in the service men who will command the respect of the entire people as well as the officers with whom they are associated. . . . We add that their conduct during the short time they have been with us, has been such as commands the respect and esteem of the entire people.[47]

A wonderful endorsement indeed, but there was always more work to be done. Sergeant Ross along with Privates J. F. Harrod and W. C. Beach went to Mason to assist the sheriff in keeping peace during the district court session. While there Private Beach arrested two men, charge not identified; they were delivered to the jail in Mason. Harrod and Beach were back in camp at Alice on the twenty-eighth of March.

Traveling to another part of the state in order to enlist Herff A. Carnes may have been the occasion for John R. Hughes to also meet up with a young lady whom he intended to make his wife. She remains mysterious, as Hughes never mentioned her in any of the numerous interviews he gave later in life, nor has her name been found in any of Hughes's personal papers. Jack Martin, Hughes's early biographer, identified the woman as Elizabeth Todd although he knew this was not her real name. Martin may, in reality, have known her true identity, but instead coyly referred to her simply as "a gay, spirited brunette of twenty, whom we shall know as Elizabeth Todd." [48] To cause further confusion for later historians, Martin indicated Hughes had met the woman prior to the time of the murder of the Williamson family in 1889, but while he was dealing with the investigation resulting in the legal hanging of Dick Duncan two years later, the young lady fell victim to an unspecified illness and died. Her body was taken to an unnamed small town on the Gulf Coast for burial. Supposedly his friends had tried to communicate with Hughes to inform him of the tragedy, but he was on the move so much they had been unable to do so. Martin also credits Ira Aten with knowing why Hughes never married, that "the tragic death of Elizabeth Todd was largely responsible for his remaining a bachelor."[49]

But in spite of Martin wishing Hughes's love interest to remain a lady of mystery, enough clues have been uncovered to determine her real name. She was Elfreda G. Wuerschmidt, a native of South Dakota, the daughter of Christian H. and Anna M. Wuerschmidt. A photograph of her and members of Company D including Captain Hughes is in the Manuel T. "Lone Wolf" Gonzaullas Collection. Gonzaullas identified the individuals in the photograph. The others were fellow Company D men Milam H. Wright, Harry Moore Sr., Charles "Little" Moore, Charles Craighead, and a young lady only identified by Gonzaullas as "Miss Wuerschmidt." She is, perhaps as a mild exhibition of her strength as a woman and to reveal the lightheartedness of the occasion, wearing a cartridge belt with holster and pistol prominently displayed. The weaponry is no doubt that of Captain Hughes himself, as the side arms of the other Rangers in the photograph appear, almost on display. The photograph also appears in Maude T. Gilliland's book *Wilson County Texas Rangers: 1837–1977*. Gilliland stated the picture was made in Ysleta in 1904 by Ranger Herff Carnes, "who told of Captain Hughes' annual pilgrimage to his sweetheart's grave in Rockport on the date that would have been their wedding anniversary."[50] At least one other photograph was made of the young lady: standing alone with Captain Hughes on what appears to be a shoreline. This photograph appears in *Horsebackers of the Brush Country: A Story of the Texas Rangers and Mexican Liquor Smugglers*, also by Maude Gilliland. The caption by Ms Gilliland shows that it was taken by Herff Carnes near the coastal city Rockport in 1904.[51]

Christian Wuerschmidt and his wife were natives of Germany. The 1900 census shows they had been married for twenty-three years, providing a marriage date of 1877. In 1900 the family was living in Adams County, Nebraska, the father's occupation given as minister. Why the family moved to El Paso is unknown, but the 1910 El Paso County census shows the head of household is now the widower Christian Wuerschmidt;

it also reveals the family had immigrated to the United States in 1883. Their son George P. (actually Paul G.) was born in South Dakota in December 1885, daughter Elfreda G. was born in October 1887 and another son, Marcus A., was born in March 1890. By 1920 son Paul G. Wuerschmidt worked as an electrician for "Govt Shop," residing in Ysleta Village. But he had worked at more than being an electrician in a government shop, as on April 21, 1918, he had enlisted as a Special Ranger, then giving his previous occupation as a mechanic, and to the question about previous service: "Deputy Sheriff many years." The ques-

tion as to why he wanted to become a Special Ranger was not asked on this form, but perhaps he was like so many others who became Rangers: he wanted to enforce the laws of the state and protect his own property and that of his neighbors. He also was permitted to carry a weapon legally. Paul Wuerschmidt was issued a warrant of authority as a Special Texas Ranger to serve without pay. He was not assigned to a specific company.[52]

It is certain that the lost love of John R. Hughes was Elfreda G. Wuerschmidt.[53] Their wedding date was to be one day in June, as Hughes's journals, which he kept in later years, at least three of which are known to exist, reveal that in some years in

John R. Hughes and the woman he was to marry, Elfreda Wuerschmidt. Photograph taken in 1904 near Rockport, Texas, by Herff Carnes. *From the M. T. Gonzaullas Collection; courtesy the Texas Ranger Hall of Fame and Museum, Waco, Texas.*

the month of June he traveled to Rockport in Aransas County on the Gulf of Mexico, less than 150 miles southeast of San Antonio. In the spring of 1903 the men of Company D did much work that was little different from that done three decades before. Captain Hughes with four men scouted down in the Brownsville area to determine if there was a need to place a detachment there. This took thirteen days and 250 miles of traveling. In early April Hughes scouted between Brownsville and Alice, then to the border region of Hebbronville, as well as San Antonio. He scouted sometimes with Private Herff Carnes and sometimes with Private W. C. Beach.[54]

The Rangers proved to be successful in May as they made arrests and recovered stolen cattle. Sergeant Ross with two Rangers and a deputy sheriff scouted for several nights in Cameron County. Their night work paid off as on May 24 they arrested Pedro Mireles for cattle theft, and on the next night arrested Will and Charles Dorsett for the same offense. They were all delivered to the county jail in Brownsville. During the same month Privates J. H. Baker and Sam McKenzie helped Sergeant Ross recover stolen cattle.[55]

In June Privates Albert R. Mace and Herff A. Carnes responded to the report of a fence being cut on Lasiter's Ranch in Starr County. The pair picked up the trail, which led them to the Santa Rosa ranch where they arrested a Mexican who they believed had cut the fence. He was delivered to jail in Hidalgo and turned over to a deputy sheriff. In addition Private Mace arrested a black man and delivered him as well to Hidalgo.

Two years before, an incident that should have been a peaceful arrest turned deadly and a drama began, which ultimately drew Captain Hughes into it. Several men lost their lives, an obscure Mexican became a hero to many of his people, and a popular *corrido*, or border ballad, was created. The tragedy began on June 12, 1901, when Karnes County Sheriff William T. "Brack" Morris with a small posse attempted the arrest of a suspected horse thief named Gregorio Cortez. An apparent misunderstanding caused by an imperfect translation between the parties resulted in gunfire: Gregorio Cortez shot Morris; in turn Morris shot Romaldo Cortez, Gregorio's brother. Both Morris and Romaldo

Cortez died from their wounds. Many men of South Texas then became man hunters to track down Cortez. Two days later near the small community of Belmont in Gonzales County a posse caught up with Cortez. He answered the demand to surrender with gunfire and in the ensuing gun battle Gonzales County sheriff Richard M. Glover and posse member Henry Schnabel were both killed. Cortez, now wanted for three murders in two counties, headed south intending to lose himself in Mexico. He never made the Rio Grande, as on June 22, ironically his twenty-sixth birthday, ten days after the initial gunfight that had made him a wanted man, Cortez was found and arrested by Ranger Capt. John H. Rogers. Cortez stood trial and was found guilty but due to numerous appeals and changes of venue he spent long months in jail waiting for the final verdict of the three murder charges. In all Cortez endured eleven trials, and spent time in eleven different Texas jails.[56] Hughes's involvement came when he and Rangers Mace and Carnes had to be present to maintain peace and order.

Besides the arrests and scouts during June 1903, seventy-three head of cattle were recovered and delivered to the rightful owners.[57] Also during that month Hughes, Privates Tom Ross,[58] Sam McKenzie,[59] Crosby Marsden[60] and R. E. Smith [61] were present at the trial of Antonio Cabrara.[62]

Little real action occurred during the month of July. Twenty-five head of stolen cattle were recovered and delivered to the Cameron County sheriff. The Rangers also assisted a customs inspector, although no details were provided. August was similar, but September proved to be different as now Pvts. J. F. Harrod and Herff A. Carnes were sent to Laredo to enforce the quarantine during the yellow fever scare. At the same time Privates Baker and Beach were sent to Brownsville during the yellow fever scare in that place. During this period the public had a legitimate reason to fear the epidemic. There were nearly 800 cases in Laredo alone, with seventy-five deaths reported. Fortunately, none of the Rangers enforcing the quarantine suffered from the dread disease.[63] Later, in October, Captain Hughes reported that besides the recovered property and the arrests, two of his men, Ross and Beach, had "served the whole month less the 5 days that they have reported on scout [duty] in state service [on quarantine duty]."⁶⁴

A most unusual theft occurred in October. No details were reported but on the twenty-third Sergeant Ross with several Mexican officials searched an area in Cameron County and "found 4 scrapers that had been stolen from Brownsville Land and Irrigation Co. in Texas." The recovered scrapers, large mule-drawn implements used to move earth from one place to another, frequently used in the construction of roads, were delivered to the Custom House in Matamoros, Mexico. They were then returned to the rightful owners.⁶⁵ In November Hughes with Privates J. H. Baker,⁶⁶ Sam McKenzie, and Earl R. Yeary⁶⁷ started on a lengthy scout in Nueces, Hidalgo, and Cameron counties. Among the ten ranches they visited or scouted in was the Chicago Ranch, which John B. Armstrong, a Texas Ranger of the 1870s, now owned and operated.⁶⁸ Armstrong had served under famed Ranger Captain L. H. McNelly in the mid-1870s, had accompanied him in the invasion of Mexico to recover cattle stolen from the King Ranch, and most notably, in 1877, captured John Wesley Hardin and delivered him back safely to Texas to stand trial for one of his many murders. Did Captain Hughes and Rancher Armstrong discuss past accomplishments? Armstrong "knew" Hardin from the capture; Hughes had known him after his pardon from Huntsville prison in 1894.

The new year of 1904 brought considerable positive press for Hughes in particular and the Ranger Force in general. The *Alice Echo* noted he had arrested "a bunch of bad men" and explained that he was "acting in concert with Sheriff Mike Wright and inspector of Customs H. H. Jeffries, [and] after a long and tiresome search, succeeded in making four important arrests" during the past week. One man was arrested at Arroyo Colorado, for theft of mules; one at Brownsville on the same charge, and two at Corpus Christi, one of whom was charged with defacing brands and the other with receiving and concealing some of the same mules.⁶⁹

Whereas the arrest of these four men drew little notice, the arrest of a New York fugitive in February 1904, did. The arrest of New York singer and actor Charles F. Dodge may have been one of the more peaceful arrests in Hughes's career, but it brought about much publicity for him. In 1900 Mrs. Rose Dodge, actress, obtained a divorce decree from her husband, and then married Charles W. Morse, a banker. Then in 1904 she brought suit for annulment of her marriage to Morse on the grounds that her marriage was not legal, since previous husband Charles F. Dodge claimed he had never been served with the proper legal documents for the divorce. Consequently she wanted the marriage to Morse annulled to prevent charges of bigamy against herself. However, her attorney, after a thorough investigation, determined that Charles F. Dodge had indeed been served with the proper legal documents and he was guilty of perjury. Upon learning he was under investigation, Dodge left the grand jury's jurisdiction; it was believed he was headed for Mexico.[70]

The law firm of Baker, Botts, Parker & Garwood in Houston contacted Hughes concerning the fugitive, first by telephone and then in a telegram and on the thirteenth of February via a long letter, giving a physical description of Dodge—"a man about 58 years of age,[71] with light mustache, rather inclined to baldness, weighs about 180 pounds and is something under the medium height"—along with the fact that he was "accompanied by a Jew lawyer named Kaffenberger" as well as a man named Bradley. In case Hughes had any question as to why Dodge was wanted, the letter stated Dodge was under indictment in New York for perjury, under a $10,000 bond, pending an appeal against requisition papers in federal court. At that point Dodge and associates had left Brownsville to go to Alice by stage and then, presumably, to Laredo to cross into Mexico, probably heading for Mexico City. What the three fugitives were unaware of was that Sgt. Thomas M. Ross was already in the stagecoach with them, a horse-back undercover agent. [72]

Absent the telephone record and the telegram, what was said and telegraphed is unknown, but four days after the letter was sent, Hughes was ready. Governor S. W. T. Lanham now telegraphed Hughes to act: no details were provided, but a news item headline said it all: "Charles F. Dodge Arrested Before Reaching Mexico." The news came from Alice, dated February 17, simply stating that Hughes had arrested Dodge "on a telegram from Governor Lanham, authorizing him to do so and hold him for requisition papers."[73] The Dodge saga continued to make headlines. The New York governor forwarded a requisition to Governor Lanham to have Dodge returned to New York. On February 19 Captain Hughes had his prisoner in Houston, but kept him in his personal custody. Naturally Dodge's attorneys prepared for another battle in court to keep him in Texas. They denied their client was planning to enter Mexico. In spite of various unofficial attempts to convince Hughes he should turn his prisoner over to them, Hughes was resolute and kept Dodge close until he received orders from Governor Lanham to release him to New York authorities.

Hughes kept his prisoner in comfortable quarters, not a remote dry camp in the brush but in what to Hughes must have been considered a "luxury hotel." Did Hughes have Dodge in handcuffs all the time? That is unknown, but he did not lose his prisoner. During this period he had time to catch up on some correspondence. One letter to the Honorable W. W. Turney of El Paso is revealing, as it shows he was considering a change in his career, although we do not know specifically what other position Hughes had in mind. The position would pay as much if not more than his captain's pay, but Hughes only indicated he would consider the offer. "Now what I want to ask you is for your opinion of the future of the Ranger Force, as that will have something to do with my accepting the new position," Hughes wrote. He expressed his opinion to Turney that the Ranger Force had plenty of friends in Alice, Brownsville, and Corpus Christi, in his district in other words. "I am getting along smoothly in my District—Have made lots of friends and have done lots of good work," he continued, but there was "lots of work layed [*sic*] out ahead of me to be done. Rangers are badly needed in my District." Now he allowed a moment of self-praise: "I have caught every band of thieves that I have started after and have every thing coming my way." He confided in Turney that if the Ranger Force was "going to be kept up" he would not want the new position, "even if it pays a little more." It is obvious Hughes was considering the new position seriously; if he did accept it he realized he would be required to live in Mexico, "I expect at Monterey [*sic*]." As for the reason he was in Houston: "I suppose you have read about the Dodge case. I still have him a prisoner and we have rooms at the [Rice] Hotel. He is a sociable old fellow and we like him."[74] Of course Turney was aware of the Dodge case, as it was front-page news.

Ultimately Dodge was returned to New York where his testimony convicted the corrupt attorney Abraham H. Hummel of suborning perjury. Hummel was ultimately sentenced to one year in prison, and disbarred.[75] This was one arrest by Hughes that resulted in national publicity because of the subsequent legal battles in New York. Hughes no doubt paid little attention to the matter after Dodge was placed on a ship to return him to New York.

Meanwhile, closer to home, Daniel S. Booth, editor of the *Alice Echo*, gave continuous attention to the activities of Captain Hughes and his Rangers, as nearly every issue of the *Echo* carried a report of some action, or even inaction. The June 30 edition reported Captain Hughes was back at headquarters "for a while"; it also reported that Sam McKenzie had left the previous week for Brownsville, and he had "fully recovered from his recent illness." In July Sgt. Tom M. Ross was back in town after "a trip up the country." In the August 4 edition the *Echo* reported Captain Hughes "left Monday for—somewhere. Rangers don't give out their destination in advance." Then in the next issue the reader learned that Earl R. Yeary returned on August 7 from a visit to his folks in Runge, Karnes County; he was quoted as saying "the cotton crop is about a failure in that section." In September Captain Hughes returned from Brownsville and Herff Carnes left for Floresville "on a visit to home folks." One envisions *Alice Echo* Editor Daniel S. Booth making a point to provide weekly news of the Rangers' activities.[76]

The new year of 1905 proved to be no different as Hughes and his men continued to receive positive publicity. On Christmas Day 1904, Herff Carnes and Milam Wright scouted in Starr County on the Rancho Nuevo. They arrested one Casimiro Garcia who had in his possession three head of mules, which were believed to be the property of Rulio Garcia, a Starr County rancher. The Rangers delivered the suspected mule thief to San Diego and turned him over to Sheriff Manuel

Rogers. He was able to give bond in the sum of $500 to await the action of the grand jury. The Rangers, the *Echo* reported, "were on the scout during Christmas, but say [they] do not mind that as the arrest made fully compensates them for the hardship endured and that they believe the arrest will lead to other important discoveries and arrests."[77]

In mid-January 1905, Editor Booth provided in his columns a history of the Rangers stationed at Alice, remarking that when the town was founded about sixteen years previously, it had been headquarters for a Ranger company. It was chosen for that purpose due to its central location and its railroads and telegraph lines, and "within easy reach of the various trails or routes usually traveled by outlaws, especially stock thieves making their way to Mexico or from that country to the interior of Texas." The first company was that of Capt. J. S. McNeel; then Capt. J. H. Rogers; then after he was removed to Laredo, Capt. J. A. Brooks "and his efficient ranger boys" were sent to Alice. Then Brooks's company was sent to Laredo and Hughes's company was sent to Alice. Now Hughes's company was ordered to Harlingen, but "in all probability" Captain Hughes would have one or two men stationed there, just as his predecessors did. Booth concluded with additional praise: "These brave officers—and their records prove that they were fearless in the discharge of duty wherever stationed, were a terror to a class of outlaws that is fast disappearing or rather, perhaps, moving westward as the line of civilization advances toward the sparsely [*sic*] settled frontier.[78]

The attention continued, as in mid-March Editor Booth wrote:

Capt. J. R. Hughes returned from Austin Friday [March 10]. The headquarters of his ranger force were recently transferred from Alice to Harlingen, hence we do not see the genial and efficient ranger captain as frequently as formerly.[79]

In April Theodore Roosevelt, having being placed in the highest office due to the assassination of President McKinley in 1901, and recently elected in his own right, visited the state, which brought additional attention in the columns of the *Echo*. Editor Booth pointed out that Rangers Sam McKenzie and Milam H. Wright had left on

April 4 for Austin "to see Teddy," then in the middle of his eight years as president. The monthly return recorded that Captain Hughes and five men went to Austin to meet President Roosevelt, suggesting more than a mere sight of the country's chief executive.[80] Then in the following week attention was again brought to the Rangers, as in the "Personals" column this notice appeared:

> Capt. John R. Hughes, Sergt. Ross, W. C. Beach, Sam McKenzie and M. A. Wright [sic, M. H.] had the honor of being the only company of rangers on special duty on the occasion of the President's visit to San Antonio.[81]

Captain Hughes was visiting San Antonio to see the president, but another well-known lawman was there as well: Patrick F. Garrett, the man who broke up the Billy the Kid gang of Lincoln County, New Mexico. He was then the collector of customs at El Paso and was in San Antonio "upon the special invitation" of the president.[82] Judge Clarence Martin of Fredericksburg, who had expressed so well the satisfaction when Hughes's men assisted in keeping order at Gillespie County's district court, was also there. It may well have been an occasion for Hughes to renew acquaintance with many other lawmen, besides seeing the president, if not actually getting close enough to shake his hand.[83]

On May 14 McKenzie and Wright went from Brownsville to Corpus Christi "to keep peace on an excursion train." McKenzie, the monthly return noted, had been in Brownsville "all this month" at the request of the St. Louis, Brownsville & Mexico Railroad Company, keeping hack drivers and boys off of the cars.[84] This was in the beginning days of the railroad going from Corpus Christi; some individuals apparently felt they deserved a free ride.

In May 1905 Adj. Gen. John A. Hulen ordered another change in the makeup of the Ranger Force. General Order No. 1 now ordered Captain Hughes to move his headquarters from Alice to Austin; his territory of operations would be district one, which was all that part of the state east of the counties of Clay, Jack, Palo Pinto, Erath, Hamilton, San Saba, Mason, Gillespie, Kerr, Medina, Bandera, Atascosa, Live Oak, and San Patricio. He was "to proceed to Austin overland using wagons and teams" and then he was to "arrange to dismount his command as no mounts for it will be foraged at the State's expense after July 1, 1905, except for one mount for commanding officer."[85]

How much attention Hughes and his "efficient ranger boys" gave to the accolades in the *Alice Echo* is uncertain but probably very little. Hughes and his boys were more concerned with recovering stolen stock and capturing fugitives. In July Sam McKenzie with two deputy sheriffs of Cameron County recovered twenty-five head of stolen cattle that had been placed on the Henry Edd ranch, in Starr County, 160 miles from Brownsville. Investigation convinced Cameron County Sheriff Celedonio Garza that Edd had purchased the cattle, not knowing they had been stolen by Charles Dorsett. There were about fifty complaints against Dorsett. Whether Dorsett ever had to pay for his thievery is not recorded, but many ranchers were able to recover cattle stolen from their land. The *Herald* of Brownsville provided this concluding comment praising the Rangers as well as local lawmen: "Sheriff Garza and deputies and Captain Hughes and rangers have done some good work in recovering these cattle and the good citizens of Cameron county will duly appreciate their services."[86]

During the summer of 1905 there was nearly an overwhelming amount of work in the huge new area of Company D's responsibility. There were riots at Humble, north of Houston. In June Carnes and Wright arrested twenty men on various charges there. All were placed in the Harris County jail. On July 15 Captain Hughes went to Groveton, via Humble, to investigate matters there. Then on August 8 he was needed in Lampasas, one hundred miles northeast of Austin. On August 22 he needed to return to Groveton; he was there five days. And Carnes and Beach and new recruit W. O. Dale were still at Humble, making arrests. Then on October 2 (the September monthly return is missing), Hughes and two men with Adjutant General Hulen journeyed to Edna in Jackson County to protect a black man, known as Monk Gibson, from a mob intending to give him lynch rope justice. Gibson was suspected of an unusually brutal crime: Lora Conditt and four of her children were murdered on September 28, 1905. In addition, one of the four children, her oldest daughter, had been raped. Young Monk Gibson, a black field hand who worked on the farm, was suspected almost immediately, as he had blood on his clothes. While moving him from Edna to Hallettsville for safe keeping, he managed to escape from the guards. Gibson remained "at large" until October 9. Ultimately Gibson and another man, Felix Powell, were found guilty of the murders. Powell was legally hanged in 1907 in Victoria; Gibson was legally hanged in Cuero in 1908.[87]

During October Captain Hughes as well as Rangers J. C. White[88] and W. O. Dale[89] helped preserve order during the Gibson troubles. On October 20 Hughes settled accounts in Edna, and then on the twenty-sixth he went to Port Lavaca to assist the State Fish and Oysters Commissioner I. P. Kibbs. There were disagreements over paying taxes on oysters. Hughes returned to Austin on October 27, leaving W. O. Dale at Port Lavaca to assist Kibbs. He was there from October 24 to November 17 enforcing the law.

~ 10 ~

From East Texas to the Texas Panhandle

"CAPT. HUGHES . . . IS MORE THAN ANY OTHER, PERHAPS,
THE IDOL OF THE FORCE . . ."

— *Editor J. C. Howerton in the* Cuero Daily Record,
July 3, 1908

An urgent call for help from Wood County began the new year of 1906. Sheriff William J. Ray[1] had brought an accused murderer to the jail at county seat Quitman, a small community located in far east Texas. He had been held in the Dallas County jail while preparations were made for his trial. The sheriff feared a lynch mob would storm the jail; he understood completely what the mob would do once his prisoner was in its hands. Captain Hughes with three Rangers left Austin headquarters on January 3 to assist the sheriff in protecting his prisoner during his court proceedings. Not surprisingly the presence of Hughes and his three men prevented any mob violence, which was appreciated by Wood County authorities, especially the district judge. They were back in Austin on the thirteenth, having logged 531 miles in all. On the same day Robert W. Simpson, judge of the 7th Judicial District, wrote Governor Lanham to compliment the work of Captain Hughes and his men. "I desire to thank you for your prompt action in sending the Rangers to this place," he began. There had been no trouble, and of course maybe there would not have been anyway, but, he added, "I feel sure that the presence of Capt. Hughes and his efficient force had a very desirable effect." Simpson continued: "Permit me to say in behalf of Capt. Hughes and each of his men here, that they are estimable gentlemen, and have so conducted themselves that every one is complimenting them." The judge believed the service of the Rangers would not be needed again, and expressed to the governor the idea that the Rangers were "more efficient" than the local militias. In addition he recommended the force should be increased and perpetuated "as long as mob violence is threatened in this state."[2] Mob violence was a very real fear in Texas, as elsewhere in the country. Many blacks suffered at the hands of mobs, as did suspected horse thieves in many western counties.

In early January 1906, a strike at the Humble Oil field near Houston caused great concern among the officials. Oil had been discovered in 1904 resulting in a boom which brought in a great influx of men of all types, causing the population to grow in excess of 10,000 by 1905. But by 1906 production declined, and with it unrest increased among the workers. The strike did not remain peaceful; W. H. Lyne of the Producers Oil Company feared violence and called for help. Captain Hughes sent three Rangers to maintain peace: Herff Carnes, J. C. "Doc" White, and Milam Wright. This trio prevented violence until the strike ended. Lyne sent Hughes a letter expressing his heartfelt appreciation, thanking him "for the admirable conduct of your men at this place during the recent strike troubles here." Lyne continued with his praise: "We feel that the cool, determined stand made by Rangers Carnes, White and Wright on the night of the visit of the mob to the company's property, was the means of stopping the intended destruction of property." Further, Lyne was relieved the Rangers had accomplished their mission without bloodshed. Most noteworthy of all perhaps was Lyne's statement that "it takes more than what is commonly called nerve for the three men to face a mob of 300 determined men, intent on destroying property." Fine words indeed from a relieved company superintendent.[3]

During the late 1880s, the decade of the 1890s, and the early years of the twentieth century, John R. Hughes had little time to consider events taking place in East Texas. Now that his territory included East Texas he became fully aware of the history of the place. Among the bloodiest incidents was the smoldering feud between two related families, which had begun during the 1898 sheriff's race in Columbus, Colorado County, a small community located some fifty miles west of Houston. Occasional killings and attempts to kill kept the trouble alive until the Rangers arrived and established order. The two factions most directly involved were the Reese and Townsend families and their supporters, resulting in a conflict often called the Reese-Townsend Feud, or also known as the Colorado County Feud. According to the late Colorado County historian Bill Stein, who spent a lifetime gathering, promoting, and writing about events in Colorado County's history, the feud began when the 1898 sheriff's race pitted the incumbent sheriff—Sam H. Reese—against his one-time deputy, Larkin Hope. The two men were related by marriage and had once been friends. Former senator Mark H. Townsend had backed the winning candidate in each of the previous nine elections, but now dropped his support of Reese and endorsed candidate Hope. This act practically guaranteed a Hope victory, but on August 3, 1898, an unknown assailant shot and killed Larkin Hope in downtown Columbus, the county seat. Suspicion fell on Jim Coleman, a close friend of Walter and Herbert Reese, sons of Sheriff Sam Reese. The influential Townsend now picked a new candidate—a brother-in-law, Will T. Burford—who won the election, amidst strong feelings between those who had backed one candidate over the other.

The community was peaceful for about nine months, but on March 16, 1899, Sam Reese lost his life in a gun battle near where Larkin Hope had been shot. Among the individuals involved in the shooting on the town square were Will D. Clements, Marion Hope, Mark Townsend, and Sam Reese. The victims included Reese and two bystanders, Charles Boehme, killed instantly by a stray bullet, and an infant son of Mayor Williams, little Johnny Williams. Had Reese provoked the very fight in which he was killed? Perhaps, but as typical of family feuds all over Texas and other states, his sons vowed vengeance. At least five more gunfights took place during the following years, in which at least five men were killed and several others wounded. The dead included Dick Reese, brother of Sam Reese, along with his buggy driver; Sheriff

Burford's son Arthur; Hiram Clements, brother of Will D. Clements; and Jim Coleman. The court never convicted anyone for these killings.[4]

The event that drew Captain Hughes into the Colorado County troubles occurred on June 30, 1906. About eleven o'clock in the morning, "after enjoying a period of several months tranquility from the deadly popping of the six-shooter, . . . Columbus was again brought to the front as the scene of a pitched battle between opposing factions." The incident began earlier that morning when Marion Hope and Herbert Reese got into a fist-fight in which Reese "got the worst of it." To no one's surprise Reese went home and got his brother, Walter Reese, and now with deadly weapons in hand they approached the downtown area where they expected Hope to be. In the interim Hope had armed himself and was waiting with a shotgun. These men did not miss with their shotguns: when the shooting stopped Herbert and brother Walter Reese both were wounded; Hiram Clements was mortally wounded, although it was said he did not fire a shot in the melee. Dr. Joseph F. Lessing, a brother-in-law of the Reese brothers and a half-brother of Marion Hope, was charged with the murder of Hiram Clements.[5] Commented the editor of the *La Grange Journal*, in neighboring Fayette County, reporting on the "deplorable event": "It is to be regretted that after the public had been led to believe that all was well, to have the old wound bleeding again."[6]

Naturally Colorado County Sheriff Walter E. Bridge[7] knew he needed help if he intended to maintain any semblance of control. Nothing in his background prepared him to deal with feuding families; in 1900 he was a landlord, and did some farming as well. Now a bloody feud between two prominent families was taking place in the center of his town, and Sheriff Bridge knew whom to contact for help. On the seventeenth of July the sheriff met with District Judge Munford Kennon.[8] They discussed the troubles and concluded the state had to provide help. Sheriff Bridge sent the following message to Governor Lanham:

> Condition of affairs such here that local authorities cannot handle the situation. Send four or five rangers at once.

Governor Lanham answered favorably:

Will comply with your request and send rangers on first train.[9]

Four Rangers reached Columbus the night of July 17: Captain Hughes, Sergeant Tom M. Ross, and two privates, Herff A. Carnes and James C. "Doc" White. What they did exactly is not detailed in the records, but certainly their first action was to let the townspeople see they were there to keep the peace. Certainly they were present at the mass meeting called by concerned citizen Joseph J. Odom on the morning of the nineteenth. The purpose of the meeting was "to express the disapproval of the citizens of the town of the existence of the feud and to devise means to prevent further fighting within the limits of the town." A circular, no doubt read by Hughes, was distributed to inform the citizens, which we have today as it was later printed in the *Mercury* of the neighboring town of Weimer:

> Mass Meeting—Deploring the existing conditions in Columbus, it is desired and earnestly urged that every good citizen of this city assemble in the court house at 9 o'clock in the morning, Thursday, July 19, then and there to discuss ways and means for the betterment and relief of the depression which has settled upon all our people. Therefore, all citizens interested in the good and welfare of the town are not only warmly asked to attend, but they will be expected to be present.— Many Citizens.[10]

Such violence on the main streets of an eastern community, far from what many may have still considered the frontier and far from Hughes's former area of enforcement, provided great copy for other newspapers. The *Dallas Times Herald* stated that the citizens of Colorado County had "decided that the feudists at that section must put up their guns. A wise act, and one that commends itself to every loyal Texas citizen." The *Express* of San Antonio also commented on the situation, that if the feudists did not cease their violence, then "the citizens of Columbus should 'put up' their feudists in a safe place where their guns can no longer make it impossible for law-abiding people to preserve the peace."[11]

Captain Hughes was called back to Austin, but he ordered Ranger Milam H. Wright, then in Navasota, to join his men at Columbus; Sergeant Ross remained there until July 21 and Private Carnes for five more days before being called back to Austin. Hughes had been away from headquarters four days; Herff Carnes had been out nine days. But Hughes knew the trouble was not over and sent J. C. White to Columbus on August 23. To assist him in keeping order at district court Carnes and Wright joined White on September 9.[12]

Ranger White remained in Columbus until October 10, guaranteeing the peace would hold for a period of two months. White then was ordered to Karnes City in Karnes County, "to keep peace at a murder trial."[13] Meanwhile, a mob threatened to storm the jail and lynch a prisoner in McLennan County, a hundred miles north of Austin. Captain Hughes and Sergeant Ross rushed to county seat Waco to assist Sheriff George W. Tilley[14] in protecting the black prisoner from the mob. Instead of simply dispersing the mob and ordering the would-be lynchers to go on about their business, Hughes delivered his prisoner to Austin for safe keeping, knowing the Travis County jail was more secure and there were sufficient officers to prevent a mob from storming the jail. Milam H. Wright left his duties in Houston to provide assistance to Captain Hughes and Sergeant Ross. This action of saving the prisoner's life forced Hughes to be away from headquarters from September 19 through September 27.[15]

Captain Hughes and three men then started to Waller County to assist authorities in keeping the peace during an election. While there, an assassination occurred in Rio Grande City, on the Rio Grande in Starr County, causing Hughes to leave the Waller County situation and assist authorities there. Stanley Welch, judge of the 28th Judicial District and known as the "Silver Tongued Orator of the Southwest," a resident of Corpus Christi, was in Rio Grande City investigating charges of voter fraud. It was alleged that political clubs were supplying Mexican citizens in Starr County with poll tax receipts and insisting that they be allowed to vote. Judge Welch wanted to be there on election day. During the night of November 5 he was murdered while he slept.[16]

Hughes left two men in Hempstead, Waller County, while he and one other Ranger returned to Austin the next day; then on the eighth he and J. C. White with Ivan Murchison[17] scouted down in Starr County with the sheriff, helping to keep the peace and investigate the assassination. Ten days later Hughes with newly elected Starr County Sheriff Deodoro Guerra, traveled as far as Mier, Mexico, to further investigate the Welch case. Guerra had been elected on November 6; other than taking the oath of office this investigation of Welch's assassination may have been his first official duty.[18] On December 4 Hughes had to return to Austin to make out a report on the work Company D had accomplished in November, then he returned to Rio Grande City. On December 26 Hughes with Ranger Charles B. Brown[19] returned to Austin. They arrived on the twenty-ninth, ready for anything in the new year.[20]

Now Captain Hughes assigned Ranger White and new recruit Desiderio Perez[21] to continue working the Welch case. In addition they were to scout to the small community of Samfordyce in southwest Hidalgo County, scarcely a mile from the Rio Grande. White and Perez crossed the river, scouting farther down into Mexico, where they arrested "some Mexicans for theft of horses" and delivered them to the jail at Rio Grande City. The Rangers had been out scouting for five days in their search. The arrested men had been "for a long time a source of annoyance to the citizens of Starr and Zapata Counties by stealing horses and cattle," Hughes reported. He added, "their capture was a great relief."

Calls were continuous for Ranger assistance. Herff A. Carnes and M. H. Wright were sent to Karnes City to help Sheriff E. Calloway Seale preserve peace during the meeting of district court, a murder having recently been committed "that had caused considerable feeling and about which trouble might have arisen at anytime." One wonders if Hughes and his men ever had the chance to sit down and just relax.

Then in April 1907, trouble flared up in Groveton in Trinity County, some 150 miles northeast of Austin. Attorney at law R. O. Kinley[22] shot Texas Ranger James D. Dunaway of Company B.[23] On April 26 Ranger Dunaway telegraphed Governor Thomas Mitchell Campbell the following from Groveton: "Send rangers at once. Waylaid and shot all to pieces. Not serious." Governor Campbell no doubt wondered how a Ranger could be shot "all to pieces" but yet be "Not serious." His wonderment certainly increased when he received the following from Sheriff George H. Kirkwood of Trinity County: "H. L. Robb and Jim Dunaway assassinated. Shots fired from R. O. Kinley's building upstairs." The governor discussed the matter with Sheriff Kirkwood by telephone, but now the sheriff said that Dunaway "might recover, but there was no hope for Robb."

R. O. Kinley himself sent a telegram later that same day: "Dunaway came in today and I had to shoot him. Send Capt. Hughes immediately." Governor Campbell sent Captain Hughes, along with Sergeant Carnes and Private Wright. Hughes explained simply that they were there "to assist the sheriff in keeping the peace, there having been a shooting at that place." The report that Dunaway had been assassinated was premature, although Kinley's intent was to kill him. That H. L. Robb had been shot as well was accidental. Kinley was able to give bond in the amount of $2,000 and gave an explanation of the shooting. He reportedly explained that "for several years" he and Ranger Dunaway had "been unfriendly and that Dunaway has shown a disposition to seek trouble. He said a few nights ago at Trinity he met Dunaway on the street and Dunaway jumped on him and beat him." Supposedly Dunaway also threatened him with his life if he said anything about it.[24]

This shooting grew out of an incident from the previous fall when a detective named Myers was murdered as he was gathering evidence against various bootleggers. After presenting his findings in the form of testimony at the Groveton courthouse he was ambushed that evening while walking home. Howard L. Robb was the prosecuting attorney at Trinity County when Myers was killed. Kinley, who had defended the alleged bootleggers, now admitted he had shot Dunaway. Carnes and Wright arrested four men in connection with the shooting of Robb and Dunaway: R. O. Kinley, Carrol Kinley, R. E. Minton, and Ollie Freeman.

Kinley's shotgun blast had severely wounded Dunaway, nine balls hitting him in the abdomen alone. He was taken into Trinity on stretchers, his wounds dressed, and he was sent home to rest. Hughes returned to Austin on May 1, confident that Carnes and Wright could keep the peace at Groveton.

Later that week Carnes and Ranger Parker M. Weston, a young man from Fort Bend County[25] recently enlisted in Captain Brooks's Company A and now detached to work with Hughes's company, were still with the recovering Dunaway "while he was sick from wounds received at Groveton." Apparently they feared another assassination attempt while he was in bed and virtually helpless. Dunaway remained in Trinity until he was sufficiently recovered to return to Llano, his home county. The Rangers stayed with him until they reached Austin, then he continued on alone.

In May Captain Hughes moved the Alpine camp to Marfa, getting the new headquarters established by May 24. Hughes may have felt more comfortable back in West Texas, working in surroundings he had already spent years scouting. On June 6 Captain Hughes and Sergeant Carnes with J. C. White and C. B. Brown began a thirteen-day scout down to Candelaria on the edge of the Rio Grande, via L. C. Brite's[26] Ranch, then on to Ruidosa, Hot Springs, Presidio, and Shafter Mines. On his return to Marfa, Hughes wrote, absent proper grammar:

> This scout was made to learn the new men of Co "D" the country and to learn the condition of the country generally in regard to lawlessness. We found the country to be in a fairly good condition.[27]

On June 21 Captain Hughes went to Fort Hancock, El Paso, and Ysleta, "for the purpose of laying plans to capture a Mexican who is wanted in New Mexico and is supposed to be hiding in Old Mexico and comes across to the American side sometimes." On June 25 Carnes with former Company E Ranger and now Presidio County Sheriff M. B. Chastain[28] brought back a Mexican prisoner, Santano Filamona, possibly the subject of Hughes's scout. On July 18 Hughes, Carnes, J. C. White, and Alexander Ross,[29] who had re-enlisted on July 9, scouted down to the Rio Grande to the mining district to determine where a detachment was needed. They went by Lajitas, Marfa, and Mariposa Mines, Los Chisos Mines, Dallas Mines, and the Big Bend Mines, then over several cattle ranches on this eight-day scout.

There was great variety of action during the summer months. On July 28 Hughes and Carnes went to Valentine in response to citizens' request "to keep down drunken rows during pay day." They were back at headquarters on July 30.[30] On August 13 Hughes was in El Paso consulting with Sheriff Florence J. Hall[31] as to the best place to station a detachment of Rangers. Then he was on to Sierra Blanca to investigate the report of freight cars being robbed. On the nineteenth he and Sheriff M. B. Chastain with L. C. Brite investigated a report that thieves were stealing Brite's cattle and driving them into Mexico. He then went to Del Rio in Val Verde County as there was "trouble over the office of County judge." He then stopped at Comstock and spent a few days with the detachment stationed there. He was out six days and had covered a total of 584 miles.

On August 27 Sergeant Carnes went to Van Horn "to assist local officers in keeping the peace at an Old Settlers Reunion." [32] Were the "old" settlers still young enough to create a disturbance that the local officers could not control? The "one riot, one Ranger" is a myth, but apparently "one old settlers reunion, one Ranger" was reality. At the reunion Carnes did arrest a man named McClellan for disturbing the peace and delivered him to the El Paso jail, but whether he was an "old settler" or not is unknown. Perhaps this was the core of the concern for a Texas Ranger to be present at the Old Settlers Reunion?

On September 1, 1907, John T. Priddy[33] and R. E. Bryant were enlisted in Company D. Four days later Hughes went to Valentine where he arrested two men for murder: A. B. Medley and C. F. Barber. They were placed in the El Paso jail. On the fifteenth Hughes went from Marfa to Santa Fe, New Mexico, at the request of Judge Van Sickle of Alpine, "to accompany a witness who was afraid to go on alone." This took four days and covered 684 miles.[34]

In October Hughes and Priddy scouted down on the Rio Grande; on November 30 R. E. Bryant was discharged at his own request, no reason given. Then Hughes went to Marfa and consulted with the sheriff at Comstock, then moved headquarters on to Ysleta. On December 12 Rangers Milam H. Wright and J. T. Priddy started from Comstock to investigate a report of cattle being stolen from the J. M. Talley ranch. They spent several days at Boquillas and in different mining camps in the Chisos Mountains. They were back in Comstock on December 31, having covered 540 miles.[35]

The troubles in Groveton forced Hughes to return in January 1908. He left Ysleta to first appear in Laredo in a murder case and then traveled from Laredo via Austin and Houston to Groveton to attend court as a witness. He was kept busy in the various courts, not returning to Ysleta until February 5, away a total of twenty-eight days. He had traveled 2,194 miles in all. While Captain Hughes was busy in court Sergeant Carnes was assisting the G.H. & S.A. Railroad district superintendent to guard the train between El Paso and Valentine. After four days of guard duty Carnes was relieved on the twenty-third by Alexander Ross.[36]

Strangely the monthly report of February does not describe any activities of Captain Hughes. He did not return to headquarters until February 5, and the rest of the month seems to have been quiet for him. But elsewhere M. H. Wright was working in Del Rio, consulting with Sheriff John F. Robinson about how best to deal with cattle thieves. While there Wright learned of two Mexicans stealing a cow from an area ranchman. Wright with a deputy sheriff began pursuit, tracking them into Edwards County, then back into Val Verde County. There they arrested the pair and delivered them into jail at Del Rio. In El Paso a prisoner had to be moved from the jail to Taylor County on a change of venue for murder. Ranger F. M. Ascarate[37] and a deputy sheriff delivered the prisoner to Abilene. On February 26 Private C. A. Craighead investigated a report of the robbery of boxcars at Valentine. There Craighead arrested a black man and delivered him to jail in Fort Davis, but he managed to escape.[38]

Just how much detective work Captain Hughes contributed in the investigation of the murder of Judge Stanley Welch cannot be ascertained, but on March 17 he traveled from Ysleta to Rio Grande City as a witness. Antonio Cabrera was charged with the murder of Welch. The trial was to take place in Cuero, DeWitt County, on a change of venue from Starr County, and was set to begin in June. Hughes now returned to Ysleta. That same month M. H. Wright and J. T. Priddy scouted on Devil's River to investigate cattle theft. They determined the identity of the guilty party, arrested him, and delivered him to the Del Rio jail where he was indicted. On March 21 Wright started on a scout after a man wanted in Val Verde for arson. The man was captured near Ozona, and delivered to the Del Rio jail.[39]

In April Captain Hughes, Sergeant Carnes, and Private Priddy began a lengthy scout, starting from Ysleta on the fourteenth with their hack, mules, and saddle horses to go down into the cattle country around Sierra Blanca, Valentine, and Marfa seeking signs of cattle thieves and lost cattle and horses. On April 3 Wright and Craighead followed a man who was wanted at Del Rio for forgery; they arrested him about four miles from Langtry and delivered him to the Del Rio jail.[40] Being that close to Langtry did they perhaps stop into old Judge Roy Bean's Jersey Lilly Saloon? If so they could only talk about the beginning myths about Bean, the "Law West of the Pecos." Judge Roy Bean had died on March 16, 1903, just over five years before.[41]

Company D's activity in May was sparse, as Hughes reported "During this month the members of Co. 'D' made twenty-three scouts." He reported no arrests or recovery of stolen stock or property. June proved to be a busy month, however. Captain Hughes and Sergeant Carnes left Ysleta on June 8 to attend court in Houston as witnesses in a murder case. M. H. Wright joined them at Comstock. After six days in court Carnes and Wright returned to camp but Captain Hughes was needed in Cuero to attend the trial of Antonio Cabrera. The trial proved to be an example of an early twentieth-century media circus, the *Victoria Advocate* only one of numerous newspapers finding it great copy. The *Advocate* headlined its page one article, "A Strong Case Against Cabrera" in large bold type, reporting there was much interest in the trial.

During the trial of Cabrera, Monk Gibson, a convicted multiple murderer, was waiting to be legally hanged in Cuero. The *Advocate* managed to tie the two cases together, pointing out that the state had made "a strong case against" Cabrera, and "Cuero may have another neck tie party." To witness an execution of Gibson and Cabrera was an event not to be missed by the morbid, and the reporting would undoubtedly sell many copies of the newspapers. Cabrera's victim, Judge Welch, was well-known in Victoria and Cuero, Victoria and DeWitt counties respectively, and if Cabrera was found guilty, "as the evidence seems to conclusively show, he will be given the extreme penalty." Although the prosecution summoned seventy-five witnesses, only eighteen were placed on the stand. Captain Hughes, Thomas M. Ross (only named captain on February 1, 1907) and A. Y. Baker were three of those who testified. Besides those three Rangers, others testifying were identified as "prominent citizens and officials of the Rio Grande Country." Testimony in the Cabrera case was finished on July 1. The citizens who had wished for another "neck-tie party" were disappointed however, as the jury, finding Cabrera guilty, assessed his punishment at life imprisonment instead of death by hanging.[42] Hughes and his men may have remained in Cuero until July 2, until assured there would be no trouble. Rangers Captain Ross, R. E. Smith, Sam McKenzie, and Crosby Marsden left for their headquarters the evening of July 2. James C. Howerton, editor-publisher of the *Cuero Daily Record*, found the presence of the Rangers an excellent opportunity to praise their work[43] :

> They have been here since the Cabrera trial began, quietly watching the situation and their presence doubtless had a tendency to keep down trouble between the opposing factions. If there is any man the average Mexican stands more in awe of than another it is a ranger. Their calmness in danger, their ready grasp of the situation and their ability to place a bullet just where wanted, conspire to render them a terror to the excitable or the cowardly. There are only thirty-two rangers on the state force, divided into four commands of eight each.

Then the four captains and their location were noted, and Howerton continued with attention given to Hughes:

> Capt. Hughes was here the greater part of the trail [*sic*, trial] of Cabrera. He is more than any other, perhaps, the idol of the

force and not one of them but would go to him at any time at any risk. . . . [Captains Ross and Hughes] are quiet men and know no fear. In fact, a coward would soon be run out of the ranks. At the same time the ranger must be cool under all circumstances. A rash man would cause trouble quickly. As a consequence, two or three rangers will quiet a disturbance quicker than twenty ordinary men. The evil doers, at least, know what a ranger is.[44]

Hughes was not able to return to camp until July 6, after being out twenty-eight days and traveling a total of 1,824 miles.[45] While he was in Cuero, Ranger Wright was on the train passing Del Rio when Sheriff Robinson requested him to stop and assist him in preventing Mexicans from crossing the Rio Grande from Del Rio to Las Vacas, Mexico, "for the purpose of joining the Revolutionists." Craighead had earlier come down at Sheriff Robinson's request, so there were now Robinson, Wright, Craighead, as well as several deputies and custom inspectors present. Several on the Mexican side fired twenty-five or thirty shots at them, but they did not return fire, as the parties who did the firing were "well hidden behind an adobe wall."[46]

In July Captain Hughes with Carnes and new recruit Ray E. King[47] spent most of the month on two different scouts: first to Jeff Davis and Presidio counties, out sixteen days and traveling 398 miles. Then on July 25 the same three scouted from Chocar up through the Diablo Mountains to the 2 Ranch, then through Apache Canyon to the Sierra Oscura and up near the Salt Lake, and then to Sierra Blanca and Ysleta, out eleven days and traveling 350 miles. Milam Wright and Charles Craighead in the meantime scouted from Comstock to Devil's River seeking some stolen goats, seventeen of which they recovered and returned to the owner. On the thirtieth Wright and one other scouted to Shumla Station and found tools belonging to the railroad. They returned the tools and arrested one man for the theft and delivered him to the Del Rio jail.[48]

After such heavy traveling in August, the return of September shows Captain Hughes consulting with William B. Anthony of the State Land Office in Austin and Presidio County Sheriff M. B. Chastain, "in regard to trouble that was brewing over settlement on state lands." They were able to make "arrangements that prevented any trouble over State Land."[49]

The remainder of the year was relatively quiet for Hughes, but for Alexander Ross, Sergeant Dunaway of Company B—sufficiently recovered from his shotgun wounds—Sam McKenzie, and a justice of the peace from Shafter Mines, excitement was at a high level in late October. On the twenty-eighth the quartet scouted from Shafter Mines to San Antonio Canyon in the Chinati Mountains to arrest S. W. Wright who had been charged with killing a Mexican, as well as to hold an inquest on the body of the deceased Mexican. The arrest was peaceful but then about thirty-five armed Mexicans arrived and demanded the prisoner— intending to give him a "neck-tie party"—such as the Rangers had in their revenge hunt for the killers of Captain Frank Jones. "The Rangers refused to give him up," Hughes reported, "and it looked for a while like there was going to be war between the Rangers and the Mexicans." But then the Mexicans backed off and the prisoner was delivered to the jail in Shafter. He was later taken to the jail in Marfa.[50]

The young Frank M. Ascarate did accomplish something while a Ranger, as he and Craighead assisted an El Paso County deputy sheriff at Sierra Blanca. They arrested four men charged with theft of cattle and horses, recovering six head of stolen horses and two stolen saddles. Rather than being satisfied with that, they continued to work on the case, and were out while Hughes prepared his return, "at present out after more stolen stock which they expect to recover." Hughes stressed that the "band of men have been depredating for a long time; they are quite notorious and we think we shall be able to break them up this time." No names of gang members were given.

That month's return contained some rare comments by Hughes on the quality of people who made up his district. "The majority of the ranchers in this district are good citizens and are on the side of law and order" he began, noting that although the thieves and murderers were "few as compared to the number of people" in the area, "still the country's being so sparsely settled, rough and mountainous [its nature] affords thieves an opportunity to escape." He believed that every sheriff in the El Paso district was friendly toward the Rangers, and often called on them for assistance. "Most of the sheriffs are Ex-Rangers; and while they are all good officers, their counties are so large and so thinly settled that they need the Rangers to help work them."

Hughes continued with commenting on a movement that concerned him greatly. He had noticed in the newspapers that one of the representatives-elect was preparing a Civil Service Law, which he intended to apply to state, district, and county officers. Hughes wrote: "I hope that the Ranger Force be exempt, if this law is passed; for the reason that the majority of the Rangers have spent so much time out on the range learning horsemanship, workmanship, trailing and reading brands that their scholarship has been very much neglected." Hughes gave an example of what concerned him. Several years before, the federal authorities tried putting their Mounted Inspectors of Customs under Civil Service, and "found it such a failure that it was abandoned." The anecdotal incident: a herd of cattle had been smuggled across the river in the Big Bend Country. The inspectors knew of the theft but "were at a loss to know how to find them, when some ranchman told them to get a Ranger to trail them up. This they did, taking a man from my camp at Marathon." They took the Ranger to the place where the cattle had crossed about three weeks prior; he took up the trail and followed it about 120 miles and found the cattle. The Ranger remained unidentified, but Hughes recalled him, as the Collector of Customs appointed that Ranger to be a Mounted Inspector, "regardless of the Civil Service." That Ranger was still on the force and "is one of the best Mounted Inspectors on the Rio Grande."

Hughes concluded his lengthy report by stating there were more calls for help than he could possibly fill, pointing out: "I could find places for twice as many men as I have in my company." He added that he hoped the Legislature would raise the pay of the sergeants and privates so that they would not "always be looking for something better, and leave the Service when they find a better paying position."[51] He knew of what he spoke, as many of his former Rangers were now sheriffs or Inspectors for the Customs.

One important crime in El Paso that Captain Hughes certainly investigated, although he left no report of his findings, was the mysterious killing of Mannen Clements, occasional constable of the county and occasional bad man. Hughes had met him years before during the Frazer-Miller Feud in Pecos City, he being one of the three men arrested in the conspiracy to kill Sheriff George A. Frazer. Clements was shot in the back of the head the night of December 29, 1908, in the popular Coney Island Saloon. The headlines screamed "No Arrests Made" and "Police Are Mystified" and the mystery was never solved, although there were numerous theories as to the identity of the assassin. Ironically his father-in-law, James Brown Miller, intended to determine who was guilty of killing Clements and then kill him. But Miller was unable to avenge the death of young Clements, as he himself was lynched before he could determine who the guilty party was. In April 1909, Miller and three associates were taken from their jail cell in Ada, Oklahoma, and strung up in an old livery barn for a murder he committed there. Although Hughes's name does not appear in the voluminous newspaper reports of Clements's assassination, he may have spent part of January investigating. His report for January indicates he made frequent trips to El Paso to consult with ranchmen and authorities.[52]

Hughes was again concerned with potential train robbers during the month of March; he consulted with the district superintendent of the G.H. & S.A. Railroad and sent Rangers down the tracks to investigate robberies of boxcars. Rangers Wright of Company D and Sergeant J. A. Dunaway of Company B both worked as quarantine guards at Del Rio in Val Verde. They worked the quarantine twenty-four days.[53]

Captain Hughes certainly worked harder as he had fewer men and probably it seemed as if much of his time now, in 1909, was spent traveling from one point to another as well as finishing reports. In April he made four trips to El Paso to consult with the sheriff, no specific details provided as to what was the concern. Alexander Ross was discharged on April 16. On April 24 Hughes arrested S. L. Hackett for theft of horses at Ysleta and placed him in the El Paso jail. Then on April 30 Captain Hughes was needed at district court in Victoria. He reached Victoria on

May 2 and was there until May 9. Harry Moore had enlisted on May 1; then on May 22, Ray E. King re-enlisted. From June 3 to 8 Captain Hughes was in Barstow in Ward County as a witness in a murder case. On June 12 he began a lengthy scout, summarizing it as follows:

> Capt. Hughes and Privates King and Harry Moore started on scout down the Rio Grande on horseback, went via Fabens, Fort Hancock, Old Fort Quitman and old Barney's place, out up the old overland stage route through Quitman Canon to Red Light, and via Eagle Springs, Chocar, Lobo, Chispa, and Double Wells to Valentine, where I left King and Moore with the horses while I came to Ysleta on 20th out 12 days, traveled 350 miles.[54]

Perhaps this lengthy scout was in part to "learn" the recruits the country while looking for possible fugitives as well. July continued with frequent trips to El Paso "on Ranger business." A serious crime now occupied Captain Hughes's time with the report of a train wreck in July. On the twelfth he sent Sergeant Herff Carnes and C. A. Craighead to Aragon to investigate the wreckage. On July 14 they arrested three men—Pantelion Ramos, Rosolio Esquibel, and Taborcio Esquibel. The Rangers charged the trio with train wrecking in Presidio County and then placed them in the hands of the El Paso authorities. The next day, the fourteenth, Craighead arrested Francisco Ramos for the same offense; he was arrested at Valentine and then delivered to the El Paso jail.[55]

August and September were relatively quiet for the captain. His main action was traveling to Midland where he was called to testify in a murder case. But October proved to be a much busier month, as he was part of the planning committee for the significant visit of two presidents to El Paso: U.S. President William Howard Taft and Mexican President Porfirio Díaz. To some historians the meeting proved to be of no great historical significance, as one Taft biographer merely summed up the event with less than one paragraph.[56] However, for Presidents Taft and Díaz, and El Paso citizens especially, the meeting was of supreme importance. Taft hoped the meeting would strengthen President Díaz in the eyes of his own people, thus discouraging—hopefully—revolutionary activity. He also was aware of the billions of dollars of American capital invested in Mexico. Díaz, the aging dictator, wanted to impress the American people. Great expense and energy was expended by the many committees to observe the proper political protocol; among all the other factors of guaranteeing safety for the presidents, were such showmanship observances as draping every building in El Paso with red, white, and blue flags along with green flags representing Mexico.[57]

Most importantly for the city of El Paso, however, it was a very newsworthy event. Officials wisely believed they needed the presence of the Rangers, and Hughes was not merely present but was on one of more than a dozen committees preparing for the visit. The committees were determined by attorney and mayor Joseph U. Sweeney of El Paso and Mayor Felix Barcenas of Juarez. Real estate businessman Zachary T. White chaired the Public Safety Committee and had, besides Captain Hughes, lawmen Frank B. Simmons, Florence J. Hall, T. C. Lyons, and Col. Joseph F. Huston whom White delegated to work out the safety details. These lawmen planned together with the purposes of guaranteeing the safety of the two presidents as well as keeping the citizens safe. The presidential visit of Taft and Díaz lasted only one day, but it was the result of several weeks of hard work and careful planning.

Captain Hughes certainly made an impressive figure as he led the presidents' carriages through the controversial El Chamizal zone, that section of the city under dispute due to the changing bed of the Rio Grande. The Rangers rode along the alleys on either side of the streets where the presidents passed. Hughes had with him Rangers Herff Carnes, Charles Craighead, Harry Moore,[58] and Charles R. "Little" Moore. But there were many more guardians than those five: C. C. Hartley, sheriff at Del Rio, rode along with the Rangers. In addition there were over 200 men sworn in as deputy sheriffs and 250 extra police sworn in to protect the presidents. A similar amount of protection was provided President Díaz in the form of his elite military unit, soldiers known as *Zapadores*. Many of the visiting dignitaries and officials of the city, state, and nation attended a ball at Fort Bliss the evening of October 15. Present, among other notables, were Texas Governor Thomas M. Campbell

and Secretary of War J. M. Dickinson. The post hall was "prettily deco-
rated with the national colors while the infantry, cavalry and artillery
officers appeared in their regalia," and to further beautify the El Paso
evening, the "gold braid of the military was intermingled with the beautiful varicolored gowns of El Paso's society women," presenting in all "a
picture long to be remembered." There was no indication that any of
Captain Hughes's men who had spent so much energy preparing for the
visit attended this dress ball.[59]

Hughes in his monthly report summed it all up with few words:
"Capt. Hughes and all members of Co 'D' went to El Paso to assist
in protecting the two Presidents and to keep the Peace generally—
returned to Ysleta 17th some of the men came from Del Rio." Reading Hughes's report one might think that nothing out of the ordinary
had happened during the visit of the two presidents. Actually one of
Hughes's Rangers, Charles R. Moore, working with guard Frederick
Russell Burnham, prevented the assassination of one or both presidents.
What Hughes so calmly described as a pencil pistol was recognized as
an assassin's weapon, as it could be held in the palm of one's hand, out
of sight until the precise moment when the assassin chose to fire the
single shot. Private Moore, working with guard F. R. Burnham, noticed
a man acting suspiciously and held him defenseless, Moore grabbing his
arm while Burnham grabbed his wrist, revealing the weapon. Describing the "Mexican as an activist," the pair believed he may have intended
to shoot one of the two distinguished presidents, probably Díaz. The
man was jailed overnight, and after the presidents had gone on their
respective ways he was released, apparently as he had made no overt
act such as firing the weapon.[60] What could have been an embarrass-
ing international incident was prevented by the sharp eyes of two of
the hundreds of men acting as guards. Private Moore did not consider
his actions heroic at all, as Hughes obviously did, probably thinking he
was just doing his job. Company D at this time had an aggregate of six:
Captain Hughes, one sergeant, and four privates.[61]

After perhaps a day or so of resting men and horses after the grand
event, it was time to move camp again. Now Company D was ordered

to establish camp at Amarillo, over four hundred miles northeast of El Paso. On November 8 Hughes, with M. H. Wright, C. A. Craighead, and C. R. Moore, all began the work of exchanging the camp location with Company B who were to be stationed elsewhere. Exactly what date this was completed is uncertain, but certainly by mid-November. On November 23 Craighead and Moore were fully at work: the pair with Mr. Stewart, Special Agent of the Atchison, Topeka and Santa Fe Railroad, went to Pampa in Gray County where they arrested H. C. Satterwhite for murder. He was taken to Canadian and jailed. On December 15 Captain Hughes left Amarillo to go to Austin for a consultation with the adjutant general and Governor Campbell about work at Amarillo; he then went to San Antonio, as there were more men applying to become members of his Ranger Force.[62]

~ 11 ~

A Ranger in the Panhandle

"UPON COMING UP WITH THE HOWE'S [*sic*] . . . THEY
OPENED FIRE ON THE POSSE, AND IN THE FIGHT FOLLOWING
BOTH OF THE HOWE'S WERE KILLED."

— *Sgt. Herff A. Carnes, January 30, 1911, Scout Report*

Amarillo's newspaper, the *Daily Panhandle*, interviewed Captain Hughes as soon as possible and headlined the write-up as if the man had been totally silent previously: "Capt. Hughes of Rangers Talks" the sub-headline read, noting that he was a "Fine Type of the Real Texas Ranger of Olden Days." Hughes stated, with reference to Amarillo,

> I am thoroughly well pleased with Amarillo, and more so to note the quiet trend in the peace [police?] departments of the city and county. I am grateful to note that the local option situation is being cared for in a thorough manner by local officers. I hope and believe that they will continue in the course now outlined. I trust I shall not be forced to send a report to headquarters having on it a case of the class indicated. I am convinced that the local officers are equal to the task of caring for the policing of the city and the county, and shall not feel badly if the situation remains such that my force will not be compelled to make an arrest in this line. A blank report will not hurt me with the department.

Hughes continued, pointing out that he had been in the Ranger service for twenty-two years, and during those years had "manufactured" all

216

the reputation he desired. Thus, he assured the *Panhandle* reporter, "there will be no reputation plays, either by myself or my men. . . . Amarillo, so far as I am able to determine from the limited acquaintance with the city, is quiet and peaceable, with a promise for unbroken record of the same character." Hughes continued with his praise of the region as well as informing the reading public of his background. He pointed out that this was the first time he had been stationed away from the Rio Grande region, with the exception of the relatively brief stay in Austin. He noted the Panhandle region "appears to me to be a fertile and most desirable one. I am glad to say that I have been cordially received in Amarillo and that the Citizenship meets my highest expectation." Hughes knew he was presenting a positive image of himself and letting the *Panhandle* readers know he thought highly of them as a class. He noted he had already made "a little scout into the country" and with what he learned his knowledge and his appreciation of the Texas Plains and its people increased. The *Panhandle* editor described Hughes as "sociable and thoroughly posted in matters in his line, with a rather liberal knowledge of everyday affairs in general." He further noted that he was not interested in "petty work" and that he and his men much preferred "to face and conquer situations on a greater scale" such as the "old-time work of the rangers," and "taking care of the big cattle thieves and criminal cases where much was involved."[1]

A few weeks later, in early December, Captain Hughes received more positive publicity in the columns of the *Panhandle*. Described as a "splendid tribute," a petition addressed to the citizens of Amarillo and Potter County was prepared by El Paso citizens and sent to Amarillo and was then published in the newspaper. The petition in essence praised Captain Hughes and his men, stating the company had been in El Paso County for the previous two years and during that time "won the respect and regard of our people for their manly demeanor, sober conduct and absolute attention to official duties at all times." Further, the community of El Paso regretted the circumstances that caused the command to move elsewhere. The petition was signed by over forty El Pasoans, including Chief of Police R. F. Jenkins and his assistant chief W. J. Ten Eyck; Chief Deputy Sheriff R. E. Bryant; W. W. Turney;

Sheriff Florence J. Hall; and many other county and city officers. Most had known Hughes professionally as well as socially.[2]

In spite of Hughes's stated desire to be above the minor elements of law enforcement, he spent ten days between January 15 and 25 in Fort Worth hunting information on a murder, and then two days in Austin seeing the adjutant general in regards to the possibility of placing a detachment in Colorado City, the county seat of Mitchell County, over 200 miles south of Amarillo. Placing a detachment would be equivalent to placing one, or two men at the most, as the aggregate of Company D was then only six men. Possibly a man from a different company could also be placed there. Much of the initial work was perhaps "petty" in Hughes's mind. On January 20 Ranger Charles R. Moore scouted to Texico, a small community just inside the New Mexico border some hundred miles southwest of Amarillo, and arrested C. M. Swayne for robbing a boxcar. On January 21 household goods valued at $10 were returned, but it is not clear if this is what had been stolen from the boxcar or something else. No doubt Ranger Moore considered Texico close enough to Texas land to travel there and exert his authority. On January 24 Ranger Moore traveled to Fort Worth with Mrs. G. Hill to get physical possession of her child awarded her by the 47th District Court. He returned two days later, having traveled 668 miles by rail. No doubt this was one of the actions that Hughes would have preferred be accomplished by a county deputy sheriff, rather than a Ranger. Sergeant Carnes arrested L. B. Lancaster for "Falsely personating Ranger" and arrested one other man for rape. In all Hughes noted there had been arrests for vagrancy, disturbing the peace, and "gaming" in the month of January, certainly most of them what he considered petty violations of the law. With delivering prisoners, Captain Hughes and his men were becoming acquainted with the Potter County jail.[3]

On February 10 Captain Hughes and Sergeant Carnes were in Colorado City to determine if placing a detachment there was necessary. It was the largest city in the county and second only to Amarillo in the broader area; Colorado City could boast a population of over one thousand, a new public school, waterworks, and an electric plant, and the promise of continued growth, soon adding banks and a newspaper, the *Colorado Record*.[4] Then on February 23 Hughes started a trip to El Paso and Juarez at the request of the district attorney. A man named Bob Bishop had forfeited his bond in a felony case and he was also wanted before the Potter County Grand Jury to testify in a murder case. Regrettably, Captain Hughes did not find Bishop.

But, while there, due to the early stages of aviation development, Captain Hughes, like many others, took the opportunity to see Charles K. Hamilton, known as "the Bird Man," in action as he flew a bi-plane over the city's popular Washington Park. The presence of both Hughes and Hamilton was noted in the *Herald*, although the brief item was somewhat misleading as Hughes was not there solely to see Hamilton: "Capt. J. R. Hughes, formerly stationed at Ysleta with his ranger company, but now at Amarillo, is in the city to see Charles K. Hamilton, the bird man."[5] No details were provided on Hughes's official business, nor was he asked about what he thought of the "Bird Man."

No doubt Captain Hughes did miss El Paso and its environs, as he found work at Amarillo less rewarding. Now back in Amarillo, he had nothing worth reporting in March; and in early April he spent a day in Austin, then three days in Marlin, the seat of Falls County, reason not specified, and then was back in Amarillo on April 11. The only arrest he recorded was one made in Amarillo, that of a man "running a disorderly house." This character was also placed in the Potter County jail.[6]

May was quite different as Captain Hughes, Herff Carnes, Charles A. Craighead, and Charles R. Moore scouted with a hack, mules, and saddle horses down into scenic Palo Duro Canyon, then to Tulia in Swisher County. They were back in Amarillo by May 16. Two days later Captain Hughes "started at night" to Marlin, and was back in Colorado City on May 29. Sergeant Carnes, Craighead, and Moore were already there attending district court, assisting Sheriff G. B. Coughran in keeping the peace. The four Rangers were there to assist the sheriff from June 1 to 11, then on the eleventh left Colorado City.[7]

In July Captain Hughes left Amarillo for Austin to consult with the adjutant general, then journeyed to El Paso County. He assisted

Sheriff Florence J. Hall in keeping the peace at Fort Hancock and Ysleta during an election; then he continued on to Del Rio and then to San Antonio. He was back in Colorado City on July 26, having traveled 1,794 miles. Then three days later he returned to Amarillo. During his absence, Rangers Herff Carnes and Charles R. Moore had arrested L. S. Mast for embezzling the huge sum of $5,000. He was turned over to Sheriff Archie R. Anderson of Harris County. On the same day, July 6, Craighead and Harry Moore arrested C. Piatt in Dalhart for carrying a pistol as well as impersonating a Ranger. He was tossed into the Potter County jail. How curious it must have been to Hughes, as now in 1910 two men had been arrested for impersonating a Ranger, whereas in previous monthly returns this had never been recorded.[8]

One horrific incident occurred in July, which certainly affected Captain Hughes. The tragedy was part of the troubles in San Benito in Cameron County on the Rio Grande. On May 27 James Darwin, an engineer for the San Benito Land and Water Company, was shot down in cold blood. Authorities ultimately believed Jacinto Trevino was the guilty party, but he had crossed over into Mexico. Trevino returned to Texas in late July, but an informant supposedly tipped off the Rangers where he was. On the night of July 31, the Rangers formed a posse of ten men to make the arrest. It consisted of Ranger Quirl Carnes, brother of Sergeant Herff Carnes of Hughes's company; Pat Craighead, brother of Charles A. Craighead, also of Hughes's company; deputy sheriffs Ben Lawrence and Earl West; and six employees of the San Benito Company. After the initial call to surrender, there was gunfire: Deputy Lawrence fell, killed outright; Ranger Quirl Carnes received wounds that resulted in his death later that night. On his way to gather help, other lawmen accidentally shot Pat Craighead, giving him a serious wound in the left leg. The wound cost him part of his leg but he would continue to work. Herff Carnes and Charles Craighead went to San Benito to help with the funeral and care for the severely wounded Pat Craighead.[9] The fugitive Jacinto Trevino never was captured by Texas lawmen, and his fate remains unknown.

More unusual incidents occurred in the month of August, forcing Hughes to travel to attend to them. On August 3, Hughes, with Rangers

Pat Craighead, still a Texas Ranger even after the loss of his left leg in a gunfight. Note wooden leg held in his left hand. *From the Hughes Personal Photo Album, courtesy the Texas Ranger Hall of Fame & Museum, Waco, Texas.*

Charles R. Moore and Harry Moore (no relation), went back to Marlin in Falls County to attend the trial of Ben Wyatt, charged with murdering his wife. The murder had been committed in an adjacent county but moved to Falls County on a change of venue. Hughes remained in Marlin with his two men guarding the jail, as "a large number of men from an adjoining county . . . had declared their intention of lynching our prisoner." The mob was afraid to challenge the Rangers and the trial took place. The wife-murderer was convicted and sentenced to death. Due to the possibility of continued mob action, Hughes delivered the prisoner to the stronger Navarro County jail in Corsicana. Later Ben Wyatt escaped from that "stronger" jail.[10]

For the first time John R. Hughes had to deal with an aspect of the Ku Klux Klan, although the term used in the Panhandle area was "whitecapping," mob action really no different than the methods used by the Klan. He had dealt with mobs before, he or his men facing a group of men intending to commit violence on a prisoner. This time it was in the Panhandle town of Post City, in Garza County, over 300 miles west of Navarro County where Hughes had just saved a prisoner from a mob. The victim in this instance was County Attorney Martin Luther Harkey, who had been savagely whipped the night of August 10, about three miles from county seat Post City, today simply Post.

The details of what Attorney Harkey had experienced were reported in the *Amarillo Daily News*:

> [Attorney Harkey was] with Dr. Ponton, one of the leading physicians of Post City. . . . [and they were] returning from plover shooting on Cap Rock plateau. They had been out all day and in chasing flocks of the festive birds had gone further than they had expected. It was late when they turned their automobile towards home and it was nearing 10 o'clock, when they dropped down off the plateau into the valley in which Post City is located.[11]

The lights of Post City were visible when the automobile stopped, the engine apparently stalling out. As Harkey was in the passenger seat he volunteered to get out and crank the engine to start it up. After he gave it a few cranks, suddenly several men, dressed in white hoods and white shirts, "seemingly out of the ground," took Harkey, rendering him defenseless. At the same time they dragged Dr. Ponton out of the automobile. Both were dragged a ways off the road, their hands tied and their eyes blindfolded. The leader told Harkey he would be whipped, "within an inch of his life" and if he did not leave town he would be killed. Two men held Harkey so he would not fall, while another held the barrel of a pistol to his head, "while others lashed him with blacksnakes until the blood poured from his body."

The next day Harkey slipped out of town, presumably with his family,[12] fearing danger to them if left alone, and went to Big Spring, sixty miles south in Howard County. On August 12 Harkey telegraphed Gov. Thomas Campbell the following:

> Situation in Garza County serious[.] mob law prevails[.] people are waylaid and brutally beaten and driven from their homes through fear of death[.] anonymous letters with threats of violence sent through the mail[,] no peace officer will act. Send [Company] D Rangers at once[.] Wire answer to Big Springs, Texas.[13]

The governor informed Adjutant General James O. Newton, who ordered Captain Hughes to investigate. On the thirteenth Hughes responded from Amarillo that he would "go to Garza County on first train." He met Harkey at Big Springs and together they returned to Post City. Harkey said there were six men in the white capping group, while Dr. Ponton said there were twelve or fifteen. Hughes accompanied Attorney Harkey to Amarillo, then Harkey went to Channing to attend court. At this point Captain Hughes may have strongly suspected Dr. Ponton was not Harkey's friend but an accomplice to the white cappers.

At that point it appeared John R. Hughes was to be the legendary one Ranger to face one mob. Hughes was certainly aware that generally the "White Caps" operated at night, dressed in white hoods. He could just as easily prepared to investigate a case of "Ku Kluxing" as the intent of both the KKK and the white cappers was the same.

Captain Hughes with Rangers Charles R. Moore and Harry Moore traveled to Post City via automobile, arriving there on the fifteenth of August. Although only three years old, the town had a post office, a school, a bank, and a newspaper. Instead of having been born as an oil boom town, or a cattle town, the town was the creation of cereal king Charles W. Post. He intended it to be a model city, an example for the rest of the country to emulate.[14] He certainly had not expected acts of violence to a leading citizen, such as Attorney Harkey.

Perhaps Harkey suspected who had made up the party of white cappers, and may have shared his suspicions with Hughes, but the captain, in his report, did not indicate his process of determining who were the suspects. Hughes did realize that Dr. Ponton, who was riding with Harkey when he was attacked, was "a supposed friend, and at a lonely spot near the cap-rock, taken from the automobile by masked men armed with rifles, and severely beaten with switches, and warned to leave the country at once."[15] Hughes and the Moores determined who the white cappers were and on August 17 they arrested six men: Dr. A. Ponton, S. C. Wilkes Jr., W. A. Wilkes, Perry Crownly, Joe Smith, and H. B. Murray. Presumably Hughes initially suspected Dr. Ponton since the automobile conveniently stalled exactly where the hidden mob was. These six were turned over to Garza County Sheriff Oscar B. Kelley. Harkey believed the reason for the attack was that he had prosecuted "horsethieves, gamblers and other breakers of the law."[16] More likely Harkey's prosecutorial efforts had gotten too close to influential men of the community and this was their way of sending him the message to back off. The men did stand their trial before Judge J. N. Boren, but were found not guilty.[17]

Attorney Martin L. Harkey had good reason to locate his practice as well as his family elsewhere and he did. He next found the need for his legal services in distant Zavala County, several hundred miles south of the scene of his failed effort for justice. There in county seat Crystal City he continued his practice of general law, spending the remainder of his life there.[18]

Captain Hughes could not spend time pondering why the men he had arrested were found not guilty of the charges, as he had more work to do and more miles to travel. After a stop in Austin on September 5 he went to San Benito and Brownsville to determine if Rangers Craighead and Carnes should remain or go elsewhere. Both had scouted Cameron County in search of the men involved in the deadly gunfight resulting in the death of Carnes and the wounding of Craighead. Then he was back in Austin on the fourteenth where he and Adjutant General Newton along with Capt. John H. Rogers went to San Antonio to investigate reports of gambling in San Pedro Park. He gave no particulars in his monthly return, but he was back in Austin the next day.[19]

In the meantime matters were growing worse in Coahoma, some ten miles northeast of Big Spring, where men were feuding with their neighbors to the point of violence. Hughes, occupied with other matters and unable to go there himself, sent Charles Moore and Harry Moore "to keep the peace there in a Feud case," which they did. They found that five men had been shot down in the streets of Coahoma using rifles and shotguns. An innocent victim of the street shooting was a young girl returning home from school; she was hit in the face with birdshot. Men of both factions did not leave home without their weapons and peaceable citizens were fearful of being on the streets. Men were ambushed; witnesses were intimidated, and no one would assist the sheriff in helping to settle the feud.[20] Pvt. Charles R. Moore reported his activities as follows:

> [September 20] Started from Amarillo to Coahoma, on telegraph request of sheriff of Howard Co., to suppress feud in which five men had been shot. Arrived in Coahoma on the 21st, accompanied by Private Harry Moore. Disarmed all parties concerned in the trouble, and restored peace and quiet in Coahoma.

Over the next few days Moore and Sgt. Joseph L. Anders of Company C, Ranger Force, consulted with the sheriff and district attorney. On the twenty-third, Moore went to Big Spring to protect witnesses summoned to appear before the grand jury. Four days later he produced the evidence he and Harry Moore had gathered in the case. The next day he met B. Echols and Ab. Echols at their ranch and accompanied them to Big Spring "to protect them from an ambuscade." Then he and Harry Moore arrested three men: C. Black, T. J. Johnson, and J. L. Johnson. Charged with assault to murder, the three were turned over to Howard County Sheriff E. M. Mobley. Moore concluded his report: "Prisoners delivered to sheriff of Howard County. Arrested on Sept 29. Traveled 482 [miles]." Actually he had covered many more miles, but explained, "I dont know mileage from Austin to Amarillo." Captain Hughes was now there and remained in attendance during the trial of Clayton Black. Every person who entered the courtroom was searched and if carrying a weapon was disarmed. Hughes left Big Spring on October 6.[21]

An unfortunate incident happened in Brownsville on October 1, when Ranger Craighead was attacked by Valentine Noyala with a Bowie knife; Craighead killed the man in self-defense.[22] He then asked to be indicted, confident he would be cleared of any and all charges. Hughes wanted to be at the trial and he traveled from one end of Texas to the other to be there. Craighead stood his trial; his confidence in the legal system was assured when the jury was charged by the judge to acquit him, which it did without leaving the jury box.[23]

Although Captain Hughes traveled extensively by railroad now, the constant moving must have been tiring and stressful. Having established headquarters in Amarillo not long before, and spending much time in Austin, he was now ordered to establish camp back in Ysleta in West Texas.[24] His presence was noted in the *El Paso Herald*, which also pointed out that he would return to Amarillo "preparatory to moving his camp here. He and his rangers will reach here about Oct. 10." Plans didn't work out, as it was not until mid-November that the move was nearly finished. Hughes had intended to move to Ysleta in October, the *Herald* explained, "but owing to strenuous times in other parts of the state he was delayed."[25] The *Herald* again followed Captain Hughes's actions, reporting that the company would "arrive soon."

The "strenuous times" included the normal cattle theft and other offenses, but now revolutionists were at work again. In November Captain Hughes was called to Marfa at the request of Presidio County Sheriff M. B. Chastain. Reports had reached him that Mexican revolutionists were crossing the river and trouble was expected. Captain Hughes consulted with Sheriff Chastain and learned his main concern was at the Ruidosa crossing point. Hughes rode the rails to Marfa, arriving there on December 13, and then down to Presidio to investigate. Hughes had said that he and his Rangers did not "apprehend any serious trouble on the American side." [26] Hughes and Chastain were at Presidio on the fourteenth "to watch actions of revolutionists." Many Mexican and Anglo outlaws were anxious for turmoil and during December much of the work of the Rangers was caused by the unrest. Hughes wrote that during December "Mexican bandits, calling themselves revolutionists, were very active along the border, driving off stock into Mexico, robbing small stores, and committing other depredations." Hughes, Carnes, and

Craighead rode many miles along the Rio Grande in Presidio County and scouted in El Paso County as well. Pvt. Charles R. Moore scouted Brewster and Presidio counties also. Pvt. Harry Moore investigated the robbery of some boxcars at Valentine. He and some U.S. officials ran down and captured sixteen alien Chinese; they were ordered deported by a U.S. court. The two men who smuggled the Chinese were also arrested and both were convicted. Besides the border trouble, the sheriff of Potter County requested Sergeant Carnes to go to Waxahachie to identify a man wanted in Potter County for forgery. He summed up his report of operations: "During the month there was a great deal of robbery and disorder, and we had more calls for assistance than we were able to answer."[27] During the same period Herff Carnes and Charles Moore investigated the robbery of a G.H. & S.A. train.[28]

At the beginning of the new year, Sgt. Herff A. Carnes was on detached duty working in El Paso County; he also covered many miles as did Hughes, and the incidents in which he participated varied from the mundane to the exciting and deadly. On January 16, Carnes with Deputy Sheriff B. Alderete scouted from Ysleta down the Rio Grande. After ten miles they recovered one Jersey cow, which was certainly tame enough but was worthy of noting in his monthly report to Captain Hughes. The Jersey must have been very special as it was valued at $100. The recovered bovine was returned to the owner who must have been very pleased.[29]

In contrast to the peaceful recovery of a Jersey cow, on January 30 Sergeant Carnes with Rangers Charles R. Moore and Charles H. Webster,[30] with several other posse members, went on scout to locate Benjamin F. Howe and his sons, Robert and Guy Howe.[31] Carnes, Moore, and Webster were all experienced peace officers, and presumably their posse members had some experience as well, in addition to knowing the country. The Howe men had developed a reputation as tough criminals in their home neighborhood of Abo,[32] in Torrance County, New Mexico Territory. Neighbors feared them and refused to cooperate with authorities. Prior to the Howe men coming to the attention of the Texas authorities, New Mexico authorities suspected them of stealing goods from railroad boxcars.

On January 25, 1911, John A. McClure, a special officer of the Atchison, Topeka & Santa Fe Railroad, went to the Howe farm to investigate and possibly recover stolen goods. His mistake was to enter into the Howe territory alone. When he did not return authorities became concerned, and suspicions were aroused for his safety. On investigation New Mexico authorities discovered his body; he had been murdered and his body dropped down a well on the Howe farm. They also discovered a great variety of stolen goods taken from the railroad boxcars. The Howes were now strong suspects for not only the relatively minor act of boxcar thievery but also the murder of McClure. Authorities in Santa Fe offered a reward of $500. The flight of the Howes led them towards Mexico, partly on foot and partly on the railroad. Near Fort Hancock, Texas, the trio was discovered by a railroad officer who threw them off the train. Now again on foot, they headed for Sierra Blanca, intending to cross into Mexico. What they could not have known was that the railroad officials had alerted the Rangers. In addition they were unaware that New Mexico lawmen were trailing them, and they would soon face a combined group of Texas and New Mexico lawmen, perhaps eager to shoot to kill.

The posse, numbering eight men, included three of Hughes's men: Sergeant Carnes and Ranger privates C. R. Moore and C. H. Webster; the New Mexico lawmen included Customs Agent Thomas L. O'Connor; Myron R. Hemly, a Justice of the Peace; and the noted lawman and friend of Hughes, Ben Williams, special agent for the railroad. Their combined expertise provided the wherewithal to catch up with the three fugitives. Which lawman yelled out to them to surrender: Sergeant Carnes? Ben Williams? Private Webster? Whoever demanded them to give up is not in the record, but both sides were ready: the Howes to make a stand, a final stand if necessary, and the Rangers to capture or kill, the latter being the easiest and probably their preferred finale for the Howe crime spree.

No one could account for the number of shots fired when the gun battle ended. Initially posse member Hemly shot at Robert Howe who fell wounded, but he himself was hit by shots from Howe, so both were wounded and at least temporarily out of the fight. Robert Howe's shots also hit customs agent Thomas L. O'Connor; the wounds proved fatal. After this initial firefight the two remaining Howes abandoned their wounded partner and fled into the thick brush intending to lose themselves from the eyes of the posse. The lawmen, too quick for them, surrounded the Howes and prepared to lay siege if necessary to capture or kill the pair. The remaining lawmen did not have to lie in wait long, as the Howes, thinking it was better to fight it out, burst out with guns blazing. Both Benjamin F. and son Guy, as Sergeant Carnes expressed the final outcome, "opened fire on the posse, and in the fight following both . . . were killed."[33] Hughes reported that "[The Howes] were surrounded during the night, and refusing to surrender, opened fire on the officer. In the fight that followed, two of the men were killed, and the third wounded and captured and taken to El Paso and placed in jail."[34] Of the criminal Howe family, only one son remained alive, and he was wounded.

Pvt. Charles R. Moore delivered prisoner Robert Howe to El Paso, the wounded man probably feeling fortunate to be alive. He later confessed that he, his father, and brother had killed John A. McClure as he had determined they had robbed the boxcars; he also confessed to the killing of Thomas O'Connor. He stood trial and was sentenced to five years in the Texas prison at Huntsville.[35]

Hughes missed out on the gunfight with the Howes as he was away from camp in Austin, in "a long conference with Governor Colquitt for his regular station at Ysleta." Hughes had been away from Ysleta since January 13, and, according to the report from Austin was "eager to get back for closer scrutiny of the Mexican revolutionists who have been making that section interesting territory during the past few weeks." Hughes, as well as the other captains, received "explicit instructions" relative to the course of action he and his six-man company were to follow: that the State of Texas would not tolerate anything but the strictest of neutrality and that Captain Hughes as well as every other representative of the State had received those orders. Besides Captain Hughes working on the Rio Grande, Capt. J. H. Rogers, now a Deputy U. S.

Marshal, would be there. Captain Hughes was interviewed regarding his thoughts on the "Mexican revolutionists." He said: "I am sure there will be little fomenting of discord on this side the border hereafter. The State authorities are active and I know personally that the Federal Government has a large number of secret service men specially detailed to watch disturbers along the river." He continued:

> They may get a headquarters and try to do some agitating, but they will have to move frequently and too fast to accomplish much. Both the State and National authorities are determined the boundary of the United States shall not be used as a place for the designing of schemes against the government of a friendly power. Strict neutrality is our watchword, and we mean to see that it is made effective.[36]

There was no further comment from Captain Hughes or Governor Colquitt regarding the border situation. Rumors however did continue about troubles on the Rio Grande. El Paso's *Herald* was happy to report that Captain Hughes expected an increase in the Ranger Force, due to the "strained conditions" in Mexico.[37]

Unfortunately there was no increase in the Ranger Force. General Orders No. 5, issued by Adj. Gen. Henry Hutchings on October 2, 1911, was "published for the information and government of all concerned." Really just a change in terminology, it was really no different from the preceding orders from 1901 when the Frontier Battalion was eliminated, to be replaced by the Ranger Force. The pay was $100 per captain per month; $50 per sergeant per month; and $40 per private per month. Each man had to provide his own horse, horse equipment, and clothing; the state would provide each man with one improved carbine and pistol at cost—"the price of which shall be deducted from the first money due such officer or man," but the state would supply the ammunition. But significantly, the Ranger Force was re-organized as of October 1. There would be three companies, each consisting of one captain, one sergeant, and twelve privates. John R. Hughes would now command Company A, John J. Sanders would command Company B, and James M. Fox would command Company C. Curiously, a fourth

Four twentieth-century Texas Rangers. From left: Leo P. "Lucky" Bishop, Captain James Monroe Fox, Jefferson Eagle Vaughn, and Capt. John R. Hughes. Photo made probably in Austin in 1914. *From the Flachmeier Collection, Courtesy the Austin History Center, Austin, Texas.*

company, Company D, was to consist of only the captain. Of the three captains, only Hughes by name was given specific orders, in Section 15, point 3: "Captain John R. Hughes will proceed to enlist the quota of men designated above. He will select only such men as are courageous, discreet, honest, of temperate habits and respectable families." As of this date the Ranger Force would consist in its entirety of an aggregate of forty-three men.[38]

Apparently the *Herald* of El Paso obtained a copy of General Orders No. 5, as the item specifying all Rangers were to be mounted, where it had not been so long before that only captains were to have a mount ready at all times, was reported.[39] Hughes took at least some of the rumors of revolutionary activity seriously, as in mid-November he notified Governor Colquitt "of threatened trouble" and warned the governor "he had evidence that a Mexican revolt will be launched."[40]

Captain Hughes further corresponded with Governor Colquitt on November 23, advising that the situation in El Paso "at present is not alarming" but there was "considerable revolutionary talk"; and he had further noticed "a great many strange Mexicans in town" dressed as laborers who were purchasing railway tickets "for points in the interior." Hughes admitted that these men did not seem to be in charge of any particular person, and there was nothing in their appearance to indicate they were "revolutionary recruits." He had visited the Mexican Consulate but the vice-consul was unable to provide any information. After visiting "several other parties" the vice-consul provided some information which he—Hughes—had not yet followed up on. Hughes concluded his report praising his men: "I find that my men had been zealous and faithful in the discharge of their duty and had scouted the river thoroughly," and he would keep the governor "fully advised as to conditions."[41]

One of the things Captain Hughes did early in 1912 was to correspond with Ben C. Cabell, Chairman of the Board of Directors, Huntsville Prison. His reason for so doing was to request prisoner Howe be turned over to New Mexico authorities to be tried for the crimes committed there. Hughes stated the belief of the New Mexico authorities that he would receive "at least a life sentence." Howe had received a sentence of only five years, which Hughes found "too light a sentence for a man guilty of the offenses committed by Howe and his brother."[42] No record of Cabell's response has been located or the final outcome of the crimes committed by Howe.

A few days later Captain Hughes, signing his correspondence as Captain of Company A, wrote Governor Colquitt regarding a matter concerning the Japanese. The governor apparently had been informed of possible cases of destitution among Japanese citizens in Texas and asked Hughes to investigate. The captain, now acting again as a detective, visited several business places owned or operated by Japanese and found, "after diligent inquiry," no cases of destitution among the Japanese people, or any "refugees from Mexico among those people."[43]

Frequently during the next months Captain Hughes and his men had to deal to some degree with the potential of trouble from the

Mexican revolution. Due to the nature of his dangerous work along the Rio Grande, Hughes usually took another Ranger with him on scouts. Frequently Pvt. Charles R. Moore accompanied him, and generally their movements became news items for the El Paso newspapers. In June Captain Hughes, "accompanied by ranger Charles Moore, has left for Brownsville on special duty."[44] Their return to El Paso was also duly noted in early August, reporting "everything in that section was quiet."[45]

But the typical concerns of the Rangers continued to be theft against property. Frequently complaints from citizens along the border counties identified the thieves as Mexicans crossing the river and stealing livestock. In addition to this, Captain Hughes and his Rangers as well as customs agents had to be constantly looking out for Mexicans dealing in revolutionary activity on Texas soil. In September Captain Hughes was in El Paso to observe the passage of Mexican troops through the state. One troop passed the evening of September 11 and another the next morning. A Ranger was on each train, while the guns of the Mexicans were in a baggage car and in charge of United States troops.

On September 11 Sergeant Moore and Pvt. Pat Craighead left Ysleta to go to Pirate Island where they captured one "revolutionist" who was placed in jail in El Paso. There were as many as forty of these revolutionists on the island who stole some horses and drove them into Mexico. "My men got there a little too late to catch the main bunch," Hughes complained, "but succeeded in catching the one." Moore and Craighead were to remain two more days on the island. Farther down the river Hughes had learned of a band of revolutionists on the Mexican side; he intended to send a man down to observe their actions. He was unaware of any other group of revolutionists except those at Ojinaga across the river from Presidio.[46]

But the calls for Ranger assistance continued, as after a fight in Fort Stockton in November Sheriff Dudley S. Barker[47] appealed to Hughes to send Rangers there. He needed Rangers "to prevent further trouble" following the fight in which two Mexicans were killed and three "fatally hurt last night."[48]

How busy were the Rangers and what did they accomplish was a legitimate question, raised mainly by politicians in the eastern counties where the county sheriffs did not have such huge areas to patrol, nor did they have the Rio Grande for fugitives to cross virtually at will. At the end of the period from September 1, 1909, to June 30, 1911, Captain Hughes reported the company had made 377 arrests, the crimes including murder, rape, robbery and burglary, highway robbery, white capping, kidnapping, various felony thefts, and a dozen or more other offenses. Their duties included assisting at district court sessions, keeping the peace at elections, assisting the sheriff in subduing a feud, to guarding jails and assisting local officers during a revolution. The value of property recovered and returned to owners (excluding livestock), was placed at $551.50. In all the company had made 273 scouts and had covered a total of 88,637 miles, many by horseback. Captain Hughes explained in his report that the details of their accomplishments represented probably one-third of the work of the Ranger Force, as Company C, which had been abolished and Company B, which had changed captains very recently, "probably will not send in any report." The area Hughes worked had the extra problem of revolutionists and men who claimed to be. "Lawless characters, both Americans and Mexicans, took advantage of the unsettled conditions along the border to steal a great many horses and cattle, and commit other depredations, such as robbing small stores, remote from the railway and having no telephone or telegraph connections." In conclusion, Hughes wrote: "I expect to receive a great many calls from these counties [along the river]."[49]

Apparently the news about revolutionists from Texas was considered detrimental to the state's reputation, and in response to this Governor Colquitt dictated an article that was published in the popular *Leslie's Illustrated Weekly Newspaper* in its issue of April 16, 1914. Entitled "The Texas Ranger as He Is" the one-page article reviewed the purpose of the Texas Rangers, its legal foundation, and a brief history of the force. Colquitt explained that he continued to encourage cooperation with Mexican authorities in dealing with criminals on either side of the Rio Grande; further, he explained that the Rangers were not subject to local influences or political pressures, but answered only to the governor. He concluded his piece: "The Texas Ranger is a tremendous force to this end [to uphold the law]. . . . he is a capable, sober, courageous man, a good horseman, and a good marksman." To illustrate his article he had provided photographs of Capt. J. J. Sanders alongside his horse; one of Captain Sanders and three of his men resting on the bank of the Rio Grande; and a photograph of Captain Hughes mounted. Included in the caption was the fact that he had been in the service for twenty-four years, actually closer to twenty-seven years. Additionally there were three small oval portraits of Governor Colquitt himself, Captain Sanders, and Captain Hughes, the commander of Company A.[50] At the time *Leslie's* was perhaps the most influential publication in America, having a circulation of nearly 100,000. Although Captain Sanders did not gain the recognition nor the respect of his contemporaries that Captain Hughes did, this article certainly confirmed in the minds of many Americans the unique nature of the Texas Ranger.[51]

～ 12 ～

Capt. John R. Hughes—
Lone Star Ranger

"I HAVE ENDEAVORED TO PERFORM MY FULL DUTY TO MY
STATE, TO MY GOD, AND TO MYSELF . . .

—John R. Hughes to Miss B. Mathews, February 3, 1915

W ith such frequent visits to Brownsville, some 800 miles down the river from El Paso, at times Hughes must have considered other opportunities to earn his livelihood. He had been in the dangerous work of being a Ranger since 1887, and was now nearing the age of sixty in 1914. The position of county sheriff attracted him. In June Cameron County voters were excited about the possibility of who would become sheriff if former Ranger Carl T. Ryan, the incumbent, chose not to run. Ryan had served five years under Capt. W. J. "Bill" McDonald prior to running for sheriff. Captain Hughes would make the sheriff's race very interesting if he threw his hat in the ring: he certainly had the name recognition as well as the experience behind him to be a strong candidate. If Sheriff Ryan announced his intended resignation at the end of the year, the field would be open for the primaries.

On June 7, 1914, Hughes arrived in Brownsville and checked into the San Carlos Hotel "for a few days." He gave a brief interview to a reporter of the *Brownsville Daily Herald*, stating that there was still considerable cattle and horse stealing along the border, and that "it was particularly bad at the last new moon." This the reporter must have already realized, but Captain Hughes always proved to be good copy.[1]

236

John R. Hughes in his later years, in 1935 still wearing his six-gun. *Courtesy Robert G. McCubbin Collection.*

What Hughes did not state explicitly to the *Herald* reporter was that he was considering a run for the office of Cameron County sheriff. He only hinted at this possibility and it quickly became headline news. The initial headline read that he *might* run; a smaller headline pointed out that the "famous ranger captain" would announce his intention on or before the following Saturday. The article briefly reviewed his career, that he had been a Ranger for twenty-seven years and a captain for twenty-one of those years. He had the matter "under consideration" and informed the *Herald* that he would announce within a few days. Further, Hughes revealed, "a number of influential citizens" of the town and the county had spoken with him and encouraged him to enter the race. The *Herald* pointed out that if he devoted himself to the race for sheriff he would necessarily have to give up his position as Ranger. Hughes had a "wide and varied experience in dealing with the border criminal" and that, assured the *Herald*, in stating the obvious, would assure the law-abiding that if elected he would "make Cameron county an excellent officer."[2]

Now the race did indeed become interesting, when the *Herald* announced that William T. Vann, now a deputy U.S. marshal, was a candidate. Vann was an experienced lawman, having served six terms as sheriff of Leon County, Texas. On June 12 Vann announced that he was "going to be in the race to the finish regardless of the number of candidates." That number included Sheriff Carl T. Ryan, apparently changing his mind about resigning, Frank E. Hill, and Frank Carr. Now the *Herald* reported that Captain Hughes had decided he would not be a candidate. In spite of these reports, which must have confused some voters, the *Herald* two days later printed the names of all seeking election to the various county officers: sheriff, tax collector, tax assessor, surveyor, county commissioners, and justices of the peace as well as constable. The list for sheriff included besides the name of John R. Hughes, W. T. Vann, Frank E. Hill, J. F. Carr, C. T. Ryan, and J. D. Scrivner.[3]

By July the *Herald* was openly stating that Vann would receive the full support of the Democratic Party, and that the other candidates would probably withdraw their names very soon. The race for the sheriff's office attracted much attention, more than any other office. The two leaders at that point were Vann and Ryan. The *Herald* failed to cover the political "back room" maneuverings, but on October 9, the county commissioners boosted Vann's chances by appointing him to fill out the unexpired term of Sheriff C. T. Ryan, who had by this time resigned.

Captain Hughes at his Ysleta farm. *From the Hughes Personal Photo Album, courtesy the Texas Ranger Hall of Fame & Museum, Waco, Texas.*

Vann took the oath of office the next day, and would continue to campaign for the next term, the election to be held on November 3. On that day, the voters elected Vann the new sheriff of Cameron County.[4] John R. Hughes would continue to be a Texas Ranger.

As the year of 1914 closed, an important announcement appeared in the *San Antonio Light*, stating that Captain Hughes, while in Austin, was making his report and conferring with Adj. Gen. Henry Hutchings. Hughes had gone directly from headquarters at Ysleta, and informed Hutchings "the situation on the border is now excellent."[5] At least for a brief time the border, in Hughes's opinion, was quiet. Whatever trouble the revolutionists may have been brewing was held in check.

Less than a week later, those reading the *Light* were surprised to find that Captain Hughes was ready to retire. The sub-headline stated simply that he "Was Not Reappointed as Ranger Captain by New Governor."

The article reminded its readers that Hughes had spent twenty-seven years of continuous service as a state Ranger, and that he was captain for most of those years. Hughes would retire "when the new administration is inducted about the middle of next month." The *Light* reminded its readers that Hughes had "been stationed at various portions of the state and has been a fearless officer in the discharge of his duties. . . . He is well known throughout the state, due to his long service in the employ of the state."[6]

The new governor who chose to dismiss the most effective Ranger in the history of the state was James Edward "Pa" Ferguson, whose term began on January 19, 1915, and ended August 25, 1917, after the Senate impeached him. Governor Ferguson made it clear to Captain Hughes he would not renew his position, but presented no reasons for his decision in writing. Hughes was approaching the age of sixty and Ferguson used age as an excuse to drop his name. He ignored the quality work Hughes had given the state for nearly three decades and appointed a political crony to take his place. Hughes certainly could find a degree of satisfaction when the new governor, having endured a term wracked by scandal, among other "accomplishments" nearly destroying the Ranger Force, suffered the ignominy of impeachment. Instead of selecting men for their abilities to enforce the law in Texas, Ferguson had filled the ranks with political appointees.

Although the degree of disappointment experienced by Captain Hughes in being "cashiered" is unknown, the year of 1915 began with good news, which brightened him—in the form of a letter from an unknown admirer. The remaining years would provide a near succession of good news, compliments from friends as well as strangers, awards, accolades, honors, birthday wishes, all resulting in positive publicity for himself and the Texas Rangers.

On January 17, 1915, a Fort Worth resident, who unfortunately we know only as "Miss B. Mathews," learned of Hughes's retirement and wrote him a lengthy letter, complimenting him on his service to the state. She wrote him "to congratulate you on your excellent record of bravery and daring deeds while in the ranger service. You are a man that all of Texas should be proud of." She further complimented him, adding that he "should also be commended for your religious and moral principals [*sic*]." Miss Mathews apologized for writing "to a total stranger" but she begged his pardon in taking the liberty to do so. She believed that her letter "will doubtless be only one of many letters you will receive from people throughout the state of Texas congratulating you." She further confided to Hughes that she once worked with an old Texas Ranger there in Fort Worth, but did not identify him by name and he was now dead. "I have also had the pleasure of meeting Captain McDonald. There is nothing that interests me more than to hear rangers speak of pioneer days in Texas."[7]

Hughes's response to Miss Mathews reveals his own mastery of the language, his gentle manners and humility, in spite of a misquotation. "Permit me to assure you of my sincere appreciation of your kind expressions of regard for my simple services to the state of Texas," his letter began. Waxing poetic, the context approaching the character of a *billet doux*, Hughes wrote that her "kind letter . . . comes as a caress most grateful to all my sensibilities." He then explained his basic philosophy of life: "I have endeavored to perform my full duty to my state, To my god, and to myself, Believing with the bard, Honor and shame from no condition rise, Act well thy part, There all the honor lies." He concluded that it would be his "earnest endeavor in the walks of private life" to maintain the esteem and confidence of his friends; of course he now included Miss B. Mathews among his friends.[8]

As if he had not gained enough recognition during his active Ranger years, Hughes now started to become a celebrity. In mid-June of that first year of retirement the *El Paso Herald* composed a lengthy article about him and his home in nearby Ysleta, treating it as a journalistic scoop with the headline, "Capt. John R. Hughes, Oldest Texas Ranger, Retired at Ysleta, Recounts His Life History." The reporter stressed that after his twenty-seven years "of continuous service" (not quite true due to the several months' resignation to work in the Fronteriza Mines of Mexico), Hughes was now "living quietly on a ranch at Ysleta near El Paso." In case the reader did not already realize it,

Hughes had "made for himself a name that was a terror to evil doers, particularly those who inhabited the Big Bend region of the state and made a business of 'cattle rustling.'"

Whenever Hughes recounted his life history, he only touched on the highlights: his living in Indian Territory where he "grew to know the wilds and the prairies with all the instinctive knowledge that the red man could teach." A brief summary of his capture of the horses stolen from his ranch followed, how he joined the Rangers, how he "was always a horseback ranger" and had "worked horseback in every county on the Rio Grande from El Paso to Brownsville and was quite successful." In summary, he related how he advanced in the ranks: "I got my promotions all the way from private to captain by my superior officers being killed by Mexican bandits" starting with Sgt. Charles Fusselman and then Capt. Frank Jones. He added, "For several years I expected to be killed by criminals."

Hughes revealed in the conclusion to the article that he had kept a scrapbook "that is very interesting to all old timers, and a great many of my friends want me to write a book of my life as a ranger, but I don't expect to do so for several reasons." One reason given was that he did not crave notoriety; and further, he acknowledged that he did not need the money. He had "accumulated enough of this world's goods to be able to keep the wolf from the door," he explained, but he then clarified his situation: "I am not rich however."[9] He indeed was able "to keep the wolf from the door" as during his years living and working in El Paso County he had purchased land cheaply, and the value of course through the years had increased. In 1929 Hughes had also purchased stock in the Citizen's Industrial Bank of Austin. With no wife or children to support and living frugally, he was able to live comfortably. Through the years he was invested and by the 1940s was chairman and largest stockholder of the Citizens' Industrial Bank of Austin. The *Austin Statesman* in fact informed its readers that during his post-Ranger years Hughes "became a prominent business man here, and was chairman of the board of the Citizens' Industrial Bank and at the time of his death, the [chairman of the] board of the Motor and Industrial Finance Corporation."[10]

However, even while living comfortably in his retirement years he was constantly reminded of the dangers he had experienced, and the sudden death that could come to him and his friends. The shooting in Seminole, Gaines County, Texas, in the Panhandle adjacent to the southeastern border of New Mexico, on the evening of April 1, 1923, must have brought back terrible memories. Two career criminals ambushed and instantly killed William Davis "Dave" Allison, former sergeant of Company D, along with Horace L. Roberson. The murderers, two cattle thieves with extensive criminal pasts, were Hill Loftus, alias Tom Ross, and Milt Good. Both victims were members of the Texas and Southwestern Cattle Raisers Association and had gathered enough evidence against Loftus and Good that would undoubtedly send them to the penitentiary for years. The rustlers ambushed the two officers the night before the trial was scheduled to begin.

The double killing of two cattle inspectors, both well-known by Hughes as well as most other lawmen, garnered headlines across the state. As Rangers, both had worked under Hughes, and often, in reporting the deaths of the two men, newspapers could not resist concluding their reports with retelling briefly just who Captain Hughes was. "As Texas Rangers they worked under Capt. J. R. Hughes of Ysleta, who was a ranger for 28 years, retiring from service in 1915. The slain men left the ranger service for the more lucrative opportunities with the Texas and Southwest Cattle Raisers Association." Hughes described the men as "natural-born peace officers," men who had returned to service "because of the thrill and the good they accomplished[.]"[11]

Although Hughes had retired from active service, the prosecution called him to be a character witness, requiring him to take the stand to speak about the murdered men. The trial for the murder of Allison was held in Lubbock; the trial for the murder of Roberson was held in Abilene. In spite of the best efforts of the defense attorneys, the juries found both men guilty. What Hughes had to say at the trial in Abilene has not been preserved, but an Abilene reporter interviewed him, pointing out that he had spent almost two weeks there, having come in his automobile "which he has substituted for the rollicking deck of a frisky horse, and which he drives himself like a veteran of the game."[12]

The judge, staring at the convicted murderers Loftus and Good, sentenced them to long terms in prison. The defense attorneys appealed the conviction of course, but the court of appeals affirmed the lower court's decision. Sentenced to spend time in Huntsville penitentiary, on November 29, 1925, the pair managed to escape after overpowering a guard. Ultimately, they would have lived happier lives if they had remained in prison. Tom Ross later committed suicide by shooting himself in the head; Milt Good was recaptured and sent back to prison, but in 1934, Gov. Miriam "Ma" Ferguson, wife of the impeached predecessor, pardoned him. A few years later, after writing his autobiography, which failed to bring him the success or financial gain he craved, he again committed a crime and was returned to Huntsville. In 1960, again a free man, his life ended in an automobile accident in LaSalle County.[13]

By 1923, Hughes was experiencing what it felt like to be a celebrity. Instead of explaining just what Hughes contributed to the prosecution of Ross and Good, the reporter found a physical description more newsworthy. Although he was "seventy years old," he looked more like he was fifty-five "and gets about like fifty." It was his "vigorous outdoor life as a ranger for twenty-eight years [which] gave him a vigor of limb and constitution that many a man half his age would envy. His frame is straight and square, his complexion is tanned and healthy, and the friendly eyes hold a sparkle that speaks of plenty of 'pep.' "[14]

Although Hughes was encouraged by some to write his life story, he never did; nevertheless he became the subject of many articles by other writers, in both newspapers and periodicals. He also became a veiled character in western novels. Zane Grey was among the most popular western novelists during this time and he befriended Hughes. Grey was so impressed with the man that he dedicated his novel *Lone Star Ranger* to him and the Texas Rangers. Grey's dedication concluded with this statement to all Rangers:

Gentlemen,—I have the honor to dedicate this book to you, and the hope that it shall fall to my lot to tell the world the truth about a strange, unique, and misunderstood body of men—the Texas Rangers—who made the great Lone Star State habitable, who never knew peaceful rest and sleep, who are passing, who surely will not be forgotten and will some day come into their own.

The book, first published by Harper & Row in 1915, remains in print. Almost fifteen years later the names of Grey and Hughes were

John R. Hughes at Judge Roy Bean's Jersey Lilly Saloon in Langtry. *University of Texas at El Paso Library, Special Collections Department.*

again joined when Hughes visited Austin in 1929. The *Statesman* head-lined its article "Zane Grey's Texan Who Cleaned up Early Border Badmen Back on Austin Visit." Hughes was described as "one of the early and most famous Texas peace officers who helped wrest the com-monwealth from the bandits and Indians." The *Statesman* described him as not only a "picturesque ranger" but also a "soldier of fortune" who gave twenty-eight years of his life to the Texas Rangers, and who "still walks as straight and steadily as men half his years, and spends a lot of his time traveling." Hughes was in Austin to visit relatives as well as numerous friends, one of whom was former Travis County sheriff Robert Emmett White,[15] a highly respected officer "who was with Capt. Hughes on many occasions," and whose son James C. had served in Company D under Hughes. Other friends Hughes visited on his travels included rancher and self-created detective J. Frank Norfleet,[16] and the man who was perhaps his best friend, Ira Aten, described as "another Travis county pioneer, [now living] in the Impe-rial Valley in California." The *Statesman* also pointed out that Hughes traveled mainly in the summer months, as he "stays at home during the rest of the year in El Paso." But occasionally "the urge to take up arms is too strong, and he helps the federal agents take prisoners by the carload from El Paso to [the prison in] Leavenworth."[17]

On one of the captain's trips around Texas he visited his nephew Emery H., son of brother Emery S. Hughes who had passed away on April 21, 1916. It was in the 1930s when the captain had a candid, and unusual, photograph made. It shows John R. Hughes, a broad smile clearly seen amidst his white beard, standing behind a grand nephew and two grand nieces, Louis Bond Hughes, Patricia Irene Hughes ("Tinker"), and Katherine Nell Hughes. The young Louis Bond is shoeless and shirtless while his younger sisters are wearing dresses and shoes. "Uncle John," proudly standing behind with arms on the shoul-ders of Louis and Katherine, is wearing a white dress shirt, neck tie, suspenders—and is barefoot! The original photograph is not dated but from the appearance of the children it was probably made in Austin in 1937 or 1938.[18]

In addition to Zane Grey and his novel dealing with the Rangers, Eugene Cunningham could not resist including some of the exploits of Captain Hughes in his writings. Cunningham is best known for his book *Triggernometry: A Gallery of Gunfighters*, first published in 1934.[19] *Triggernometry* contains chapters on seventeen gunfighters such as Bill Longley, John Wesley Hardin, and Ben Thompson. Cunningham also included El Paso's marshal, Dallas Stoudenmire, Ranger and rancher James B. Gillett, and other well-known figures including Baz L. "Bass" Outlaw and Captain Bill McDonald. Perhaps to show his knowledge of Renaissance literature, he entitled the chapter on Hughes "Bayard of the Chaparral," suggesting that Hughes was the bravest of the brave, only in the brush country rather than on the fields of Europe when knighthood

Among the more unusual photographs of Captain Hughes is this one with the three children of Hughes's nephew, Emery H. Hughes. The children from left: Louis Bond Hughes, Patricia Irene Hughes, and Katherine Nell Hughes. Photo made circa 1937-1938. The photograph was made at the Emery Hughes home on Riverside Drive in Austin. "He was over for lunch or dinner and mother said 'Come and let me take a picture with you and the kids'" hence the unusual nature of the picture, Hughes wearing white shirt and tie but having removed his footwear. Photo by Katherine Hughes, mother of the children. *Courtesy Louis B. Hughes, M.D.*

was in flower. Hughes and Cunningham did become friends, and Cunningham sent a copy of the published book to the captain. By December of that year, Hughes had read the book—"enjoyed it very much"—and chose to write the author. He noted he had known many of the characters discussed in the book: "I knew John Wesley Hardin. He came to Pecos . . . at the time of the Miller Frazer feud. He was a friend of Jim Miller and Mannie Clements. I knew all three of these men up to the time of their death."[20] Hughes complimented Cunningham on his portrayal of Hardin, saying he had "described John Wesley Hardin just as I would have described him—only better." Hughes stated he knew Ben Thompson in Austin in 1878, but made no further comment about the gambler-gunfighter who also served as city marshal of Austin.[21]

Besides mentioning he had known Jim Gillett since 1890, adding, "he is the very best," Hughes had also read Gillett's book *Six Years With the Texas Rangers*, saying that he believed "every word of it." In reading Cunningham's chapter on Baz L. "Bass" Outlaw, titled "The Little Wolf," Hughes recalled the Ranger who could not avoid liquor. "I knew Bass Outlaw and was in the Ranger company with him; made many scouts with him and slept under the same blanket with him many nights—and I approve everything you say about him." Hughes concluded his complimentary letter stating that he would keep *Triggernometry* with him "as reference so I can go back over it and look at it as history." Hughes obviously was a reader of western books, novels as well as history, and other types of literature. His final paragraph in the Cunningham letter makes it clear: "There was a time when I thought William McLeod Rayne[22] [*sic*, Raine] was at the very top as a writer but now I will have to hand it to Eugene Cunningham."[23] There is no way of knowing how many books the captain had in his personal library, assuming he had a shelf or two containing novels and biographies along with Cunningham's *Triggernometry*.[24]

Hughes also corresponded with author-photographer Dane Coolidge but how extensive it may have been is unknown. One intriguing letter remains from July 1935. Coolidge's letter suggests he had written a story dealing with a Texas Ranger, but as of that date he had received no indication of it being accepted by a publisher. His "Mexican novel" was just out, published as *Wolf's Candle*,[25] but another book on the Mexican revolution "hasn't come off." Perhaps Coolidge was feeling somewhat depressed as he concluded his letter, "Times are pretty good

John R. Hughes and western writer Eugene Cunningham, author of *Triggernometry*. Hughes here explains the making of a hangman's noose. *University of Texas at El Paso Library, Special Collections Department..*

only there are thousands of men out of work and on relief. As long as Mr. [Franklin Delano] Roosevelt keeps on playing around in Washington I can't see much chance of improvement, but all the same things are picking up." He assured Hughes that he wanted to remain friends and that he would notify him if he did get anything published. Coolidge ended his letter: "My bum foot is pretty good now and I may fix it up, some day, if I live long enough. I remember how you used to walk right away from me, last summer, and I hope you are still keeping it up." Was this a veiled reference to Hughes's own accidentally self-inflicted bullet wound, or a later problem?[26]

Later that year a history of the Rangers appeared, which has been—and occasionally still is—considered a "classic" work: *The Texas Rangers: A Century of Frontier Defense* by Walter Prescott Webb. Dr. C. L. Sonnichsen, having been recently named head of the English Department at the University of Texas at El Paso, reviewed Webb's book for the *El*

"Taken at Dallas at the Ranger Loghouse at the Centennial Exposition August 1936—Capt. John R. Hughes and Capt. W W Wright both old time Texas Ranger Captains." This was Hughes's identification of this photo. Photo by Paul R. Clegg Studio, Dallas. *Courtesy The Centennial Collection, Archives of the Big Bend, Bryan Wildenthal Memorial Library, Sul Ross State University, Alpine, Texas.*

Paso Herald-Post and Captain Hughes found the remarks of interest. Hughes, an avid newspaper reader, cut out the review, writing the name of the newspaper and the date on the clipping. Not surprisingly, the editors chose to illustrate the review with a photograph of the captain himself: "Capt. John R. Hughes, our own veteran of the Texas Rangers," showing the frequently published bust photograph of Hughes wearing a sweater and Stetson, with his shadow on the wall.[27]

In preparing his work, Dr. Webb interviewed Harbert Davenport, a highly respected lawyer and historian and who would become president of the Texas State Historical Association. Webb accepted Davenport's opinion of Hughes, as he quotes Davenport as saying that the old Ranger "had a mixed reputation. With many of those who knew him, he took a place next to McNelly amongst border captains and peace officers." This was high praise indeed, although Davenport went on to say that some others who were knowledgeable of the situation along the border rated him "below [Captain] Brooks and [Captain] Rogers. Their charge against him was that he was susceptible of being influenced by clever stories and lacked the ability of McNelly, Brooks, and Rogers to distinguish, in this regard, between the true and the false."[28] Apparently this opinion influenced Dr. Webb as he did not give Captain Hughes much attention in his book, little more than a fine photo illustration. However, if the unequal treatment drew any disappointment on the part of Hughes it was never expressed.

The 1936 Centennial Year of Texas proved to be an important year for the state as well as for John R. Hughes. El Paso was making plans

Hughes identified this photo: "This picture of the Sun Bowl Parade Jan 1st 1936—Picture taken by Mr. H. A. King a good citizen and a good old time Ranger, El Paso Texas." *University of Texas at El Paso Library, Special Collections Department.*

early for the Sun Carnival Parade, an event that became an institution. Sheriff Chris P. Fox[29] was chair of the parade committee, and in mid-December 1935, he delegated to County Clerk W. D. Greet the responsibility of seeing that Captain Hughes was in position at the head of the parade. He was to be ready at the corner of Campbell and Texas Streets no later than 9:30 a.m. on New Year's Day. Greet was to "see that he is mounted on a horse that is suitable for parade work and that he is properly attired for the affair." Sheriff Fox admitted that in turning this responsibility over to Clerk Greet, "I am getting a great load off of my mind, as he is one of the most important figures in the parade."[30]

At first, Captain Hughes did not wish to play the part of parade marshal, as at the time he was in Austin. The initial request was a telegram delivered to Hughes:

> The people of the Southwest are requesting that you honor them by being the grand marshall [sic] of the Sun Carnival Pageant of History Parade to be held in this city for the people of the southwest on the morning of January first nineteen hundred thirty-six. This will be the greatest affair in the history of this part of the country, and they pray that you will honor them with your acceptance[.] Advise by wire collect[.][31]

Hughes initially did not want be part of the "greatest affair in the history of" El Paso County, and responded that his pressing business prevented him from participating. Sheriff Fox followed the rejected telegram with a telephone call; again, Hughes turned him down with the same "undesirable result." Hughes obviously did not appreciate whom he was dealing with at the time, as a few days later he looked up from his desk to see Sheriff Fox and Clerk W. D. Greet standing before him. These were old friends of the captain, and no doubt smiled when they announced, "Captain, you are going to be grand marshal of the El Paso Sun Pageant. You'd better come along with us—or else."

A third refusal of their request was impossible, as Hughes explained: "I went along. No use trying to buck Texans when their minds are made up. They took me to El Paso, provided me a fine horse and an appropriate costume, and I was grand marshal of the parade. It was a lot of fun and a grand time."[32] Part of the fun certainly was the fact that grand nephew Louis Bond Hughes rode a little pony by or slightly behind Captain Hughes.[33]

This was not the only parade Hughes led in 1936. The Texas Centennial Exposition wanted him to lead the Ranger Division at the opening of the Centennial parade in Dallas on June 6. George B. Black,[34] a Ranger of the Frontier Battalion days who had served in Captain Bill McDonald's Company B, was head of the Ranger Division of the parade. He began corresponding with the captain in April. Black requested Hughes to lead the parade, but also wanted him to bring his gun,[35] and his new hat that Hughes had purchased for sôme special occasion. Black would furnish him a horse and saddle. In a later communication Black asked him to bring his pistol, carbine, and scabbards. "We are going to wear khaki pants and shirts and large hats; you bring the hat." By May 21 it was all confirmed: Hughes would arrive in Dallas on June 4 or 5. He was to report to Ranger headquarters on the Centennial grounds, where Black would have a cot for him. Now Black added one more item: he wanted Hughes to use the S. D. Myres saddle. Hughes of course knew Myres perhaps the most famous leather-goods maker of the twentieth century, formerly of Sweetwater, Texas, but now in El Paso. This was an especially ornate saddle, valued at the huge amount of $1,500. Hughes was to be well armed with pistol in scabbard, carbine in scabbard, special hat, khaki shirt and pants, and riding on a special saddle. Black would furnish him a "gentle horse" and now he added one more item: "I am also expecting you to bring that knife that was picked up on the battlefield in Old Mexico, and the history of it you may give me more details about when I see you here."[36]

Dallas was thrilled with Hughes leading the parade. Besides the real-life Ranger, an important part of the Centennial was the display of a large statue of a Texas Ranger, unveiled by Senator John Morris Sheppard.[37] The *Dallas Morning News* commented that the unveiling of the Ranger statue was "the high light of the Texas Rangers' and Ex-Rangers' Day at the exposition and members of the great law enforcement body of

This 1936 oil portrait of John R. Hughes by El Paso artist Leola Freeman was a key exhibit at the 1936 Centennial in Dallas. It is now proudly displayed in the home of Hughes's grand-nephew, John R. Hughes. Artist Freeman was considered El Paso's "premier portrait painter." *Photo by Pat Parsons.*

days gone exchanged experiences with present members." Other celebrities were present, as well as members of the motion picture industry. Most notable was King Vidor himself who directed the motion picture *The Texas Rangers.* Vidor also "presented the statue to the ranger log cabin headquarters in the Centennial grounds." Also in attendance were members of the cast, including Jean Parker, who played the heroine of the film, Lloyd Nolan, Jack Oakie, Fred MacMurray, and George "Gabby" Hayes. King Vidor made a short speech in which he eulogized the Texas Rangers. Senator Morris Sheppard "outlined briefly the meaning of the word ranger in his address."[38]

While Hughes was enjoying life in Dallas during the Centennial, professional photographer L. A. Wilke was concerned with getting his article about Hughes into print. Wilke had just received a telegram from his literary agent asking for Hughes's authority to use the material given Wilke for the story. "This indicates," Wilke wrote, "he has

found a magazine which is
going to buy it. I am not sure,
but I think it is Real Detective, which is probably the
best magazine of its kind
published." He added that he
hoped Hughes was "having
the time of your young life in
Dallas."[39]

The dangers to life and
limb seemingly were all in the
past at this period of Hughes's
life as these were very happy
years for the old Ranger
Captain. As he was an avid
newspaper reader, he became
aware of the movement to
do something special in
honor of Capt. Frank Jones,
whose early death at the age
of thirty-seven resulted in

L. A. Wilke, journalist and photographer. As a good friend of John R. Hughes he took numerous photographs of the retired Texas Ranger. *Courtesy Mike Cox.*

Hughes becoming captain of Company D. The first publicity in this
matter was in September 1936, when Edwin B. Hill, tax assessor for
the El Paso County Water Improvement District No. 1, recommended
that "the State ought to move the grave to a place of honor." The grave
was located "a short distance from the Ysleta High School" on property
owned by C. G. Willhoite of Las Cruces, a superintendent of the New
Mexico State Highway Department.[40] Nelson Avery Rector, a cousin
of Jones and a highly successful attorney, also noticed the initial report
and became interested, stating he would communicate with other family members "in an effort to have the body moved."[41] All this would cost
money, and to mark the grave properly would require time and effort.
There were no more headlines about the Frank Jones monument story
in the centennial year, but the plans would come to fruition in 1937.

The "Model T" Hughes owned received attention along with its owner in the 1936 issue of *Ford News*, a 220-page magazine devoted to all things relevant to Henry Ford's invention. In the "Snapshots of Ford Folks" section appeared a small black and white photograph of the eighty-one-year-old retired Texas Ranger standing alongside the vehicle. The caption informed the reader that Hughes "drove his twelve-year-old Model T from his home in El Paso to the Texas Centennial."[42] It was this automobile that nephew Emery H. considered an antique, and which Hughes later gave to him. Hughes replaced it with a Ford V-8.

As the Texas Centennial year ended, William Parker Hughes, younger brother by two years, came to Texas for a visit in December. The pair may have talked about their days as Rangers, as W. P. had served under Lt. Nelson O. Reynolds in Company E of the Frontier Battalion back in 1877. William had served only a short time and then devoted the remainder of his life in the printing and publishing

John R. Hughes, left, and brother William Parker Hughes, 1936. They may have been more like strangers than brothers as they had not seen each other for many years. Photo by L. A. Wilke. *University of Texas at El Paso Library, Special Collections Department.*

business. In December 1936, plans were in the works for the January Southwestern Sun Carnival Parade in El Paso, with John R. Hughes once again serving as parade marshal. The Rotary Club planned, as part of the activities, a special luncheon in honor of the Texas governor, James V. Allred at the historic Paso del Norte Hotel. Captain Hughes was willing to attend but brother William declined the invitation. This was not a difficult decision for the governor who wanted both Hughes brothers in attendance. Governor Allred pulled rank and issued an order to the former Ranger captain. The "riot order" read in part:

> Inasmuch as a state of insurrection and revolt exists today in El Paso in the vicinity of the Rotary meeting at Hotel Paso del Norte, as Governor of Texas and Commander in Chief of the Texas Rangers, I hereby call upon your return into active service.
>
> In the interest of the people and welfare and the dignity of the State of Texas and the City of El Paso, in connection with the Southwestern Sun Carnival, I also hereby call upon you to enlist and have present at said point of insurrection one William Hughes, also a former Ranger of the sovereign State of Texas.[43]

In case Hughes missed the subtlety, Governor Allred concluded his order by stating, "this is a command" over his signature and the seal of the state. December 31, 1936, was the date. The executive order was hand delivered, addressed to "Senior Captain Texas Rangers" John Hughes. On the envelope, Hughes wrote: "The Governors order to me to Bring Brother Bill in." Hughes did bring in his brother, suffering from "timidity" as the cause of his initially declining the invitation; Governor Allred and the Rotarians were pleased.[44] This was the occasion when both William P. and John R. were photographed together, providing us with one of the very few photographs of William Parker Hughes.

Captain Hughes was not the only Ranger whose life was of interest to writers and reporters. Alonzo Van Oden now became the subject of a biography of sorts. He had kept a diary through his years as a Ranger, preserving clippings and poems, much like Hughes had done. In that Centennial year Oden's daughter, Ann Jensen, who had lost her father when she was only eight years old, published his diary. She explained her reasoning:

> I have assembled this diary and scrapbook of my father's with the belief that it will reveal the soul of a Texas Ranger—of all Texas Rangers—good, honest men, who are men of culture, refinement and understanding, men who are bravely trying to do their best for a common good.

George B. Black, former member of Company B and then a Special Ranger assigned to Company D, provided an introduction, in which he stated that even though Oden's diary and scrapbook was a "personal record," it was "a history of the life of any Texas Ranger, and it makes us in the service feel that it might be our record, too."[45] Black also included in his introduction an explanation of how he learned about this historical treasure:

> Not long ago a tattered, marble board-covered book was laid in my hands. . . . Opening it, I found the pages yellowed, and frayed with much handling. . . . The pages were covered with penscript in the neat Spencerian style of a half-century ago. I found what I believe to be the only diary and scrapbook ever kept by a member of the Ranger force—the record kept by Alonzo Van Oden from the day he entered the Ranger service.[46]

It was of course not the only diary of a Ranger, but it remains an important contribution to the history of the Rangers.

Ann Jensen sent Hughes a copy of her father's "diary and scrapbook." He later wrote her about it, explaining that at first he did not think he would appreciate the book, "Because I was in the Ranger service all the time that your father was. But I have found it was interesting." He continued, writing that he knew her father, that he was a smart man, "but I had almost forgot him and did not think your book would be very interesting to me." But when he started reading it, "it brought back old times and old Ranger adventures that I had forgotten and now when I get to thinking of the old Ranger days in the big bend of the Rio Grande I get the book out and read it and enjoy it very much." He ended his letter saying, "your father was a smart man and a loss to the state of Texas." He signed his letter "Capt. John R. Hughes Texas Ranger."[47] No doubt some of those memories of "old times" that were brought back to him included the gunfight at Tillie Howard's parlor, which resulted in the deaths of Joe McKidrict and Baz L. "Bass" Outlaw, back in 1894.

Writer Dane Coolidge sent Hughes a copy of his book *Ranger Two Rifles* and asked for his opinion. Hughes read it, sent him a "nice letter," and called the book "a good story." Coolidge sent the letter to his publisher, "telling them it isn't every day a Western author gets a Ranger to say his stuff is good." He hoped the publishers would print the letter, perhaps as an endorsement on the dust jacket.[48]

The Rangers of the horseback era were frequently subjects of newspaper articles, often a lengthy story in a Sunday edition. The Texas Ex-Rangers Association was formed in 1920, with the initial gathering held in Weatherford, Texas, on August 20 of that year. Over the years the reunion was held in different towns, its purpose "for social benefit, to meet once a year, to live over again as far as possible the days of our boyhood," but also to gather and provide proof for them or their widows to obtain a pension. Membership was $1.00 per year.[49] How many of the reunions Hughes may have attended is unknown, but he did attend some. His membership certificate is dated July 28, 1927. It records his date and place of birth, when he joined and when he retired from the Ranger Service, and place of residence. It was signed by Commander William M. Green, and his daughter, secretary Ruby Green. Hughes kept among his personal effects a program dated August 1–3, 1928, when the reunion was held at Colorado, Texas. His name is listed among the nearly 180 members. Other prominent names include Capt. D. W. Roberts, Capt. Junius "June" Peak, Nat B. Jones, J. V. Latham, J. B. Gillett, and S. O. Durst.[50]

In 1937, the community of Santa Anna, in Coleman County, hosted the reunion. It was exceptional that on this occasion Hughes suffered sunstroke on his way to Santa Anna and was in "critical condition" in a hospital in San Antonio.[51] Whether Hughes actually made it to the

Men of the horseback Ranger days as they appeared in 1936. Standing from left: James B. Gibson who served in Company A under Capt. G.W. Arrington, and John R. Hughes; seated are brothers Ira and Ed Aten. *University of Texas at El Paso Library, Special Collections Department.*

reunion is doubtful, although once released he may have continued his journey just to see old friends. George B. Black was president that year, and Black "pushed the program through," at least on the first day, and began making plans for the following year's event.[52]

When not enjoying trips to Dallas and leading parades, John R. Hughes enjoyed traveling and drove out to California more than once to visit his old Ranger companion, former sheriff and longtime friend Ira Aten. Just before the celebration of his eighty-third birthday, reporters visited him, and he was feeling jovial. He said he was going on a "big toot" to celebrate, "just to show how young he feels. He doesn't even drink." Although he had been "denned up" during the winter, he was "looking younger than ever, despite his 83 years and white whiskers." As an example of his "youthful spirit" he pointed out that he long ago abandoned horseback riding for a fourteen-year-old Model T Ford. He drove it twice to California to visit Aten and several times to Austin and Corpus Christi. He was quite proud of it also. He left a typed note, undated, expressing pride: "This car is a model 1924 and was bought out of the salesroom on January 1st, 1924. It has been driven to the Pacific Ocean and back twice and to the Gulf of Mexico about six times. One time to Hot Springs, Arkansas and several times to Hot Springs, New Mexico." He added that he lived "on the road in this car every summer and travel all summer."[53] According to his later journals, the trip to the Gulf of Mexico may have been to visit the grave of his beloved Elfreda Wuerschmidt, as on several occasions in the month of June Hughes drove to Rockport, on the Gulf, where she had been laid to rest, although her grave remains unmarked. Unfortunately, none of the numerous newspaper reporters ever directly asked Hughes about the love of his life, or if they did his response was not recorded. Perhaps he felt it was none of the public's business about who he loved and lost and remained silent on the subject, at least for the press. Dr. Louis B. Hughes, nephew of Hughes, did however relate to this author in an interview that as a young boy at least on one occasion he drove Hughes's car part of the time on a visit to Rockport to visit her grave. He fondly recalled how he was barely able to see over the steering wheel, but it was great adventure for him. He recalled that at the cemetery he let "Uncle John" go off to the grave alone, that it was unmarked at the time and he could not recall how to locate it today. Captain Hughes had loved, and lost—not to another man did he lose her, but to death—and he chose to hold that in his heart. Whether he ever seriously attempted to find a replacement for her is unknown, but apparently she was irreplaceable.

It was in Austin that his nephew, Emery H. Hughes, the son of brother Emery S. Hughes, "cast covetous eyes on the vehicle, desiring to acquire it as an antique." When Captain Hughes understood Emery considered his vehicle an antique he gave it to him, and then replaced it with a "streamlined 85-horse-power automobile which he drives at present." He was not one to maintain an "antique" automobile.

At the time of the interview Hughes was in a jovial mood. Regarding his youthful feelings, he commented: "Why, I'm even thinking of getting married. I've got a girl picked out. She's eight years old, and she's promised to wait 25 years and then marry me."[54]

But even with all the wonderful things happening to the old Ranger, life's normal events brought occasional sadness. His old friend and Ranger companion Sheriff Milam Harper Wright died while in office; he was fifty-nine years of age. After his Ranger career, the voters elected him sheriff of Hudspeth County, and he served from November 8, 1932, until his death on February 12, 1938. Wright had joined the Rangers in 1907 and had served most of the time with Hughes. He also served as a member of the U.S. Customs Mounted Patrol. Hughes clipped the obituary from the El Paso newspaper, enclosing it with a letter to nephew Emery H., adding that it was "about the death of our good old friend Milam Wright. I am sorry to loose [*sic*] him—his brother Will is here and a lot of his people are coming from Corpus Christi and Floresville." Within this letter Hughes revealed he kept his nephew well informed of where he was and his health; because he had no children of his own he may have considered Emery H. Hughes the son he never had.[55]

The famous Ernie Pyle, described as a "Roving Reporter" for Scripps-Howard, also was proud to be able to interview Hughes. Pyle termed Hughes the "best-known man in El Paso" and called him "an institution, like the Fourth of July or the Rio Grande." Pyle declared that Hughes "loved it." Pyle described him "as spry as a cricket," adding that he was one who "hears perfectly, sees well, walks miles around town every day, thinks straight, has a grand sense of humor, drives his own car, and thousands of people speak to him on the street." Further, Pyle visited his quarters and found them of interest, saying he had "a small corner room in a side-street hotel. Hanging on the walls are his extra clothes. In the corner sits a rifle he had when a Ranger. On the desk are scrapbooks of pictures and clippings about his career. On the floor are two or three suitcases, all packed." At this point in his life, Hughes "spends his days monkeying around town, talking to cronies."

But Pyle also described Hughes's early years, how he had spent time with the Indians in the Oklahoma Territory, how he had been shot by an Indian when he was but seventeen, the shot shattering his right arm.

He suffered from that wound "to this day." That arm was weak and smaller than his left, Pyle wrote, stating that Hughes "had to learn to do everything with his left hand, even shoot." Hughes let Pyle handle his six-shooter, one with a "beautiful pearl handle, with an eagle carved on one side." Pyle looked at it, pointed it, and then "swung it around" but only then realized it was loaded, the bullets to him "looked like cannon balls." Pyle quickly laid it down on the bed saying, "Gee whiz, the thing's loaded!" To which Captain Hughes responded: "You bet it is. There's no sense in having a gun that isn't loaded." Hughes explained that he did not carry it around town but did take it with him on his auto trips.

After the visit to Hughes's room, the two men drove out to Ysleta to see an old adobe house built to house Company D some years before. They drove twelve miles, stopping every now and then while Hughes did most of the talking. Pyle said that Hughes was "very friendly and

Rangers at Frank Jones monument on May 12, 1938. Ed Aten, Ira Aten, and R.E. Bryant, standing. Hughes pointing to name. Inscription reads: "Captain Frank Jones Born in Austin, Texas 1856 Killed by Bandits June 30, 1893 near San Elizario while commanding Company D Texas Rangers." The monument was erected by the state of Texas in 1936. *From the M. T. Gonzaullas Collection. Courtesy the Texas Ranger Hall of Fame and Museum, Waco, Texas.*

thoughtful, and you don't feel that he's old at all. Despite his local renown he is just the opposite of pompous or blustery." Pyle ended his article stating that he had "never spent a calmer, pleasanter half-day with anybody in my life."[56]

In May 1938, Hughes and three other Ranger comrades, brothers Ira and Ed Aten and R. E. "Ed" Bryant, traced the route of the pursuit of the Olguin Gang, the outlaws who were responsible for the death of Capt. Frank Jones back in June 1893. James J. Kaster accompanied the group, perhaps as their driver. They ended where the large memorial stone stood, marking the spot where Jones fell. Ed Aten, at the age of sixty-eight, was the youngest of the quartet. Bryant and Ed Aten had been members of the five-man posse that tracked the Olguins, but inadvertently had crossed the line into Old Mexico where members of the gang waited in ambush. It was the death of Captain Jones that resulted in Hughes being named captain of Company D.

The 1,200-pound stone had been placed in early November 1937, paid for by an unknown amount of donations. The *El Paso Times* was supportive of the effort to honor the fallen captain, and placed a large photograph of the marker on page one of their Monday, November 8, issue. The ceremony was scheduled for the following Sunday, November 14, 1937, when Jack Funk, great-grandson of Capt. Pat Dolan, under whom Frank Jones had served, unveiled the marker by removing the Texas state flag. More than 200 El Pasoans and residents of the Valley attended the ceremony, among them, Ed Bryant. C. E. "Billy Smith" Matthews and James B. Gibson, the latter a former Ranger under Captains G. W. Arrington and L. P. Sieker, were also in attendance.[57] There is no indication that Hughes or the Aten brothers attended the unveiling. The neighborhood had changed since 1893, but reportedly the marker was placed within a hundred feet of the actual grave of Jones. Ed Bryant, who participated in the fight and knew where the body had fallen, was quoted as saying that Jones's "grave is on private property back of the Ysleta Grade school to the left of the old county road."[58]

The reunion of these four veterans of course made news, and later they were gathered there for at least one photograph, on May 12, 1938, showing Hughes kneeling on the ground pointing to the name of Frank Jones, the others standing. That photograph has been reproduced numerous times in works devoted to the Texas Rangers. L. A. Wilke was there and took at least one photograph.

Honors began to accumulate on the old Ranger. On May 31 Horace H. Carmichael, Director of the Department of Public Safety (DPS), issued a declaration. He had appointed Hughes Honorary Captain in the Texas Ranger Force, granting him "all the rights, privileges, and emoluments appertaining to said appointment." Veteran Ranger captain and quartermaster Roy W. Aldrich also signed the declaration. It was indeed a unique honor. The old Ranger's physical description was also included: he was eighty-three-years-old, five foot ten inches tall, weighed 180 pounds, had grey hair, brown eyes, and a fair complexion.[59]

Honors continued in the following year of 1939. Fort Worth made preparations for the Forty-Third Annual Fat Stock Show from March 10 through March 19. On January 9, Secretary-Treasurer John B. Davis invited him to participate. With Hughes as a key figure, the event's organizers now planned to inaugurate the "Parade of the Purebreds," which amounted to some 600 or 700 purebred cattle being driven before the coliseum audience. In addition to the purebreds, Davis explained to Hughes, it was their "intention to dramatize this event" by adding a "small" herd of buffalo and a herd of Texas longhorn steers as well. At the same time, the crowd would pay tribute to the "old time cowmen and cowboys who have had a part in the founding and evolution of the cattle industry." To accomplish that, the planning committee invited "four or five cowmen and cowboys typical of the industry half a century ago" to be their guests. Davis was confident that Hughes and the other cowmen would participate as well; then along with the other cowmen he would ride into the arena after the steers and buffalo had exited. At that point, the master of ceremonies would introduce Hughes and the others and the purebreds with their herdsmen would pass in review. Gentle mounts would be provided, with saddles, "and it will not be necessary for you to enter the arena at a gallop." Davis estimated this display would take less than thirty minutes. To add to the attraction, Hughes would be one of around 1,000 Texas cowmen as guests of the Fat Stock Show, "at a chuck wagon dinner on the grounds." The other celebrities invited were veteran cattlemen John Arnott of Amarillo, Ab Blocker of Big Wells, John Ellison Carroll of Big Lake, and Bob Beverly of Lovington, New Mexico.[60]

Captain Hughes received the invitation and on the twelfth responded in the affirmative to John B. Davis, signing his reply "Old time Cowboy and Texas Ranger." He took the opportunity to review his younger years as a cowboy:

> For your information I will say that I went up the Chisholm trail with long horn cattle in the spring of 1877. The cattle were from the Santa Gertrudes Ranch (The King Ranch). I did not go from the King Ranch with these cattle, but was working at the Comanche and Kiowa Indian Agency near Fort Sill[,] Indian territory, delivering beef to the Indians. As the government was trying to keep the Indians from hunting buffalo, as the buffalo were so scarce that if the Indians went out on the hunt they would not find enough buffalo to satisfy them, and they might stampede the herds on the trail and kill some of the cattle, also some of the cowboys.

And Hughes continued to reminiscence:

> In the spring of 1877 the contractors that I was working for, lost the contract and we drove what cattle they had on hand, to Kansas and held them until November when they were sold and shipped east. I returned to Fort Sill and in the spring of 1878 went to Austin, Texas, and went up the trail in 1878 with cattle of Snider and Drum [sic, Snyder and Drumm]. Major Drum was boss of the herd.[61]

Hughes looked forward to celebrating his eighty-fourth birthday on February 11, as did El Paso's *Herald-Post*. "Hughes Pleasure Bent at Youthful Age, 84" read the headline on page seven of the Thursday, February 9, issue. In addition to the large headline a recent photograph, with Hughes wearing, appropriately, a white hat. The news was that the "straight, tall white-haired El Pasoan" would eat chicken dinner with his friend of thirty years, H. F. Greggerson, described as a prominent farmer of the Lower Valley, a former customs guard, border patrolman, and deputy sheriff. The two old lawmen shared the same birthday. They were reportedly going to talk of other days and of their first meeting. Journalist L. A. Wilke was to be a guest.

Hughes shared his further plans with the readers of the *Herald-Post*. He said he would leave home on March 1 and drive his car on his annual "jaunt" to South and East Texas, and then attend the Fort Worth Fat Stock Show, riding daily in the rodeo arena as a special guest. The *Herald-Post* quoted Hughes as saying: "I will soon be 84. I realize I have not much longer to live. I am not going to let anything interfere with my pleasure." He intended to drive each day until he became tired, then stop at a tourist camp and cook his own meals. "I like to eat my own cooking," he added.[62]

This comment inspired the reporter to add that Hughes had cooked many meals over a campfire "in the sagebrush of the West Texas plains, . . . bent over a fire thinking of the trail of the criminal he was following as one of the crack Rangers in the service of the he-man early west law."[63] If the readers did not realize they were reading about a western celebrity yet, the *Herald-Post* was educating them that El Paso indeed owned an icon.

Having his physical needs taken care of in appreciation of his presence in the Fat Stock Show was not enough. John M. Hendrix, director of Special Events, now requested him to bring along his "pet Winchester and scabbard" as well as his "six-shooter and scabbard," no doubt intending those implements of law enforcement to be prominently displayed in photographs. Hendrix assured Hughes his room at the Hotel Westbrook was reserved for him, as well as rooms for the other cowmen who were going to attend. Mr. and Mrs. Hendrix lived in the Hotel Westbrook.[64]

On the same day, birthday February 11, T. M. Presley, manager of the Fort Worth office of the Texas Livestock Marketing Association, expressed his interest in meeting Hughes and his eagerness to show him the "vast changes" that had taken place in the livestock industry. The

Photographer L. A. Wilke wrote this on a print given to Hughes: "Here Capt. Hughes is shown today as he lived, with rifle and six-shooter, sitting among the rugged waste lands of West Texas, where he used to watch for bad men trying to cross the Rio Grande." *University of Texas at El Paso Library, Special Collections Department.*

offices would be turned over to Hughes for as long as he wished to remain in Fort Worth.[65] Tarrant County Sheriff Arthur B. Carter made Hughes a "Special Deputy Sheriff" and offered the sheriff's headquarters for his use, advising Hughes he should consider himself one of them.[66]

Certainly, the visit to Fort Worth was a wonderful experience for Hughes. He posed casually for numerous photographs and visited with reporters. One photograph, which later appeared in the popular book *Trail Driving Days* by Dee Brown and Martin F. Schmitt, shows Hughes showing his "old pistol" to "veteran cattlemen" J. Ellison Carroll, Ab Blocker, and Bob Beverly. Carroll was a celebrity of sorts, as he had established the world steer roping championship record in San Antonio in 1908. An article in the *Fort Worth Star-Telegram* was headlined "Oldest Retired Ranger Captain Peps Up Tales" and explained that with Hughes's arrival at the Stock Show, "new life was given stories of the early day cattle business and criminals of Texas," suggesting that the stories the old men now were telling were getting better and bigger with each re-telling. As for the .45-caliber pistol Hughes displayed for the photographer, he said a rancher, whose identity he did not disclose, had given it to him in 1903. "He thought that I saved his life and he presented me the pistol." Hughes refused to divulge further details on the incident.[67] Two other photographs appeared in Fort Worth's *Star-Telegram:* Hughes with J. Ellison Carroll and John Arnott, and one with Bob Beverly with Ab Blocker. Blocker had spent years in the business, herding cattle in Texas, Wyoming, Canada, and Mexico. They all shared similar experiences from the cattle driving days; none however had had such an exciting life as Ranger Hughes. The quintet were guests at a luncheon in their honor at the Blackstone Hotel.[68]

There were distinguished notables besides the Ranger and old cattlemen at the luncheon: John Kenzie of Denver, Colorado, manager of the huge Matador Land and Cattle Company was there; John Scharbauer of Fort Worth, eighty-four years old, "who made cattle history in the Midland area"; Leon Gross of Fort Worth, a merchant who had dealt with cowmen for many years; James D. Farmer, pioneer cattleman who sold his first steers to Armour and Swift Packing plants; and Sam R. McKelvie, former governor of Nebraska. John M. Hendrix, director of Special Events, in speaking of the quintet, said: "When we were kids these men were our heroes. They are old now, but they are still our heroes when we realize how much they have contributed to our country." The men were reticent to talk at first, but then Bess Coughlin, Fort Worth's "cowgirl songbird," sang some songs of the trail, including "Open Range Ahead" and "The Last Roundup," after which the men "opened up." How excellent a singer the nearing-forty-year-old actually was is impossible to say, but her voice was beautiful to the ears of these old-timers. All who heard her no doubt thought "she sho' can sing," as did Hughes.[69]

Added Bob Beverly, "The only thing I've ever learned is that I'll never get out of this world alive, but I'm glad I'm not dead yet." John Scharbauer, apparently having no quotable words, got up and sang a song, "Gee, Ain't It Great to Meet a Friend from Your Old Home Town."

Then Hughes began to reminisce. "About 61 years ago I came through a little town named Fort Worth with a herd of cattle. I saw some boys on the creek bank digging for fish bait. I don't recognize any of you boys here as the ones I saw then, and I'm not even sure this is the same city, with these skyscrapers."

Bob Beverly was not to be outdone.

I was educated on the trail and always thought that any man who could count to 100 qualified to be a school teacher. I figured that if I could learn to count to 100 I could get a job driving cattle. You see, I could count to 100 cattle, then put a stone in my pocket. Then count another 100. As long as there weren't more'n about 50,000 head I'd be all right.

And Bob Beverly wasn't through with his tale:

I was up in Wyoming when I found out that they were actually shipping cattle in railroad cars. Well, they were hanging rustlers up there and rustlers were making it hot for cattlemen, so I headed for the Mexican border. I got there and found Captain Hughes making people behave. So I had to reform.

Did the room rock with laughter at these old-timers' remarks? Perhaps so. Maybe the humor is lost to us today, not knowing the old-timers or hearing their manner of becoming *raconteurs*. Then former governor Sam R. McKelvie "struck a serious note": "When I have attained the age of these men and hold the respect that they command I will feel I have lived a good life. I don't know that we will ever have another such race of men. If we could be certain that their race will be perpetuated we could be certain of the security of our country in the future."[70] The awareness of the growing war in Europe certainly motivated the governor to mention security.

Hughes, as did the others, thoroughly enjoyed the Fort Worth visit. After the drive back home, he learned that William Ward Turney, another old friend and prominent El Paso resident, had died on March 23, at the age of seventy-seven years. In the 1890s Hughes with his Rangers had often crossed Turney's ranch land in pursuit of fugitives. The highly successful lawyer was the first county attorney of Brewster County. He had served in the Texas Legislature, both in the House and the Senate.[71]

Hughes's life story had now reached a new level, higher than all the other old-time Frontier Battalion Rangers. Paul Havens, a pseudonym of Jack Martin, had sold his story to *True Detective Magazine*, and Lloyd B. Rust of Republic Pictures Corporation found it "most interesting." After reading the first installment, he wrote Hughes and believed that because of the Ranger's "colorful career," a motion picture could be made from his story. Rust first wanted to know if Hughes was interested in such a project, and was confident he could "negotiate a deal" with Republic's executives, but wanted to know Hughes's response. Hughes responded in the affirmative, and Rust followed up with inquiring if the rights to the story in *True Detective* were available.[72] If Republic did produce a motion picture based on Hughes's life there is no mention of it in the Hughes papers. Perhaps Republic did produce such a motion picture, but the film life was not recognizable as the life of Hughes.

The magazine serial did produce one tangible reward: Bernarr MacFadden of MacFadden Publications determined Hughes should receive an award for valor. This was to be the first certificate of valor given by the company, and the decision was based on the content of the Paul Havens/Jack Martin article in *True Detective*. Others involved in the decision-making process resulting in the choice of Hughes included Lewis J. Valentine, police commissioner of New York City; Col. Homer Garrison Jr., director of the Department of Public Safety of Texas (DPS); Chief of Police Edward B. Hansen of Duluth, Minnesota, and members of the MacFadden staff.[73] MacFadden obviously wanted to gain further recognition on Hughes's reputation, but traveling to New York to receive an award was not in Hughes's plans. He felt compelled to turn down the request, feeling it "unwise for a man of my years to consider traveling to New York for the presentation." He explained that although he was enjoying good health "considering my age" the problem was that "old wounds that I have suffered years ago bother me some, and I prefer to remain among my friends here in Texas." [74] The rejection was not a total defeat for the publishing mogul, however, as they still received publicity for their story. The *El Paso Herald-Post*, earlier that year, had reported that "the captain's adventures in the years he patrolled Texas are told in the current issue of True Detective Mysteries."[75]

MacFadden provided not only a certificate of honor but a medal as well. He shipped it to Austin where on December 14 Hughes accepted the honor in a ceremony presided over by Colonel Garrison. He was one of five receiving the award due to their standing as a "noted peace officer," based on their entire career.[76]

Brother William Parker Hughes died on April 5, 1940. The two brothers had been apart most of their adult lives, William P. living in Northport, Washington, while John R. remained in Texas, although they occasionally corresponded. William had visited only four years earlier and the two had appeared at El Paso's Sun Carnival the end of that year. W. P. Hughes Jr. wrote his uncle of William's passing, informing him his father was buried "in a beautiful little cemetery overlooking the Columbia River, which he loved so much during the past 40 years." W. P. Hughes Sr. was proud of his brother John. Probably to John's surprise, he had kept a large picture of him hanging in his "shack." The son would now preserve it.[77]

The New York trip was not the only one Hughes did not take. Later that year W. Lon Johnson, judge of the Superior Court of the State of Washington, wrote the captain, apologizing that he had intended to write sooner but hadn't, although he had often thought of Hughes. Judge Johnson explained that as William P. Hughes had "passed away some time ago" and that he had "a great many close, personal friends who regret his passing" Johnson felt it necessary to explain that William Jr. intended to travel to El Paso and visit him "next year," or sometime in 1941. The judge described William's final days, when he had made a trip to Kansas to undergo some unnamed medical treatment. The son objected to this, but Hughes Sr. was determined and made the trip. After a few days, with death clearly imminent, his son was called, but nothing could be done. William Parker Hughes Sr.'s body was returned to his home in Northport where it was interred in the place he himself had chosen. Johnson concluded his letter by inviting Hughes to travel to

Washington to visit, "but it may be that now, with your brother having passed away, that you would not care to make the trip up here."[78] He was correct in his surmise, as Hughes did not travel to Washington.

The old captain did journey to Las Cruces, New Mexico, the following year to participate in a parade, however. Claude Everett, president of the Dona Ana County Sheriff's posse, proudly announced that Hughes, described as a "widely-famed former Texas Ranger," would lead the parade marking the opening event of the Ranch Hands-College Students Round-Up. That was on the opening Friday, and on the following Saturday morning another parade would begin the day's activities. Following the rodeo, the Block and Bridle club of the college invited the guests to attend the "chuck wagon supper." Hughes had no trouble attending this event as Las Cruces was scarcely fifty miles from El Paso.[79]

United States Congressman Robert Ewing Thomason noted Hughes's eighty-seventh birthday on February 11, 1942, and sent him birthday wishes from Washington, D.C. Thomason may have simply sent Hughes birthday greetings as a political gesture, or he and Hughes may have had previous contact. Thomason had served on the committee investigating the alleged misconduct of Gov. James E. "Pa" Ferguson, whose report led to his impeachment.[80] Hughes responded to Thomason's letter, stating he was "pleased" with his work in Washington. Hughes remarked he was particularly interested in the bill introduced by Thomason to provide a pension for those who "worked" in the Catarina Garza War. He quickly pointed out that he himself was not interested in a pension, but he took the opportunity to explain his interest:

> I arrested Catarina Garza in the summer of 1888, when he was trying to start his revolution. Victor Sebree made a complaint and I arrested him. When I arrested him he pulled his pistol to shoot us. I was then 54 years younger than I am now and I thought I was some man. I just grabbed him and took his pistol away from him. I did not want to kill him.

Hughes then reminded Thomason that it was only a short time later that Victor Sebree did shoot Garza twice, once through his liver, which "stopped the revolution for two or three years, as it takes about that long for a person to recover from a bad wound." Curiously, Hughes added a regretful and very personal comment about his arrest of Garza, that the United States had spent considerable money to capture him, admitting he had "often thought how much money I would have saved the United States and Texas if I had just killed him."[81] . . . *if I had just killed him.*

Since his 1915 retirement, Hughes had become more and more a Texas institution, if not an American institution. By July 1942, he had become an icon, as headlines announced his story was now available in book form. "Texas Ranger 'Rides Again'" headlined the report in El Paso, followed with slightly smaller headline: "Story of John R. Hughes in Print." The book, entitled *Border Boss*, by Jack Martin, was now available, and Hughes was described in the combination book review-mini biography as "one of Texas' most colorful living characters"; accepting the reviewer's statement El Paso must have been satisfied that his story "finally has been placed between the covers of a book." The unidentified reviewer stressed that the book was not a history of the Ranger organization "as such," but recounted "countless anecdotes which are a part of that organization's history." The reviewer explained how Hughes established a ranch near Liberty Hill, how he recovered stolen horses in New Mexico, and how he rose in the Ranger ranks to the captaincy. "Incident follows incident and anecdote follows anecdote" we learn, and at book's end, "Martin tells how he has only two marks of that long service—the hearing in one ear lost because of inflammation caused when a tick crawled into it when he was sleeping on the range, and one bent right arm."[82] No mention was made of the accidental bullet wound in his foot, which certainly left some type of lasting scar.

With the biography available to the public (a copy then sold for $2.50), recognized as an important figure wherever he went, John Reynolds Hughes must have deep down realized he was an important part of Texas. And he was indeed.

~ 13 ~

Texas State Cemetery

"EVERY SCHOOL BOY IN TEXAS CUTS HIS EYE TEETH ON STO-
RIES ABOUT THE TEXAS RANGERS. I WASN'T ANY EXCEPTION."

—*Lyndon Baines Johnson to John R. Hughes, May 31, 1946*

Among the first, if not *the* first, to review Martin's *Border Boss* was noted Texas folklorist J. Frank Dobie. He provided a lengthy review for the *Houston Post*, certainly one of the highest circulating newspapers of the state in 1942. Dobie's review linked the Rangers with the men fighting in World War II: "Texas Rangers Operated on Lines Now Used by Commandos" the headline read. Hughes, in smaller type, is described as "One of the Best." Dobie's review actually summarizes Hughes's life as told in *Border Boss*, again pointing out how the Rangers enforced their own brand of justice in the vigilante killings of the eighteen men of the Olguin gang who had killed Capt. Frank Jones. Not Hughes, but an unidentified "remarkable undercover man" was responsible for the detective work that identified the men who killed Jones.

Dobie was more interested in comparing the unidentified Ranger's undercover work with the current British Commandos than naming him: he was Ernest St. Leon. St. Leon's plan and its execution afforded "a precise precedent for British Commando raids on continental Europe and for the Commando tactics that General MacArthur is said to be training large numbers of men in Australia for," Dobie wrote. He did quickly point out, however, that to "imagine all Texas Rangers" to be "lone wolves, acting on the spur of the moment without planned coordination" would show a misunderstanding of them.

Other Rangers such as Thalis T. Cook, James B. Gillett, and Joe Sitter as well as lawman George Scarborough received attention in Dobie's book review. Even Pancho Villa was identified as a friend of Hughes. Dobie concluded with Hughes's belief that because Villa "never went back on his word or on a friend" that he, in that regard, would "have made a good Texas ranger."[1]

John R. Hughes was not the only Ranger who could now look back on his younger days and reminisce. Ira Aten, from his home in El Centro, California, prepared an autobiography that J. Marvin Hunter serialized in *Frontier Times* in 1945. Old Frontier Battalion Ranger Doc Gourley, one of Captain Sieker's Company D boys from the 1880s, had also relocated to California. At least occasionally he and Hughes corresponded; a long letter signed "The Gourleys" must have brought back many memories for John Hughes. A warm feeling of being loved also emanated from that letter.

[W]e just love you and your letters a lot and . . . we always marvel that we can have your letters and that you are so well and able to wrote [*sic*] them nice letters. . . . I met you in that year 1892 in Alpine, Texas. You and Jim Putman were camped at the old Chambers place right close to Alpine. . . . Poor old Jim has been dead these long years now[2]. . . . Another old friend came from that same neck of the woods and that was Wood Saunders[3] —peace to his ashes. Another neighbor of them Putmans, Saunders, Gourleys was the Jones Family—Capt. Frank Jones family. He was a neighbor too. Another dear departed one of the rangers boys was Ike Herrin[4] . . . Capt. I have wondered just how many of the old fellows are left. I guess you and Mr. Ira Aten are the only ones. I am sure that I know of no others.[5]

The families mentioned in this letter all lived on Curry's Creek, a settlement several miles west of the present town of Kendalia in Kendall County, and some thirty miles north of San Antonio. Unfortunately few of the letters exchanged between the Gourleys and Hughes remain.

While Hughes celebrated his eighty-eighth birthday, the *Austin Statesman* presented a lengthy article headlined "Veteran of 28 Years as Ranger" to its readers. The *Statesman* reporter, Wick Fowler, had read *Border Boss* and could not contain his excitement or resist writing in a style more thrilling than author Jack Martin himself. Hughes's "blazing six-guns abruptly ended the careers of many murderous bad men in his capacity as a Texas Ranger," wrote Fowler. Continuing in the same breathless style, Fowler described how Hughes, in his "quiet and efficient way," earned the sobriquet of "Border Boss" from "the cattle rustlers, stage robbers and law-abiding citizenry alike." He "fought and whipped many of the nation's toughest criminals, outshooting the surest shots even after they were already drawing a bead."[6] Fowler's prose reads like the gaudiest of dust jacket blurbs on a western shoot-'em-up novel.

Later that year biographer Jack Martin himself, now a resident of Ann Arbor, Michigan, wrote to Hughes and apologized for the delay between letters, but suggested his longer letter now would be his Christmas communiqué. He had had his "annual bout" with the flu, and was so far behind in his work that he would not be able to visit again soon. Of concern were the sales of *Border Boss*. He had not heard from his publisher, the Naylor Company of San Antonio, in several months, but could only assume sales were "about as he expects." He said that from time to time he received letters from readers around the country, and "in every case they mention what a fine career" Hughes had. Of course many said they would like the opportunity of meeting Hughes.[7]

A very positive review of *Border Boss* by Joseph Dixon Matlock appeared soon after publication in the prestigious *Southwestern Historical Quarterly*. A professional researcher and professor of American history at the University of Texas, Matlock described Martin's biography as "another essential volume to the recorded history and lore of the Texas Rangers, [and] can be put on the popular reading list of all types and ages of readers, as it is biography, adventure, romance, and history enacted upon the large, colorful stage of Texas." It was further defined as "an excellent supplement" to *The Texas Rangers: A Century of Frontier Defense* by University of Texas professor Walter Prescott Webb.[8]

El Paso County Sheriff Allen G. Falby[9] now invited Hughes to be a guest at the annual Law Enforcement Educational Exhibit to be held in El Paso's Liberty Hall January 18–19, 1944. Among other distinguished guests were Col. Homer Garrison Jr., head of the Department of Public Safety (DPS) and past president of the Texas Police Association; Capt. C. E. Aldrich, the oldest Ranger captain in service; and Manuel T. "Lone Wolf" Gonzaullas, well-known lawman.[10] Garrison was scheduled to give a speech both nights of the exhibit; apparently Hughes's only purpose was to be present and enjoy the event.[11]

John R. Hughes, in spite of his age, certainly maintained an interest in many activities and what was happening in the political world. He wrote Lyndon B. Johnson, then a member of the House of Representatives, 10th Texas District. Hughes had received a copy of the *Congressional Record*, which he read and it "proved very interesting to me" and thus he had loaned it to some of his friends and relatives. "As far as I am posted," Hughes continued, "I am in favor of your actions in the house of representatives." Hughes, in case Congressman Johnson was unaware, pointed out he had been a member of the Texas Ranger service for twenty-eight years, and was a captain for twenty-two years. He concluded by wishing the future U.S. president "all kinds of good luck the same as I had while I was in the Ranger Service." Johnson responded two days later with a letter that undoubtedly made Hughes feel proud. "Seldom do I receive a letter of which I am prouder than the one you wrote to me," Johnson began. He wrote that his "every action since you first sent me here as your Representative in 1937 has been directed toward what I feel are your best interests and the best interests of all the other folks in the Tenth District." What was most heartening to Hughes, perhaps, was Johnson's concluding remarks: "Every school boy in Texas cuts his eye teeth on stories about the Texas Rangers. I wasn't any exception and I surely would enjoy the opportunity to sit down and listen to you tell about them. I know I would enjoy it immensely." Hughes was careful to preserve this charming letter in his collection of mementoes.[12]

Two months later a letter brought sadness to the captain. Ira Aten wrote from Burlingame, California, that his oldest brother, Tom, had

passed away in June at the age of ninety. He was buried in the Round
Rock Cemetery where Aten's parents and his oldest sister were all buried. He pointed out that outlaw Sam Bass was buried in the same cemetery. Aten signed his letter, "Your Old Ranger Companion of near 60
years ago."[13]

Friendly letters came from people in the corporate world as well.
William A. George, president of Universal Metals, Inc. of Hollywood,
California, wrote Hughes in early January 1947, to apologize for the
delay between letters due to his government work. What prompted the
letter was George's trip to a Hollywood bookstore to order *Border Boss*.
Both he and his wife, Burness, found it "extremely interesting." W. A.
George was in a revelatory mood as he explained he had just loaned the
book to a girl he used to go to school with in Abilene; at the same time
he had purchased a copy of Stuart N. Lake's *Wyatt Earp Frontier Marshal*.[14] He recalled that his first trip to El Paso and "the western country"
was in 1891, and his first meeting with Hughes was in 1895 when he
had met him along with Carl Kirchner, William Schmidt, Jim Fulgham,
and Ed Aten. The Rangers then were stationed at Chispa, when the
railroad tracks were being laid from there to the San Carlos Coal Mines.
They were "very interesting days at that time," wrote George. But as
much as Mr. and Mrs. George enjoyed Martin's book, he found fault
with it and willingly pointed out what he felt were the book's weaknesses. "I think that it fails to mention so many outstanding instances of
your most interesting and outstanding career and the wide appreciation
by all law abiding citizens of the west" he wrote, and further expressed
his uncertainty as to "whether it was your individual modesty or your
collaborator that failed to get different occurrences in the book." George
believed that there "was much left out that would have certainly been
most entertaining to the reading public and as I knew so many things
of your Ranger life I feel that if I was a writer or had the inclination to
write, that I could have gotten out more pertaining to your outstanding
life of which there was no other Ranger either private or captain that
could in any way compare with you."[15] These were legitimate concerns
perhaps, but whether Hughes chose to ignore some events of his career

in working with Martin, or whether Martin simply ignored certain incidents, remains unknown. No doubt Martin felt he included enough to satisfy his publisher. No book can satisfy every reader's taste.

Ira Aten and John Hughes remained the best of friends after their days as Texas Rangers. On February 2, 1947, Aten wrote Hughes from his home in El Centro reminding him that February 11—Hughes's birthday—"is close at hand" and he would be ninety-two that day. Aten mused philosophically about life, writing that ninety-two years "is a long time to live in this beautiful world & if any one has enjoyed it you have. I congratulate you in all you have done & I think your greatest acts is your kindness & love for little children." Aten was at the time enjoying his children and grandchildren, which suggests that at some time Hughes may have expressed to Aten that he regretted not having any children himself. Did Hughes reveal his love for children so readily because he himself did not have any of his own? Aten continued: "I can remember when we would go on scouts you will [*sic*, would] fill your pocket with candy & every little child you would see you would pitch him some candy. I'll bet that many people living recollect the Ranger that pitched them some candy from off his horse as he rode by."[16]

Attorney at Law Ralph W. Yarborough sent birthday wishes to Hughes on the day after his birthday, reminding him of their first meeting in W. W. Turney's law office in El Paso "twenty years ago this fall." Since that time Yarborough wrote that he had "read with interest everything that I saw about you, have admired your fine career and have been grateful that Texas had such officials in the days of her disquietude." Besides wishing him "many more birthdays," he stated that Hughes typified the Texas Rangers, and "added a dignity and a touch of the past to the Texas Centennial celebration" back in 1936 "that would otherwise have been missing."[17]

Hughes responded to Yarborough's letter, expressing his good feelings. "It makes me feel good to know that such persons as yourself take time out to read the articles which have been written about me and it pleases me more for you to remember the first time we met, twenty years ago." Since Hughes now had an office in Austin he could easily say that he would "drop by and visit" in the near future.

Through the years John R. Hughes kept the many good wishes sent to him, as well as clippings from newspapers about him or something that interested him deeply. Considered "scrapbooks" by some archivists, in addition to these collections he kept small notebooks, small enough to fit in a shirt pocket—or a saddlebag—which in effect were a diary. It is unknown how many of these exist today. Two have been examined by this author, and they both provide a fascinating look into the life of a man of action in his final years, in which he noted things as important as the surrender of Japan and the death of President Franklin Delano Roosevelt or as simple as that a small amount of rain had fallen.[18]

Unfortunately there are few references to his Ranger activities of decades before, no description of gunfights with fugitives or detailing a pursuit of a train robber, which the average historian would greatly appreciate. The entries reveal the occasional frustrating incidents, no doubt experienced by everyone at one time or another, as well as a recording of honors. For example, on January 1, 1942, he noted: "I was Grand Marshall [*sic*] in the Sun Bowl Carnival Parade today." On January 12 he wrote: "went to Dr. Cathcart and Mason. Dr. Cathcart was out of town and I quarreled with Dr. Mason."[19] On the same day Hughes "tried to turn in my Income Tax [but] they had no blanks." The tax office did acquire the proper blanks as eight days later, on January 20 he wrote: "Turned in my Income Tax." On his birthday that year he noted how he enjoyed sharing a birthday dinner with Mr. Herbert F. Greggerson and family near Ysleta.[20]

On April 8 Hughes noted that it was the fifth day of rain and it was cold at 9:00 p.m., and the newspaper had reported twelve inches of snow had fallen at Ruidoso, New Mexico. In spite of the "good rain here" Hughes had his "picture taken with S. D. Myres" the noted saddle maker.[21] On the tenth he wrote: "Sick today pain in my left knee" but four days later he drove his car to Ysleta. On April 28 he noted he "Bought new Speckticles [*sic*] at El Paso." Ira Aten's visits were wonderful as they allowed the two former Rangers to talk about old times and simply enjoy each other's company. Ira arrived in El Paso on May 1, 1942; the next day they drove to Fabens, and then on the third day they visited Juarez, Mexico, now with Ira's brother Ed as well. They then went on to Las Cruces, New Mexico. Then on the fourth day they went to Radium Springs; three days later they all ate dinner with Arthur Jay Robertson, frequently known as "Jack Robinson" and family in Las Cruces. Robertson, a native of Lincoln County, Arkansas, had served as a regular Ranger from December 28, 1917, through March 10, 1919, and had been honorably discharged.[22] On May 29 Hughes may have felt like an active lawman again as he noted in his diary that he "went to Hatch and Rincon to help settle a row between Mr. Calcot and Mr. White." The two communities of Hatch and Rincon were northwest of Las Cruces, only a few miles apart. There was no indication as to what the "row" was about, but apparently it was settled amicably as there is no later reference to it. On June 26, Hughes met with Drs. Cathcart and Mason for "First treatment of my nose."

Hughes was proud of his automobile and he frequently mentioned it in his journal. As he did not have a garage of his own, he stored the vehicle in the garage of friend Harry Moore. He refers to it as if it was a prize possession, writing of maintenance visits to tend to it. On January 27, 1942, he "Put water in Battery of my car"; on February 24 he "went to see my car"; on March 12 "Went to Harry Moores house to see my car[.] Put water in battery." At times his journal reads as if he is writing not just for his own reference, but providing posterity with material to study or analyze. In an entry dated July 30, 1937, Hughes wrote of the vehicle's history, and chose to provide information about the previous owner:

> I bought this auto from Jack Robinson [sic] in February 1924[.] he bought it new from the Webb Motor Co. [in] Fabens Texas either late in Dec. 1923 or Jan 1924. Jack is now Deputy sheriff at Las Cruces New Mexico—was last year Chief of Police at Las Cruces.

He further noted, "I have drove this car to the Pacific Ocean and back twice. Staid [sic] at Mr. Ira Atens house near El Centro California two winters with this car—and to San Diego—one trip to Hot Springs, Arkansas." He may have paused occasionally while writing in his little notebook, as the dashes so suggest. He continued: "Several Trips to Rockport Texas to go in the Salt Water—and to Corpus Christi—Several trips from El Paso to Austin[.]"

But besides such mundane items, Hughes recorded life's tragedies, some very personal. On August 6, 1943, he wrote: "Sister Nell Died today at Mound City Kansas." Nell, twin sister of Thomas Forester, was 83 years old, and apparently had lived her entire life in Mound City.[23]

Hughes also occasionally noted doctor visits and medicine he was taking, but also revealed more troubling aspects of his personality, that of occasionally being depressed, although he didn't use that specific term. On February 22, 1945, eleven days after his ninetieth birthday, he noted: "I am in bad shape[.] I don't think I will live very long." But in contrast to some individuals who allow depression to overwhelm them, Hughes still could get out and enjoy life and family and friends. On March 4 he and nephew Emery with his family visited the Longhorn Cavern in Burnet County, now a state park. He did not miss what was happening in the world, as on April 12 he wrote "Pres. Roosevelt died" and on May 7 he noted "Germany surrendered" and on August 15 he wrote "The Japs surrendered." On September 1, 1945, he visited Camp Mabry in Austin and noted that Fred C. Olsen had been made captain of the Texas Rangers. Two months later, on November 14, he returned to Camp Mabry "to get cartridges" but also noted he "failed to get cartridges." Hughes made no additional entry as to why he wanted cartridges.

The subject of death did occupy the thoughts of John R. Hughes more and more. On an undated page, Hughes listed men he had known who had passed on, and not from natural causes. He wrote at the top of the page: "my old companions Killed" and then listed Charles Fusselman, John F. "Smoker" Gravis, Capt. Frank Jones, Joe McKidrict, Baz L. "Bass" Outlaw, Pat Garrett, Joe Sitter, Dave Allison, H. L. Roberson, Herff Carnes, Ernest St. Leon, and George Scarborough. All had died by the gun; some murdered in cold blood, most killed in the line of duty.

The remembering of old friends killed in action as a Ranger, such as Charles Fusselman, or killed in a drunken brawl, such as Baz L. Outlaw, and the occasional friend or family member who died of natural causes, appears to have weighed heavily on Hughes's mind. He was also experiencing typical health problems of a man in his nineties.[24]

On April 15, 1947, he noted that he had bought five cartridges at seven cents each, but gave no indication of why he needed such a small number of cartridges. On May 20 Captain Olsen took him to visit the state Legislature, and on the following day they made a return visit. This second appearance received statewide notice courtesy the United Press. A report reached Amarillo from Austin headlined "Oldest, Youngest Texas Rangers Meet Legislature." In contrast to Captain Hughes's ninety-two years, Capt. Fred Olson was a mere forty-seven years old. He had been promoted to the rank of captain two years before on September 1, 1945, and Hughes, described as a "sturdy, white-whiskered, gold-badged 90-year-old Ranger" witnessed the honor.[25]

The reasons for the legislative visit were not merely to see or be seen. On the twentieth of May 1947, John R. Hughes accepted a singular honor: the House adopted Resolution No. 238 that day. It began by stating that the organization of the Texas Rangers was 124 years old, "giving it the distinction of being one of the oldest continuous organized constabularies in the World"; and that whereas John R. Hughes had served from 1887 to 1915 and that his service record "will vouchsafe to him a place high on the honor roll of officers and men of the Texas Rangers who have served Texas with honor and distinction to themselves," and that Hughes, the "patriarch of Texas Rangers" was now ninety-two and "yet is hale and hearty under the weight of years" and that he was the "pride of the Texas people" that he was invited to be the guest of the House on Wednesday May 21, and the privileges of the floor be extended to him.[26]

Not to be outdone, on the next day the Senate passed Resolution No. 113, placing him "high on the honor roll of officers and men who have served the State of Texas as Rangers, with honor and distinction." This resolution was signed by Allan Shivers, President of the Senate who would soon become the governor of Texas.[27] The press release that appeared in numerous newspapers pointed out that Hughes was the oldest Texas Ranger captain and Fred Olson, who had been promoted to that rank two years before, was the youngest captain. Both young and old Ranger captains were given a hearty welcome.[28]

What exactly happened between the honors bestowed upon him near the end of May and the beginning of June will be forever unknown. On Saturday, May 31, Hughes traveled out to his old ranch, the Running H, and went over the grounds, probably not changed greatly since the late 1880s when he was raising horses there. The family members were aware that he was not feeling well and that at times he was despondent. [29]

Three days later, on Tuesday, June 3, John Reynolds Hughes took his pearl-handled Colt .45 pistol with him into the garage of the Austin home of his niece at 4215 Avenue H. He placed the end of the barrel against the roof of his mouth. No one heard the shot, apparently, as no one investigated. That single shot ended the life of the oldest Texas Ranger and the last of the "Four Great Captains." When family members missed him at dinnertime they investigated and found him in the garage, lying on his back. Austin police were called, as was Justice of the Peace Mace Thurman. The police photographed the body, and Thurman conducted an inquest and determined the cause of death as suicide. He noted in his record book:

> On June 3, 1947 I was called to hold an inquest over the body of John R. Hughes. He was found dead in the garage of his home located at 4215 Ave. H Austin, Texas. He had a bullet wound thru his head—the bullet went in his mouth and came out the back upper part of the skull. He had told the family and neighbors that he was ready to die, and did not see why he should linger so long. A gun was found beside his body.

Thurman's final notation was his official finding: "Suicide—Due to Gunshot Wound." According to one early notice he had been in ill-health "for some time." In ill health perhaps, but he had rallied enough strength the previous week to visit the Legislature where he received the resolutions praising his career.[30]

Survivors of the old Ranger were listed as sister-in-law Mrs. Selma Hughes; a niece Miss Johanna Hughes, with whom he made his home; a nephew Emery H. Hughes of Austin; Tom and Fritz Hughes, living in Marshall Ford Dam; and nieces Mrs. Raymond Flachmeier of Austin, Mrs. Gene Ballanger of Tulsa, Oklahoma, Mrs. Mack George of Orange Grove, and Mrs. B. T. Collins of Alvin, Texas. The Weed-Corley Funeral Home of Austin handled the arrangements.[31] The pallbearers were C. M. Rogers, J. Albert Thompson, Lloyd W. Taylor, B. T. Collins, M. J. Jones, and Raymond H. Flachmeier, the latter the husband of John's niece, Valentine Hughes. John R. Hughes was buried in the State Cemetery alongside governors, senators, fellow Texas Rangers, and other distinguished heroes of Texas.

Hughes left no note explaining why he would take his own life, so one must always wonder. The fact that many of his old Ranger friends and companions were gone either from gun battles with outlaws or from natural causes, was at least occasionally on his thoughts is beyond question. His health was slowly deteriorating, and in all likelihood, he felt there was no reason to continue his life, knowing his failing health would not improve. His family mourned, and certainly his good friend Ira Aten mourned as well. Presumably, he learned of Hughes's death within a few days, perhaps by telephone. As far as known, he made no public comment on the suicide, but he wrote a letter to a friend to whom he revealed that learning of the passing of Hughes by his own hand, tested his optimistic nature, and raised the unanswerable question: "Oh, why did he want to leave this beautiful world."[32] Ira Aten, who was responsible more than anyone else for Hughes's becoming a Texas Ranger, lived many more years, surviving with his wife amidst children and grandchildren until his own death from natural causes on August 6, 1953, at his home in Burlingame, California.[33]

But like so many historical figures, such as Jesse James, Billy the Kid, and Meriwether Lewis, there was controversy over his death, as in the minds of some the declared suicide was in reality a homicide. The belief that there was foul play involved was not publicized in 1947, however. Apparently at least one family member doubted the suicide theory, not willing to accept the verdict of the official inquest. In 1981, historian James M. Day, then the director of the El Paso Centennial Museum, began researching Hughes's life with the intent of writing a full-length biography. He worked with nephew Emery H. Hughes, then eighty-one years old. Nephew Emery Hughes declared he did not believe his uncle's death was a suicide. "I just don't believe it," he said. The nephew's view of his uncle's passing was a surprise to Day, as he had always believed the "aging, despondent ranger shot himself while sitting on his porch swing in 1947."[34]

Emery Hughes maintained that he was closer to his uncle than anyone else and thus was in a position to know things that perhaps had been overlooked by the medical examiner and the police. Emery Hughes was quoted as saying, "They said he was despondent and they didn't make any further investigation. I guess they figured a 93-year-old man ought to be dead anyway."

Hughes further elaborated on the situation, pointing out that the old Ranger "often sat on the porch swing at his El Paso home with his pistol in his lap covered with a sweater. He said police found the gun at Hughes's side with a rag covering the handle—leading them to believe the death a suicide." Emery maintained that Hughes "was shot from a distance of a foot or so and a tooth was knocked out. Why didn't he just put the gun in his mouth?" At this point Emery Hughes made a statement that must have surprised other family members and friends, and certainly Justice of the Peace Mace Thurman: "He could have been 'tussling' with her (the woman who found out about his money)."

But according to the official report, prepared by S. H. Rosen of the Austin Police Department, the gun had been placed *inside* the mouth. Officer Rosen certainly had no reason to record anything other than what he observed as he was the first person outside the family who saw the body. Rosen wrote that he had responded to the call that there was a deceased person at 4215 Avenue H, and that he found the body lying on the ground with a bullet wound piercing the upper roof of his mouth exiting the crown of his skull. Lying at his feet was his cap with a part of his skull in it and hair from his head wedged to the cap where the bullet made the exit. A .45 Colt Revolver was also found at his feet with one of the shells fired, there were four unfired shells.[35]

Also at the scene were Dr. J. J. Brady who performed a "medical examination" at the scene, and Justice of the Peace Mace B. Thurman who held an official inquest. His verdict was the deceased came to his death, a suicide, "due to self-inflicted wound." Two other officers arrived

The impressive headstone for John R. Hughes in the Texas State Cemetery in Austin. The headstone is correct but the footstone (not shown) is in error by stating he was born in Kansas. *Photo courtesy Pat Parsons.*

at the scene, George Smith and J. C. Hester, who "took pictures, later going to Weed Corley Funeral Home to take more."[36]

Officer Rosen interviewed Mrs. Carlson, the nurse for Mrs. Selma Hughes, a widow in her eighties. Mrs. Carlson informed the officer that Captain Hughes was "first missed" at 4:30 p.m. as "he usually comes around for his supper [but] this evening he did not show up." They started looking for him within twenty minutes and then found his body in the garage. Dr. Brady had treated him "in the past" and said that "Capt. Hughes has been sick some lately and was sort of despondent."

The death of John R. Hughes remained a mystery, at least according to the headlines of various newspapers that carried the United Press story. The woman who Hughes may have been "tussling" with was never identified, and it is doubtful that any of the immediate family were even aware of the unidentified woman being in or near the house when the fatal shot was fired—if indeed she even existed. Apparently nephew Emery H. Hughes was the sole person who believed the death of Hughes was not a suicide. James M. Day certainly did not accept the homicide theory. When the homicide theory broke, Hughes had been dead for over thirty years.

Day was collaborating with Emery Hughes on his uncle's life story, and was working to have his papers and correspondence donated to the University of Texas at El Paso. "Most of the documents originated in El Paso," Day explained, "[as] Hughes served with Company D along the border from El Paso to Brownsville and after his retirement, he spent most of his life here."[37] Day continued to gather material about John R. Hughes for the book, but if he ever finished a manuscript, it never became the book he envisioned and if he did finish a manuscript its whereabouts is unknown. Some of the material John R. Hughes left was placed with the University of Texas in El Paso, now archived in the Special Collections of the C. L. Sonnichsen Room. Other original documents found their way to the Austin History Center as well as the Texas Ranger Hall of Fame and Museum in Waco. In the final analysis, each of those repositories was an appropriate place for the personal papers of Texas Ranger Captain John R. Hughes to be preserved.

~ 14 ~

The Great Captains

"TEXAS RANGER. [T]HERE IS A SORT OF MAGIC ABOUT THE WORD. THERE IS SOMETHING ABOUT IT THAT MARKS THE MAN SO TITLED AS AN ELEMENT APART FROM THE GENERAL TERM OFFICER; SOMETHING THAT MARKS HIM IN THE PUBLIC MIND AS A SUPER-LAW ENFORCER. AND THERE IS SOMETHING MORE THAN MEN BEHIND IT ALL; THERE IS A TRADITION, AND EACH MAN—LIKE CAPTAIN JOHN HUGHES—CONTRIBUTES SOME PART TO THAT TRADITION."

—*C. L. Douglas*, The Gentlemen in White Hats, *1934*

In the history of the Texas Rangers there were many captains; the names of Jack Hays, Samuel Walker, Ben McCulloch, Rip Ford, Sul Ross, John B. Jones, and L. H. McNelly deserve the title of great as much perhaps as Brooks, Hughes, McDonald, and Rogers.[1] Of those featured in chapters in the 1996 *Rangers of Texas*, all were deceased prior to the "great captains" beginning their careers. They were Rangers during the heyday of the horseback Ranger while the careers of the four "great captains" transitioned from the horseback days into the beginning years of the automobile. All were instrumental in creating the mystique of the Texas Ranger, the recognition of which exists perhaps more so today.

On November 10, 1930, John H. Rogers collapsed and passed to the heavenly reward in which he believed all his life. One obituary described him as one of the bravest of the brave who never tarnished his oath of office, never turned his back upon a criminal fleeing from justice, never showed the white feather in the hour of conflict and in deportment and practice and custom and habit was a model for his kind. . . . Men said he bore a charmed life. He served with a whole host of the daring rough riders of Texas who battled for law observance with their sixshooters and made the resorts of smugglers and cattle thieves and robbers and gunmen places for the habitation for civilized men and women.[2]

These words described John H. Rogers, but they equally describe the contribution of Brooks, Hughes, and McDonald. Each of the four was great in his way; each contributed mightily in establishing a greater respect for the law. The quartet, working separately as well as occasionally together, became the transition pieces between one era and the next, each providing an essential link between the two. Each Texas Ranger of the twenty-first century can look back upon the service of these four as a model.

Walter Prescott Webb was not the first to write a history of the Texas Rangers, but his study was the most comprehensive to that date, 1935. He wrote of the numerous captains in the organization's long history, focusing more on their role and influence than that of the enlisted men who risked their lives fighting Comanches, Kiowas, Mexican bandits, or Anglo fugitives from justice.

The bulk of Webb's *The Texas Rangers* was pre-twentieth century, tracing the history of the organization from its founding in 1823 when Stephen F. Austin employed ten men to service. The individual considered as a Texas Ranger continued through the days of the Republic, statehood, the Civil War, and State Police, although the term "Texas Ranger" was not always used. Following the end of Reconstruction in Texas, in 1874 Gov. Richard Coke, created the Frontier Battalion that in the early twentieth century became the Ranger Force. Entering the twentieth century in his history, Webb coined the phrase "The Four Captains," which has evolved into the

"Four Great Captains," in effect unintentionally minimizing the role and contribution of previous captains.

From the amount of space Webb devoted to Capt. William Jesse McDonald, it is apparent that he considered Captain Bill the "greatest" of the four. This begs the question: how can an individual measure greatness when the subjects are all doing similar work during the same time and same place? If one considers length of service, Rogers holds the record of the four. J. A. Brooks served from 1882 until 1906: twenty-four years. J. H. Rogers served from 1882 until 1911: twenty-nine years. W. J. McDonald served from 1891 until the end of 1906: fifteen years. And J.R. Hughes served from 1887 until early 1915: twenty-eight years. They served an aggregate of ninety-six years, with an average of twenty-four.

All four captains served long years during dangerous times, patrolling a huge area of the state with very few men. The period of their service followed the days when patrols scouted after "Indian sign," with the intent of engaging a band of Kiowas or Comanches in a fight. To most of the young men who joined in the early 1870s, an Indian fight represented adventure and it was their purpose for joining. By the end of the decade, however, the frontier had pushed westward and the once nomadic tribes survived on reservations. By the time Brooks, Hughes, McDonald, and Rogers entered the service the former threat to the advancement of white civilization was gone; now the Frontier Battalion's main concern was maintaining law and order throughout the state.

It was dangerous to be a Texas Ranger, as evidenced by the fact that three of the four captains received wounds at least once in gunfights with outlaws. Brooks and Rogers were seriously wounded in the 1887 gunfight against the Connor gang in Sabine County; one Ranger lost his life in that engagement.[3] McDonald received wounds in a gunfight with the sheriff of Childress County in 1893.[4] Ironically, Hughes was wounded only once during his twenty-eight years as a Ranger, and that was by accident when he dropped his pistol and it discharged into his foot.

The four great captains made up a stalwart quartet of honest law enforcement individuals. Whereas the four had similar experiences patrolling huge areas, they were seldom together. Governor Culberson's order to prevent the prizefight in El Paso in 1896 placed not only the four captains but the adjutant general together as well. Today it seems strange that the governor would order over thirty Rangers to El Paso to prevent a prizefight, which would harm neither person nor property. Brooks and Hughes did work together at the Temple railroad strike of 1894, but the only time the four captains worked together was in El Paso in 1896.

One may be tempted to ask which of the four was the greatest. This is a difficult question to even consider, as what constitutes greatness is subjective. Length of service would suggest a degree of greatness, perhaps, but all four served a long time. However, the number of years as a Texas Ranger is only part of the equation. All but Hughes served in various law enforcement capacities after leaving the Rangers.

Captain Brooks began his career on January 15, 1883, as a private in Company F, commanded by Charles B. McKinney. He ended his Ranger career twenty-four years later as a captain. As a sergeant in 1886, Brooks and two other Rangers crossed the Red River into Oklahoma Territory in search of horse thieves. In the Chickasaw nation, the Rangers challenged the alleged horse thief: Brooks killed him to preserve his own life. Curiously, in spite of the three acting in the line of duty, they quickly faced a murder charge. The Ranger trio stood their trial before the famous "Hanging Judge" Isaac C. Parker at Fort Smith, Arkansas. After a ten-day trial, the jury found them guilty of manslaughter. Judge Parker fortunately believed the verdict was unjust and suspended the sentence. On September 13, 1887, President Grover Cleveland issued them a pardon.[5] Ironically, during August that same year, in Williamson County, John R. Hughes joined the Rangers to begin his long career. He was certainly aware of Brooks's stressful experience, and recalled it in 1915 when he told a newspaper reporter, with possibly a hint of pride, "I have never been indicted by a grand jury." He could have said the same about John H. Rogers. After retiring from the Ranger service,

Brooks served many years as county judge of Brooks County, named in his honor.

Rogers, who served more years as a Ranger than the others, continued in law enforcement as a United States marshal. Rogers and Brooks worked together more often than the other two, and both were seriously wounded in the gunfight against the Connor gang. A bullet wounded Rogers in the left arm and rib cage; Brooks lost three fingers of his left hand and received a severe wound in his right hand in this fight. Captain Rogers gained his greatest fame in capturing the fugitive Gregorio Cortez in 1901. Later he worked in Colorado County to reduce the amount of violence the Reese-Townsend feudists created.

Captain McDonald began his career as a Special Ranger in 1889. When an opening appeared, he applied and Governor Hogg named him captain of Company B on February 1, 1891. Among his most noteworthy incidents was the capture of the two men who robbed the bank in Wichita Falls, killing a cashier in the process. McDonald and several of his Rangers captured the pair the following day. During the night of February 26, 1896, a mob stormed the jail and lynched the two prisoners. McDonald could not have prevented this as he and his men had already left Wichita Falls.[6] He served a mere fifteen years as a Ranger, but before and after his Ranger experience, he had worked in various law enforcement capacities. McDonald as well worked in Colorado County during the Reese-Townsend feud. All four of the Great Captains worked in Colorado County, preventing further mob violence, but not all together. The feud was carried on by two generations, covered action in three counties, lasted four decades, and caused numerous killings, but there were no convictions. It was not the bloodiest of the great feuds of Texas, but no other feud brought in the four captains as did the troubles in Colorado County.

John R. Hughes began as a private and earned promotion to the rank of captain. He worked twenty-eight years, less about six months when he worked as a mine guard in Mexico, and worked every county along the Rio Grande border as well as in East Texas, Central Texas, the Panhandle, and in virtually every corner of the state. His work occasionally took him beyond the border of Texas into Arkansas as well as New Mexico, and into Mexico.

Even though he served fewer years than Brooks, Hughes, and Rogers, some have named McDonald as the premier Ranger captain, although with no official endorsement. Virgil E. Baugh wrote of McDonald and Hughes together, but provided no clues as to why he chose those two captains over Brooks or Rogers. Was it because McDonald was fortunate enough to have befriended two U.S. presidents—Theodore Roosevelt and Woodrow Wilson—and in so doing, became a guest at the White House? Thanks to Albert Bigelow Paine, his biography appeared during his lifetime, in 1909, thus bringing his name to the forefront in the mind of many. Neither Rogers nor Brooks nor Hughes had an amanuensis such as McDonald had, and they probably would have rejected one if one had appeared. Besides the book, his official biographer penned articles about the man, thus making his name nearly a household word.

Neither Brooks nor Rogers experienced working with a publisher, although Brooks attempted to write his memoirs in 1935 but did not finish; no publisher deemed his autobiography worthy of publication, although it was utilized by his biographer decades later. Writers such as W. W. Sterling and W. P. Webb were able to interview them and accepted their version of events as accurate. While still an active Ranger and during retirement, Hughes cooperated with newspaper reporters and gave interviews, although much of what did appear in print dealt with his experiences prior to enlisting in the Ranger service. Interviews with a Ranger captain always made good newspaper copy.

As historians examine the lives of their subjects, they discover their personalities. History portrays McDonald as somewhat of a showman. The expression "One Riot, One Ranger" continues to be associated with McDonald's name, as if he had indeed stopped a riot by himself. In addition, an officer of the U.S. Army described McDonald as a man who would "charge Hell with a bucket of water," which of course may evoke a smile, but nothing more. Only McDonald had such quotations attached to his name.

History considers John H. Rogers the "Christian Ranger" in that his faith was on display, whereas it was the bravado of McDonald that was on display. Rogers may have indeed carried a Bible in his pocket or saddlebag, and considered it of greater value than his Winchester or six-shooter. He was devoted to his career, but more so to his faith and family. On the other hand, James A. Brooks was an alcoholic who neglected his wife and family, to the extent that he was a near stranger to his children. He gained the respect of South Texans nevertheless, as residents of the county elected him judge of the county that bears his name today. He served two years in the state Legislature and served as county judge for twenty-eight years.

John Reynolds Hughes never wrote his autobiography, although by granting reporters interviews he provided details of his life, which otherwise would have been lost. He experienced many incidents similar to those Brooks, Rogers, and McDonald experienced, but no president ever invited him to the White House, nor did a president ever invite him to participate in a wolf hunt, as Theodore Roosevelt invited McDonald to do.[7] Hughes was, however, part of a group providing security for President Díaz of Mexico and President William H. Taft, and later for Theodore Roosevelt. No newspaper reporter mentioned him carrying a Bible in his pocket as Rogers did, but in his later years, he taught Sunday School classes in Ysleta, thus one can surmise he was as much a true Christian as Rogers was. Moreover, Hughes avoided alcohol as Rogers and McDonald did, but Brooks did not.

In the final analysis, attempting to measure the greatness of these four men will result in many differing opinions. Walter Prescott Webb considered McDonald the greatest of the four; Virgil E. Baugh apparently had a fondness for both McDonald and Hughes. Jack Martin certainly considered Hughes most worthy of a biography. Zane Grey chose to dedicate his *Lone Star Ranger* to Hughes. Artist Leona Freeman convinced Hughes to sit for a full-length portrait in oils, which resulted in furthering his importance as an iconic figure in Texas history. Each of the four Ranger captains was great in his own way, and each was considered great by the people who knew them. Each was also considered great by the individuals who had cattle or horses stolen by thieves or bandits, and saw their property returned safely. Each was considered great by the individual whose life was saved by a Texas Ranger captain, be his name Brooks, Hughes, McDonald, or Rogers.

Endnotes

Notes to Introduction

1. *San Antonio Daily Express*, January 17, 1915. The headline read "Sunday School Superintendent Has More Battles with Outlaws than any Other Man in the U.S."

2. *San Antonio Light*, May 30, 1915. The *Light* article carries only one illustration, a bust photograph showing a clean-shaven Hughes with black hat, suit, and tie. Cropped from a group photo showing Hughes, Captain Monroe Fox, Jefferson E. Vaughn and Leo P. Bishop, it hardly represented the expected image of a Ranger.

3. *San Antonio Daily Express*, January 17, 1915.

4. Ibid., October 11, 1925. Pearl Virginia Jourdin, born about 1885 in Texas, married Samuel W. Crossley on December 31, 1908, in San Antonio. S. W. Crossley practiced medicine while Pearl taught school. By 1920 their two children were Grace A., age nine years, and son Wallace, age seven years. Her mother, Mollie "Giordano" [*sic*], age sixty years, lived with them. Pearl V. J. Crossley died March 14, 1945, at the age of sixty-nine in Del Rio, Texas. Texas Death Certificate # 9969. 14th U.S. Census, El Paso County, Texas. Enumerated January 27, 1920. ED 94, sheet 17A. Interestingly, Pearl's aunt, Virginia R. Jourdin, married Augustine Montaigue Gildea, a one-time fugitive wanted in Lincoln County, New Mexico. After Gildea became a respectable citizen in Texas, he and Ranger Hughes met on official business, Hughes apparently unaware of Gildea's past. Obituary for Mollie Jourdin in the *San Antonio Daily Express*, April 23, 1933.

5. John R. Hughes, as told to L.A. Wilke, "The Wide Loop of a Ranger Noose," *Real Detective* 38, no. 2, September 1936.

6. Dane Coolidge, *Fighting Men of the West* (New York: E. P. Dutton & Co., 1932). The Hughes chapter covers pages 137–63 and includes two photographs of Hughes, one which Coolidge claims to have taken himself, showing an aged Hughes with his shadow on the wall. The book also contains the famous group photograph of Hughes with Oden, Speaks, and Putman. See also the Haley book review appearing in the *Southwestern Historical Quarterly* 36, no. 1 (July 1932): 75–76.

7. C. L. Douglas, *The Gentlemen in the White Hats: Dramatic Episodes in the History of the Texas Rangers* (1934; repr., Austin: State House Press, 1992).

8. Eugene Cunningham, *Triggernometry: A Gallery of Gunfighters* (1941; repr., Caldwell, ID: The Caxton Printers, Ltd., 1982). Cunningham dedicated his book "Affectionately and Appreciatively" to Hughes and James B. Gillett, "Two Great Horseback Rangers friends of mine."

9. William Warren Sterling, *Trails and Trials of a Texas Ranger* (1959; repr., Norman: University of Oklahoma Press, 1969).

10. Virgil E. Baugh, *A Pair of Texas Rangers: Bill McDonald and John Hughes*, The Great Western Series, No. 9 (Washington, D.C.: Potomac Corral of The Westerners, December 1970).

11. Jack Martin, *Border Boss: Captain John R. Hughes—Texas Ranger* (San Antonio: Naylor Company, 1942; repr., Austin: State House Press, 1990, with introduction by Mike Cox).

12. Harold Preece, *Lone Star Man: Ira Aten Last of the Old Time Rangers* (New York: Hastings House, 1960), 160.

13. Ibid.

14. G. W. Ogden, "The Watch on the Rio Grande," *Everybody's Magazine*, September 1911, 353–65. The publication was founded in 1899 by John O'Hara Cosgrave and frequently had a circulation of well over 100,000. Hughes's reputation could only have been increased with this article praising him and the Texas Rangers as a protective force in society. George Washington Ogden gained considerable recognition for his western themed articles and novels, of which *The Trail Rider*, published in 1925, is his best known.

Chapter 1: A Terror to all the Bad Men

1. Obituary for Thomas Hughes in the Wickham Scrapbook Collection, vol. 9, page 99. Hannah Wickham created these scrapbooks, a total of nineteen notebooks of newspaper clippings pertaining to individuals and happenings in and about Mound City and Linn County, Kansas. Wickham clipped from various newspapers for fifty years until her death in 1935. The originals are archived in the Sommerville Free Library of Mound City; duplicates are housed in the Linn County Museum and Genealogy Library in Pleasanton, Linn County, Kansas. Hereafter cited as WSB Collection.

2. Hughes and Sargent genealogical records from archives in Linn County, Kansas Historical Museum and Genealogical Library. Copy of the Hughes-Bond-Sargent Family Trees researched and recorded by Mrs. Clifton Hughes Taylor, Houston, Texas. Mr. Clifton H. Taylor was a grandson of Emery S. Hughes, a brother of John R. Hughes.

3. Thomas Hughes obituary, WSB Collection, Vol. 9, 99–100.

4. The date of their marriage was either 1846 or 1847. The research of Mrs. C. H. Taylor shows June 1, 1847, whereas the obituaries for Thomas and Jane Sargent Bond Hughes both indicate their marriage took place on June 1, 1846.

5. Jane Bond Hughes obituary, WSB Collection, Vol. 11, 14.

6. Ibid.

7. Deed Records, Henry County, Illinois. Vol. 22, 533–34. The date of the sale was October 20, 1855.

8. Ibid., Vol. 25, 153–54. The date of this sale was October 3, 1856. Jack Martin, in *Border Boss*, relates the family was living in Dixon, Lee County, Illinois, some seventy miles northeast, but no official record of this move has been located.

9. Thomas Hughes obituary, WSB Collection, Vol. 11, 14.

10. Ibid.

11. Undated newspaper clipping, but October, 1909, in the WSB Collection.

12. *Border Sentinel*, Mound City, Kansas, December 24, 1869.

13. Undated newspaper clipping, but October, 1909, in the WSB Collections.

14. The Marais des Cygnes "massacre" was an atrocity led by a band of guerrillas under command of Charles Hamilton. He and some forty of his followers captured a group of eleven "free-state" men who were unarmed. Hamilton ordered the free-state men shot, but only five of them actually were killed, the others managing to escape. This occurred on May 19, 1858, and was merely one of many acts of brutality committed by men with opposing political views over the question of slavery. *Southeast Kansas Adventures & Day Trips*, 31–33. *Southeast Kansas Living Magazine*, Humboldt, Kansas, 2009. For a balanced treatment of events in Kansas prior to the war see *Border Warfare in Southeastern Kansas: 1856–1859* by G. Murlin Welch (Pleasanton, Kans.: Linn County Historical Society, 1977).

15. *El Paso Herald-Post*, June 4, 1947. This article reporting the death of Hughes provides a brief summary of his life and career. The obituary gives no indication as to who informed the *Herald-Post* that Hughes's fascination with the Indian Territory "made him run away" nor does it give any indication of Hughes's survivors. The *Austin-American* of June 4, 1947, however does provide such a list, naming a sister-in-law and numerous nieces and nephews.

16. Martin, *Border Boss*, 8.

17. 9th U.S. Census, Linn County, Kansas. Enumerated June 2, 1870, 64.

18. 1875 Kansas state census of Linn County, 26. Here Thomas Hughes is shown to be a hotel keeper with real property valued at $5,000 and personal property valued at $1,000. In 1875, at least on the day of the census, the hotel had four boarders. The hotel keeper was successful enough to hire a cook, a twenty-four-year-old black woman, curiously from Texas.

19. *Austin-American*, June 4, 1947.

20. Ibid., June 5, 1947. The Austin newspaper reports that Hughes lived with the Choctaws and Osage for four years, whereas the *Herald-Post* of El Paso obituary reports only "he lived with the Indians." The *Oxford Times* of July 6, 1871, bemoans the fact that "loose stock" were quickly destroying the "few remaining tepees" where once the "leading chiefs of the Osage tribe" dwelled. An article announcing his retirement from the Rangers and based on an interview with Hughes indicated that after leaving home "he lived for six years with different tribes of red men" prior to moving to Central Texas. *San Antonio Daily Express*, January 17, 1915, reprinted in *Frontier Times* 5, no. 1 (October 1927): 4–8.

21. Martin, *Border Boss*, 17–18.

22. Jo Ella Powell Exley, *Frontier Blood: The Saga of the Parker Family* (College Station: Texas A&M University Press, 2001), 261.

23. The photographs are preserved in the "John R. Hughes Scrapbook" in the C. L. Sonnichsen Special Collections Department of the University of Texas at El Paso. Hereafter cited as Hughes Scrapbook.

24. *El Paso Herald-Post*, April 12, 1938. The article, "No Thief Is Going to Take the Captain's Automobile," was one of a series in Pyle's regular "Touring with Pyle" column. Pyle spent several hours in his interview with Hughes, concluding his article: "I've never spent a calmer, pleasanter half-day with anybody in my life."

25. "Capt. John R. Hughes, Fighting Ranger; Force of Circumstances Made a Peace Officer," *El Paso Herald*, January 13–14, 1923 (weekend edition). In contrast, Martin relates that Hughes's arm was injured in an unusual manner: his employer, identified as Art Rivers, was fighting with an Indian and about to be killed. Hughes stepped in and saved Rivers's life, but in the process he was injured. "The white lad threw up his arm to deflect the blow. The weapon shattered the bones in his arm, but he thus saved himself from more critical injuries." *Border Boss*, 3. It is doubtful if such an individual as Art Rivers existed as no contemporary record of the man has been found.

26. William Cx Hancock, "Ranger's Ranger," *True West* 8, no. 4 (March–April 1961): 23–24. Hancock spent some time interviewing Emery H. Hughes and gathered some photographs from him as well. Three of the illustrations in this article are from the Emery H. Hughes Collection: one showing Hughes's rifle and boots, one showing Emery holding his uncle's rifle, and one showing the portrait of John R. Hughes painted for the 1936 Texas Centennial celebration held in Dallas. The items have since been separated, but remain in the family's private collections.

27. Pearl Virginia Crossley in the *San Antonio Express*, October 11, 1925.

28. Roy Wilkerson Aldrich was born in Quincy, Illinois, in 1869. During the Spanish-American War he was commissioned a 2nd Lieutenant. He served with the British Army during the Boer War in South Africa. From 1903–7 he was sheriff of Kiowa County, Oklahoma Territory, and then from 1907–15 he worked in real estate in Corpus Christi and San Antonio. In 1915, the year Hughes was forcibly retired from the service, he enlisted in Company A, Ranger Force. In 1918 he was promoted to captain and quartermaster. He retired from the service in 1947. He assisted Walter Prescott Webb substantially during his work on his book *The Texas Rangers: A Century of Frontier Defense* (1935). He died January 29, 1955, and was buried in Oakwood Cemetery in Austin. His 10,000-volume library was acquisitioned by Sul Ross State University. *New Handbook of Texas*, s.v. "Roy Wilkerson Aldrich," by Morris G. Cook.

29. *Ellis County Star*, May 17, 1877.

30. Ibid., May 24, 1877.

31. Gary Kraisinger and Margaret Kraisinger, *The Western: The Greatest Texas Cattle Trail 1874–1886* (Newton, Kans.: Mennonite Press, 2004), 133–35. This work cites the *Ellis County Star* of June 7, 1877.

32. Jim French and John Middleton both attained notoriety due to their involvement in the Lincoln County War, although both remain mysterious figures. French may have been half-Cherokee, suggesting he was a native of the Indian Territory where Hughes spent some time. He was in Lincoln, New Mexico Territory, on March 31, 1878, when Billy the Kid and others ambushed Sheriff William Brady and four of his deputies. The gunfire killed Sheriff Brady and one deputy, but in turn, French was wounded. He, as well as Middleton, was one of the men defending the home of Alexander McSween during the "Five Day Battle" that left McSween and several others dead. French, Middleton, and Billy the Kid escaped. French's fate is unknown; Middleton died of smallpox in New Mexico on November 19, 1882. Frederick W. Nolan, *The Lincoln County War: A Documentary History* (Norman: The University of Oklahoma Press, 1992), 461, 475. Nothing more is known of Charles Nebo.

33. Hughes here refers to the Richard King Ranch of South Texas. The appellation of Santa Gertrudis Ranch was natural, as King had purchased the 15,000-acre *Rincon de Santa Gertrudis* land grant as well as the 53,000-acre *Santa Gertrudis de la Garza* land grant in 1853 and 1854 respectively. In 1877, when Hughes was driving cattle, what we know today as the King Ranch was called the Santa Gertrudis Ranch. King's brand of the Running W appeared in the 1860s but was not officially recorded until February 9, 1869. *New Handbook of Texas*, s.v. "King Ranch," by John Ashton and Edgar

P. Sneed; and Ibid., "Richard King," by Bruce S. Cheeseman; and Ibid., "Santa Gertrudis Cattle," by Art Leatherwood.

34. Although considered non-combatants by Lincoln County War historian Frederick W. Nolan, during the "Five Day Battle" several of the fighting men stationed themselves in the Ellis home. On February 19, 1878, Benjamin Ellis served on the coroner's jury on the body of John H. Tunstall, whose death began the shooting phase of the Lincoln County War that resulted in notoriety for Billy the Kid. Nolan, *The Life and Death of John Henry Tunstall* (Albuquerque: University of New Mexico Press, 1965), 285. In one of the more intriguing ironies of Wild West history, not only did Hughes know the Ellis family when in Linn County, but also was at least aware of the Olinger family, who lived there in 1860 and perhaps through the decade. Head of household William Olinger died in Mound City in 1861; he was survived by his wife Rebecca and three children: John Wallace, Amerideth R. B., and Rosanna Amanda. Amerideth R. B. Olinger, known as "Pecos Bob," with brother John, were in Lincoln County at least by 1876. John moved on to California while Bob remained. Lincoln County Sheriff Pat Garrett employed Robert Olinger and James Bell to guard the imprisoned Billy the Kid while he waited for the hangman's noose for the Sheriff Brady killing. On April 28, 1881, the Kid killed both during his escape. Frederick W. Nolan, *The Lincoln County War: A Documentary History*, 477, and e-mail to author from Nolan, January 9, 2010.

35. See note 17, *supra*.

36. This was the firm of Major Andrew Drumm, a well-known cattleman of Ohio. He had purchased cattle in Texas and had them driven overland to Kansas markets. Major Drumm was in Dallas attending the Texas Cattleman's Convention in 1919 and became ill. Friends rushed him to San Antonio but he died there on April 14, 1919. His widow survived him; the couple had no children, and he had bequeathed part of his fortune to endow a home for homeless and friendless children in Kansas City. Born February 6, 1828, in Ohio, he was ninety-one at the time of his death. *San Antonio Express*, April 14, 1919. The "Snider" firm was that of Mississippi brothers Dudley H. and John W. Snyder, successful cattle dealers. 10th U.S. Census, Williamson County, Texas. Enumerated June 14, 1880, 437. Their cattle operations covered lands from the Gulf of Mexico to the Pacific shore. John M. Sharpe, "Experiences of a Texas Pioneer," in *The Trail Drivers of Texas*, comp. and ed. J. Marvin Hunter (Austin: University of Texas Press, 1986), 721–29.

37. *Oxford Times*, June 22, 1871. This issue was volume one, number one.

38. Ibid., July 13, 1871.

39. 10th U.S. Census, Linn County, Kansas. Enumerated June 2, 1880, 62. His occupation is now given simply as "printer." The Thomas Hughes household is number 79 while the Chandler household is number 80.

40. *Oxford Times*, August 31, 1871.

41. Ibid., September 21, 1871.

42. Ibid., October 7, 1871.

43. Ranger Service Record of W. P. Hughes; *Frontier Times* 5, no. 2 (November 1927): 88; *El Paso Herald-Post*, December 1, 1936; *Northport News*, April 12, 1940. Hughes today rests in the Forest Home Cemetery in Northport, Washington.

44. The information about Hughes's life on the Fort Sill reservation and cattle driving years is principally from his untitled recollections dated September 18, 1932, while living in Austin. The two-page typed memoir is in the Roy Aldrich Collection, Archives of the Big Bend, Sul Ross University, Alpine, Texas.

45. *Austin Daily Democratic Statesman*, October 23, 1878.

46. The "Hughes Brothers' Horse record" is preserved in the Archives of the Texas Ranger Hall of Fame & Museum in Waco. This ledger has no pagination.

47. *Austin Daily Democratic Statesman*, January 5, 1879.

48. Hughes Brothers' Horse Record.

49. The description and location appears on a bill of sale signed by Emery S. Hughes, dated December 25, 1881. Original in Hughes Scrapbook. The original town of Bagdad became a ghost town when the railroad bypassed it to lay tracks at nearby Leander; today what was Bagdad is part of Leander.

50. Williamson County Deed Records, Vol. 37, July 1885, 484–85. Emery S. Hughes, according to one obituary, left Kansas and went to Austin "forty-five years ago" which would date his arrival as 1871. WSB Collection, Vol. 10, 90.

51. Hughes Brothers' Horse Record.

52. *Morrison & Fourney's General Directory of the City of Austin For 1881–82*. Printed by E. W. Swindels, 1881. "Fritz" Bastian is listed on page 52 as proprietor of the *Statesman* book bindery, located on the northwest corner of Congress Avenue and Mulberry (today 10th Street). Emery S. Hughes is listed on page 100 as foreman of the Book and Job Department, *Austin Daily Statesman*. He roomed at the Congress Avenue Hotel.

53. Hughes Brothers' Horse Record.

54. *Austin Daily Statesman*, October 11, 1882. The announcement also appeared in the *Waco Examiner*, as John R. Hughes kept a clipping announcing the marriage in his scrapbook. The quotations are from the *Waco Daily Examiner* of October 10, 1882. Governor S. W. T. Lanham named Emery S. Hughes

Texas State Printer. He died April 21, 1916, in Austin and is buried in Austin's Oakwood Cemetery. The Travis County census of 1880 shows the Fred and Johanna Bastian family, all born in Prussia, included Helen, Emile, Selma, Julia, and Alma. The 1875 City of Austin census, however, shows the last child, Alma, as American born, suggesting the family arrived in the United States between 1866 and 1869. "Schedule of Inhabitants in the City of Austin, County of Travis, State of Texas." Original ledger in Austin History Center, Austin, 107–8.

55. Hughes Brothers' Horse Record.

56. G. W. Ogden, "The Watch on the Rio Grande," *Everybody's Magazine* 25, no. 3 (September 1911): 353–65. Ogden apparently interviewed not only Hughes but other Rangers working on the border for this lengthy article. Since Hughes was still an active Ranger at this time, the interview must be considered more accurate than the writings of later years by such popular writers as Jack Martin. To contrast this apparently accurate portrayal of Hughes's recovering the stolen horses, Dane Coolidge described how Hughes had trailed the gang to the southwest corner of New Mexico Territory, and with an unidentified sheriff "jumped them; and when the smoke had cleared away four horse-thieves were stretched out dead." Hughes, Coolidge explained correctly, returned home a year after he had left, with seventy-five horses, including his own favorite stallion, Moscow. Ogden was born about 1862 in New Jersey but when he moved to Texas is unknown. 10th U.S. Census, Union County, New Jersey. Enumerated June 10, 1880, 370.

57. *Houston Chronicle*, December 27, 1914. "Bandit Hunter for 28 Years to Retire; Capt. Hughes's Story" is the headline of this interview. The *Chronicle* sent one of their reporters to interview Hughes on the occasion of his retirement. Of the interview, the reporter wrote: "He told his story modestly, under pressure from his visitor. In his telling he related a simple narrative of facts. He left out the grand-coloring because it is 'all in a day's work' with him—this catching of murderers and cutthroats upon 'the last frontier.'"

58. *San Antonio Daily Express*, January 17, 1915. "Sunday School Superintendent Has More Battles with Outlaws Than any Other Man in the U.S." The article followed Hughes's retirement after twenty-eight years in the service of the state. A version of this article appeared in the *Kansas City Star* of January 1915, which a Mound City newspaper later reprinted with additional family information. What little is known of Bond Hughes is here: "[Bond and sister Nellie Coleman] are still residents of Mound City, the latter conducting a hotel in the same site on which her father and mother began the hotel business. While Bond Hughes has been Mound

City's principal stock shipper many years, and it is truthfully said of him that 'his word is as good as his bond.'"

59. Willian Cx Hancock, "Ranger's Ranger," see note 34 *supra*.

60. *San Antonio Light*, May 30, 1915. This lengthy interview, with no indication of the reporter's identity, was entitled "Oldest Texas Ranger Modestly Recounts His Early Exploits." It is illustrated with a photograph of Hughes wearing a black hat, white shirt, and tie, and clean-shaven. Only after he left the Ranger service did Hughes grow the beard that later became his trademark.

61. Transcript of undated WPA Interview with Captain John R. Hughes by Vera P. Elliott. No further information has been learned about Miss Elliott, other than that her address during the time of the interview was 40-110 Locust Street, El Paso.

62. 9th U.S. Census, Williamson County, Texas. Enumerated [June?] 1870, 411.

63. The letter is in the form of an undated clipping from the *Texas Farm and Ranch*, preserved in the Hughes Scrapbook. The periodical, *Texas Farm and Ranch*, continued publication under different titles until November 1963. *New Handbook of Texas*, s.v. "Farm and Ranch," by Diana J. Kleiner. Reports of the murder of Mr. and Mrs. Merrill appeared in numerous newspapers. See *Galveston Daily News* of December 29, 1884, citing specials from Big Springs and Fort Worth.

64. Article in unidentified newspaper in Hughes's Scrapbook, but originating from Austin, January 21, 1907.

65. From available sources it is apparent that the meeting between Hughes and the rustlers must have taken place in Sierra County, New Mexico Territory. Prolific author Carl W. Breihan wrote in his sketch of Hughes: "Down the Gila River Hughes went, and east to Silver City and Hillsboro." Research has not yet pinned down the exact location of the gunfight between Hughes and the rustlers, however. Carl W. Breihan, "Ranger John Hughes," *Real West* 18, no. 141 (September 1975): 22–27.

66. *San Antonio Light*, May 30, 1915. A lengthy account, in part an interview with Hughes: "Oldest Texas Ranger Modestly Recounts His Early Exploits."

Chapter 2: "Hold up, Wesley!"

1. Alice Braeutigam Sauer, "Mr. and Mrs. John Wolfgang Braeutigam," in *Pioneers in God's Hills: A History of Fredericksburg and Gillespie County People and Events* (Austin: The Gillespie County Historical Society, printed by Von Boeckmann-Jones, 1974), 2: 9–11. The Braeutigam family is enumerated

in the 1860 census showing the head of household John, born in Saxony, as 31 years of age; his wife Christine, born in Hanover, age 28. Their five children ranged in age from six months to eight years. His real estate was valued at $800 and his personal estate at $1,270. 8th U.S. Census, Gillespie County, Texas. Enumerated July 28, 1860, 29. Enumerator George Max spelled the name *Brautigan* and others spelled the name *Brandigan*. I have used the spelling as it appears on the headstone in *Der Stadt Friedhof*, or City Cemetery, in Fredericksburg. The stone, chiseled in German, provides the dates of March 17, 1829, to September 3, 1884, for his lifespan. See also Esther Mueller, "Old Fort Martin Scott, at Fredericksburg," *Frontier Times* 14, no. 11 (August 1937): 463–68. Mueller gives the date of Braeutigam's death incorrectly as September 10, 1884.

2. Alice Braeutigam Sauer, in *Pioneers in God's Hills*, 9–11.

3. District Court Records of Gillespie County. The Grand Jury found an indictment against Collier, that on or about September 3, 1884, he did "with malice aforethought kill and murder one J. W. Brantigan [*sic*] by shooting him Said J. W. Brantigan with a certain fire arm the description is to the Grand Jury unknown." The numerous court documents are readily available for examination in Fredericksburg. On the end of the envelope for Collier is written: "Disposed of Sept Term 1886—Deft had died."

4. *San Antonio Light*, November 24, 1884.

5. Ira Aten, "Six and One Half Years in the Ranger Service Fifty Years Ago," 13. Typed copy in the Briscoe Center for American History. These memoirs were prepared by Aten in 1941. Hereafter cited as Aten, "Six and One Half Years." See also *Galveston Daily News*, November 25, 1884. Harold Preece, in his fictionalized biography of Ira Aten, followed Jack Martin in identifying the leader of the gang as Judd Roberts, stating that it was Roberts who "led a gang of four men who robbed and killed an old ranchman named Brautigen [*sic*] . . . ." Harold Preece, *Lone Star Man: Ira Aten Last of the Old Texas Rangers* (New York: Hastings House Publishers, 1960), 144.

6. "Six and One Half Years," 13.

7. Wilburn Hill King was born in Georgia but during the Civil War moved to Texas and rose to the rank of brigadier general. Following the war he was elected to two terms in the Texas House of Representatives, serving Hopkins County. From July 25, 1881, to January 23, 1891, he served as adjutant general. He authored a "History of the Texas Rangers," which was included in Dudley G. Wooten's *Comprehensive History of Texas* (1898). Hill died October 12, 1910. *New Handbook of Texas*, s.v. "Wilburn Hill King," by David S. Walkup.

8. Aten, "Six and One Half Years," 39.

9. Ibid., 42.

10. Hughes and Aten remained friends throughout their lifetime, no doubt because of Hughes's assistance to Aten in the 1880s, and being involved in life and death situations.

11. Ohio-born Nicolas Dayton was in 1860 working with D. B. Hicks in Morgan County, Missouri, as an apprentice saddler. In 1866, having moved to Johnson County, Missouri, he married Mary Louisa Jackson, also of Johnson County. Their first three children were born in Missouri. Sometime in the late 1870s he moved and began farming near Liberty Hill. He remained there the balance of his long life. His wife Mary Louisa died on August 16, 1904. In 1920 he was living with his son George P. and his family, post office Liberty Hill. He was eighty-one years of age. He died on April 30, 1923, and is buried in Hopewell Cemetery in Williamson County beside his wife of nearly forty years.

12. Ira D. Aten was one of three Aten boys who served with the Texas Rangers, the others being Edwin Dunlap and Calvin Grant. All were born in Hughes's home state of Illinois. Aten joined Company D Frontier Battalion on June 1, 1883, enlisted by Capt. L. P. Sieker. After his Ranger days Aten served as sheriff of two Texas counties, and then moved to El Centro, California. Hughes and Aten maintained their friendship through the years, even though many miles apart. Ira D. Aten died on August 5, 1953, and is buried in Evergreen Cemetery near El Centro.

13. From the *Burnet Bulletin*, reprinting a lengthy article in the "43 Years Ago" column, which was itself a reprint of an article from a newspaper identified simply as the *Observer*, no date or place given. The *Bulletin* article was in the issue of May 30, 1929, so it was originally from an issue of late May 1886.

14. Aten to Adj. Gen. W. H. King, May 3, 1886. Sergeant Aten wrote this letter to King on May 3, stating he was writing from "E. S. Hughes rancho." This strongly suggests Aten and Hughes became acquainted only *after* Hughes had returned from the pursuit after horsethieves in New Mexico Territory. Jack Martin, in his *Border Boss*, identifies this fugitive as Judd Roberts, who in reality was Collier, supposedly a relative of "those men who died in New Mexico," or the two Hughes had supposedly killed to recover his stolen horses. Further to confound the issue, Martin has "Roberts" wounded in the head by Aten. Martin, 34.

15. The newspaper account identifies the man only as Dr. Thorp. His name appears as Thorpe on both the 1880 and 1900 Williamson County census, the latter as a physician. 10th U.S. Census, Williamson County, Texas. Enumerated June 3, 1880, 476; 12th U.S. Census, Williamson County, Texas. Enumerated June 30, 1900, ED 126, Sheet 19.

16. *Burnet Bulletin*, May 30, 1929.

17. Captain Jones's Monthly Return, June 30, 1886.

18. The story of the imprisoning of young George P. Dayton is from an undated account found in the vertical file in the Burnet County Library in May 2009. This is a single sheet printed in longhand, addressed to "Edna" and signed simply "Harold," apparently a response to a query about an early family story. Harold was the grandson of George Porter Dayton, the boy confined in the corn-crib while Aten and Hughes confronted Collier. The 10th U.S. Census, Williamson County, Texas, enumerated June 22–23, 1880, 473, shows the family, misspelled "Daten" consisting of Nicolas and Mary L., the parents, and children William Lee, Mary L., Nicolas C., and George P. George is one year old, thus he would be about seven when the killing of Collier took place.

19. Robert Penniger, *Fredericksburg, Texas . . . The First Fifty Years*, Festival Edition, trans. C. L. Wisseman (Fredericksburg: Arwed Hillmann, 1896). The article, "The Murder of John W. Braeutigam," is on page 79.

20. Aten, "Six and One Half Years," 42.

21. John R. Hughes Ranger Service Record.

22. [J. Marvin Hunter], *Frontier Times* 5, no. 1 (October 1927): 4–8. In this issue Hunter describes a visit with Hughes and reprints an article from the *San Antonio Express* of January 17, 1915.

23. Sgt. Ira Aten to W. H. King, August 11, 1887, written from Georgetown, Williamson County.

24. *San Antonio Express*, January 17, 1915. The physical description is from a later "Oath of Service Ranger Force" dated July 9, 1903.

25. Robert W. Stephens, *Texas Ranger Sketches* (Dallas: Self-published, nd), 63–75. See also Candice DuCoin's *Lawmen on the Texas Frontier: Rangers and Sheriffs*. This work by a Jones descendant relates the story of the various Jones family members, focusing especially on those who served as Texas Rangers. (Round Rock, Tex.: Riata Books, 2007).

26. Capt. Frank Jones's report dated February 29, 1888, reporting on Aten's work while on detached service.

27. *Galveston Daily News*, August 8 and 9, 1887. Farmer and deputy sheriff William J. Stanley was born about 1832 in Tennessee and had relocated to Texas by the early 1850s. By 1880 he and his wife Martha provided a home for five of their own children and one orphan, and had one man working as a laborer. 10th U.S. Census, Williamson County, Texas. Enumerated June 21, 1880, 504.

28. Report of Capt. Frank Jones from Camp Savage, February 29, 1888.

29. The *Austin Daily Statesman*, May 19 and 20, 1887; and the *New York Times*, May 20 and 21, 1887.

30. The *Austin Daily Statesman*, June 19; *New York Times*, June 19, 1887.

31. Hughes never did catch up with members of the Cornett-Whitley-Barber gang, but eventually the law took their lives. William H. Whitley was killed resisting arrest near Floresville in Wilson County on September 25, 1888. John T. Rankin, U.S. Marshal for the Western District of Texas, received the credit. John Barber fled Texas to the Indian Territory of what is today Oklahoma. On December 7, 1889, a posse of deputy marshals out of "Hanging Judge" Parker's court shot him to death. Braxton "Brack" Cornett was cornered by Alfred Allee, a Frio County deputy sheriff, on February 11, 1888, and was shot to death while resisting arrest.

32. Capt. Frank Jones's report, February 29, 1888.

33. Zane Grey developed such respect for the Rangers that he entitled one of his novels, *Lone Star Ranger*, which he dedicated to Captain Hughes "and his Texas Rangers." First published by Harper & Row in 1915, the book remains one of Grey's most popular titles.

34. Capt. Frank Jones's report, February 29, 1888.

35. Record of Scouts, Frontier Battalion, Ledger # 401-1096, giving date of gunfight as August 9, 1886, 68–70. See also Annette Martin Ludeman, *A History of La Salle County: South Texas Brush Country 1856–1975* (Quanah, Tex.: Nortex Press, 1975), 118–20. J. M. Mize was born about 1858 and enlisted in Capt. J. T. Gillespie's Company E on June 30, 1886. He was honorably discharged August 31, 1886. Ranger Service Records. Perhaps the wound suffered in the fight with Davenport convinced Mize to leave the Ranger service. Davenport was born January 29, 1864, in Arkansas. His first known trouble with the law was the killing of Elkanah M. Herford, known as "Old Man Hereford" in 1886. He was captured, stood trial for the killing, found guilty of manslaughter, and sentenced to five years in Huntsville penitentiary. On March 6, 1894, Gov. J. S. Hogg restored full citizenship rights to him and he was a free man. In spite of that experience Davenport continued in his hard lifestyle. He and Texas Ranger William L. Wright got into a difficulty in Cotulla, La Salle County, on October 24, 1900. Wright killed Davenport. Unpublished biography by Donald C. Crawford, grandson of James Richard Davenport. Copy in author's possession.

36. These communities are in Uvalde County, Dimmit County, Webb County, and Zapata County, respectively. What was Carrizo is today under the waters of Falcon Reservoir, the town having been moved in 1898 and is now named Zapata, the county seat. It is located some fifty miles south of Laredo in Webb County. See *New Handbook of Texas*, s.v. "Zapata, Texas," by Jean Y. Fish.

37. Monthly Returns of Capt. Frank Jones, October and November, 1887. The one teamster was Bob Patton who had been enlisted September 10 by

Captain Jones. All muster rolls, monthly returns, and scouting reports cited in notes are from the Texas State Library and Archives Adjutant General files, in Austin.

38. Sieker to Hughes and reply, December 24, 1887, and Sieker to Hughes, December 31, 1887. From "Quartermaster Captain L. P. Sieker" Ledger 401-1107 Letter Press Book, 84, 86 and 92.

39. Monthly Return of Capt. Frank Jones, dated December 31, 1887.

40. Details of the kidnapping of Barrera are from the *Galveston Daily News*, December 7, 1887.

41. William W. Shely was a Missouri native born about 1867. His terms as sheriff of Starr County began with his election on November 4, 1884. He served continually until November 6, 1906, a total of twenty-two consecutive years. Sammy Tise, *Texas County Sheriffs*, 473. Hereafter cited as Tise.

42. *Galveston Daily News*, December 10, 1887.

43. Ibid., December 11, 1887.

44. Ibid.

45. Capt. Frank Jones Monthly Return, prepared at Camp Savage, January 31, 1888.

46. Hughes to Capt. L. P. Sieker, January 15, 1888.

47. *Fort Worth Daily Gazette*, August 4, 1883, article headlined "The Fence Cutters."

48. Ibid., August 31, 1883.

49. Ibid., September 8, 1883, citing an item from the *Statesman*.

50. Hans Peter Nielson Gammel, comp., *The Laws of Texas*, vol. 9 (Austin: Gammel Book Co., 1898), 566, 569. R. D. Holt, "The Introduction of Barbed Wire into Texas and the Fence Cutting War," *The West Texas Historical Association Yearbook* 6 (June 1930): 65–79. Holt listed ten causes for the "war," one of which was that fences "hindered" stealing and rustling. He wrote that the counties that had the most severe fence cutting troubles were Clay, Brown, Coleman, Frio, and Medina. Apparently Company D Rangers dealt with fence cutting problems mainly in Navarro and Brown counties.

51. Jim King had an extensive career as a Ranger, beginning service under Lt. Charles B. McKinney in Company F, then under Lt. Joseph Shely, then under Capt. George H. Schmitt of Company C and finally enlisting under Capt. Frank Jones in Company D on September 1, 1889. Ranger Service record. He was killed at Loma Vista, Zavala County, on February 11, 1890. Robert W. Stephens, *Texas Ranger Sketches*, 77.

52. Aten, "Six and One Half Years," 53. The quotation, "which pleased me mightily," is added in the serialization that appears in *Frontier Times* 22, no. 5 (February 1945): 127-42.

53. Special Orders Ledger, "August 1870 to April 2 1897," Adj. Gen. Orders Book 401-1012, 221.

54. L. E. Daniell, "Samuel R. Frost," *Personnel of the Texas State Government, with Sketches of Distinguished Texans* (Austin: Smith, Hicks & Jones, State Printers, 1889), 322–24; and *New Handbook of Texas*, s.v. "Samuel R. Frost," by Julie G. Miller.

55. The date of Hughes's departure from camp is in "Record of Scouts and Arrests of Corp[.] Durbin's detachment from Mch 15 1888, to Sept. 30 1888." Box 401-1180 folder 16.

56. Ledger 401-1084, "Vol. 3 Operations of Front. Battalion and Report of Special Rangers from December 1 1885 to November 30 1892," 98.

57. *New Handbook of Texas*, s.v. "Rio Grande City Riot of 1888," by Alicia A. Garza.

58. Victor Sebree was mustered into Company F of the Frontier Battalion Texas Rangers on September 1, 1883, as a private, under Joseph Shely, a brother of Sheriff W. W. Shely. He remained in the service with Company F until honorably discharged with the rank of corporal on January 1, 1885. His record shows he was again mustered in on October 20, 1889, and honorably discharged on March 15, 1890, serving under Capt. J. A. Brooks, Frontier Battalion.

59. *New Handbook of Texas*, s.v. "Rio Grande City Riot of 1888," by Alicia A. Garza.

60. Hughes's early biographer, Jack Martin, devotes considerable attention to the arrest of Garza, describing the confrontation as if it were a classic example of two deadly gunfighters facing each other at high noon on a dusty street of a trail town. According to Martin, Garza attempted to draw his pistol but Hughes was quicker and "With a quick wrench he got it away from the startled editor, and in another instant had him and his companions covered. The fight was over without a shot being fired." This appears to be yet another example of Martin's addition of "color" to his narrative with little basis in fact. Martin, *Border Boss*, 44–48. Martin's influence is obvious in "Catarina E. Garza and the Garza War" by Gilbert M. Cuthbertson, in *Texana* 12, no. 4 (1973): 335–348.

61. *San Antonio Light*, May 30, 1915. Sebree afterwards shot Garza and two companies of Rangers were sent there to attend to the mob.

62. Tennessee native James R. Robinson served first under Capt. George H. Schmitt prior to enlisting in Company D under Captain Jones on July 1,

1888. The tall—one inch over six feet—dark Ranger struck an imposing figure on the streets of Austin where he enlisted. He was born about 1856. In the famous photograph of Captain Jones's company at Realitos, he is seated in the front row with the captain.

63. Monthly Return of Capt. Frank Jones, August 31, 1888.

64. *Galveston Daily News*, September 27, 1888.

65. Victor Sebree had served in Company F of the Frontier Battalion, first under Capt. W. W. Shely and then under Capt. J. A. Brooks. Ranger Service Record.

66. *New York Times*, September 25, 1888, citing a report from San Antonio dated September 24, 1888.

67. *Galveston Daily News*, September 24, 1888, citing a report from Brownsville dated September 23, 1888.

68. Ibid., citing a report from Rio Grande City dated September 23, 1888.

69. Ibid., citing a report from Rio Grande City dated September 24, 1888.

70. Ibid., September 28, citing a report from Brownsville dated September 27, 1888.

71. For a complete biography of Captain Rogers see Paul N. Spellman, *Captain John H. Rogers, Texas Ranger* (Denton: University of North Texas Press, 2003).

72. *Galveston Daily News*, citing a report from Austin dated September 27, 1888.

73. Ibid., September 30, 1888, citing a report from Rio Grande City of September 29, 1888.

74. *Galveston Weekly News*, October 23, and "Recapitulation of arrests" by the Frontier Battalion, October 22, 1888.

75. The date of the stagecoach robbery is uncertain, but J. Walter Durbin's letter of October 29, 1888, indicated "stage robbed by one man between here & Pena last Saturday." "Operations of Front. Battalion and Report of Special Rangers. From December 1 1885 to November 30, 1892." Vol. 3, 102 and 104.

Chapter 3: Challenging the Odles

1. Charles B. Barton was born in October 1865, the son of E. B. and Santos Barton. In 1880, the Barton family, the parents and their fourteen children, ranched in Nueces County, Texas, their residence listed as Rancho Los Indios. Older brother Riley also served in Company D with Charles, and was born in March 1854. In 1900, Charles and Riley (Reiley) were living

in Hidalgo County, as was their mother, now a widow. The census shows she had given birth to sixteen children, thirteen of whom were still living in 1900. Of interest is that both Barton brothers were in camp the day the photographer came to make the now famous photograph of Captain Jones and his men near Realitos. 10th U.S. Census, Nueces County, Texas. Enumerated June 9, 1880, 51; 12th U.S. Census, Hidalgo County, Texas. Enumerated June 15, 1900, 261, 235 and 239.

2. February 1889 Monthly Return of Capt. Frank Jones. Ira L. Wheat first served as sheriff from September 10, 1883, until November 4, 1884. He was later elected on November 6, 1888, re-elected two more terms and served until November 3, 1896. Tise, 169. In 1880 he was farming in Edwards County, twenty-four-years of age with a wife and two small children. Edwards County census, enumerated June 16, 1880, 338.

3. March 1889 Monthly Return of Capt. Frank Jones.

4. The ages are approximate, according to the San Saba County census, enumerated June 9, 1880, 431. According to the census, the head of household, in 1880, was Mike Williamson, a farmer born in Georgia where his wife Mary Ann was also born. The census shows another son, Columbus, age eleven in 1880. Daughter Levonia Williamson Homes had two children at the time of the census: Maggie, six years old, and "Jonnie," one year old. Apparently, Mrs. Williamson and her daughter both were widows by the time of the 1880 census. A summary of the case by J. Marvin Hunter, "The Famous Dick Duncan Murder Case," appears in *Frontier Times* 16, no. 5 (February 1939): 197–98.

5. Samuel B. Howard was elected sheriff on November 2, 1886, re-elected on November 6, 1888, and served until November 4, 1890. Tise, 454. The census records show he was born in October 1838 in Tennessee. In 1860, his occupation is given as farm hand; in 1870, living in Alabama, his occupation is given as mechanic. In 1880 he is in San Saba County with his wife and five children, his occupation given as "Mill Wright." The final census shows him as a sixty-two-year-old carpenter in San Saba County.

6. William N. Cooke was appointed Maverick County sheriff on January 17, 1887, elected November 6, 1888, again on November 4, 1890, and served until November 8, 1892. Tise, 363.

7. Born February 4, 1869, Tap Duncan lived a long and successful life working in the cattle industry, on ranches from Texas to Colorado and Idaho and Arizona. He died after being struck by an automobile on November 19, 1944, in Kingman, Arizona.

8. The Duncan boys were sons of Abijah and Martha M. Duncan. In 1880 the parents had five children at home: Harriett, Richard, Nancy, George T., and

Fanny, ranging in age from Harriett, twenty, down to Fanny, seven years old. 10th U.S. Census, San Saba County, Texas. Enumerated June 5, 1880, 439.

9. J. Marvin Hunter, "The Famous Dick Duncan Murder Case" in *Frontier Times*, February 1939; the *El Paso Daily Times*, September 19, 1891, reporting the news from Eagle Pass of the execution of Duncan. Jack Martin, in his biography of Hughes, devotes pages 66–75 to the Duncan murder case, stating that when Hughes and Aten received the orders to work up the case, the "two men stared at one another. Here was probably the most difficult assignment they had ever been given."

10. April 1889, Monthly Return of Capt. Frank Jones. J. T. Gillespie had an enviable record of law enforcement service. He first joined the Rangers as a private on January 14, 1879, in N. O. Reynolds's Company E. During his service he rose from private to captain of Company E, having also served under Charles L. Nevill in the same company. He was honorably discharged from the service on April 15, 1887, having been elected the first sheriff of Brewster County on February 14, 1887. He was re-elected on November 6, 1888. Tise, 65. Sheriff Gillespie died in office in January 1890, although the exact date is not given in the Commissioners Court minutes. Those minutes, held in Murphyville (now Alpine), Brewster County, dated January 18, record the following: "Whereas it appears to the satisfaction of this court that a vacancy exists in the office of the Sheriff and Collector of this county by reason of the death of J. T. Gillespie, and whereas it is an important public necessity that some suitable person be appointed to fill said vacancy during the unexpired term of said J. T. Gillespie, deceased, It is therefore the order of the Court that John Rooney be and is hereby appointed Sheriff . . . ." Minutes, Book 1, 111. Curiously, his headstone gives the death year as 1891, obviously an error. The headstone shows he was born on April 28, 1856, which date is presumably correct. His death date should be given as January 14, 1890. Barry Scobee, Fort Davis historian, wrote that Gillespie's death was caused by pneumonia. *The Steer Branded Murder*, 45.

11. John G. O'Grady was the son of Irish parents John and Kate O'Grady. The father arrived with his family in America and joined the U.S. Army; he died in 1879. In 1880, Kate O'Grady, now a widow with her children, operated a hotel in Boerne, the county seat of Kendall County. Son John was listed as twenty-one years old, but no occupation is listed. 10th U.S. Census, Kendall County, Texas. Enumerated June 23, 1880 by Captain Jones's brother Pinckney Jones, 219. Grace O'Grady, older sister of John G., and Frank Jones were married on December 15, 1885. Grace O'Grady Jones died in 1889. Widower Jones then married Mrs. Helen Baylor Gillett, the daughter of famous Ranger George W. Baylor, on October 3, 1892. Candice DuCoin,

Lawmen on the Texas Frontier: Rangers and Sheriffs (Round Rock, Tex.: Riata Books, 2007), 117, 124.

12. Monthly Return of Capt. Frank Jones, May 1889.

13. *Walter Durbin Texas Ranger and Sheriff* by Robert W. Stephens, quoting from the Durbin manuscript, page 78. This book was published by Clarendon Press, of Clarendon, Texas, in 1970.

14. Ibid., 78–81; December 1889 Monthly Return of Capt. Frank Jones.

15. Robert W. Stephens, *Texas Ranger Sketches* (Np: Privately printed, 1972), 125–31.

16. Burnet County Marriage Record Book F, 1880–1888, showing license was obtained on July 20, 1882.

17. Farmer B. V. McCarty left a large family to mourn his loss. In 1880 the family consisted of McCarty, wife Susan A., and seven children ranging in age from sixteen-year-old James C. V. to eight-month-old Bryant F. Bryant V. McCarty was born in Mississippi while wife Susan A. was from Tennessee. All the children were Texas born. 10th U.S. Census, Burnet County, Texas. Enumerated June 22, 1880, 118.

18. William M. Spitler correspondence with petition to Gov. John Ireland, December 18, 1885. Interestingly, Spitler was the Assistant Marshal who conducted the 1880 Burnet County census.

19. Sheriff J. W. Wolf to Gov. John Ireland, May 4, 1886. John W. Wolf was appointed Burnet County sheriff on June 1, 1884, and elected November 4, 1884. He was re-elected on November 2, 1886 and served until November 6, 1888. Tise, 76.

20. Sheriff J. W. Wolf to Gov. L. S. Ross, April 26, 1887.

21. Ibid., May 18, 1888.

22. The census lists William E. McCarty as a fifteen-year-old in 1880. 10th U.S. Census, Burnet County, Texas. Enumerated June 22, 1880, 118. Captain Jones and Private Aten had arrested Alvin and Will Odle and delivered them to the jail in Uvalde. Sheriff Wolf then returned them to the Burnet jail. April 1887 Monthly Return of Capt. Frank Jones.

23. Calvin G. Aten had enlisted in Company D on April 1, 1888, and remained in the service until August 31, 1890. Born in Abingdon, Illinois, on December 7, 1868, he was in Texas with the family in 1876 where he established residence in Round Rock, Williamson County. Conflicted, he apparently remained on the family farm out of respect for his father's wishes, but opted to join the Ranger service to experience adventure. After leaving the service he returned home where he married Mattie Jo Kennedy on May 2, 1894. They moved to the Texas Panhandle where Cal worked on the huge

XIT Ranch. C. G. Aten died on April 1, 1939, and is buried in Citizens Cemetery in Clarendon, Texas. Stephens, *Texas Ranger Sketches*, 14–16.

24. Capt. Jones to Adj. Gen. L. P. Sieker, December 29, 1889.

25. Adjutant General Records, "Record of Scouts" Record Group 401-1180-17.

26. W. J. Lockhart, "The Odle Brothers," in *Wagons, Ho! A History of Real County, Texas*, ed. Marjorie Kellner (Dallas: Curtis Media, Inc., 1995), 77. In 1930 Walter J. Lockhart was a sixty-one-year old stockman. 15th U.S. Census, Edwards County, Texas. Enumerated April 5, 1930, Enumerator District No. 69-3, Sheet 3-A.

27. Calvin G. Aten to brother Ira Aten, letter dated December 12, 1936. This is a fifteen-page letter on lined notebook paper; copy courtesy Robert W. Stephens in author's possession.

28. Marjorie Kellner, in *Wagons, Ho! A History of Real County*, 6. Just when Zach H. Eppler carved the names and placed the fence around the graves is unrecorded. 14th U.S. Census, Uvalde County, Texas. Enumerated January 9, 1920, E.D. # 161, sheet 10. Eppler is shown to be a thirty-seven-year old ranchman. See also Allan A. Stovall, *Nueces Headwater Country: A Regional History* (San Antonio: The Naylor Company, 1959), 109–10.

29. Pvt. Charles H. Fusselman to L. P. Sieker, July 20, 1889. This is a five-page letter from "Headquarters Detachment Company 'D'" on Frontier Battalion letterhead, showing Jones as captain, Ira Aten as 1st sergeant, and Fusselman as 1st corporal. The report is a listing of "a few of the crimes commited [*sic*] on the river," mainly murder and theft of livestock, most of which had resulted in no arrests.

30. Ibid., February 29, 1890.

31. Service Record of Charles H. Fusselman; Captain Jones to L.P. Sieker, May 21, 1889; Muster Roll, August 31, 1889.

32. Charles H. Fusselman Ranger Service Record.

33. C. H. Fusselman to Adjutant General King, written from Shafter, November 26, 1889.

34. U.S. Marshal Paul Fricke to Adjutant General King, December 12, 1889.

35. James H. White was elected sheriff on November 4, 1884, re-elected November 2, 1886, and November 6, 1888, and served until November 4, 1890. The Virginia-born lawman also served as Tax Collector. Tise, 172. 12th U.S. Census. El Paso County, Texas. Enumerated June 1, 1920. E.D. # 21, Sheet 2.

36. *Galveston Daily News*, April 18, 1890.

37. George Herold's extensive career is discussed briefly in Robert W. Stephens's *Texas Ranger Sketches*, 59–61.

38. The identity of this bandit is from the *El Paso Herald*, April 18, 1890.
39. Fusselman's quote before death is from the *El Paso Times*, April 19, 1890.
40. *Galveston Daily News*, April 18, citing a report from El Paso of April 17, 1890.
41. Ibid.
42. Captain John R. Hughes as told to L. A. Wilke, "The Wide Loop of a Ranger Noose," *Real Detective* 38, no. 3 (September 1936): 24–29, 82–85.
43. Capt. Frank Jones to L.P. Sieker, April 18, 1890.
44. C. G. Aten to L. P. Sieker, from Marfa, April 22, 1890.
45. *Galveston Daily News*, April 20, 1890. The governor's reward notice is dated April 22, 1890. Original in the Flachmeier Collection, Austin History Center.
46. Date of appointment from Captain Jones's Muster and Pay Roll prepared on May 31, 1890, at Cotulla, La Salle County.

Chapter 4: Another Ranger Killed

1. Sieker to Sgt. C. H. Fusselman, March 2, 1890.
2. Ibid., April 11, 1890.
3. Captain Jones's Monthly Return, June 30, 1890, prepared at Marfa.
4. Captain Jones's Monthly Return, July 31, 1890, prepared at Presidio.
5. Isaac N. "Ike" Lee was born in Kentucky in November 1852. By 1870 he was working as a farm laborer in Atascosa County, Texas, near Somerset. He was mustered into C. L. Nevill's Company E Frontier Battalion as a private on November 16, 1880. He served until July 7, 1886, and was discharged honorably with a rank of 1st Corporal. In 1900 Lee was living in Fannin County, a widower, forty-seven years old, with five children ranging in age from eight years to nineteen years. Ranger Service Record and 12th U.S. Census, Fannin County, Texas. Enumerated June 22, 1900, E.D. # 59, Sheet 11.
6. *Galveston Daily News*, August 5, 1890. Gravis was the son of Charles K. and Elizabeth Gravis. In 1880 he was raising sheep while younger brother John F. was attending school. 10th U.S. Census, Duval County, Texas. Enumerated June 3, 1880, 224.
7. Walter W. Jones was mustered into Company D on May 1, 1887, and honorably discharged on February 14, 1891. Ranger Service Records. He was not one of the brothers of Captain Frank Jones. In 1900 W. W. Jones operated a saloon in Val Verde County, by then with a wife and two children.

8. William Kipling was mustered into Company D on May 1, 1890, and honorably discharged on August 31, 1890. He was indebted to the State of Texas "on account of Cash advanced by John R. Hughes." Ranger Service Record.

9. John C. Mayfield was mustered into Company D on August 26, 1889, and served honorably until August 20, 1890. Ranger Service Records. When honorably discharged he was indebted to the State of Texas for one Winchester carbine ($12); one Colt's pistol ($12); one gun scabbard ($1.25) and one pistol belt and holster ($1.50).

10. Captain Jones's Monthly Return, August 31, 1890, prepared at Presidio.

11. Ibid.

12. In 1870 Patrick Dolan was residing in the 4th Ward of Galveston with his wife Mary whom he had married in January. He was listed as a thirty-two-year-old laborer, born in Ireland. 9th U.S. Census, Galveston County, Texas. Enumerated August 1, 1870, 293. Dolan was appointed a 1st Sergeant in Capt. John R. Kelso's Company D of the Frontier Forces, serving from September 10 to December 21, 1870; appointed private in the State Police on July 26, serving until August 26, 1870; appointed 1st Lieutenant in Capt. Neal Coldwell's Company F of the Frontier Battalion May 5–December 1, 1874, apparently served continually and then on November 30, 1877, appointed Captain of Company F, serving until April 30, 1879. Ranger Service Record.

13. Ranger Service Record of Thalis T. Cook.

14. Captain Jones's Monthly Return, September 30, 1890, prepared at Presidio.

15. Ibid., October 31, 1890, at Camp Hogg, Brewster County.

16. Tise, 424.

17. Carl Kirchner was born in Bee County, Texas, on November 19, 1867, the son of Saxony-born Christian and Tennessee-born Martha Kirchner. He mustered into Company D on May 18, 1889, and remained in that company until July 24, 1895, retiring with the rank of 1st Sergeant. Kirchner died on January 28, 1911, in El Paso and was buried in Concordia Cemetery. 9th U.S. Census, Bee County, Texas. Enumerated August 16, 1870, 582. In 1900 he was working as a saloon keeper; in 1910 his occupation was given as "Manager Ice & Brewery Co." 12th U.S. Census, El Paso County, Texas. Enumerated April 28, 1910. E.D. 16, Sheet 19.

18. Captain Jones's Monthly Return, November 30, 1890, prepared at Camp Hogg, Brewster County.

19. James Buchanan Gillett was elected Brewster County sheriff on November 4, 1890, and served one term until November 8, 1892. He was city marshal of El Paso from spring of 1882 until April 1, 1885. Tise, 65. See also Gillett's autobiography *Six Years with the Texas Rangers: 1875 to 1881.*

20. Details on the life and career of Thalis T. Cook are from Stephens, *Texas Ranger Sketches*, 43–47. The killing of H. H. Powe by Gilliland is discussed in Barry Scobee, *The Steer Branded Murder* (Houston: Frontier Press of Texas, 1952). A frequently published photograph of Captain Hughes and the men of Company D in 1894 shows Hughes seated with Ranger Cook standing behind him holding his Winchester.

21. Captain Jones's Monthly Return, January 31, 1891.

22. Captain Jones's Monthly Return, February 28, 1891. Also see Ledger 401–1084, "Operations of Front. Battalion and Report of Special Rangers," Vol. 3, 125.

23. Alonzo Van Oden, *Texas Ranger's Diary and Scrapbook*, ed. Ann Jensen (Dallas: The Kaleidograph Press, 1936), 11.

24. Ibid., 23.

25. Ledger 401-1084, "Operations of Frontier Battalion" of Quartermaster L. P. Sieker identified the pair only as "J. and C. Flores" and were arrested for disorderly conduct. Two other events not listed in the monthly return include the arrest by Hughes of J. Terva and G. Lubia for fornication.

26. Captain Jones's Monthly Return, April 30, 1891; and "Operations of Frontier Battalion," 126.

27. Ibid., May 31, and June 31, 1891, Monthly Returns.

28. "Operations of Frontier Battalion," 127.

29. Captain Jones's Monthly Return, July 31, 1891. Polvo exists today as a small village within the Big Bend National Park.

30. Ibid., August 31, 1891.

31. Ibid., October 31, 1891.

32. DuCoin, *Lawmen on the Texas Frontier: Rangers and Sheriffs*, 192.

33. Captain Jones's Monthly Return, October 31, 1891.

34. Ibid.

35. Ibid., November 31, 1891.

36. Ibid., December 31, 1891.

37. Buchel County was abolished in 1897 and attached to Brewster County; this legislative act made Brewster County the largest in the State of Texas.

38. The spelling of this private's name is problematic. His service records, signed by Captain Brooks and Captain Jones, show Danniel, Daniels, and Daniells. His own signatures show similar variations.

39. Ibid., January 31, 1892.

40. Captain Jones's Monthly Return, January 31, 1892. The variation in names of the deceased is due to the imprecision of the spelling of Mexican names by Rangers. The "Operations of Frontier Battalion" identifies the deceased ore

thieves as Matildo Carrisco, Jose Velata, and Guintino Chavez. The Monthly Return spells them as Matildo Carrasco, Jose Villeto, and Quinlino Chaves.

41. *Border Boss*, 96–100.

42. Captain Jones's Monthly Return, February 29, 1892.

43. Robert Speaks began his Ranger career with Company E, when he mustered into Lt. Charles L. Nevill's company on August 3, 1880, at Fort Davis, and served until August 6, 1880. He next joined as a private in Frank Jones's Company D, mustering in on September 9, 1890. He was honorably discharged on August 31, 1893, from Captain Hughes's Company D. Prior to joining Nevill's Ranger Company he was a laborer, with no further occupation shown. The census shows he was a native of Missouri, his parents both born in Kentucky. 10th U.S. Census. Pecos County, Texas. Enumerated June 19, 1880, 496.

44. Captain Jones's Monthly Return, March 31, 1892.

45. Alonzo Van Oden, *Texas Ranger's Diary and Scrapbook*, ed. Ann Jensen, 59.

46. Ibid.

47. Captain Jones's Monthly Return, June 31, 1892.

48. Ibid., August 31, 1892.

49. Undated newspaper clipping, probably either the *Times* or the *Herald* of El Paso, preserved in Hughes Scrapbook.

50. Alonzo Van Oden, *Texas Ranger's Diary and Scrapbook*, 36.

51. As yet no historian has written a full-length biography of Baz L. Outlaw although he is a well-known Texas Ranger and deserves one. Two reliable articles have appeared, however: "Bass Outlaw: Myth and Man" by Philip J. Rasch, published in the now-defunct periodical *Real West* of July 1979, pages 13–15, 55, 60; and "The Latest on 'Bass' Outlaw" by Bill O'Neal in *Real West* of August 1982, pages 40–43. Eugene Cunningham devoted a chapter, "The Little Wolf: Bass Outlaw," in his *Triggernometry: A Gallery of Gunfighters* (236–48). O'Neal wrote, in regards to Outlaw's resignation, that Captain Jones had "repeatedly warned Baz to curb his drinking. But when Baz was discovered drunk while on duty, Jones forced him to resign," 41.

52. Captain Jones's Monthly Return, September 30, 1892.

Chapter 5: Battling the Olguins

1. Captain Jones's Monthly Return, January 1893, and "Operations of Front[ier] Batt[alion] & Reports of Special Rangers . . . ," 74. Hereafter cited as "Operations."

2. Captain Jones to W. H. Mabry, from Camp Cleveland, January 17, 1893.

3. Native Texan Wigfall Van Sickle, born December 19, 1863, was county judge serving Brewster, Buchel, and Foley counties at this time. As late as 1920, he was still practicing law in Brewster County. By then Buchel and Foley counties had been disorganized and had become part of Brewster County. Judge Van Sickle died September 14, 1941. His family laid him to rest in the Elm Grove Cemetery in Alpine where Sheriff J. T. Gillespie, D. W. Gourley, R. L. Nevill, and Joseph B. Townsend, men who knew and worked with Hughes, are also buried.

4. Baz L. Outlaw to General W. H. Mabry, January 26, 1893; Application for Special Ranger, dated February 6, 1893, and sworn to and subscribed February 10 before W. Van Sickle, County Judge, witnessed and signed by W. W. Turney, A. S. Gage, and Frank Jones. Here, besides his physical description, Outlaw listed his occupation as "Dept U.S. Marshall" [*sic*].

5. Captain Jones's Monthly Return, February 1893, and "Operations," 75.

6. George W. Baylor to Adj. Gen. W. H. Mabry, February 15, 1893.

7. Captain Jones to Adj. Gen. W. H. Mabry, March 9, 1893.

8. Ibid., April 22, 1893.

9. Ibid., April 16, 1893.

10. Frazer was elected sheriff on November 4, 1890, and was re-elected on November 8. 1892. He lost the race to Daniel Murphy on November 6, 1894. Tise, 436.

11. Sheriff G. A. Frazer to Hon. J. S. Hogg, June 13, 1893.

12. Bill Leftwich, *Tracks Along the Pecos* (Pecos, Tex.: The Pecos Press, 1957), 48. Leftwich quotes portions of the court document, case # 150. The *El Paso Times* of July 13 reports Frazer's version of the plot from an interview with a *Times* reporter.

13. J. M. Dean to Adj. Gen. W. H. Mabry, June 19, 1893. John M. Dean, frequently known as Colonel or Senator, entered politics initially when appointed Presidio County Attorney in 1879. He later ranched with former Texas Rangers James B. Gillett and Charles L. Nevill. He was state senator from 1892 to 1896. *New Handbook of Texas*, s.v. "John M. Dean," by Julia Cauble Smith.

14. Captain Jones to Adj. Gen. W. H. Mabry, June 2, 1893.

15. *El Paso Daily Times*, June 30, 1893.

16. Robert Edward "Ed" Bryant was born on March 5, 1866, in Ysleta, and was a resident of El Paso County his entire life. His first experience as a Ranger was under Capt. George W. Baylor, enlisting on November 6, 1883, at Murphyville (now Alpine) and serving until his honorable discharge on

August 31, 1884. He again became a Ranger by enlisting in Company D under Capt. John R. Hughes on June 26, 1893. He served through much of the decade until May 31, 1900, when he was discharged because of the reduction in the Ranger Force. From 1900 through 1929, he served as a deputy sheriff or a deputy U.S. Marshal. His obituary in the *El Paso Herald* praised his work in law enforcement, noting especially his fluency in both English and Spanish. "Because of his ability to speak Spanish, and because of the respect Juarez and other Mexican officials had for him, he was of great help in aiding Americans." Bryant died while visiting his children in Los Angeles, California, on August 20, 1940. He was buried in El Paso's Evergreen Cemetery. *El Paso Herald*, August 21, 1940; Stephens, *Texas Ranger Sketches*, 32–34.

17. *San Antonio Daily Express*, July 1, 1893.

18. The description of the initial action of Jones is from the lengthy report of George Wythe Baylor written to Adjutant General Mabry, July 9, 1893.

19. Carl Kirchner to Adj. Gen. Mabry, July 2, 1893.

20. George W. Baylor to Adj. Gen. W. H. Mabry, July 9, 1893. Baylor's account of the fight also contained his hand-drawn sketch of the scene where Jones was killed.

21. Ibid.

22. The telegrams dealing with Jones's death are all archived in the Adjutant General's Papers, Texas State Archives, dated June 30 and July 1, 1893.

23. Richard Bascom Chastain was born in Texas in June 1862. His Ranger service began when he was mustered into Capt. Frank Jones's Company D on January 1, 1891. His honorable discharge is dated August 31, 1893. Following his Ranger service he worked as a carpenter in Presidio. 12th U.S. Census, Presidio County, Texas. Enumerated June 23, 1900. E.D. # 66, Sheet 13. His application for pension shows he was living in Sierra Blanca, Hudspeth County. In 1930 he gave his occupation as County Officer.

24. *El Paso Daily Times*, June 30, 1893. The International edition of the *Times* reported that ex-police Capt. Chester Helm also was in the posse.

25. Baylor to Mabry, July 9, 1893. The Winchester, watch, and badge are now in the possession of Old West memorabilia collector and artist Donald M. Yena.

26. *San Antonio Daily Express*, July 2, 1893. William Kenner and his twin brother James Russell Jones were born in Seguin, Guadalupe County, on April 2, 1849. They were the first-born children of William E. and Keziah Jones. Around 1850 the family moved to Kendall County where the other children were born. William K. studied law and was admitted to the bar in 1873.

Prior to beginning law practice he and brother Pinckney enlisted in Neal Coldwell's Company F for one year. They were both honorably discharged on June 4, 1875. Jones ran for the office of Val Verde County Judge and was elected in 1884 and re-elected four times, serving through May 1894. He then was appointed Deputy Collector of Customs at Del Rio and held that position until 1898. William Kenner Jones died on December 9, 1925, while serving as county attorney of Val Verde County. DuCoin, *Lawmen on the Texas Frontier: Rangers and Sheriffs*, 73–77.

27. Baz L. Outlaw to Adj. Gen. Mabry, July 2, 1893, writing from the Lindell Hotel in El Paso.

28. John R. Hughes to Adj. Gen. W. H. Mabry, July 1, 1893.

29. "Operations," 77.

30. *El Paso Times,* July 6, 1893.

Chapter 6: Scouting on Pirate Island

1. J. M. Dean to Gov. J. S. Hogg, July 2, 1893.

2. W. H. Austin to Gov. J. S. Hogg, July 3, 1893.

3. T. T. Teel to Gov. J. S. Hogg, July 3, 1893.

4. Robert Cross to Gov. J. S. Hogg, July 3, 1893.

5. Jeff McLemore to Gov. J. S. Hogg, July 3, 1893.

6. Peyton F. Edwards Sr. to Gov. J. S. Hogg, July 3, 1893.

7. W. W. Turney to Gov. J.S. Hogg, July 3, 1893. William Ward Turney was the son of Albert G. and Salina Ward Turney and was born July 11, 1861, at Marshall, Texas. He moved to Fort Davis in 1886 and taught school, then in 1887 he was admitted to the bar. He became the first county attorney of Brewster County. In 1892 and again in 1894, he was elected to the House of Representatives, where he was serving when he made his recommendation. In 1896 he was elected to the Senate from which he retired in 1902. He increased his ranching interests so that at one time his O-2 Ranch covered 200,000 acres. He died in El Paso on March 23, 1939. His complete obituary appeared in the *Alpine Avalanche*, March 31, 1939. He will reappear later in Hughes's life story as a longtime supporter of the captain.

8. Sheriff F. B. Simmons to Gov. J. S. Hogg and Adj. Gen. W. H. Mabry, both July 3, 1903.

9. J. D. Escajeda to Gov. J. S. Hogg, July 3, 1893.

10. H. H. Kirkpatrick et al., to Adj. Gen. W. H. Mabry, July 3, 1893.

11. W. Van Sickle et al., to Adj. Gen. W. H. Mabry, July 3, 1893.

12. George Wythe Baylor to Adj. Gen. W. H. Mabry, July 5, 1893.

13. Baz L. Outlaw to Adj. Gen. W. H. Mabry, July 5, 1893.

14. William Noyes to Adj. Gen. W. H. Mabry, July 5, 1893.

15. James H. Faubion, of the firm of Faubion & Son, dealers in shingles, laths, doors, blinds, and building material of all types, including coffins, farm implements, and barbed wire, to Adj. Gen. W. H. Mabry, July 5, 1893. Faubion must have been friends with Hughes while Hughes ranched in Williamson County. In 1880 Tennessee native Faubion had a wife and children there, and by 1890 he was still farming at sixty-five years of age. His wife had passed on, and three of his children lived with him. Decades later, in 1930, eighty-five years of age, he continued in general farming, with daughters Maude M. and Kate M. still residing with him. 15th U.S. Census, Williamson County, Texas. Enumerated April 2, 1930, E.D. # 246-13, sheet 7.

16. Isaac N. "Ike" Herrin began his Ranger career under Capt. Frank Jones, enlisting on March 27, 1892, then served under Hughes. His service record does not indicate when he was discharged. He was born in September 1870, in Texas; following his Ranger career he and Ed Aten operated a saloon in El Paso, and then operated a saloon in Shafter, where he worked as a bartender. 12th U.S. Census, Presidio County, Texas. Enumerated June 30, 1900, E.D. # 67, Sheet 23; *New Handbook of Texas*, s.v. "Edwin Dunlap Aten," by H. Allen Anderson. Herrin died in Leon County on August 6, 1903. Texas death certificate # 41376.

17. Corporal Carl Kirchner and petition to Adj. Gen. W. H. Mabry, July 5, 1893.

18. S. R. Miller to Adj. Gen. W. H. Mabry, July 7, 1893. Samuel R. Miller claimed to be ex-sheriff in this letter. Sammy Tise's *Texas County Sheriffs* does not list him holding that office. However, in the election of November 6, 1888, William Russell was elected but died before qualification. As a stop-gap measure, S. R. Miller was appointed and qualified. He also served as Collector of Taxes. Miller was born in England in June 1847; in 1900 he was living in Marfa with his wife and seven children. 12th U.S. Census, Presidio County, Texas. Enumerated June 27, 1900. E.D. # 66, Sheet 16; State of Texas Election Returns, Presidio County, Texas State Library & Archives, letter of B. F. Adams, County Judge, May 29, 1891, to George W. Smith, Secretary of State. Denton G. Knight replaced Miller as sheriff in the November 8, 1892, election.

19. John R. Hughes to Adj. Gen. W. H. Mabry, July 5, 1893.

20. Sheriff F. B. Simmons to Gov. J. S. Hogg, July 7, 1893.

21. Sheriff F. B. Simmons to Adj. Gen. W. H. Mabry, July 7, 1893. Simmons had wanted Rangers in El Paso County all that year, and perhaps before. Back on February 1 he had sent a petition to Mabry requesting Rangers, pointing out "this County is very much in need of the Rangers as depredations are being committed which cannot be stopped without the Rangers as they can give their time to this matter." Simmons was elected on November 8, 1892, was re-elected and served until November 8, 1898. Tise, 172; *El Paso Times*, July 6, 1893.

22. John R. Hughes to Adj. Gen. W. H. Mabry, July 8, 1893.

23. Ira Aten to Adj. Gen. W. H. Mabry, July 10, 1893. This was the second Texas county Aten served. He was appointed sheriff of Fort Bend County on August 21, 1889, serving until November 4, 1890. He became sheriff of Castro County by appointment, serving from May 9, 1893, until his election November 6, 1894. He served until January 1895. Tise, 94, 188.

24. *El Paso Daily Times*, July 13, 1893.

25. *San Antonio Daily Express*, July 17, 1893; *El Paso Herald-Post*, May 13, 1938.

26. "Pioneer Rangers Trace Route of Gang That Killed Jones," *El Paso Herald-Post*, May 13, 1938.

27. C. L. Sonnichsen. "Last of the Great Rangers—Captain John R. Hughes," typed manuscript, dated 1946. Original in the Special Collections Department, University of Texas at El Paso.

28. Captain Hughes Monthly Return, July 31, 1893; and Hughes to Adj. Gen. W. H. Mabry, July 26, 1893.

29. Ibid.

30. Ibid.

31. C. L. Sonnichsen. "The Miller-Frazer Feud," unpublished manuscript prepared by Sonnichsen in 1946, archived in Special Collections, University of Texas at El Paso Library. For works on Miller see also Glenn Shirley's *Shotgun for Hire: The Story of "Deacon" Jim Miller, Killer of Pat Garrett* (Norman: University of Oklahoma Press, 1970); Bill C. James, *Jim Miller: The Untold Story of a Texas Badman* (Wolfe City, Tex.: Henington Publishing Company, 2001). For a treatment of Miller's final killing and the resultant lynching see this author's *James Brown Miller and Death in Oklahoma: Was Justice Denied in Ada?* (Gonzales, Tex.: Reese's Print Shop, 2009).

32. Judge C. N. Buckler to Gov. J. S. Hogg, July 14, 1893.

33. George M. Frazer was a Tennessee native, born there in January 1828, and became Pecos County judge. In 1900 he was head of his family, working

as a merchant with three daughters: Emma, age thirty; Ella, age twenty-eight; and F. A. Lucas and her child. 12th U.S. Census, Pecos County, Texas. Enumerated June 14–15, 1900, ironically by J. M. Gibson, brother of the murdered Con Gibson. E.D. # 69, Sheet 6.

34. Captain Hughes Monthly Return, July 31, 1893. See also a lengthy summary of the Frazer-Miller feud by "Old Timer" which appeared in the *El Paso Times,* June 17, 1920, a belated reminiscence inspired by the lynching of J. B. Miller and three of his associates in Ada, Oklahoma, in 1909.

35. Baz L. Outlaw to Adj. Gen. W. H. Mabry, September 6, 1893.

36. *El Paso Daily Times,* September 17, 1893.

37. Captain Hughes Monthly Return, August 31, 1893.

38. *El Paso Times,* August 25 and September 2, 1893.

39. Captain Hughes to Adj. Gen. W. H. Mabry, August 25, 1893.

40. *San Antonio Semi-Weekly Express,* August 29, 1893.

41. Ibid., August 16, 1893.

42. Ibid., September 30, 1893; the *El Paso Times* of September 9 reported the arrest, identifying the man arrested as Nita, "who murdered Victoriano Hernandez in Presidio county in January of last year." This article included the name of Frank Gaspey Jr. as also involved in the arrest.

43. Captain Hughes to Adj. Gen. W. H. Mabry, November 18, 1893.

44. Ibid., November 24, 1893.

45. Quartermaster G. H. Wheatley "Ledger" of letters sent, February 13, 1894, to Capt. J. R. Hughes, 150. A. V. Oden enlisted on March 1, 1891, and served until May 18, 1894. Oden Ranger Service Record.

46. *Galveston Daily News,* March 23, 1894.

47. Ibid., March 28, 1894.

48. H. Gordon Frost, *The Gentlemen's Club: The Story of Prostitution in El Paso* (El Paso: Mangan Books, 1983), 72.

49. Report of Captain Hughes to Adj. Gen. W. H. Mabry telling of the deaths of Baz L. Outlaw and Joe McKidrict, dated April 6, 1894. Hughes's report agrees with Oden's, pointing out that Selman was hit in the right leg. The well-known photograph of Selman made at this time shows him with a cane, due to the wounds received in that gunfight.

50. Alonzo Van Oden, *Texas Ranger's Diary and Scrapbook,* 40–41. The gunfight is discussed in great detail in Leon C. Metz, *John Selman: Texas Gunfighter,* in the chapter "The Death of Bass Outlaw" (New York: Hastings House, 1966), 139–50; as well as in Robert K. DeArment, *George Scarborough: The Life and Death of a Lawman on the Closing Frontier* (Norman: University of

Oklahoma Press, 1992), 60–76. The well-known photograph of John Selman Sr. with the cane appears in Metz's *John Wesley Hardin: Dark Angel of
Texas*, 271; Metz's *John Selman: Texas Gunfighter*, facing 128; and in DeArment's *George Scarborough*, 142.

51. Captain Hughes's Monthly Return, April 30, 1894, and telegram from
    Hughes to Adj. Gen. W. H. Mabry, April 6, 1894. Outlaw was buried in
    El Paso's Concordia Cemetery, his grave only recently marked. McKid-
    rict is buried in Austin's Oakwood Cemetery, his grave marked shortly
    after interment.

52. Daniel Murphy to Adj. Gen. W. H. Mabry, February 21, 1895.

53. G. A. Frazer to Gov. Charles A. Culberson, February 24, 1895.

54. Captain Hughes to Adj. Gen. W. H. Mabry, March 4, 1895.

55. Captain Hughes Monthly Return, March 31, 1895.

56. Robert M. Utley, *Lone Star Justice: The First Century of the Texas Rangers*
    (New York: Oxford University Press, 2008), 259–60. The various newspaper
    reports dealing with the strike fail to mention the presence of the Rangers.
    See the *Galveston Daily News* of June 6, 9, 11, and 12, 1894, for example.

57. Capt. J. A. Brooks of Company F had with him G. J. Cook, G. N. Horton,
    Joseph Natus, and E. E. Coleman; from Company E were John Nix, T. M.
    Ross, and Dan Coleman; from Company B were Edward F. "Ed" Connell,
    R. L. "Lee" Queen, Adolphus A. Neely, Jack Harwell, and C. B. Fullerton.
    The name of the photographer is unknown.

58. Captain Hughes Monthly Return, July 31, 1894. The Temple city marshal at
    this time was William Taylor who served from 1885 to 1897. Born in Ber-
    ryville, Virginia, in 1860 he came to Texas in 1877, worked as a cowboy for
    five years and then came to Temple in 1882, where he engaged in the meat
    business. After his career as city marshal, he spent two years in the Klon-
    dike searching for gold and then returned to Temple where he established
    the Taylor Undertaking Company. He remained in this occupation until his
    death in December 1919. Although the *Temple Daily Telegram* of December
    1, 1907, printed an extensive interview with him, there is no mention of
    Hughes or the arrest of Gifford.

59. Quartermaster Report, 1894, Ledger, 89.

60. Ibid., 91.

61. Ibid., 92.

62. For a brief biography of Riggs see Bill C. James's *Barney K. Riggs: A West
    Texas Gunman* (Privately printed, 1982).

63. The Fort Stockton troubles are thoroughly reviewed in Bill C. James's
    Sheriff A .J. Royal: Fort Stockton, Texas (Privately printed, 1984); see also

Barney Riggs: The Yuma and Pecos Avenger, by Ellis Lindsey and Gene Riggs (Xlibris Corp., 2002).

64. Charles H. Harris III and Louis R. Sadler, *The Secret War in El Paso*, 92–97; Bill C. James and Mary Kay Shannon, *Sheriff A. J. Royal: Fort Stockton, Texas*, 21–22; Robert K. DeArment, *George Scarborough: The Life and Death of a Lawman on the Closing Frontier*, 53–56.

65. *Times-Democrat*, Muskogee, Oklahoma, March 16, 1914. There is no apparent explanation for this illustrated article; possibly it was used as filler. The illustrations depict "Typical Texas Rangers," one mounted with no identification, one showing Wood Saunders on horseback pulling a water barrel, and one identified as Hughes on a white horse. The caption states that Captain Hughes "never takes the trail of a man that he doesn't land dead or alive."

66. Glenn Shirley, *Marauders of the Indian Nations: The Bill Cook Gang and Cherokee Bill* (Stillwater, Okla.: Barbed Wire Press, 1994), 1.

67. The only work on Sullivan remains his autobiography. The most recent reprint is by Bison Books, an imprint of University of Nebraska Press, with an introduction by John Miller Morris (2001).

68. The best treatment of Thomas D. Love and his pursuit of Cook and other outlaws remains Bob Alexander, "An Outlaw Tripped Up by Love" in the *Quarterly* of the National Association for Outlaw and Lawman History 26, no. 3 (July–September 2002): 1, 7–16. This includes a remarkable photograph of the captured outlaw Cook with lawmen C. C. Perry, T. D. Love, and Mitchell County, Texas, Sheriff Young Douglas McMurry. By the various authors who discuss some aspect of Perry's career, he is identified as C. C. or simply Charles Perry. Glenn Shirley identifies him as Christopher Columbus Perry, with "Charles" as a nickname. Sullivan may have gained some satisfaction after his hard luck of losing out on the reward money for Cook when he learned that in 1896 C. C. Perry absconded with $7,000 of Chaves County tax funds and disappeared in South Africa. His final fate remains unknown. Larry D. Ball, *Desert Lawmen: The High Sheriffs of New Mexico and Arizona 1846–1912* (Albuquerque: University of New Mexico Press, 1992), 287.

69. Telegraph item from El Paso of January 14 printed in the *Galveston Daily News*, January 15, 1895.

70. W. J. L. Sullivan, *Twelve Years in the Saddle with the Texas Rangers* (1909; repr. Lincoln: University of Nebraska, 2001), 102. The book was originally published under the title *Twelve Years in the Saddle for Law and Order on the Frontiers of Texas*.

71. Ibid., 104.

72. Henry W. Reynolds, Deputy Collector of Customs, to Judge W. Van Sickle, January 26, 1895.

73. Judge W. Van Sickle to W. W. Turney, January 30, 1895.

74. Extract from letter to Adjutant General's office from J. L. McAleer and forwarded to Captain Hughes. Extract dated February 1, 1895.

75. Captain Hughes to Adj. Gen. W. H. Mabry, February 15, 1895.

76. Sheriff Denton G. Knight's request is described in a letter from Hughes to Mabry, February 7, 1895, also a letter from Robert B. Neighbors to Hughes, February 4, 1895. Chispa was founded in 1882 when the Southern Pacific Railroad laid its track some sixteen miles northwest of Valentine. Although at one time it had a post office, by the 1970s it was only a stop on the railroad. A branch line once ran to a coal mining settlement south. Ed Bartholomew wrote Chispa was "bare now." Ed Bartholomew, *Texas Ghost Town Encyclopedia* (Fort Davis, Tex.: Frontier Press, 1982), 25.

77. Sheriff R. B. Neighbors to Captain Hughes, February 4, 1895.

78. Captain Hughes to Adj. Gen. W. H. Mabry, February 7, 1895.

79. Ibid., February 8, 1895. Little further information has been found regarding this killing. A report from Pecos indicated that "an unknown man was killed to-day by Ranger Fulgham of Captain Hughes' company." When ordered to surrender he "offered resistance and was thereupon shot by the officer." The only clue to his identification was found in a small book in his pocket bearing the name of Charles Carroll, Suggs, Indian Territory. His body was turned over to the county for burial. *San Antonio Semi-Weekly Express*, August 29, 1895.

80. Captain Hughes to Adj. Gen. W. H. Mabry, February 18, 1895.

81. Judge W.H. Harris to Adj. Gen. W. H. Mabry, February 25, 1895.

82. Captain Hughes to Adj. Gen. W. H. Mabry, March 11, 1895.

83. Ibid., March 21, 28, 29, 1895.

84. H. H. Kilpatrick to Adj. Gen. W.H. Mabry, March 30, 1895.

85. Captain Hughes to W. H. Mabry, April 2, 1895.

86. David Dorado Romo, *Ringside Seat to a Revolution: An Underground Cultural History of El Paso and Juarez: 1893–1923* (El Paso: Cinco Puntos Press, 2005), 18.

87. Captain Hughes to W. H. Mabry, April 2, 1895.

88. *Galveston Daily News*, April 23, 1895.

89. Captain Hughes to Adj. Gen. W. H. Mabry, April 5, 1895.

90. J.D. Milton to Hughes, April 23 and Hughes to Adj. Gen. W. H. Mabry dated April 24, 1895.

91. Captain Hughes to Adj. Gen. W. H. Mabry, June 11, 1895; see also *San Antonio Daily Express* of July 1, 1895, for coverage of the killing, reporting news from El Paso.

92. J. M. Dean to Adj. Gen. Mabry June 13 and Captain Hughes to Mabry, June 19, 1895.

93. Captain Hughes Monthly Return, June 30; and Hughes to Mabry July 3, 1895. San Antonio's *Express* provides an excellent review of the killing based on reports from El Paso. Headlines reflect the belief that Mrs. Mrose was used as a decoy to entice the man to his death. *San Antonio Daily Express,* July 1, 1895. For treatments of the Mrose killing see Leon C. Metz, *John Selman, Texas Gunman* and Robert K. DeArment *George Scarborough: The Life and Death of a Lawman on the Closing Frontier.*

94. J. D. Milton to Mabry, on letterhead of El Paso County Sheriff Simmons, June 30, 1895.

95. Captain Hughes Monthly Return, July 31, 1895.

96. E. E. Townsend's Journal entry dated Saturday August 17, 1895. The journal entries were written on the pages of a large single-entry account book, with his handwritten notation "Eagle Pass E. E. Townsend U.S. Inspector." The entry regarding the store robbery is found on pages 44–46. Original journal in Townsend Papers in Archives of the Big Bend, Sul Ross University, Alpine.

97. *Galveston Daily News,* August 17, 1895; Captain Hughes Monthly Return, September 30, 1895.

98. 12th U.S. Census, Burnet County, Texas. Enumerated June 5, 1880, 124.

99. E. E. Townsend, "The Robbery of the Valentine Store," *Voice of the Mexican Border* (published at Marfa, Tex.), 1, no. 4 (December 1933): 180–82. Townsend had a distinguished career in law enforcement. On October 2, 1899, he filled out his application to be a Special Ranger, "To look out for interest of W. W. Turney & other stockmen of Brewster Co. Tex." He detailed his previous experience as serving as a Ranger in Company E, 1891–1892; 1893–1894 a Deputy U.S. Marshal; 1894–1898 Inspector of U.S. Customs, was "sober and temperate" in habits and had never been convicted of any crime. The six-foot-tall officer was enlisted in Hughes's Company D on June 1, 1899, and served until September 25, 1899, receiving an honorable discharge on that date. Townsend was later elected sheriff of Brewster County, serving three terms. In 1932 he was instrumental in making the Big Bend a state park, now part of the National Park Service. He died on November 14, 1948. His younger brother Joseph B. Townsend also served as a Ranger under Captain Hughes, serving from May 8, 1899, through December 10, 1902.

100. Captain Hughes to Quartermaster W. H. Owen, October 1, 1895.

Chapter 7: Spectators on the Rio Grande

1. Leo. N. Miletich, *Dan Stuart's Fistic Carnival* (College Station: Texas A&M University Press, 1994), 18–20.
2. *New Handbook of Texas,* s.v. "Charles Allen Culberson," by Robert L. Wagner.
3. Leo N. Miletich. *Dan Stuart's Fistic Carnival,* 220, citing *The General Laws of Texas.*
4. Ibid., 58–59.
5. Captain Hughes to Adj. Gen. W. H. Mabry, November 1, 1895.
6. William Schmitt to Adj. Gen. W. H. Mabry, November 4, 1895.
7. Captain Hughes to Adj. Gen. W. H. Mabry from Ysleta, November 8, 1895.
8. Ibid., November 11, 1895.
9. Ibid., December 27, 1895.
10. *San Antonio Daily Express,* February 11, 1896.
11. Captain Hughes Monthly Return, February 1896.
12. *El Paso Daily Herald,* February 11, 1896.
13. Miletich, *Dan Stuart's Fistic Carnival,* 141. Rector was born in 1863 in West Virginia. He saw the development of motion pictures from the earliest days of film making until his death on January 26, 1957. Although his filming of the Fitzsimmons-Maher fight was a failure due to weather conditions, his filming of the Corbett-Fitzsimmons fight in 1897 has survived, at least in part. Obituary in the *New York Times,* January 27, 1957.
14. *El Paso Daily Herald,* February 12, 1896.
15. *San Antonio Daily Express,* February 14, 1896.
16. Ibid., February 13, 1896.
17. Ibid., February 15, 1896.
18. J. C. Burge remains virtually unknown except for his photography. He was born in 1839 and died in 1897. He was in Arizona from 1881–1884 and then in New Mexico from 1885–1891. In 1895 and 1896 he was in El Paso. David Haynes, *Catching Shadows: A Directory of 19th Century Texas Photographers* (Austin: Texas State Historical Association, 1993), 18. Besides the two exposures of the Ranger group at El Paso, the death photographs of John Wesley Hardin and Martin Mrose were both made by Burge.
19. *San Antonio Daily Express,* February 20, 1896.
20. Ibid., February 21, 1896.
21. Ibid., February 22, 1896.

22. Private R. M. Loeser to Adj. Gen. W. H. Mabry, February 28, 1896. Little is known of Robert M. Loeser. He first served under Captain Brooks in Company F from September 1, 1890, through March 3, 1891. He then served under Capt. Frank Jones in Company D from April 1 to June 20, 1891, then under Captain Hughes. His application for Special Ranger indicated he was born in New York City in 1864. His occupation is shown to be a "Chemist." To the question as to where he had resided the previous ten years he wrote 1890–1897 in Texas and then 1897–1900 in California. He stated he had served as a Deputy U.S. Marshal, a deputy sheriff, and a State Ranger. As to why he wanted a commission as Special Ranger he gave "For outdoor work," certainly an unusual request, as most men requesting such a commission indicated they wanted to reduce crime.

23. *El Paso Daily Herald*, February 21, 1896.

24. Sullivan, *Twelve Years in the Saddle with the Texas Rangers*, 146-48.

25. *El Paso Daily Herald*, February 21, 1896.

26. James G. Reagan was born in Texas in 1865 and when enumerated in the 1900 Val Verde County census gave his occupation as stock raiser. Perhaps he served as a deputy on a part-time basis. 12th U.S. Census, Val Verde County, Texas. Enumerated June 5, 1900, E.D. # 74 sheet 6. The first person enumerated in the 1900 census for Val Verde County was Roy Bean, living with his two sons Sam and John. He gave his occupation as stock man.

27. J. G. Reagan to Governor Culberson, February 21, 1896.

28. *El Paso Daily Herald*, February 22, 1896. Today there is a Texas State Historical Marker commemorating the site: "Fitzsimmons-Maher Prizefight." This was erected in 2003 by the Texas Historical Commission and is in Langtry, Val Verde County.

29. *El Paso Daily Herald*, February 22, 1896.

30. Ibid.

31. Mabry's telegram to Hughes to curtail expenses is responded to in a telegram by Hughes dated January 17, 1896; the telegram to Mabry "regardless of consequences" is from Culberson to Mabry, February 12, 1896.

32. Robert K. DeArment, *Broadway Bat: Gunfighter in Gotham. The New York City Years of Bat Masterson* (Honolulu, Hawaii: Talei Publishers, Inc., 2005), 18–19. The Masterson quotations are from the *Morning Telegraph* of October 30, 1917.

33. W. W. Turney to Adj. Gen. W. H. Mabry, December 4, 1895.

34. Captain Hughes to Adj. Gen. W. H. Mabry, December 20, 1895.

35. Ibid., February 17, 1896.

36. *New Handbook of Texas*, s.v. "Texas Fever," by Tamara Miner Haygood.

37. Proclamation by C. A. Culberson and Allison Mayfield, Secretary of State. The printed copy is dated February 10, but a copy was not forwarded to General W. H. Mabry until February 20, 1896.

38. Steven W. Pipkin was a Texas-born stock herder, born in July 1863. 12th U.S. Census, El Paso County, Texas. Enumerated June 2–4, 1900, 248A.

39. *Galveston Daily News*, March 20, 1896.

40. *San Antonio Daily Express*, March 12, 1896.

41. Captain Hughes to Adj. Gen. W. H. Mabry, undated March, March 11, March 19, April 4, 1896, letters and telegrams.

42. W. B. Tullis recommended R. M. Clayton to be a Special Ranger, based on his experience and knowledge of the livestock industry. He took the oath on March 24, 1896. He was from Parker County, Texas, and was forty years of age. Tullis, a member of the livestock commission, was a dealer in cattle and horses with headquarters in Quanah, Texas, and ranches in Hardeman and Greer counties. (Greer County became part of Oklahoma in 1906.)

43. Captain Hughes to Adj. Gen. W. H. Mabry, May 9 and 10, 1896.

44. W. B. Tullis to Adj. Gen. W. H. Mabry, March 31, 1896.

45. For a treatment of Spanish-language editors and their newspapers see David Dorado Romo, *Ringside Seat to a Revolution: An Underground Cultural History of El Paso and Juarez, 1893–1923* (El Paso: Cinco Puntos Press, 2005), 23–32.

46. *San Antonio Daily Express*, March 11 and 12 and April 3, 1896. See also DeArment's biography of George Scarborough, 57–59. Lauro Aguirre's name is spelled in a variety of ways; I have used the spelling in Romo's *Ringside Seat to a Revolution.*

47. Captain Hughes to Adj. Gen. W. H. Mabry, April 11, 1896.

48. Captain Hughes to Quartermaster W. H. Owen, May 29, 1896. Bell served in Company D until his honorable discharge dated January 31, 1897. Bell, suffering from tuberculosis, died on July 29, 1897, and is buried in Stockdale, Wilson County.

49. Captain Hughes to Quartermaster Owen, June 30, 1896.

50. Captain Hughes to Adj. Gen. Mabry, August 28, 1896.

51. W. W. Turney to Adj. Gen. W. H. Mabry, May 26, 1896. The trial did not take place until April 1897.

52. James B. Gillett later wrote of his adventures in *Six Years with the Texas Rangers*, first published in 1921 and kept in print by many later editions. Unfortunately he makes no mention of this incident against the Friers

although he had provided an important tip to other lawmen. Gillett was elected sheriff of Brewster County on November 4, 1890, and served one term until November 8, 1892. He was replaced by another former Ranger, Doctor W. Gourley. Tise, 65.

53. Captain Hughes to Adj. Gen. W. H. Mabry, October 4, 1896. Of interest is that someone, perhaps in the adjutant general's office, made "editorial corrections" on Hughes's original letter. Any quotations I have used are from Hughes's own pre-edited version.

54. *New Handbook of Texas*, s.v. "Glass Mountains." Today U.S. Highway 385 runs through the eastern portion of the range.

55. Captain Hughes to Adj. Gen. W. H. Mabry, October 4, 1896.

56. Ibid.

57. Jubus C. and Arthur S. Frier were the sons of Isham C. and Mary J. Frier. The family is found in the 1880 McCulloch County, Texas, census. The parents were Missouri-born as was Isham's step-daughter, then twelve years of age. The others were all born in Texas. In 1880 Jubus C. "Jube" was nine years old and brother Arthur ten months old. 10th U.S. Census McCulloch County, Texas. Enumerated June 2–3, 1880, 537. Their post office was Brady. Hughes spelled the name "Frier" in his report, although it is seen as "Friar" as well. Their bodies were placed in simple wooden coffins, with their boots on, "some distance east of other interments in the old cemetery" at Fort Davis. The county paid the burial expenses: $13.00 for the coffins and $1.00 for the two graves. Deputy Sheriff J. P. Weatherby, Tom Granger, and John Pool of Marfa witnessed the burial. On their way to the cemetery they met a former buffalo soldier, Randolph Wiggins, who now was a "professed Baptist preacher." It was Preacher Wiggins who knelt in the dust and prayed for the souls of the Frier brothers. Weatherby placed a wooden headboard on the graves the following day with their names. Lucy Miller Jacobson and Mildred Bloys Nored, *Jeff Davis County, Texas* (Fort Davis, Tex.: Fort Davis Historical Society, 1993). One of the illustrations shows Tom Granger painting the name of "J. Frier" on a wooden headboard. The gunfight with the Friers is described on pages 163–65. Today the original wooden marker is housed in the Fort Davis Museum. A large modern stone has been recently placed in the Fort Davis Pioneer Cemetery.

58. Captain Hughes to Adj. Gen. W. H. Mabry, October 4, 1896.

59. Captain Hughes Monthly Return, September 1896.

60. *San Antonio Daily Express*, October 1, 1896.

61. Postcard reward notice from Lindley Brothers of Sherwood, Texas (then seat of Irion County), to Sheriff D. G. Knight, Presidio County. Original in the Flachmeier Collection, Austin History Center.

62. Ernest St. Leon to Adj. Gen. W. H. Mabry, September 30, 1896. The *Daily Express* of San Antonio provided a lengthy report of this fight, probably having interviewed Captain Hughes at Fort Davis. Here Combs's wound is described: "the lead in its passage carrying away the small piece that projects in front of the ear, then passed through the back part, leaving a small hole, marking him for life."

63. Captain Hughes to Adj. Gen. W. H. Mabry, October 13, 1896.

64. Captain Hughes to Adj. Gen. W. H. Mabry, December 20 and 31, 1896.

65. Copies of official court records of Tom Green County provided by Suzanne Campbell, Director of the West Texas Collection, Angelo State University. Details of Humphreys's life after sentencing are undetermined.

66. Ibid., December 31, 1896.

67. Ibid., January 1, 1897.

68. *San Antonio Daily Express*, January 1, 1897.

69. For a brief sketch of Augustine Montaigue Gildea see Philip J. Rasch, "Gus Gildea—An Arizone [*sic*] Pioneer" in the *Brand Book* of the English Westerners Society 23, no. 2 (Summer 1985).

70. *San Antonio Daily Express*, January 1, 1897.

71. Captain Hughes to Adj. Gen. W. H. Mabry, December 31, 1896.

72. J. Marvin Hunter. This article, in part, originally appeared in the *Galveston Daily News*, date not provided, and reprinted with additional introductory material in *Frontier Times*, December, 1944. The article is entitled "The Outstanding Texas Ranger," 76–79. There is no indication where the visit took place, but perhaps in Bandera where Hunter had his Frontier Times Museum.

Chapter 8: The Hardest Man to Catch

1. Ranger service record and the *Galveston Daily News*, April 24, 1896. George P. Leakey was born in Edwards County in 1862, and began his career as a Ranger in Company F under Lt. William Scott, mustered in the service on June 27, 1885, and honorably discharged on October 5 of the same year. He then was mustered into Company D under Hughes on May 8, 1894, and received an honorable discharge on May 1, 1895. On July 19, 1895, he applied for an appointment as a Special Ranger, listing his occupation as an inspector for the Cattle Raisers Association of Texas. His application was approved by Reeves County Judge James E. Bowen. His several reports as a Special Ranger indicate he worked in the Pecos and Reeves County area. Leakey died on the Texas and Pacific train on April 21, 1896, at 3:00 a.m.

"while being taken from Pecos City to his home at Leakey, Tex." Tuberculosis was given as the cause of his death.

2. Author's visit to the grave of James Maddox Bell, 2008.

3. Captain Hughes to Captain W. H. Owen, Quartermaster, January 11, 1897.

4. Tennessee native Philip S. Elkins in 1880 resided in Limestone County, Texas, with his wife and two children, his occupation given as a butcher. In 1900 he was in Reeves County, post office Pecos City, his occupation now given as a carpenter. His son Claude, twenty-four, gave his occupation as hotel keeper. 10th U.S. Census, Limestone County, Texas. Enumerated June 28, 1880, 310; 12th U.S. Census, Reeves County, Texas. Enumerated June 27, 1900, E.D. #68 sheet 5.

5. Captain Hughes to P. S. Elkins, January 17, 1897.

6. Judson Heard was a Mississippi native born in 1855; in both the 1880 and the 1900 census he appears as a single male and a boarder, with no occupation given in 1880 and in 1900 a "miner." 10th U.S. Census, McLennan County, Texas. Enumerated June 4, 1880, 81, and 12th U.S. Census, Reeves County, Texas. Enumerated June 30, 1900, E.D. # 68 sheet 8.

7. T. J. Hefner served as Reeves County attorney from May 12, 1886 to November 14, 1894. He was elected county judge in 1896 and served in that office for fourteen years. In 1898 he defeated George M. Frazer in the race for county judge. Born April 29, 1858, in La Grange, Texas, he died on October 3, 1915, and is buried in Pecos. Alton Hughes, *Pecos: A History of the Pioneer West* (Seagraves, Tex.: Pioneer Book Publishers, 1978), 317–18.

8. Captain Hughes to Quartermaster W. H. Owen, January 20, 1897.

9. Judson Heard to Quartermaster W. H. Owen, February 6, 1897.

10. P. S. Elkins to Capt. John R. Hughes, February 5, 1897.

11. Edwin Dunlap Aten, born September 5, 1870, in Illinois, developed a "wild streak" and was forced to join the Rangers at the insistence of older brother Ira. He enlisted in Capt. Frank Jones's Company D on September 16, 1892. Aten married Elena Benavides and the couple had one child who died young. Not long after, the Atens separated. He operated a saloon in Ysleta where he lived, and later was located at Shafter where he tended bar and dealt faro in Ike Herrin's saloon, he also a former Ranger of Company D. Aten became a Ranger again in 1901 and also performed undercover work for Captain Hughes. His second marriage was to Mrs. Gertrude Bacus Aiello, a young widow. E. D. Aten overcame the recklessness of his youth and served the Rangers admirably. He died in El Paso on January 31, 1953, and is buried there in Rest Lawn Cemetery. Robert W. Stephens, *Texas Ranger Sketches*, 16–20.

12. Captain John R. Hughes to Quartermaster W. H. Owen, February 10, 1897.

13. J. C. Yeates to Adj. Gen. W. H. Mabry, February 1, 1897.

14. Captain Hughes to Adj. Gen. W. H. Mabry, October 31, 1896. This is a nine-page letter on Company D's letterhead.

15. Ranger service record of John C. Yeates. After his career under Captain Hughes, Yeates did serve as a Special Ranger, without pay, but was never assigned to Captain Brooks's Company F. In 1900 he was living in Kinney County in the household of his father-in-law with a wife and son, his occupation listed as a farm laborer. He also served as a post master in the small community of Tularosa, Kinney County, listed in that position on December 13, 1901. See Jim Wheat's *Postmasters and Post Offices of Texas, 1846–1930.* Compiled Records from the National Archives and the Library of Congress, microfilm reel # 3163. Texas State Archives. In 1910 Yeates was living with his wife and six children in San Antonio. He now was proprietor of a pawn shop. Yeates became a San Antonio police officer and served for twelve years on the force. On May 16, 1928, he walked his 3:00–11:00 p.m. beat, returned home and was stricken and died almost immediately. His obituary in the *San Antonio Light* states he had served as a deputy sheriff in Kinney County for fourteen years and a Ranger for four years. He was survived by his widow, the daughter of William S. Hutchinson, the founder of Tularosa, four sons and four daughters. *San Antonio Light*, May 16, 1928. 12th U.S. Census, Kinney County, Texas. Enumerated June 5, 1900, 162; and 13th U.S. Census, Bexar County, Texas. Enumerated April 29, 1910, E.D. # 13 sheet 29. The official death certificate (Bexar County # 19703) gives his date of birth as April 14, 1857. The cause of death was listed as *angina pectoris*; he was found in a dying condition when medical assistance arrived. Donaly E. Brice, Research Specialist at the Texas State Archives, found no record that Yeates served time in a Texas penitentiary as was apparently believed by some during his lifetime.

16. Doctor W. Gourley was elected sheriff of Brewster County on November 6, 1892, and served until November 4, 1902. He followed Ranger James B. Gillett as Brewster County sheriff. Tise, 65; *San Antonio Daily Express*, March 10, 1896. D. W. "Doc" Gourley was born in December 1858 and by 1900 resided in Alpine with his wife, mother-in-law Laura A. Toler, a sixty-six-year-old widow, his six children, a nephew, and a boarder. 12th U.S. Census, Brewster County, Texas. Enumerated June 1, 1900. E.D. # 9, sheet one.

17. The name of the saloon, absent from most accounts concerning the killing, is from a brief notice appearing in the *San Angelo Standard*, September 19, 1896, citing a report from Toyah dated September 14.

18. Bill Leftwich, *Tracks Along the Pecos* (Pecos, Tex.: The Pecos Press, 1957), 51–59; and Bill C. James, *Jim Miller* (Wolfe City, Tex.: Henington Publishing Company, 2001), 7–9; Ellis Lindsey and Gene Riggs, *Barney K. Riggs: The Yuma and Pecos Avenger* (NP: Xlibris, 2002), 155–61.

19. Ira J. Bush, *Gringo Doctor* (Caldwell, Idaho: The Caxton Printers, 1939), 71.

20. Captain Hughes Monthly Return for March, 1897.

21. Sheriff D. W. Gourley to Captain Hughes, April 11, 1897.

22. R. M. Clayton to Adj. Gen. W.H. Mabry, May 5, 1897.

23. *San Antonio Daily Express*, May 15, 1897; also see R. Michael Wilson, *Great Train Robberies of the Old West* (Guilford, Conn.: Globe Pequot Press, 2007), 137–38. Who the actual participants were remains speculative. Hughes believed the robbers were members of the Ketchum gang, as does R. Michael Wilson and also Wild Bunch historian Donna B. Ernst. See Ernst's *From Cowboy to Outlaw: The True Story of Will Carver* (Sonora, Tex.: Sutton County Historical Society, 1995).

24. Captain Hughes to Adj. Gen. W. H. Mabry, May 18, 1897.

25. *San Antonio Daily Express*, May 20, 1897.

26. Captain Hughes to Adj. Gen. W. H. Mabry, May 27, 1897.

27. Richard Clayton Ware was born November 11, 1851, in Rome, Georgia, and had an extensive career as a lawman. On April 1, 1876, he joined Berch S. Foster's Company E and later served under Lieutenant N. O. Reynolds before transferring to Company B under Ira Long. On January 10, 1881, he became the first sheriff of Mitchell County and served in that capacity until November 8, 1892. On May 11, 1893, he became United States Marshal for the Western District of Texas and served until January 26, 1898. Ware died on June 25, 1902, in Fort Worth. His brother Charles L. Ware also served as a Ranger. R. C. Ware's best-known exploit remains his participation in the July 1878 street fight against Sam Bass when the gang attempted to rob the bank in Round Rock, Williamson County, Texas. The historical marker on his grave credits him with giving Bass the bullet which proved to be his death wound, although George Herold is also given the credit for Bass's death wound. Ranger Service record, and Robert W. Stephens' *Texas Ranger Sketches*.

28. Captain Hughes to Adj. Gen. W. H. Mabry, June 2, 1897.

29. Captain Hughes Monthly Return, June 6, 1897.

30. Capt. W. J. McDonald to Adj. Gen. W.H. Mabry, October 12, 1897.

31. Jeffrey Burton, *The Deadliest Outlaws: The Ketchum Gang and the Wild Bunch*, 2nd ed. (Denton: University of North Texas Press, 2009). Burton has researched extensively on these outlaws. See also his *Dynamite and Six-Shooter*

(Santa Fe: Press of the Territorian, 1970), 32–34, as well as Burton's article "Tom Ketchum and his Gang," *Wild West*, December 2001, 32–37, 72–73.

32. Captain Hughes Monthly Return, July 31, 1897.

33. Ibid., August 1897; *New Handbook of Texas*, s.v. "Spofford, Texas," by Ruben E. Ochoa.

34. Captain Hughes Monthly Return, October 31, 1897.

35. Ibid., November 31, 1897.

36. For results of the legal system's dealing with the Holland brothers see Burton's *The Deadliest Outlaws*, 61; and the *El Paso Times*, January 18, 20, and 22, 1898.

37. Admission Records, Territory of New Mexico Penitentiary, Conduct Record Book I (1898–1917). New Mexico State Records Center and Archives, Santa Fe. Also the *El Paso Daily Times*, March 14, 1899.

38. Extradition Papers, Adjutant General Files, Texas State Library and Archives.

39. *El Paso Daily Times*, March 14, 1899.

40. *Santa Fe Daily New Mexican*, March 14, 1899.

41. Ibid. Hughes had indeed known Oliver Lee for several years, as in January 1896, Lee faced six indictments for alleged cattle stealing and altering brands. In that month Hughes and express messenger E. J. Fowler went to Las Cruces "to see Lee" and "the result was that he came down of his own motion" and surrendered to El Paso County Sheriff Simmons. Lee of course denied the charges. Perhaps because he knew Lee, Hughes was able to convince Lee to turn himself in without any undue publicity. *El Paso Herald*, January 9, 1896.

42. *El Paso Daily Times*, January 6, 1900.

43. James H. Boone was first elected sheriff of El Paso County on November 8, 1898, and served until he resigned in 1905 to devote more time to business interests. Boone died while visiting California on July 26, 1906; the cause of death was given as ptomaine poisoning. *El Paso Herald*, July 27, 1906.

44. *El Paso Daily Times*, January 5, 1900.

45. *Border Boss*, 146–50.

Chapter 9: From Ysleta to Alice

1. H. S. Gleim to Capt. John R. Hughes, May 11, 1900. Harry S. Gleim was a native of Illinois, born in 1856. When he and his family settled in Texas is unknown, but by 1910 the Gleim family was living in Shafter. 12th U.S.

Census, Presidio County, Texas. Enumerated May 9, 1910, E.D. # 200, Sheet 8.

2. H. S. Gleim to Capt. John R. Hughes, May 11, 1900.

3. Sheriff D. G. Knight to Capt. John R. Hughes, May 12, 1900.

4. *New Handbook of Texas*, s.v. "Shafter, Texas," by Julia Cauble Smith.

5. Robert E. Porter was born in England in May 1873. In 1900 he was working as a deputy sheriff. 12th U.S. Census, Presidio County, Texas. Enumerated June 29, 1900. E.D. # 66, Sheet 7.

6. Sheriff D. G. Knight to Capt. J. R. Hughes, May 13, 1900.

7. Captain Hughes Monthly Return, January 31, 1901.

8. On April 6, 1901, Captain Hughes wrote to Adj. Gen. Thomas Scurry recommending John J. Brooks to be named 2nd Lieutenant to replace Tom Platt who had resigned. He had earlier enlisted on November 14, 1899. He was born in 1868 in Brown County, Texas, and worked as a cowboy prior to joining the Rangers. Ranger Service record. In 1900 he was a thirty-five-year-old head of household but a widower with two sons, Tom and William, ages five and one year respectively. He gave his occupation as "State Ranger." 12th U.S. Census, El Paso County, Texas. Enumerated June 21, 1900. E.D. # 25, Sheet 15. He was not related to Captain J. A. Brooks, unless distantly.

9. Captain Hughes Monthly Return, March 31, 1901.

10. The Hotel Dieu was a hospital conducted by the Sisters of Charity. Hughes received one wound while living in the Indian Territory, and this accidentally self-inflicted wound may be the only other one received during his lifetime. Writer William Cx Hancock, however, wrote that the number was significantly higher. In the article "Ranger's Ranger," published in the popular magazine *True West*, he wrote of "countless wounds." No doubt it was a genuine canard; Hancock wrote that Hughes was "slowing down with the weight of countless wounds. Just how many outlaws he had been forced to spin into the dust with his blazing guns and how much of their lead had been pumped into him perhaps even he did not know. And he became more and more unwilling to discuss such details" (March–April 1961 issue, p. 48).

11. E. B. Jones worked as a bookkeeper prior to serving in Company D. He was born at Vicksburg, Mississippi, in 1876. He joined on August 9, 1900, and received his honorable discharge on April 7, 1902, as a private of Company D. Ranger Service Record.

12. John R. Hughes to Adj. Gen. Thomas Scurry, March 13, 1901.

13. H. E. Delany enlisted in Company D on March 10, 1901, and then was honorably discharged on December 23 of the same year. He was a native of Dry Fork, Alabama, born about 1872. Ranger Service Record.

14. John R. Hughes to Adj. Gen. Thomas Scurry, March 14, 1901; the doctor's name is given in the *El Paso Herald* of March 14, 1901. Although it was generally known that a pistol holding six shots could be safe, it was also generally understood it was much safer to load only five chambers, leaving the hammer resting on an empty chamber. It is surprising that Hughes over-looked that fact of life.

15. *San Antonio Daily Express*, October 29, 1901, citing a report from Austin dated October 28. Perhaps the reason the notice appeared in the *Express* is that Hughes was intending to visit the San Antonio Fair before returning to his command at Fort Hancock. Eight months later Hughes was "able to ride on horseback quite well now" according to the *El Paso Daily Herald* of June 13, 1902.

16. *El Paso Daily Herald*, May 15, 1901.

17. Captain Hughes Monthly Return, May 31, 1901.

18. The Act of the 27th Legislature was printed and forwarded to Ranger Captains as General Orders No. 62 from Thomas Scurry, Adjutant General. Copy of original orders in Adjutant General Papers, Record Group 401, folder 1183-1, "Ranger Force Correspondence."

19. Ibid. General Orders No. 62 is unpaginated, a mere four pages.

20. Captain Hughes Monthly Return, July 31, 1901.

21. Ibid., September 30, 1901.

22. These were merchants Charles W. Fassett and John M. Kelly, dealers operating mainly in hardware.

23. *El Paso News*, September 27, 1901. This is a clipping in the Adjutant General's Files.

24. Captain Hughes Monthly Return, October 31, 1901. William Davis Allison is the subject of a full-length biography by Bob Alexander, *Fearless Dave Allison: Border Lawman* (Silver City, N. Mex.: High-Lonesome Books, 2003).

25. Enoch Cook, born in Uvalde County, Texas, in February 1876, swore the oath as a Ranger on December 14, 1899. The oath was valid until August 31, 1900. On September 9, 1901, he again swore the oath, now in El Paso County. He was honorably discharged at Fort Hancock with the rank of sergeant on February 6, 1902. Ranger Service Record.

26. This Bill Taylor is not to be confused with the more notorious Bill Taylor of Sutton-Taylor Feud fame. This Bill Taylor was one of a trio of men who attempted a train robbery at Coleman, Texas, on June 9, 1898, in which fire-man Lee Johnson was killed and two of the robbers—Bud Newman and Pierce Keaton—were wounded. All three were later captured in Sutton

County but Taylor escaped. Newman now was willing to betray his former companion and was part of a posse intending to capture Taylor. In the ensuing gun battle Newman was killed and Taylor was wounded. Placed in the Brownwood jail he again escaped and his final fate is unknown. J. Marvin Hunter and Noah H. Rose, *The Album of Gunfighters* (Bandera, Tex.: privately printed, 1951), 87.

27. Tolbert Fanning McKinney first enlisted as a Ranger on December 14, 1899, in Company D, then transferred to Company E under Capt. J. H. Rogers on October 10, 1900. He was honorably discharged from Company E on July 8, 1901, at Laredo, and rejoined Company D, serving honorably until discharged on December 5, 1902. Ranger Service Record.

28. Captain Hughes Monthly Return, December 31, 1901.

29. Ibid., January 31, 1902.

30. Ibid., February 28, 1902.

31. Tise, 373.

32. Ranger Service Record of W. D. Allison.

33. Copy of original documents in Record Group 401, folder 1183-1, "Ranger Force Correspondence." The oaths were sworn before Maury Kemp, County Attorney for the County of El Paso.

34. *El Paso Herald*, June 13, 1902.

35. Captain Hughes Monthly Return, April 30, 1902.

36. Ibid., August 31, 1902.

37. Ibid.

38. Anderson Yancy Baker joined the Rangers on May 25, 1897, under Capt. J. A. Brooks, Company F, and was honorably discharged February 28, 1899. On his application to be a Special Ranger, Brooks wrote that "he commands the respect of all, is well liked by his associates, and is a good man to send in any official duty." Capt. J. A. Brooks to Adjutant General's office, received June 4, 1900. A. Y. Baker was elected sheriff of Hidalgo County on November 3, 1914, re-elected November 7, 1916, and elected six more times, serving until November 1, 1930. Tise, 256.

39. See Paul M. Spellman's *Captain J. A. Brooks, Texas Ranger*, 132; and Company F Monthly Return, June 1901.

40. Monthly Return Company D, April 31, 1906.

41. William L. Calohan never served as a Ranger but developed an enviable reputation as a Cattle Inspector. The son of William and Isbella Calohan, he was born in January 1867, probably in Blanco County. In 1900 he and his family resided in Midland County. 12th U.S. Census, Midland County, Texas. Enumerated June 13, 1900. E.D. # 110, Sheet 9.

42. Two letters from Allison to Captain Hughes, both dated September 28, 1902.

43. Captain Hughes's Monthly Returns, October and November 1902; Tise, 86.

44. Captain Hughes Monthly Return, December 31, 1902.

45. Herff A. Carnes first enlisted on February 13, 1903, taking his oath of office on that date in Floresville, Wilson County. He was twenty-three years old and gave his occupation as a farmer. In 1900 the family resided in Wilson County and consisted of Joseph M. and Mary E. Carnes and their children Alfred B., Herff A., Lola L., Quirl B., Viviane I., Ada B., Tommie C., and Webb. 12th U.S. Census, Wilson County, Texas. Enumerated June 18, 1900, E.D. # 120, Sheet 8.

46. "Convict Register State Penitentiary, Huntsville, Texas." Original records now archived in Texas State Archives. Locklin's record appears on page 511.

47. District Judge Clarence Martin, et al., "To Whom It May Concern," from Fredericksburg, February 26, 1903. Original in Flachmeier Collection, Austin History Center.

48. Martin, *Border Boss*, 66.

49. Ibid., 75, 207.

50. Maude Gilliland, *Wilson County Texas Rangers: 1837–1977*. The photograph appears on page 116.

51. Maude Gilliland, *Horsebackers of the Brush Country*, 166.

52. 12th U.S. Census, Adams County, Nebraska. Enumerated June 8, 1900, E.D. # 6, Sheet 9; 12th U.S. Census, El Paso County, Texas. Enumerated April 19, 1910, E.D. # 84, Sheet 3. Curiously this portion of the El Paso County census was conducted by Marcus A. Wuerschmidt, a brother of Paul; "Enlistment, Oath of Service, and Description Ranger Force" for Paul Wuerschmidt. Wuerschmidt served as a Special Ranger from April 22, 1918, until he was discharged on January 15, 1919. See Charles H. Harris III and Louis R. Sadler, *The Texas Rangers and the Mexican Revolution: The Bloodiest Decade, 1910–1920*, 574. For a brief sketch of Paul Wuerschmidt see Charles Harris III, Frances Harris and Louis R. Sadler, *Texas Ranger Biographies: Those Who Served 1910–1921* (Albuquerque: University of New Mexico Press, 2010), 419.

53. Paul G. Wuerschmidt married Ella Mary McClure and to keep the name of Paul's sister—Hughes's love—in the family memory they named their daughter El Frieda. The child was born August 7 but lived only until September 3, 1918. The cause of death was given as *Mitral Insufficiency*, according to the Standard Certificate of Death, El Paso County, # 26472.

54. Monthly Return for Company D dated April 30, 1903.

55. Ibid., dated May 31, 1903.
56. See Paul M. Spellman's biography, *Captain John H. Rogers: Texas Ranger* for a succinct summary of the Cortez incident. He was tried a number of times, survived an attempt to lynch him at Gonzales, and ultimately did spend time in prison. He was pardoned by Governor Oscar Colquitt in 1913, having become a legendary figure as a symbol of Anglo prejudice against Mexicans. For variants of the ballad as well see especially Americo Paredes. *"With His Pistol in His Hand": A Border Ballad and Its Hero* (Austin: University of Texas Press, 1958).
57. Monthly Return, dated June 30, 1903.
58. Thomas M. Ross was a San Antonio native born in August 1871. He served under Capt. J. H. Rogers with the rank of corporal, then enlisted with Captain Hughes on July 29, 1905, as a sergeant. He was appointed captain of Company B on February 1, 1907. He died January 1, 1946, at the age of seventy-four. His obituary stated he had served as interpreter for the U.S. District Court for fifteen years. Ranger Service Record.
59. Sam McKenzie was born in Live Oak County, Texas, and first enlisted in the Ranger Force on March 9, 1903. He gave his occupation as a "Peace Officer." In addition to serving under Captain Hughes, he served under W. J. McDonald, J. J. Sanders, Thomas M. Ross, H. L. Ransom, and J. L. Anders. He was discharged February 5, 1921. McKenzie died on July 13, 1941, in Laredo, Webb County. Ranger Service Record and Harris, Harris, and Sadler, *Texas Ranger Biographies*, 239.
60. Crosby Marsden, born in Beeville, Bee County, enlisted on February 1, 1908, in Company B by Capt. Thomas M. Ross, as a private. His previous occupation was given as a cowboy. Ranger Service Records. In 1880 he was one of seven children living at home, the son of T. H. and F. A. Marsden; Crosby was then one year old. 10th U.S. Census, Bee County, Texas. Enumerated June 1, 1880, 239.
61. R. E. Smith enlisted as a private in Company B of Captain Ross, on November 27, 1908, at Alice. He was born in Bastrop County about 1881. Ranger Service Record.
62. *San Antonio Light*, June 22, 1903, citing a report from Cuero.
63. *Palestine Daily Herald*, Palestine, Texas, September 25 and November 11, 1903.
64. Monthly Returns of Company D, July through October, 1903.
65. Monthly Return for Company D dated October 30, 1903.
66. J. H. Baker enlisted at Marathon on August 16, 1901, by Captain Hughes. Born in Polk County, Tennessee, he was then thirty-eight years old. In

February 1907 he enlisted in Captain Rogers's Company C. He was honorably discharged on July 8, 1907, due to forced reduction in company. Ranger Service record.

67. Earl R. Yeary was born about 1881 at Helena, Karnes County. He first enlisted under Captain Hughes on October 19, 1902, and then enlisted in Company B on October 7, 1911, under Capt. J. J. Sanders. His previous occupation was given as Stockman. Ranger Service record.

68. Ibid., dated November 30, 1903. See *John B. Armstrong: Texas Ranger and Pioneer Rancher* by this author, published by Texas A&M University Press, 2007.

69. *El Paso Daily Herald*, January 8, 1904, reprinting an item from the *Alice Echo*. Sheriff Mike B. Wright was first elected Nueces County sheriff on November 4, 1902, and served eight terms, until November 7, 1916. Tise, 395.

70. *Galveston Daily News*, December 17, 1904.

71. Charles F. Dodge was born in May 1859. In 1900 he resided with his thirty-two-year-old wife Rose, an actress. They had one daughter. 12th U.S. Census, New York County, New York. Enumerated June 8, 1900, E.D. # 250, Sheet 9.

72. Law firm letter to Capt. John Hughes, February 13, 1904. Original in Flachmeier Collection.

73. *El Paso Daily Herald*, February 17, 1904.

74. John R. Hughes to W. W. Turney, February 22, 1904. The original of this letter is framed and is now archived in the Texas Ranger Hall of Fame and Museum in Waco.

75. Martin, 166–69.

76. Louisiana native Daniel S. Booth was the editor and publisher of the *Alice Echo*. The Nueces County census shows him head of household with a wife and four children. His occupation is given simply as "Editor." 12th U.S. Census, Nueces County, Texas. Enumerated June 15, 1900. E.D. # 135, Sheet 27.

77. *Alice Echo*, January 5, 1905.

78. Ibid., January 19, 1905.

79. Ibid., March 16, 1905.

80. Captain Hughes Monthly Return April 30, 1905, prepared at Harlingen.

81. Ibid., April 13, 1905.

82. Pat Garrett and President Roosevelt may have been at one time on good terms, but after a case of very poor judgment in Garrett being photographed with the president as well as with saloon owner Tom Powers, Garrett lost his

job, termed an embarrassment to the president. See Jack DeMattos, *Garrett and Roosevelt* (College Station, Tex.: Creative Publishing Co., 1988), 109–120.

83. *San Antonio Daily Express,* April 7, 1905.

84. Captain Hughes Monthly Return, May 31, 1905.

85. Adj. Gen. John A. Hulen, General Orders, dated at Austin May 24, 1905.

86. *Brownsville Herald,* July 5 [?], 1905. Undated clipping in "Hughes Scrapbook" in Special Collection, University of Texas at El Paso.

87. The Conditt murder case, crime trial and aftermath, is expertly told in Harold J. Weiss Jr., *"Yours to Command,"* 229–42.

88. James C. White was born about 1885 in Travis County, the son of R. E. White, county sheriff from 1888 through 1900. Tise, 494. He enlisted in Company D on September 1, 1905. In his Ranger Service Record is the following note addressed to Captain Hughes: "My boy Jim Campbell White desires to enlist in the Ranger Service while he is not of age he is now acting for himself, & I have no objections to his going with you." Signed by his father R. E. White. This was dated from his home, Cedar Valley, Travis County, August 31, 1905.

89. No service record has been found for W. O. Dale. However, Hughes's muster and pay roll shows he was mustered in on August 16, 1905, with the rank of private and discharged May 31, 1906. There is a William O. Dale listed as a boarder living in Burnet, Burnet County, in the 1900 census, a twenty-two-year-old single white male, Texas born and occupation as Stock Farmer. 12th U.S. Census. Burnet County, Texas. Enumerated June 9, 1900, 281. This could very well be the same man.

Chapter 10: From East Texas to the Texas Panhandle

1. William J. Ray, the son of James L. and Martha Ray, was born in January 1876 and apparently lived in Wood County his entire life. He first appears in the census in 1880, and again in 1900 working as a teamster; then in 1910 as a farmer; in 1920 he worked as a real estate agent, and by 1930 had retired and was living in Mineola, the county seat. U.S. Census, Wood County, Texas, for years 1880, 1900, 1910, 1920, and 1930. His career as sheriff began with his election on November 4, 1902; he was re-elected on November 8, 1904, and served until November 6, 1906. Tise, 553.

2. Judge R. W. Simpson to Gov. S. W. T. Lanham, January 13, 1906. Original in Flachmeier Collection, Austin History Center.

3. W. H. Lyne to Captain Hughes, February 13, 1906. Letter in Roy Aldrich Papers, Archives of the Big Bend. By 1910 Lyne, a thirty-nine-year-old Louisiana native, was superintendent of an oil company in Houston. 12th U.S. Census, Harris County, Texas. Enumerated April 18, 1910, E.D. # 73, sheet 4. See also *New Handbook of Texas*, s.v. "Humble, Texas," by Diane J. Kleiner.

4. This summary of the Colorado County troubles is from the *Eagle Lake Headlight* of July 7, 1906, which printed a history of the feud taken from the *Galveston Daily News*; Colorado County Historical Commission, *Colorado County Chronicles: From the Beginning to 1923*, vol. 1 (Austin: Nortex Press, 1986); *New Handbook of Texas*, s.v. "Colorado County Feud," by Bill Stein.

5. "More Trouble at Columbus," *Weimer Mercury*, July 7, 1906. Weimer is a community west of Columbus in Colorado County. The *Weimer Mercury* newspaper began publishing in December 1888, and continues today still under that name.

6. *La Grange Journal*, Fayette County, July 5, 1906.

7. Walter E. Bridge was born in April, 1850, in Texas and died September 16, 1918. His career as Colorado County sheriff began on November 4, 1902; he served until November 3, 1908. Tise, 118.

8. Judge Munford Kennon had an extensive career in the judicial field. He was elected on March 1, 1897, and served until September 12, 1921. Colorado County Historical Commission, *Colorado County Chronicles: From the Beginning to 1923* (Austin: Nortex Press, 1986), 2:904.

9. *Weimer Mercury*, July 21, 1906.

10. Ibid.

11. Ibid., July 28, 1906.

12. August and September 1906, Monthly Returns of Captain Hughes.

13. Captain Hughes Monthly Return, October 31, 1906.

14. George W. Tilley was an Arkansas native, born about 1863. He was elected sheriff of McLennan County on November 8, 1904, then was re-elected three times and served until November 5, 1912. Tise, 365. In 1920 after his retirement from the sheriff's office he worked as a broker in the "oil lands" as the census enumerator identified his profession. 14th U.S. Census, McLennan County, Texas. Enumerated January 8, 1920, E.D. # 113, sheet 9.

15. Captain Hughes Monthly Return, October 31, 1906.

16. *New York Times*, November 10, 1906. *New Handbook of Texas*, s.v. "Stanley Welch," by Joe R. Baulch.

17. Ivan Murchison was born at Weimer in Fayette County, Texas about 1878. He first joined Capt. J. A. Brooks's Company A on December 2, 1905.

Ranger Service Record. In 1910, shown as age thirty-one, he was a boarder in Fort Worth living with his Arkansas-born wife Marian, age twenty-two. His occupation was given as Musician. 13th U.S. Census. Tarrant County, Texas. Enumerated April 16, 1910, E.D. # 120, sheet 3. A decade later the couple had a five-year-old child and were living in Wichita Falls, in Wichita County, his occupation now given as a furniture store buyer.

18. Guerra was elected November 6, 1906, re-elected on November 3, 1908, and served until November 8, 1910. Tise, 473.

19. Charles B. Brown was born at Seguin, Guadalupe County, about 1872, a son of James and Sally Brown. He enlisted in Company D on October 1, 1906, giving his age as thirty-four. Ranger Service Record.

20. Captain Hughes Monthly Return, December 31, 1906.

21. The enlistment, oath, and descriptive list of Desiderio Perez show he was born in San Antonio and was thirty-two-years and ten months of age when he enlisted on December 6, 1906. He was about average height, dark complexion, with gray eyes and black hair. He was married, unusual for a Ranger. He gave his occupation as a peace officer. Ranger Service Record.

22. R. O. Kinley was in his early thirties when he took the law into his own hands. 13th U.S. Census, Trinity County, Texas. Enumerated April 23, 1910, E.D. # 106, sheet 10. The census records his occupation as "Law" and "Civil Practice."

23. James D. Dunaway served under Capt. Thomas M. Ross, enlisting as a private on April 16, 1906. He was born in Manchaca, Travis County, about 1874. He later joined Company C under Capt. Edward H. Smith. Ranger Service Record.

24. *San Antonio Gazette*, April 27, 1907, citing a report from Galveston.

25. Parker M. Weston was a stockman prior to enlisting with Captain J. A. Brooks in Company A at Colorado City, Mitchell County, on October 8, 1906. He resigned on November 5, 1907. Ranger Service Record. In 1910, now married, the twenty-nine-year-old Texas native worked as a "Painter" for "Public Works" in Wilson County. 13th U.S. Census, Wilson County, Texas. Enumerated May 9, 1910. E.D. # 160, Sheet 16.

26. Lucas Charles Brite began ranching in Presidio County in October 1885, and established a Hereford ranch, which remains a working ranch to this day. On Christmas Day, 1917, the ranch was attacked by a gang of bandits. The ranch store was looted; the bandits were prepared to rob and kill anyone who chanced to pass by. Fortunately the Brite family was not at home, as it was a holiday, and neighbors heard the shooting and managed to provide help. Some two hundred members of the Eighth U.S. Cavalry crossed the Rio Grande in pursuit of the raiders; in the battle between the two groups

ten raiders were killed, and one U.S. soldier was wounded. Some of the loot was recovered, but most of the stolen horses were beyond recovery. *New Handbook of Texas*, s.v. "Brite Ranch Raid," by Julia Cauble Smith.

27. Captain Hughes Monthly Return, June 30, 1907, prepared at Marfa.

28. M. B. Chastain, born in Tennessee in October, 1850, served in Company E under Capt. J. T. Gillespie from October 1, 1886, and was honorably discharged December 1, 1886. Ranger Service Record. As sheriff he was appointed November 24, 1906, following the term of D. G. Knight, then was elected November 3, 1908, and re-elected four more times and served until January 1918. Tise, 424. Chastain in 1900 worked as a blacksmith, later a building contractor, then by 1920 was Brewster County Treasurer.

29. Alexander Ross took the oath of office on April 1, 1905, at Harlingen, Cameron County, enlisting under Captain Hughes. He was born at Rossville, Atascosa County. He re-enlisted on July 9, 1907, at Marfa, and again on September 2, 1908, at Ysleta. Hughes wrote: "This is Alex Ross Third enlistment in Co. 'D'." In 1910 he and his wife of four months were living in Atascosa County; his occupation "Manager General Store." This census was enumerated May 5, 1910, by Ross himself. E.D. # 5, sheet 11. In 1920 the Ross family still resided in Atascosa County; he and his wife Elizabeth now had three children. His occupation was given as "Laborer." 14th U.S. Census. Atascosa County, Texas. Enumerated January 17, 1920, E.D. # 9, sheet 7.

30. Captain Hughes Monthly Return, July 31, 1907.

31. Florence J. Hall was born about 1850 in Georgia, but when he came to Texas is unknown. He was elected El Paso County sheriff on November 6, 1906, re-elected on November 3, 1908, and served until November 8, 1910. He was followed in office by Peyton J. Edwards. Tise, 173, and 13th U.S. Census. El Paso County, Texas. Enumerated April 23, 1910, E.D. # 74, Sheet 14.

32. Captain Hughes Monthly Return, August 31, 1907.

33. The 1910 El Paso County census shows John T. Priddy as a thirty-three-year-old widower. He is living in the household of his brother-in-law, James Ware with his wife Ada Ware and their seven children. He now gave his occupation as "Inspector—Customs House." 13th U.S. Census, El Paso, Texas. Enumerated April 22, 1910, E.D. # 65, Sheet 11.

34. Captain Hughes Monthly Return, September 30, 1907.

35. Monthly Returns of Captain Hughes, October, November, December 1907.

36. Captain Hughes Monthly Return, January 31, 1908.

37. Frank M. Ascarate enlisted in Company D in El Paso on February 6, 1908, at the age of twenty-two. Born in Las Cruces, New Mexico Territory, in 1900

he was a student at the New Mexico College of Agriculture and Mechanic Arts in Mesilla. On his application is written "Cancelled," although that is not dated. Hughes noted in his August Monthly Return that Ascarate was discharged on August 8, but he enlisted a second time on October 1, 1908, in Company D. Ranger Service Record.

38. Captain Hughes Monthly Return, March 31, 1908.

39. Ibid.

40. Ibid., April 30, 1908.

41. Judge Bean was originally buried in the Del Rio Cemetery but later his body was removed to the grounds of the Whitehead Memorial Museum in Del Rio. His grave and that of his son, Sam, are beside the replica of Judge Bean's Jersey Lilly Saloon. His headstone bears the inscription "Judge Roy Bean/ Justice of the Peace/ Law West of the Pecos/ 1825–1903." The best work on Bean remains C. L. Sonnichsen's *Roy Bean: Law West of the Pecos*, first published in 1943 by the Macmillan Company, and reprinted by the Devin-Adair Company in several editions.

42. Cabrera's prison record shows his name as Alberto. He was born in 1882 in Texas of Mexican parents. He was sentenced on July 4, 1908, and his sentence affirmed on February 3, 1909, the offense given as murder in the first degree. He was received as prisoner number 29615 in Huntsville on May 28, 1909, but escaped on May 20, 1910. Huntsville Prison records archived in Texas State Library and Archives, Austin.

43. Glenn Rea, "The Cuero Record to Celebrate Centennial," in *The History of DeWitt County, Texas*, ed. DeWitt County Historical Commission (Dallas: Curtis Media Corp., 1991), 222–23.

44. *Cuero Daily Record*, July 3, 1908.

45. *Victoria Advocate*, June 26, 1908.

46. Captain Hughes Monthly Return, June 30, 1908.

47. Ray E. King enlisted first at Ysleta on June 1, 1908. Previously he had taught school in Stockdale, Wilson County. A later record shows he was discharged but again enlisted on May 22, 1909. The 1930 El Paso County census shows him as a native of Iowa, married with a wife and one son. The forty-seven-year-old was then a border patrolman. Ranger Service Record. 15th U.S. Census, El Paso County, Texas. Enumerated April 3, 1930, E.D. # 20, Sheet 2.

48. Captain Hughes Monthly Return, July 31, 1908.

49. Ibid., August 31, 1908.

50. Ibid., November 30, 1908. The occurrence was in October but is reported on the November Monthly Return.

51. Ibid., November 30, 1908.

52. The extensive reports of Clements's death are found in the *El Paso Morning Times* of December 30 as well as the *El Paso Herald* of same date. The January and February 1909 monthly returns merely indicate scouting, enlistment of C. R. Moore on February 23, and the resignation of F. M. Ascarate on February 1.

53. Captain Hughes Monthly Return March 31, 1909.

54. Ibid., June 30, 1909.

55. Ibid., July 31, 1909.

56. Henry F. Pringle, in *The Life and Times of William Howard Taft* (New York: Farrar Rinehart, 1939), wrote that the two presidents "formally greeted each other, formally sipped champagne and formally parted." Quoted in Charlotte Crawford, "The Border Meeting of Presidents Taft and Diaz," *Password*, July 1958.

57. For a detailed account of the Taft-Díaz visit see chapter one of Charles H. Harris III and Louis R. Sadler, *The Secret War in El Paso: Mexican Revolutionary Intrigue, 1906–1920* (Albuquerque: University of New Mexico Press, 2009).

58. W. H. "Harry" Moore was born at Center Point in Kerr County about 1887. He enlisted on May 1, 1909, in Company D in Terrell County, "for the period of two years." Ranger Service Record.

59. *El Paso Herald*, October 16 and 18, 1909; *El Paso Morning Times*, October 17, 1909; Captain Hughes Monthly Return October 31, 1909, and *Password*, July 1958, all contain important information about the visit. Among those attending the ball was Ranger Captain John H. Rogers, although his name does not appear in any of the planning committee rosters. *El Paso Herald*, October 16, 1909.

60. Captain Hughes, "Report of Operations, Company A Ranger Force, Sept 1, 1909–June 30, 1911." See also Harris and Sadler, *The Secret War in El Paso*, 16.

61. Captain Hughes Monthly Return October 31, 1909.

62. Captain Hughes Monthly Returns November 30 and December 31, 1909.

Chapter 11: A Ranger in the Panhandle

1. This lengthy interview appeared in Amarillo's only newspaper, the *Daily Panhandle*, November 19, 1909. Dated clipping in the Flachmeier Collection, Austin History Center.

2. Ibid., December 4, 1909.

3. Captain Hughes Monthly Return January 31, 1910.

4. *New Handbook of Texas*, s.v. "Colorado City," by William R. Hunt.

5. *El Paso Daily Herald*, February 24, 1910.

6. Captain Hughes Monthly Return, April 30, 1910.

7. Ibid., May 31 and June 30, 1910.

8. Ibid., July 31, 1910.

9. Harris and Sadler, *The Texas Rangers and the Mexican Revolution*, 40–44. The Carnes family of Wilson County proved to be of worthy stock. Of the children, Alfred B., Herff A., and Quirl B. all worked in law enforcement. Alfred B. Carnes was sheriff of Wilson County from 1917 until January 1937. He had followed W. L. Wright who had served as a Ranger. Sons Herff and Quirl of course served as Texas Rangers, and both died in the line of duty, Quirl in 1910 and Herff on December 4, 1932, while working as a customs agent for the Department of the Treasury. Officer Down Memorial Page (*www.odmp.org*) and Tise, 546–47.

10. Captain Hughes's Report of Operations from September 1, 1909, to June 30, 1911 [2]. This is a six-page single-spaced typed report prepared for Adj. Gen. Henry Hutchings, no pagination. Hereafter cited as "Report of Operations, 1909–1911."

11. *Amarillo Daily News*, August 23, 1910. Clipping in Hughes Collection, Special Collections, University of Texas at El Paso.

12. *Colorado Record*, August 19, 1910. Although not stated it would seem that Harkey would leave town only with his family. He did have a wife and two children, six and three years of age. 13th U.S. Census, Garza County, Texas. Enumerated April 15, 1910, E.D. # 104, Sheet 2.

13. This and subsequent telegrams relevant to the Post troubles are found in the Walter Prescott Webb Papers in the Briscoe Center for American History, Austin.

14. *New Handbook of Texas*, s.v. "Post, Texas," by Paul M. Lucko.

15. "Report of Operations, 1909–1911 [2]."

16. Ibid., and Captain Hughes August 31, 1910, Monthly Return, and Tise, 203. O. B. Kelley was the first sheriff of Garza County, as it had only been organized June 15, 1907. Kelley was elected on that day, then re-elected November 3, 1908, November 8, 1910, and November 5, 1912, and served until November 3, 1914. In 1900, the soon-to-be sheriff was a ranch foreman, identified in the Garza County census as "Osker Kelley," a 28-year-old Texas native. 12th U.S. Census. Garza County, Texas. Enumerated June 26, 1900, E.D. # 2, Sheet 11.

17. See Charles Dudley Eaves and C. A. Hutchinson's biography of the founder of Post City, *Post City, Texas: C.W. Post's Colonizing Activities in West Texas* (Austin: Texas State Historical Association, 1952), 88–90.

18. 14th U.S. Census. Zavala County, Texas. Enumerated January 12, 1920, E.D. # 200, Sheet 4. Martin Luther Harkey continued his successful career as attorney until his death on November 18, 1936, in Crystal City, Zavala County. Death was caused by a coronary occlusion according to Dr. Cary A. Poindexter of Crystal City. Texas death certificate # 57664.

19. Captain Hughes Monthly Return, September 30, 1910; Charles R. Moore September report dated October 1, 1910.

20. "Report of Operations, 1909–1911," [3].

21. Captain Hughes Monthly Return, October 31, 1910.

22. Charles Archer Craighead and his brother Patterson N. "Pat" Craighead both served as Rangers, both born near Sutherland Springs, Wilson County, sons of John S. and Mary I. Craighead; and "Report of Operations, 1909–1911," [3].

23. "Report of Operations, 1909–1911," [3].

24. *El Paso Daily Herald*, October 4, 1910.

25. Ibid., November 19, 1910.

26. Ibid., November 26, 1910; *Galveston Daily News*, December 13, 1910.

27. "Report of Operations, 1909–1911," [3].

28. Captain Hughes Monthly Return, December 31, 1910.

29. "Report of Operations, 1909–1911 [4]."

30. Charles H. Webster enlisted on January 13, 1911, in Company D upon the recommendation of Sheriff Peyton J. Edwards and Chief Deputy N. G. Good of El Paso County. He gave his previous occupation as peace officer. Curiously, Webster was also from Illinois, born there in Sterling, Whiteside County, in June of 1868. Hughes's home town and Webster's were less than fifty miles apart. When Webster left Illinois is unknown but in 1900 he and his family were living in Colorado Springs, El Paso County, Colorado, his occupation given as laborer. In 1910 he was in El Paso, Texas, forty-one years of age with wife and four children, three of whom were born in Colorado. 12th U.S. Census, El Paso County, Colorado. Enumerated June 22, 1900, E.D. # 31 sheet 34; 13th U.S. Census, El Paso County, Texas. Enumerated April 30, 1910, E.D. # 61 sheet 26.

31. In 1910 the Howe family consisted of Benjamin F. Howe, age sixty-three years, born in Ohio, and his two sons: Robert, twenty, and Guy, eighteen. Both worked on their father's farm. 13th U.S. Census, Torrance County, New Mexico. Enumerated May 14, 1910, E.D. # 272, Sheet 13.

32. Abo was also known as Abo Pass. Although at one time thriving enough to warrant a post office, today it is merely a ghost town with a few residents and several abandoned buildings.

33. Details of the Howes' career and bloody end is from Don Bullis' *Ellos Pasaron Por Aqui (They Passed by Here) 99 New Mexicans . . . and a few other Folks* (Chesterfield, Mo.: Science & Humanities, 2005), 212–13; Sergeant H. A. Carnes Monthly Return, January 31, 1911. See also the "Officer Down Memorial Page" at *www.odmp.org* for the "End of Watch" for Special Agent J. A. McClure and Inspector Thomas L. O'Connor.

34. "Report of Operations, 1909–1911," [4].

35. Captain John R. Hughes to Ben C. Cabell, Chairman, Board of Directors, Huntsville Penitentiary, March 31, 1911, Adjutant General Papers, Texas State Archives, Austin.

36. *Marfa New Era*, February 11, 1911. Original clipping in the Flachmeier Collection, Austin History Center.

37. *El Paso Herald*, September 30, 1911.

38. General Orders No. 5, issued October 2, 1911, from Adjutant General's Department, Austin. Hughes's copy is preserved in the Flachmeier Collection, Austin History Center. Not paginated.

39. *El Paso Herald*, November 9, 1911.

40. Ibid., November 17, 1911.

41. John R. Hughes to Gov. O. B. Colquitt, November 23, 1911.

42. John R. Hughes to Ben C. Cabell, March 1, 1912. Original letter in Hughes Scrapbook, Special Collections Department, University of Texas at El Paso.

43. John R. Hughes to Governor O. B. Colquitt, March 9, 1912. Original in Flachmeier Collection, Austin History Center.

44. *El Paso Daily Herald*, June 4, 1912.

45. Ibid., August 8, 1912.

46. Captain Hughes to Gov. O. R. Colquitt, September 12, 1912.

47. Dudley S. Barker was elected November 4, 1904, and re-elected ten times, serving as county sheriff until January 1, 1927, a total of twenty-two years. Tise, 410. Sanders was born April 16, 1854, in Cold Spring, Texas, and died February 6, 1924, in a hospital in Palestine, Texas. Upon Hughes's resignation, Sanders was named as his replacement. He remained captain of Company A until it was disbanded. Donaly Brice, "John Jesse Sanders: Lawman and Texas Ranger," *The Plum Creek Almanac* 26, no. 1 (Spring 2008): 45–50. A Texas Ranger cross was placed on his grave in the Lockhart Cemetery, Caldwell County, on November 19, 2006, with descendants and historians present.

48. Press release from El Paso printed in perhaps numerous newspapers; this item is from the *Wichita Daily Times* of Wichita Falls, November 10, 1912.
49. "Report of Operations, 1909–1911," [5–6].
50. Hon. O. B. Colquitt, Governor of Texas, in *Leslie's Illustrated Weekly Newspaper*, April 16, 1914. Original copy in the Flachmeier Collection, Austin History Center.
51. Harris and Sadler, in *The Texas Rangers and the Mexican Revolution*, describe Sanders as "tall, pot-bellied, accident prone, and a less than outstanding Ranger captain," 153. This is the man who "replaced" John R. Hughes.

Chapter 12: Capt. John R. Hughes—Lone Star Ranger

1. *Brownsville Daily Herald*, June 8, 1914.
2. Ibid., June 11 1914.
3. Ibid., June 13, 1914.
4. Ibid., October 10, 1914. William T. Vann was re-elected in 1916, 1918, and 1920 and served until November 1, 1923. He ran again and was elected on November 2, 1926, and served until his death on September 15, 1927. Mrs. W. T. Vann was appointed to complete her husband's term on September 20, 1927, and served until January 1, 1929. She was the only lady sheriff of Cameron County. Tise, 86.
5. *San Antonio Light*, December 9, 1914.
6. Ibid., December 15, 1914.
7. Miss B. Mathews to John R. Hughes, January 17, 1915. Regrettably it has not been possible to learn the full identity of this Miss B. Mathews. Letter found in the Flachmeier Collection.
8. The quotation comes not from William Shakespeare, but from Alexander Pope's *Essay on Man*: "Honour and shame from no condition rise; Act well your part, there all the honour lies." The letter, dated February 3, 1915, is in the Raymond H. Flachmeier Collection in the Austin History Center.
9. *El Paso Herald*, June 5, 1915.
10. *Austin Statesman*, June 4, 1947.
11. Clipping from an unidentified newspaper (*Midland Reporter-Telegram?*) in the Flachmeier Collection. Bob Alexander expertly relates Allison's career in *Fearless Dave Allison: Border Lawman* (Silver City, N. Mex.: High-Lonesome Books, 2003). Of the two lawmen, Roberson is the lesser known. Born in Staples Store, Guadalupe County, Texas, in 1876, he enlisted on May 8, 1916, as a private in Company C, stationed at Austin.

12. *Abilene Reporter*, September 23, 1923.

13. See Bob Alexander's *Fearless Dave Allison* for details on the final years of Ross and Good, 261–62.

14. Ibid.

15. Voters of Travis County elected Robert Emmett White sheriff on November 6, 1888, and then re-elected him for six more terms. He served until November 6, 1900. Tise, 494.

16. Jasper Frank Norfleet was first a successful rancher, then after con artists scammed him out of $45,000 he resolved to recover his loss, which he did; his success caused him to become a highly regarded detective, locating and identifying over one hundred confidence men in his career. *New Handbook of Texas*, s.v. "Jasper Frank Norfleet," by H. Allen Anderson.

17. *Austin Statesman*, June 26, 1929.

18. Captain Hughes's nephew, Emery H. Hughes, was born June 29, 1900, married Katherine Brady, and died June 15, 1990, in Baytown, Texas. Their three children were Louis Bond, born August 21, 1927, in Travis County; Patricia Irene, born on March 2, 1930, in Travis County; and Katherine Nell, born September 20, 1932. The original photograph is in the collection of Louis Bond Hughes.

19. *Triggernometry* remains in print, the most recent edition published by the University of Oklahoma Press in 1996 with an introduction by English historian Joseph G. Rosa. No one was ever charged with the murder of these noted individuals. For a succinct treatment of Thompson's career as city marshal of Austin, see Doug Dukes, *Ben Thompson: Iron Marshal of Austin* (Np: 2010).

20. All three of these men met violent deaths. John Wesley Hardin was shot to death in an El Paso saloon by Constable John Selman Sr. the night of August 19, 1895; James Brown Miller was lynched by an angry mob in Ada, Oklahoma, on April 19, 1909; Mannen Clements was shot to death on December 29, 1908, in the Coney Island Saloon in El Paso.

21. England-born gunfighter Ben Thompson and Uvalde County acting sheriff John King Fisher were shot to death in the Vaudeville Theater in San Antonio on March 11, 1884.

22. William McLeod Raine is best known for his non-fiction work *Famous Sheriffs and Western Outlaws* published in 1920. He also was a prolific writer of western novels between 1908 and 1954.

23. Carbon copy letter from Hughes to Eugene Cunningham, December 26, 1934. The letter was typed on letterhead of the Adjutant General's

Department showing Hughes as "Captain Commander." Original in the Flachmeier Collection.

24. Presumably Eugene Cunningham inscribed the copy of his book he sent to Captain Hughes, which would add great value to the first edition. Collector Robert G. McCubbin has several items pertaining to Cunningham, including a first edition of *Triggernometry*, but not this particular copy.

25. Coolidge's novel *Wolf's Candle* was published in 1935 by E. P. Dutton & Company.

26. Dane Coolidge to John R. Hughes, July 5, 1935. Original in the Flachmeier Collection. Coolidge, born in Massachusetts in 1873, wrote numerous novels as well as some non-fiction. Many of his short stories and articles were illustrated with photographs he had taken. Historians do not consider his non-fiction writing reliable.

27. *El Paso Herald-Post*, November 8, 1935.

28. Walter Prescott Webb, *The Texas Rangers: A Century of Frontier Defense* (Boston: Houghton Mifflin, 1935; repr. Austin: University of Texas Press, 1965), 461.

29. Chris Fox was elected November 8, 1932, and re-elected four times, serving until April 1942, when he resigned. He then became a U.S. Border Patrolman. Fox died on March 23, 1984, at the age of eighty-six. Tise, 173.

30. El Paso Sheriff Chris P. Fox to W. D. Greet, December 18, 1935. Original in Flachmeier Collection, Austin History Center.

31. Original telegram in John R. Hughes Collection.

32. *Imperial Valley Weekly* (El Centro, California, home of Ira Aten), January 16, 1936. Clipping in Flachmeier Collection. Hughes was visiting his old sergeant Ira Aten at the time of this interview. Hughes had obviously driven to El Centro immediately following the conclusion of the Sun Carnival Parade.

33. Personal interview with Louis Bond Hughes, M.D., March 13, 2010.

34. George B. Black, born in New York in 1870, joined Company B on September 1, 1891, and was honorably discharged on May 31, 1892. He later served as a Special Ranger assigned to Company D under Hughes. In 1899 he again served as a Special, his commission received due to a letter of recommendation of Hughes. His stated reason for wanting to serve was to provide "protection of my own & my neighbors property." Ranger Service Record. A frequently published photograph shows Black and Grude Britton as members of Company B. Their Winchesters, mule-ear boots, six-guns, and holsters with Bowie knives are prominently displayed.

35. In general the mention of a "gun" means a Winchester or a shotgun, not a hand-held weapon.

36. Letters of George B. Black to Capt. John R. Hughes, dated April 28, May 6, and 21, 1936. Originals in the Flachmeier Collection.

37. Senator John Morris Sheppard (1875–1941) is known as the champion of the 18th Amendment. *New Handbook of Texas*, s.v. "John Morris Sheppard," by Richard Bailey.

38. *Dallas Morning News*, August 22, 1936, headlined "Ranger Statue Given to Fair At Ceremonial." Original clipping in the Flachmeier Collection. The present whereabouts of this statue is unknown; it is *not* the Ranger statue located at the Love Field airport in Dallas, dedicated in 1960. The sculptor used retired Ranger captain Jay Banks as his model, with the legend on the base "One riot, one Ranger." In addition to the statue being unveiled, an oil painting of Hughes was on display. It was a three-quarter portrait by professional artist Leola Freeman, who painted it during the early months of 1936. According to the *El Paso Herald-Post* of March 23, 1936, it was first displayed in the lobby of the Hotel Paso del Norte of El Paso. The article, with a print of the painting, was headlined "El Paso Painting of Capt. [John] R. Hughes Will Be Shown at Dallas Centennial." According to the *Herald-Post* this four by four-and-one-half foot painting was done specifically for the "Ranger House" at the Dallas Centennial Exposition, and would be the only oil painting exhibited there. Artist Freeman named her painting "Lone Star Ranger" after the novel of the same title by Zane Grey, and "shows the white-bearded Texan seated, with a sombrero shading his piercing dark eyes wearing the gold badge presented to him by the state of Texas as the ranger longest in service, 28 years. He is holding his saddle rifle. His saddle and bridle are at his knee." In the background appear the Rio Grande, El Cristo Rey Mountain, and Hart's Mill. The frame was carved by Freeman herself and featured pistols, cacti, and rattlesnakes. This portrait was exhibited in Dallas and, according to the article, was to be kept in the Ranger House which was to be moved to Santa Anna, Coleman County, Texas, after the Dallas Exposition. The painting survived the various moves, and is now prominently displayed in the home of Captain Hughes's great nephew, his namesake, John R. Hughes. A brief article in the *Herald-Post* of May 28, 1936, used the painting as an illustration along with a photograph of Ranger James B. Gillett, as they were to be honored at the various Centennial celebrations. Of King Vidor's motion picture *The Texas Rangers*, motion picture critic William K. Everson, wrote: "Even though not a classic, *The Texas Rangers* is an exhilarating Western with a refreshing schoolboy vigor." William K. Everson, *A Pictorial History of the Western Film* (Secaucus,

N.J.: The Citadel Press, 1969), 161. King Vidor's best known motion picture remains *The Outlaw* due to its heroine, Jane Russell.

39. L. A. Wilke to Captain Hughes, undated but in June 1936, while Hughes was at the Centennial. Original in the Flachmeier Collection. Wilke's literary agent did find a publisher. "The Wide Loop of a Ranger Noose" appeared in the September 1936, issue of *Real Detective*, pages 24–29 and 82–85 with photographs of Hughes as a young man, and as an older man with white-gray beard; a portion of the famous photograph of Hughes and members of Company D with Hughes seated in a chair at one end and a Mexican prisoner at the other end; a portrait of El Paso Sheriff James H. Boone; a portrait of Pat Garrett; a cropped photograph showing Captain Frank Jones and Charles Fusselman; a portrait of Ed Bryant; and a photograph of the old El Paso County courthouse where Geronimo Parra was executed. A line drawing also illustrated the article; although the artist is not identified the work may be by Frank Anthony Stanush, illustrator of the Jack Martin biography. Curiously Hughes is listed as the author, although it was basically a product of Wilke. During this period of his career L. A. Wilke worked as the editor of a newspaper, living in Tarrant County with his wife Helen and their two children. 15th U.S. Census, Tarrant County, Texas. Enumerated April 9, 1930, E.D. # 220-61, Sheet 13. Wilke later became the city editor of the *El Paso Herald-Post*. Wilke was the grandfather of Texas historian Mike Cox who authored the introduction to the 1990 reprint of *Border Boss*. Five photographs of Hughes illustrate this edition. The photograph caption on page 5 is incorrect, as it reads "Capt. John Hughes holds the noose used when Jim Miller was lynched in Ada, Oklahoma. Photo by L. A. Wilke." There was no traditional noose involved in the lynching, as can be easily determined by examining the famous photograph of the four men hanging.

40. *El Paso Herald-Post*, September 23, 1936.

41. Ibid., September 25, 1936. Nelson Avery Rector was born in Texas in May of 1853, a son of Nelson S. and H. C. Rector; he experienced great success in the field of law, working in Travis and Lee counties much of his life. Candice DuCoin e-mail to author, April 19, 2010.

42. *Ford News*, November 1936. Original in the C. L. Sonnichsen Collection, University of Texas at El Paso.

43. Gov. James V. Allred to Captain John R. Hughes, December 31, 1936. Original in Flachmeier Collection.

44. *El Paso Herald-Post*, January 1, 1937.

45. Ann Jensen, ed., *Texas Ranger's Diary and Scrapbook* (Dallas: The Kaleidograph Press, 1936), 4.

46. Ibid., 7.

47. Capt. John R. Hughes to Ann Jensen, August 8, 1937. Original in the Flach-meier Collection.

48. Dane Coolidge to Captain Hughes, August 31, 1937. Original in the Flach-meier Collection. *Ranger Two Rifles* was published by Grosset & Dunlap of New York, 1937. Coolidge claimed this book and *The Law West of the Pecos* were both "written around" the life of John R. Hughes. *Fighting Men of the West*, 6.

49. [W. M. Green], "Origin of the Ex-Texas Rangers Association" in *Frontier Times* 1, no. 5 (February 1924): 3.

50. Membership certificate and program of 9th annual "Texas Ex-Rangers' Association" archived in the Flachmeier Collection, Austin History Center.

51. *El Paso Times*, August 4, 1937. A small full-length photograph of Hughes illustrates the article, appearing on page one, column one.

52. Ibid., August 4, 1937.

53. Undated typed note in C. L. Sonnichsen Collection, University of Texas-El Paso.

54. Undated and unidentified newspaper clipping in the Flachmeier Collection, but an El Paso paper of February 1938.

55. *El Paso Herald-Post*, dated February 12, 1938, attached to Hughes's letter to Emery H. Hughes dated February 13, 1938. Original in the C. L. Sonnich-sen Collection, University of Texas at El Paso. Milam H. Wright is buried in El Paso's Evergreen Cemetery.

56. *El Paso Herald*, April 12, 1938. Ernest Taylor "Ernie" Pyle was America's best-loved columnist of the World War II era. At one time, his column appeared in more than 300 newspapers and in this instance giving additional name recognition to Hughes in particular and the Texas Rangers in general. His coverage of the European and African theaters as a war correspondent resulted in his winning the Pulitzer Prize in 1943. Pyle was killed by a Japa-nese sniper in 1945.

57. *El Paso Times*, November 8, 1937.

58. One original print of the photograph, with L. A. Wilke's stamp in red on reverse, has a typed note taped to the back, given by Ira Aten. It reads: "Four veterans of the Texas Ranger Service, photographed on May 12, 1938, at the monument erected by the State of Texas to the memory of Captain Frank Jones, killed by bandits June 30, 1893, while commanding Company D of the Rangers. In the photograph, left to right, are: Ed. Aten, age 68; Captain John R. Hughes, age 83; Sergeant Ira Aten, age 75, and Ed. Bryant, age 74 years. Bryant and Ed. Aten are the only two living survivors of the battle

with bandits in which Captain Jones met his death." *El Paso Herald-Post,* May 13, 1938; and undated clipping, [May 22, 1938?] from *Galveston Daily News,* both in the Flachmeier Collection.

59. Original document in the Flachmeier Collection.

60. John B. Davis to Captain John Hughes, January 9, 1939. Original in the Flachmeier Collection.

61. John R. Hughes to John B. Davis, January 12, 1929. Original in the Flachmeier Collection. Dudley H. Snyder, then of Georgetown, Texas, contributed a brief summary of his life in *The Trail Drivers of Texas* ("Made Early Drives," 1029–31); also in *The Trail Drivers of Texas* is a contribution devoted to D. H. and brother J. W. Snyder, ("Experiences of a Texas Pioneer" by John M. Sharpe, 721–29).

62. *El Paso Herald-Post,* February 9, 1939.

63. Ibid.

64. John M. Hendrix to John R. Hughes, February 11, 1939. Original in the Flachmeier Collection.

65. T. M. Presley to John R. Hughes, February 11, 1939.

66. Sheriff A. B. Carter to John R. Hughes, February 21, 1939. Carter was appointed county sheriff on August 10, 1936, and served until January 1, 1943. Tise, 484.

67. Clipping from an undated *Fort Worth Star-Telegram* in the Flachmeier Collection. *Trail Driving Days* was published in 1952 by Charles Scribner's Sons, New York. The photograph of Hughes showing the pistol to John Ellison Carroll, Ab Blocker, and Bob Beverly appears on page 154.

68. Clipping from an undated *Fort Worth Star-Telegram* in the Flachmeier Collection.

69. Bess P. Coughlin was born December 13, 1899, and died February 26, 1978, having lived much of her life in the Fort Worth-Dallas area. She was born (it is believed) Bess or Elizabeth Hodges, as the 1920 census shows her as Mrs. Tom Coughlin, living in Fort Worth with her parents, Harry and Harriet Hodges. Indiana-born Tom was twenty-one, she was twenty. He clerked in a clothing store; a decade later they had their own residence and a seven-year-old daughter named Rita V. Mr. Coughlin continued working as a clothing salesman while Bess claimed no occupation. 14th U.S. Census. Tarrant County, Texas. Census. Enumerated January 3, 1920, E.D. # 117, sheet 2, and 15th U.S. Census. Tarrant County, Texas. Enumerated April 18, 1930, E.D. # 9, sheet 49.

70. Clipping from an undated *Fort Worth Star-Telegram* in the Flachmeier Collection.

71. *Alpine Avalanche,* March 31, 1939.

72. Letters of Lloyd B. Rust to Hughes, June 3 and June 21, 1940. Originals in the Flachmeier Collection.

73. Those involved in the selection are named in an unidentified and undated newspaper clipping in the Flachmeier Collection.

74. John R. Hughes to Bernarr MacFadden, December 14, 1940. Original in the Flachmeier Collection.

75. *El Paso Herald-Post*, June 12, 1940.

76. Ibid., December 14, 1940.

77. W. P. Hughes Jr. to John R. Hughes, April 13, 1940. Original in the Flachmeier Collection.

78. Judge W. Lon Johnson to John R. Hughes, December 5, 1940.

79. Unidentified and undated clipping from a Las Cruces newspaper in the Flachmeier Collection.

80. *New Handbook of Texas*, s.v. "Robert Ewing Thomason," by Joseph M. Ray. R. E. Thomason was elected mayor of El Paso in 1927. In 1930 he was elected to Congress and then re-elected thirteen times.

81. John R. Hughes to R. E. Thomason, February 21, 1942.

82. *El Paso Times*, July 10, 1942. The article also includes the frequently used photograph of Hughes wearing a white hat, white shirt and tie, and his pistol and gun belt. The Naylor Company of San Antonio published the book and illustrated it with drawings by Frank Anthony Stanush. An original copy is now difficult to find, which no doubt motivated the late Tom Munnerlyn of State House Press to reprint it in hardcover and paperback editions in 1990. Texas historian Mike Cox provided an introduction to this edition. In addition to the added introduction, the State House edition carries several photographs of Hughes, some of which were taken by L. A. Wilke.

Chapter 13: Texas State Cemetery

1. *Houston Post*, August 2, 1942. *Border Boss* originally sold for $2.50. A fine copy of the first edition commands a good price for the average collector. Available copies found on an on-line search show the prices range from a modest $150 to over $400. Several dealers offered it for $350. A copy signed by Jack Martin was priced at $450.00. Noted collector Robert G. McCubbin estimated that a "fine copy with a nice dust jacket" should retail about $250 to $300. E-mail to author, September 23, 2009. Today neither the hardcover edition nor the paperback reprint edition by State House Press is easily found.

2. James Mitchell Putman, born May 12, 1850, the son of William and Adaline Gibson Putman, was born in Texas, perhaps Gonzales County, as the family is there in 1860, when James was only two years old. The Putmans were still in Gonzales County in 1870 but by 1880 were living on Curry's Creek in Kendall County. This is where the family of Frank Jones resided as well. In 1900 Putman resided in Shafter, Presidio County, his occupation given as day laborer. Later he was located in Bexar County, as his Texas death certificate, # 34388, reveals he was living about seventeen miles south of San Antonio near the small community of Thelma. Like his old commander, James Mitchell Putman committed suicide, ending his life with a bullet on December 19, 1923, as the coroner determined.

3. John Woodard Saunders, born December 23, 1856, in Kendall County, Texas, was the son of George W. and Mary Saunders. He died in San Antonio on July 11, 1913, of "General Paresis" according to Dr. C. S. Gales. He is buried in Boerne, Kendall County.

4. Little has been learned of Isaac N. "Ike" Herrin. In 1880 he appears in the household of George W. Saunders with family members Mary (Sansom) and children John W. and Nancy. Isaac Herrin is erroneously shown to be eight years old and listed as grandson to G. W. Saunders. He was born in Arkansas. 10th U.S. Census, Kendall County, Texas. Enumerated June 4, 1880, 222, by W. K. Jones, a brother of Frank Jones. Herrin was mustered into Capt. Frank Jones's Company D on March 27, 1892, and served in that company at least through August 31, 1893. The available Ranger Service Record does not show a discharge date. Born in September 1870 in Texas, in 1900 he is shown as a single man working as a bartender in Shafter. 12th U.S. Census, Presidio County, Texas. Enumerated June 30, 1900, E.D. # 67, Sheet 23. His final fate is unknown. George W. Saunders was one of the men who originated the Old Trail Drivers' Association in 1915. Most significantly he began the process of asking trail drivers to record their memories of their trail driving days, which eventually resulted in the book *The Trail Drivers of Texas*. See Entry # 99 in John H. Jenkins, *Basic Texas Books: An Annotated Bibliography of Selected Works for a Research Library* (Austin: Texas State Historical Association, 1988), 256–61.

5. "The Gourleys" to Capt. John R. Hughes, August 10, 1942. Original in the Flachmeier Collection.

6. *Austin Statesman*, February 11, 1943.

7. Jack Martin to John R. Hughes, December 18, 1943. Original in the Flachmeier Collection. Joe Oliver Naylor built a successful publishing house in San Antonio, publishing primarily Texana books. He died January 25, 1955.

8. Joseph Dixon Matlock, reviewer, *The Southwestern Historical Quarterly* 46, no. 2 (October 1942): 188–89.

9. Allen G. Falby was elected sheriff on November 3, 1942, and was re-elected three times, serving until January 1, 1951. Tise, 173.

10. John R. Hughes was the "youthful hero and exemplar" of M. T. Gonzaullas, according to Robert M. Utley, *Lone Star Lawmen: The Second Century of the Texas Rangers* (New York: Oxford University Press, 2007), 125–26.

11. *El Paso Daily Times*, January 16, 1944.

12. Lyndon B. Johnson to John R. Hughes, May 31, 1946. Original in Flachmeier Collection. Hughes's letter to Johnson is in the LBJ Library, University of Texas, Austin.

13. Ira Aten to John R. Hughes, July 24, 1946. Original in the Flachmeier Collection.

14. William George was behind in his reading of western literature. Lake's very popular work on Wyatt Earp was first published in 1931; *Border Boss* in 1942. He was acquiring these books only in 1947.

15. William and Burness George to John R. Hughes, January 5, 1947. Original in the Flachmeier Collection. William George remains a mysterious but interesting individual. Born in 1875 in Texas, in 1920 he and Washington-born wife Burness were living in Stevens County, Washington. His occupation is given as detective for the Secret Service. 14th U.S. Census, Stevens County, Washington. Enumerated January 15, 1920, E.D. # 301, Sheet 8A.

16. William George to John R. Hughes, February 2, 1947.

17. Yarborough proved to be an effective attorney and senator, but lost twice in the race for governor of Texas. The year before the letter to Hughes he had returned from Japan after spending eight months there with the military government of occupation. Yarborough is buried in the State Cemetery, not far from John R. Hughes. *New Handbook of Texas*, s.v. "Ralph Webster Yarborough," by Mark Odintz.

18. One notebook examined by this author is archived in the C. L. Sonnichsen Collection at the University of Texas at El Paso. On the cover in white ink Hughes wrote: "1942 Diary Capt. Hughes El Paso Texas" The first portion does deal with Hughes's daily routine beginning January 1 and continues through May 21, 1947; another section covers the months from February 28, 1933, through September 30, 1933. This particular diary was not labeled accurately by Hughes.

19. Hughes visited the firm of Dr. John W. Cathcart and Dr. Claude H. Mason who practiced at 310 Roberts-Banner Building in El Paso. Their advertisement said that they provided "physicians, pathological, chemical X-Ray and radiation laboratories." Hudspeth Directory Co., Inc. *El Paso City Directory*, 1938, 175.

20. In 1910 H. F. Greggerson resided in El Paso with his wife Nettie and one-year-old son Herbert. At the time Greggerson worked for the Immigration Service. 14th U.S. Census, El Paso County, Texas. Enumerated April 19, 1910, E.D. # 94, Sheet 23.

21. Samuel Dale Myres (1871–1953) was not only a saddle maker but also a civic leader, first in Sweetwater, Texas, and later in El Paso. He purchased in 1894 his own saddle and harness business in Sweetwater and remained there until 1919 when he relocated to El Paso. He produced inexpensive saddles for the working cowboy as well as showplace saddles for movie stars, Western show performers, and Texas Rangers. In 1914 he made a "Miller $10,000 Saddle" with gold, silver, and over 300 precious gems for the famous 101 Ranch. During World War I he produced McClellan saddles for the military. With the advent of the automobile he turned his focus to producing quality holsters and gun belts. By 1950 his establishment was known as the "Cowboy Headquarters for the Southwest." *New Handbook of Texas,* s.v. "Samuel Dale Myres," by Patricia P. Kincaide. Hughes also had his picture taken with S. D. Myres's son William James, which is reproduced in the State House Press reprint of *Border Boss,* to illustrate the Introduction. Myres made at least one saddle for Hughes. See obituary for William J. Myres in the *El Paso Times,* September 16, 2001.

22. Robertson also served briefly as a Ranger from February 18 through March 5, 1921. He also served in various positions of law enforcement in New Mexico. At his death on April 3, 1951, he was a justice of the peace in Las Cruces, New Mexico. Ranger Service Record in *Texas Ranger Biographies: Those Who Served, 1910–1921,* by Charles H. Harris III, Frances E. Harris, and Louis R. Sadler. Apparently Hughes knew him as "Jack Robinson" or it may be a simple misspelling of his name.

23. Nell Hughes helped with the family hotel and taught instrumental music as well. 10th U.S. Census, Linn County, Kansas. Enumerated June 2, 1880, 62. By the time of the state census in 1885 she had married Ed Coleman and had borne him two children. When Mr. Coleman died is unknown. In 1900, besides her two children, her mother Jennie and brother Bond were living with her. After her first husband died she married J. W. Johnston in 1928, but he died the same year. She then remained a widow until her death. Her obituary noted her as being a "fine musician" and a teacher who taught "large classes" of students. She is buried in the Mound City Cemetery; the headstone lists her simply as Nellie Coleman. 1885 Kansas State census; 12th U.S. Census, Linn County, Kansas. Enumerated June 6, 1900, E.D. # 113, Sheet 6. Her obituary appears in the *Mound City Republic,* August 12, 1943.

24. Although this one notebook bears the year of 1942 on the cover, there are many pages dated 1933 and subsequent years in the final pages. There is no pagination.

25. *Amarillo Daily News*, May 23, 1947, citing a United Press International report from Austin; Olson's promotion from the *Austin Statesman*, September 2, 1945, "Olson Made Captain of Rangers."

26. Copy of H.S.R. No. 238 "Resolution" in author's possession.

27. Copy of Senate Resolution No. 133 in author's possession. Shivers was governor of Texas from July 1949 until January 1957, the first governor to be elected to three consecutive terms.

28. United Press International release from Austin dated May 22, appearing in the *Amarillo Daily News*, May 23, 1947.

29. *Austin American*, June 4, 1947.

30. *El Paso Herald-Post*, June 4, 1947. This issue is illustrated with the famous photograph of Hughes with black hat and his shadow on the wall taken by Dane Coolidge.

31. *Austin American*, June 4, 1947.

32. Lona Shawver, *Chuck Wagon Windies and True Stories* (San Antonio: Naylor Company, 1950), 76. Texas-born author Lona Thomason Shawver wrote a chapter on Ira Aten for her book, "which appears to be heavily based on correspondence between Aten and the author." Mike Cox to author, e-mail February 25, 2010. Cox uses the statement in his "Texas Tales" column in the *Austin American-Statesman*, October 8, 2009.

33. Ira Aten died from pneumonia on August 5, 1953. He is buried in the Evergreen Cemetery near El Centro, California. James A. Browning, *Violence Was No Stranger: A Guide to the Grave Sites of Famous Westerners* (Stillwater, Okla.: Barbed Wire Press, 1993), 7.

34. "Life and Mysterious Death of Texas Ranger J. R. Hughes to Be Documented in Book," *Houston Chronicle*, December 16, 1981; the *Monitor* of McAllen, December 16, 1981, headlined its article, "Death of Colorful Ranger Still Mystery." The *Monitor* of the same date has three brief paragraphs at the end which the *Chronicle* eliminated.

35. Official report of S. H. Rosen of the Austin Police Department.

36. Ibid.

37. *Houston Chronicle*, December 16, 1981.

Chapter 14: The Great Captains

1. See for example, *Rangers of Texas*, providing a biography of these seven named Rangers by Dorman H. Winfrey, James M. Day, Ben Proctor, Harold B. Simpson, Roger N. Conger, Billy Mac Jones, and Joe B. Frantz. Published in Waco by Texian Press, 1969.

2. Obituary for John H. Rogers appearing in the *Waco News-Tribune*, November 13, 1930. This appears in full in Paul N. Spellman, *Captain John H. Rogers, Texas Ranger*, 222–23.

3. Paul N. Spellman, *Captain John H. Rogers, Texas Ranger*, 48. The Ranger who lost his life in the fight was James H. Moore.

4. Harold J. Weiss Jr., *Yours to Command: The Life and Legends of Texas Ranger Captain Bill McDonald*, 89–96.

5. Paul N. Spellman. *Captain J. A. Brooks Texas Ranger*, 52–63.

6. Harold J. Weiss Jr., *Yours to Command: The Life and Legends of Texas Ranger Captain Bill McDonald*, 121–28.

7. Ronald J. Ward. *The Greatest Wolf Hunter That Ever Lived: The Story of "Catch 'em Alive" Jack Abernathy* (Amarillo: Custom Printing Co., 2005), 96–98; and Weiss, 225.

Selected Bibliography

A Note on Sources

There have been five essential archives that have held the greatest amount of material for this biography.

The Texas State Library and Archives holds the Adjutant General files among which are the records of the Texas Rangers. The muster rolls and monthly returns and scouting reports cited in this work are from those files.

The West Texas Collection at Angelo State University in San Angelo, Texas, is also a gold mine of material; its collections focus on West Texas. The photographic collection alone is worth a few days in the library.

The Special Collections in the C. L. Sonnichsen Room at the University of Texas at El Paso is also a necessary archive, as it contains what is termed the John R. Hughes Scrap Book, but in reality is a collection of photographs, a diary and newspaper clippings. The items from his diary and scrapbook cited here are from that collection.

The Austin History Center, adjacent to the Austin Public Library, also holds a wonderful amount of material dealing with John R. Hughes. This material originated with brother Emery S. Hughes who married Selma Bastian. Their daughter Valentine, called "Vallie," married Raymond H. Flachmeier, son of William and Amelia Flachmeier. A collection of clippings from various newspapers, photographs, pamphlets, letters, and other memorabilia gathered by Emery S. Hughes constitutes the Flachmeier Collection.

Finally, the Linn County Museum and Genealogical Library in Pleasanton, Linn County, Kansas, holds a wonderful collection of materials. Of great help was the Wickham newspaper clippings pertaining to people and events of Mound City and Linn County. Ms Wickham clipped from various area newspapers for fifty years until her death in 1935.

Books and Articles

Anonymous. *Southeast Kansas Adventures and Day Trips*. Humboldt, Kans.: Southeast Kansas Living Magazine, 2009.

Alexander, Bob. *Fearless Dave Allison: Border Lawman.* Silver City, N. Mex.: High-Lonesome Books, 2003.

Ball, Larry D. *Desert Lawmen: The High Sheriffs of New Mexico and Arizona 1845–1912.* Albuquerque: University of New Mexico, 1992.

Bartholomew, Ed. *Texas Ghost Town Encyclopedia.* Fort Davis: Frontier Press, 1982.

Baugh, Virgil E. *A Pair of Texas Rangers: Bill McDonald and John Hughes.* Washington, D.C.: Potomac Corral, The Westerners, 1970.

Breihan, Carl W. "Ranger John Hughes," *Real West* 18, no. 141 (September 1975).

Brown, Dee and Martin F. Schmidt. *Trail Driving Days.* New York: Charles Scribners Sons, 1952.

Browning, James A. *Violence Was No Stranger.* Stillwater, Okla.: Barbed Wire Press, 1993.

Bullis, Don. *Ellos Pasaron Par Aqui: (They Passed by Here) 99 New Mexicans . . . And a Few Other Folk.* Chesterfield, Mo.: Science and Humanities, 2005.

Burton, Jeff. *The Deadliest Outlaws: The Ketchum Gang and the Wild Bunch.* 2nd ed. Denton: University of North Texas Press, 2009.

———. *Dynamite and Six-Shooter.* Santa Fe: Press of the Territorian, 1970.

Bush, Ira J. *Gringo Doctor.* Caldwell, Idaho: Caxton Publishers, 1939.

Colorado County Historical Commission. Edward Woolery Pike, comp. *Colorado County Chronicles: From the Beginning to 1923.* 2 vols. Austin: Nortex Press, 1966.

Coolidge, Dane. *Fighting Men of the West.* New York: E. P. Dutton, 1932.

Cunningham, Eugene. *Triggernometry: A Gallery of Gunfighters.* Caldwell, Idaho: Caxton Printers, 1941; repr. Norman: University of Oklahoma Press, 1996.

Daniell, L. E. *Personnel of the Texas State Government, with Sketches of Distinguished Texans.* Austin: Smith, Hicks & Jones, State Printers, 1889.

DeArment, Robert K. *Broadway Bat: Gunfighter in Gotham. The New York City Years of Bat Masterson.* Honolulu: Talei Publishers, 2005.

———. *George Scarborough: The Life and Death of a Lawman on the Closing Frontier.* Norman: University of Oklahoma Press, 1992.

DeMattos, Jack. *Garrett and Roosevelt.* College Station: Creative Publishing, 1988.

Douglas, C. L. *The Gentlemen in White Hats: Dramatic Episodes in the History of the Texas Rangers.* Dallas: South-West Press, 1934; repr. with new material, Austin: State House Press, 1992.

DuCoin, Candice. *Lawmen on the Texas Frontier: Rangers and Sheriffs*. Round Rock, Tex.: Riata Books, 2007.

Eaves, Charles Dudley, and C. A. Hutchinson. *Post City, Texas: C. W. Post's Colonizing Activities in West Texas*. Austin: Texas State Historical Association, 1952.

Ernst, Donna B. *From Cowboy to Outlaw: The True Story of Will Carver*. Sonora, Tex.: Sutton County Historical Society, 1995.

Everson, William R. *A Pictorial History of the Western Film*. Secaucus, N.J.: The Citadel Press, 1969.

Exley, Jo Ella Powell. *Frontier Blood: The Saga of the Parker Family*. College Station: Texas A&M University Press, 2001.

Frost, H. Gordon. *The Gentlemen's Club: The Story of Prostitution in El Paso*. El Paso: Mangan Books, 1983.

Gammell, Hans Peter Marius Nielsen. *The Laws of Texas 1822–1897*. 10 vols. Austin, Tex.: Gammel Book Co., 1898.

Gillespie County Historical Society. *Pioneers in God's Hills: A History of Fredericksburg and Gillespie County People and Events*. Austin: Von-Boeckmann Jones, 1974.

Gillett, James B. *Six Years With the Texas Rangers: 1875 to 1881*. Chicago: R. R. Donnelly & Sons, 1943.

Gilliland, Maude. *Horsebackers of the Brush Country*. N.p., 1968.

———. *Rincon (Remote Dwelling Place): A Story of Life in a South Texas Ranch at the Turn of the Century*. Brownsville, Tex.: Springman-King Lithograph Co., 1964.

———. *Wilson County Texas Rangers: 1837–1977*. N.p., 1977.

Grey, Zane. *Lone Star Ranger*. New York: Harper & Row, 1915.

Hancock, William Cx. "Ranger's Ranger." *True West* 8, no. 4 (March–April 1961): 23–25, 45–48.

Harris, Charles H. III, Frances E. Harris, and Louis R. Sadler. *Texas Ranger Biographies: Those Who Served, 1910–1921*. Albuquerque: University of New Mexico Press, 2009.

Harris, Charles H. III, and Louis R. Sadler. *The Secret War in El Paso: Mexican Revolutionary Intrigue, 1906–1920*. Albuquerque: University of New Mexico Press, 2009.

———. *The Texas Rangers and the Mexican Revolution: The Bloodiest Decade, 1910–1920*. Albuquerque: University of New Mexico Press, 2004.

Haynes, David. *Catching Shadows: A Directory of 19th Century Photographers*. Austin: Texas State Historical Association, 1993.

Hughes, Alton. *Pecos: A History of the Pioneer West*. Seagraves, Tex.: Pioneer Book Publishers, 1978.

Hunter, J. Marvin, comp. and ed.. *The Trail Drivers of Texas*. Austin: University of Texas Press, 1986.

Hunter, J. Marvin, and Noah H. Rose. *The Album of Gunfighters*. Bandera, Tex.: Privately Printed, 1951.

Jacobson, Lucy Miller, and Mildred Bloys Nored. *Jeff Davis County, Texas*. Fort Davis: Fort Davis Historical Society, 1993.

James, Bill C. *Barney Riggs: A West Texas Gunman*. Privately Printed, 1982.

———. *Jim Miller: The Untold Story of a Texas Badman*. Wolfe City, Tex.: Henington Publishing Co., 2001

James, Bill C., and Mary Kay Shannon. *Sheriff A. J. Royal: Fort Stockton, Texas*. Wolfe City, Tex.: Henington Publishing Co., 1984.

Jenkins, John H. *Basic Texas Books: An Annotated Bibliography of Selected Works for a Research Library*. Austin: Texas State Historical Association, 1983.

Jensen, Ann, ed. [Alonzo Van Oden] *Texas Ranger's Diary and Scrapbook*. Dallas: The Kaleidograph Press, 1936.

Kellner, Marjorie, ed. *Wagons, Ho! A History of Real County, Texas*. Dallas: Curtis Media, Inc., 1995.

Kraisinger, Gary, and Margaret Kraisinger. *The Western: The Greatest Cattle Trail 1894–1886*. Newton, Kans.: Mennonite Press, 2004.

Lindsey, Ellis, and Gene Riggs. *Barney Riggs: The Yuma and Pecos Avenger*. Xlibris Corp., 2002.

Leftwich, Bill. *Tracks Along the Pecos*. Pecos, Tex.: The Pecos Press, 1957.

Ludeman, Annette Martin. *A History of LaSalle County: South Texas Brush Country 1856–1975*. Quanah, Tex.: Nortex Press, 1975.

Martin, Jack. *Border Boss: Captain John R. Hughes—Texas Ranger*. San Antonio: The Naylor Company, 1942. Repr. Austin: State House Press, 1990.

Mayes, Will H. "Let's Know Texas and Texans." *Frontier Times*, October 1936.

McCown, Dennis. "Two Significant Shootings in the Miller-Frazer Feud of Pecos, Texas," *Journal* of the Wild West History Association 3, no. 5 (February 2010).

Metz, Leon C. *John Selman: Texas Gunfighter*. New York: Hastings House, 1966.

Miletich Leo N. *Dan Stuart's Fistic Carnival*. College Station: Texas A&M University Press, 1994.

Moody, William. "The Taft-Diaz Visits: A Centennial Remembrance," *Password* 54, no. 2 (Summer 2009): 73–102.

Morrison & Fourney's General Directory of the City of Austin for 1881–1882. Austin: E. W. Swindels, 1881.

Nolan, Frederick W. *The Lincoln County War: A Documentary History.* Norman: University of Oklahoma Press, 1992; rev. ed. Santa Fe, New Mex.: Sunstone Press, 2009.

O'Neal, Bill. *Reel Rangers: Texas Rangers in the Movies, TV, Radio and Other Forms of Popular Culture.* Waco: Eakin Press, 2008.

Paredes, Americo. *With His Pistol in His Hand: A Border Ballad and Its Hero.* Austin: University of Texas Press, 1958.

Parsons, Chuck. *James Brown Miller and Death in Oklahoma: Was Justice Denied in Ada?* Gonzales, Tex.: Reese's Print Shop, 2009.

———. *John B. Armstrong: Texas Ranger and Pioneer Rancher.* College Station: Texas A&M University Press, 2007.

Penniger, Robert. *Fredericksburg, Texas . . . The First Fifty Years.* Trans. C. L. Wisseman. Fredericksburg: Arwed Hillmann, 1896.

Preece, Harold. *Lone Star Man: Ira Aten Last of the Old Time Rangers.* New York: Hastings House, 1960.

Rea, Glenn. "The Cuero Record to Celebrate Centennial," *The History of DeWitt County, Texas.* Dallas: Curtis Media Corp., 1991.

Romo, David Dorado. *Ringside Seat to a Revolution: An Underground Cultural History of El Paso and Juarez: 1893–1923.* El Paso: Cinco Puntos Press, 2005.

Scobee, Barry. *The Steer Branded Murder.* Houston: Frontier Press of Texas, 1952.

Shawver, Lona. *Chuck Wagon Windies and True Stories.* San Antonio: The Naylor Company, 1950.

Shirley, Glenn. *Marauders of the Indian Nations: The Bill Cook Gang and Cherokee Bill.* Stillwater, Okla.: Barbed Wire Press, 1994.

———. *Shotgun for Hire: The Story of "Deacon" Jim Miller, Killer of Pat Garrett.* Norman: University of Oklahoma Press, 1970.

Sonnichsen, C. L. *Roy Bean: Law West of the Pecos.* New York: Macmillan Company, 1943.

Spellman, Paul N. *Captain John H. Rogers, Texas Ranger.* Denton: University of North Texas Press, 2003.

———. *Captain J. A. Brooks, Texas Ranger.* Denton: University of North Texas Press, 2007.

Stephens, Robert W. *Texas Ranger Sketches.* Privately Printed, 1972.

———. *Walter Durbin: Texas Ranger and Sheriff.* Clarendon, Tex.: Clarendon Press, 1970.

Sterling, W. W. *Trails and Trials of a Texas Ranger*. Privately printed, 1959. Repr. Norman: University of Oklahoma Press, 1969.

Stovall, Allan A. *Nueces Headwater Country: A Regional History*. San Antonio: The Naylor Company, 1959.

Sullivan, W. J. L. *Twelve Years in the Saddle With the Texas Rangers*. 1909. Repr. Lincoln: University of Nebraska Press, 2001.

Tanner, Karen H. "Lon Oden: The Rhymin' Ranger." *Old West*, Summer 1998, 10–14.

Tise, Sammy. *Texas County Sheriffs*. Albuquerque, New Mex.: Oakwood Printing, 1989.

Townsend, E. E. "The Robbery of the Valentine Store." *Voice of the Mexican Border* C1, no. 4 (December 1933).

Tyler, Ron, Editor in Chief. *The New Handbook of Texas*. 6 vols. Austin: Texas State Historical Association, 1996.

Utley, Robert M. *Lone Star Justice: The First Century of the Texas Rangers*. New York: Oxford University Press, 2002.

———. *Lone Star Lawmen: The Second Century of the Texas Rangers*. New York: Oxford University Press, 2007.

Vanderwood, Paul. *The Power of God Against the Guns of Government: Religious Upheaval in Mexico at the Turn of the Nineteenth Century*. Stanford: Stanford University Press, 1998.

Webb, Walter Prescott. *The Texas Rangers: A Century of Frontier Defense*. Boston: Houghton Mifflin, 1935; repr. Austin: University of Texas Press, 1965.

Weiss, Harold J. Jr. *Yours to Command: The Life and Legend of Texas Ranger Captain Bill McDonald*. Denton: University of North Texas Press, 2009.

Welch, G. Murlin. *Border Warfare in Southeastern Kansas: 1856–1859*. Pleasanton, Kans., Linn County Historical Society, 1977.

Wilson, R. Michael. *Great Train Robberies of the Old West*. Guilford, Conn.: Globe Pequot Press, 2007.

Wooten, Dudley G. *A Comprehensive History of Texas: 1685–1897*. Dallas: William G. Scarff Publishers, 1898.

Public Records

Brewster County, Commissioners Court Minutes

Burnet County, Marriage Records

Gillespie County, District Court Records

Henry County, Illinois, Deed Records

Presidio County, State of Texas Election Returns
Texas Death Certificates:
James M. Putman #34388
El Frieda Wuerschmidt #26472
John C. Yeates #19703
Tom Green County, District Court Records
Williamson County, Texas, Deed Records

Federal Census Records
by County
Consulted online at Heritage Quest

KANSAS
Linn—1870, 1880, 1900

NEBRASKA
Adams—1900

NEW MEXICO
Torrance—1910

NEW YORK
New York—1900

TEXAS
Bee—1870
Bexar—1910
Brewster—1900
Burnet—1880
Duval—1880
Edwards—1880, 1930
El Paso—1900, 1910, 1920, 1930
Fannin—1900
Garza—1900
Gillespie—1860
Hidalgo—1900
Hudspeth—1930

Kendall—1880
Kinney—1900
Limestone—1880
McLennan—1880
McCulloch—1880
Midland—1900
Nueces—1880, 1900
Pecos—1880, 1910
Presidio—1900, 1910
Reeves—1900
San Saba—1860, 1870, 1880
Sutton—1880
Travis—1880
Uvalde—1920
Williamson—1870, 1880, 1900
Zavala—1920

WASHINGTON
Stevens—1920

OTHER CENSUS RECORDS
City of Austin—1875
Kansas State—1875

Adjutant General Papers
Texas State Library and Archives, Austin
Adjutant General Papers includes correspondence to and from, Monthly Returns prepared by Ranger Captains, Scouting Reports, Muster and Pay Rolls, Telegrams and other miscellaneous documents.

Correspondence to and from the Governors: Thomas Mitchell Campbell, Oscar Branch Colquitt, Charles Allen Culberson, James Edward Ferguson, James Stephen Hogg, John Ireland.

Ranger Service Records
Texas State Library and Archives, Austin

Allison, W. D.
Ascarate, Frank M.
Aten, Calvin G.
Aten, Edwin D.
Aten, Ira

Barton, Charles B.
Bell, James M.
Black, George B.
Bryant, R. E.

Calohan, William L.
Chastain, R. B.
Clayton, R. M.
Cook, Enoch

Daniels, M.R.

Fusselman, Charles H.

Gillespie, J.T.
Gravis, John F.

Hughes, John R.
Hughes, William P.

Jones, E. B.
Jones, Frank
Jones, Walter W.

King, J.W.

King, Ray E.
Kipling, William
Kirchner, Carl

Leakey, George P.
Lee, Isaac N.
Loeser, Robert M.

McKidrict, Joe
McKinney, T. F.

Mayfield, John C.
Mize, J. M.
Moore, C. R.

Outlaw, Baz L.

Perez, Desiderio
Priddy, John T.

Sebree, Victor
Speaks, Robert
St. Leon, Ernest

Townsend, E. E.
Townsend, Joseph B.

Ware, Richard C.

Yeates, John C.

Newspapers

CALIFORNIA
Imperial Valley Weekly

KANSAS
Border Sentinel
Ellis County Star
Kansas City Star
Mound City Republic
Oxford Times

NEW YORK
New York Times

OKLAHOMA
Muskogee Times–Democrat

TEXAS
Abilene Reporter
Alice Echo
Alpine Avalanche
Amarillo Daily News
Amarillo Daily Panhandle
Austin-American
Austin Statesman
Austin Daily Democratic Statesman
Brownsville Herald
Burnet Bulletin
Colorado Record

Cuero Daily Record
Dallas Morning News
Eagle Lake Headlight
El Paso Herald
El Paso Herald-Post
El Paso Daily Times
El Paso News
Fort Worth Daily Gazette
Galveston Daily News
Galveston Weekly News
Houston Chronicle
Houston Post
La Grange Journal
Marfa New Era
McAllen Monitor
Palestine Daily Herald
San Antonio Daily Express
San Antonio Gazette
San Antonio Light
Temple Daily Telegram
Victoria Advocate
Waco Daily Examiner
Weimer Mercury

WASHINGTON
Northport News

Periodicals

Ford News, 1936
Frontier Times
Everybody's Magazine
Leslie's Illustrated Weekly Newspaper
Old West
Password
Plum Creek Almanac
Quarterly – The National Outlaw Law-
   man History Association (NOLA)

Real Detective
Real West Magazine
Southwestern Historical Quarterly
Texana
Voices of the Mexican Border
West Texas Historical Association
Yearbook
Wild West Magazine

Miscellaneous

Aten, Ira. "Six and One Half Years in the Ranger Service Fifty Years Ago." Typed Copy in Briscoe Center for American History, Austin, Texas.

Convict Register State Penitentiary, Huntsville, Texas.

Crawford, Dwight C. "James Davenport." Unpublished manuscript in author's possession.

Hughes, John R., interview with Vera P. Elliott, date unrecorded, Works Progress Administration.

"Hughes Brothers Horse Record." Texas Ranger Hall of Fame and Museum, Waco, Texas.

[Hannah] Wickham Scrapbook Collection. 19 Vols. Linn County Museum and Genealogical Library in Pleasanton, Linn County, Kansas.

"John R. Hughes Scrapbook" in C. L. Sonnichsen Collection. Special Collections University of Texas at El Paso.

Officer Down Memorial Page – *www.odmp.org*

"Roy Aldrich Collection." Archives of the Big Bend, Sul Ross University, Alpine, Texas.

Sonnichsen, C. L. "The Miller-Frazer Feud." Unpublished manuscript. Special Collections University of Texas at El Paso.

Taylor, Mrs. Clifton Hughes. "Research of Hughes-Bond-Sargent Family Tree" Archived in Linn County, Kansas Historical Museum and Genealogy Library.

Townsend, E. E., Journal. Townsend Papers in Archives of the Big Bend, Sul Ross University, Alpine, Texas.

Wheat, Jim. "Postmasters and Post Offices of Texas, 1846–1930." Compiled Records from the National Archives and the Library of Congress. Microfilm reel #3163. Texas State Library Commission.

Index

A

Abilene, Tex., 146, 177, 205, 243, 279
Abo, N. Mex., 227
Acosta, Desadario, 99
Ada, Okla., 211
Agnew, Pat, 166
Aguirre, Lauro, 139
Aiello, Gertrude Bacus, 338 n11
Alamogordo, N. Mex., 171
Albillar, Lauro, 97
Alderete, B., 227
Aldrich, C. E., 278
Aldrich, Roy W., 8–9, 265
Alice, Tex., 173, 180, 182, 185, 188, 189, 191
Alice Echo (newspaper), 187, 190–191, 193
Allee, Alfred, 311 n31
Allen, F.R., 147
Allison, William Davis "Dave," 176–179, 243, 283
Allred, Gov. James V., 257
Alpine, Tex., 64, 66, 76, 87–88, 102, 113, 131, 138, 140, 142, 155, 156, 204, 276
Alvin, Tex., 286
Amarillas, Cisco V., 118
Amarillo, Tex., 173, 215–217, 219–220, 223, 225, 266, 284
Amarillo Daily News (newspaper), 222
Anders, Joseph L., 225
Anderson, Archie R., 220
Ann Arbor, Mich., 277
Anthony, William B., 208

Anthony, N. Mex., 95, 108
A Pair of Texas Rangers: Bill McDonald and John Hughes (pamphlet), xx
Apodaco, Mauricio, 169
Aragon, Tex., 212
Arios, Estanislado, 69
Armstrong, John B., 187
Arnott, John, 266, 269
Arrington, G. W., 260, 264
Arroyo Colorado, Tex., 187
Arthur, George, 179
Ascarate, F. M., 205, 209; service 351 n37
Aten, Calvin Grant, 36, 40–41, 53, 55–56, 61; family 317 n23
Aten, Edwin Dunlap, 42, 82, 84, 92, 107–108, 135, 138–139, 149, 151–152, 154, 171, 260, 263–264, 279, 282; family and service 338 n11
Aten, Ira, xv, xxi, 25–36, 40–42, 47; Williamson family murder, 48–50, 52–58, 94; 52–58, 94, 183, 246, 260–261, 263–264, 276, 278, 280–282, 286
Aten, Thomas 278–279
Atkins, Dave, 159
Austin, Stephen F., 291
Austin, W.H., 90
Austin, Tex., 104, 137, 160, 171, 191–195, 200–201, 203, 205, 217, 219, 224–226, 239, 242, 246, 252, 261, 266, 272, 284–286
Austin Statesman (newspaper), 15–17, 39, 242, 246, 277, 283

381